THE FBI'S UNDERCOVER "WISEGUY" GOES PUBLIC

The Insider

Donald Goddard

POCKET BOOKS

New York   London   Toronto   Sydney   Tokyo   Singapore

To Natalie

POCKET BOOKS, a division of Simon & Schuster Inc.
1230 Avenue of the Americas, New York, NY 10020

Goddard, Donald.
    The insider : the FBI's undercover "Wiseguy" goes public / Donald
Goddard.
        p.   cm.
    ISBN: 0-671-70335-8
    1. Undercover operations—United States—Case studies.   2. Breen,
Billy.   3. United States.   Federal Bureau of Investigation.
I. Title.
HV8080.U5G63   1992
363.2'52—dc20   91-29370
                                                                      CIP

First Pocket Books hardcover printing February 1992

10 9 8 7 6 5 4 3 2 1

ACKNOWLEDGMENTS

Ben Franklin, formerly with the Washington Bureau of *The New York Times*, put the idea in my head. More than that, he proved such a persuasive advocate that I now owe him, not only this book, but the friendship of Billy Breen, and certainly the best dinner that Washington can provide the next time we meet.

I also owe this book to Billy, of course, and to a large number of federal agents, prosecutors, and police officers who will not thank me if I single them out. *They* know who they are, however, and whatever useful purpose this book may serve is entirely due to their helpfulness and candor, and I thank them for it.

INTRODUCTION
by Nicholas Pileggi

On a sweltering summer night in a Knoxville, Tennessee, hotel room in 1982, William C. Breen was meeting with some mob loan sharks and their goons about a business proposition. Breen, an ex-cop and an ex-con, bragged and baited the hoods relentlessly.

There was nothing to indicate that Breen—a gray-haired, fifty-five-year-old, overweight bookie, con man, and smuggler—was also a professional undercover agent and that he was secretly recording their meeting for FBI agents hidden away across the street.

Suddenly, there was silence. The hoods kept staring at Breen's chest. Breen looked down and realized that the microphone wires taped to his chest were showing through his sweat-soaked shirt.

"I started cursing and screaming and went into the bathroom," Breen says. "And when I got back, with my shirt half-open, I kept fiddling with the wires and cursing the hospital for screwing up the monitor they installed for my pacemaker."

The ruse worked. Breen lived to tell the tale—to me, when I interviewed him a year or two back for *Parade* magazine, and now to Donald Goddard in a book that is required reading for anybody concerned about crime and the FBI's ability to cope with it.

Breen, of course, has no pacemaker, and a good thing, because, for close on thirty years, he has had the most dangerous job in the world. A man of many aliases, Breen has worked as a professional undercover agent for federal, state, and local law-enforcement agencies. He has gathered evidence against some of the nation's most elusive and dangerous murderers, racketeers, drug dealers, and arms smugglers.

Unlike most undercover agents, Breen is noisy. He swaggers. He dresses in expensive and colorful Las Vegas sportswear, flashes lots of cash, tips everyone in sight, and wears extra-heavy gold ID bracelets and rings and wafer-thin platinum-and-diamond watches. Where most undercovers are trained to hide under the covers, Billy Breen is the opposite. He gleefully calls attention to himself.

He is the loud one at the noisiest crap game on the Strip. He's at the table where they're mixing the Dom with the Pepsi and doing Frank Sinatra imitations. He's the one in the white stretch with the two hoods and six hookers. He is the big-money, ex-con Papa who has just made a score and he's looking for more. There is no greater key to the magic kingdom of crime.

Breen says that you can't catch crooks by acting like a normal person. "If they're gonna trust you enough to take you in or tell you enough to jail them, they're gonna want to see what you're made of," he told me. "I've been with crooks all my life. I know exactly how to act. In fact, in the middle of an operation, I'm not even acting. I'm into the deal. It's as though I am really the bad guy, doing what I am really pretending to be doing. It all works out in the end. And I'm always around when the arrests go down."

Billy Breen loves what he does and feels uniquely qualified for his role because he has been both a cop and a convict. Whenever there is a question about his authenticity as a crook, one phone call will usually establish that he has indeed spent seven years in prison—and no undercover cop, no matter how dedicated to law enforcement, would spend *that* much time establishing his bona fides. But the bad guys who check up on Breen aren't interested in his record or prison files. The real bad guys are only satisfied after they speak with someone who has actually spent time in prison with Breen. When the word comes back that Breen is no phony, that he did actually spend the seven years behind bars, he has invariably received the mob's gold card of acceptance.

In a way, Breen is the ultimate bounty hunter, catching crooks in the act rather than after the fact. But his impact on organized crime, as reflected in the roll call of hoodlums and racketeers he has risked his life to put away, may yet turn out to be of lesser importance than his impact on the FBI.

Always fascinating, often alarming, and in the end appalling, the story of Breen's thirty-year association with the Bureau, corroborated by agents he has worked with in the field, is not only the first independent account of how the FBI actually operates at the sharp end of law enforcement, but may just prove to be the incentive required for a long-overdue overhaul of its structure, policy, and tactics.

As Billy is fond of saying, "If those guys wanna clean up the streets, first they gotta clean up their act."

Here's where he tells them how to do it.

AUTHOR'S INTRODUCTION

Billy Breen works for the FBI in much the same way as a secret agent works for the CIA in another country.

An ex-cop who has done time for bank robbery, armed robbery, and bookmaking, he is completely at home in enemy territory. Code-named "Hawiya," from his customary telephone greeting, he moves around the criminal community with a freedom simply not open to undercover law-enforcement officers. Unencumbered by rules of conduct or considerations of due process (except when gathering evidence), Billy observes, reports, maneuvers, manipulates, sets up his targets and takes them down—sometimes to order but mostly because he feels like it.

Gray-haired, paunchy, with a face like a map of ould Boston, Billy can swagger into any lowlife bar in any state of the union and hook into the local criminal network before ordering his second Irish Cream. Next morning, wearing a wire, designer casuals, and enough gold jewelry to ballast an oceangoing yacht, he will be just as comfortable at a working breakfast in the airport Marriott setting up a million-dollar sting to take down the region's organized crime bosses.

There is no riskier line of work. Like any secret agent in another country, Billy has no official status. He knows he will be disowned if he gets into trouble. He learned that the hard way, early on, when the Massachusetts State Police major he was working for failed to persuade the courts to keep him out of jail. In other respects, too, he plays a more dangerous game than that of the government agents or police officers he will eventually take in to make the arrests. For one thing, there is usually no one around to help out if anything goes wrong. For another, he is a civilian. With his cover blown, he lacks even the protection of that momentary inhibition which most criminals still feel at the prospect of killing a cop.

But Billy is unconcerned about danger. Rather, he enjoys it, and seeks it out. Self-confident to the point of lunacy, he has built a career around the conviction that he can finesse his way into or out of anything, including a bullet behind the ear. Hooked on his own adrenaline, he has tested this proposition on a daily basis for most of his adult life, and as the passing years have dulled the "rush," so his exploits have become ever more hazardous and bizarre. And possibly all the more effective on that account, because no reasonable criminal—most of them pragmatists to the core—would suspect anybody of being crazy enough to run such risks for no apparent advantage.

It is not just the blarney that fools them, although Billy could take up a collection for B'nai B'rith in a Munich beer cellar. Nor does he physically impose. In his younger days he had to cultivate a violent streak in order to stay alive, but in recent years he has confined himself mostly to regular workouts with bottle and glass. Built like an old sofa, he has only to turn his cheerful, battered countenance on the enemy and they just *know* he is one of them.

In a sense they are right. He learned the style of criminals, their body language, outlook, and lingo, not just from observation but from shared experience. With a body count running into many hundreds of mobsters, drug traffickers, hit men, corrupt law officers, politicians and businessmen, bank robbers, con men, fences, bookmakers, pimps, and assorted criminal riffraff, Billy Breen is by far the most prolific asset the FBI has ever had, although it has lately cramped his style by declaring him "out of control."

As he was never really *under* control, Billy now feels entitled to a little public recognition for his work. (He has given up expecting money or official gratitude. Every time he presses the Bureau for what it owes him—around $250,000 in fees, rewards, and expenses, by his reckoning—all he gets is another hassle with the IRS.)

By deciding to surface after twenty-five years behind enemy lines, Billy Breen may well do for the FBI what Joe Valachi did for the mafia.

1

Anything for a friend.

When Special Agent Dave Jellison called from Miami to ask for help with a couple of dopers, Billy put everybody on hold—the New York mafia, thirty-odd bookies in Dallas, and organized crime in Hawaii—and flew down to oblige.

FBI intelligence sources indicated that Lennie Wald and his partner, Bruce Litsky, were dealing heavily in cocaine out of a jewelry store in Coral Springs, and reading the reports had reminded Jellison that Billy knew Wald from a previous undercover assignment.

Pressed for time, Billy wrapped up the case with such dazzling speed that only Jellison, undercover agent Richard Giannotti and the arrest team ever gave him enough credit for a textbook exercise that opened the way to the biggest cocaine bust in history.

STEP 1

When Billy dropped in unannounced one afternoon at the jewelry store, Wald called him through to the back room, where he was playing cards with Litsky and a former bookmaker named Mike who knew Billy from the old days. They chatted sociably for a while, filling him in on the local gossip, and after half an hour or so, Billy made his excuses and got up to go.

"You want anything?" Wald asked affably as he walked him to the door.

"Nah," said Billy. "Well . . . Yeah. Maybe. I'd like to look at some gold chains sometime."

"No problem. Lemme know when you're gonna be in the neighborhood again, and I'll get a bunch of stuff over here."

"Thanks, Lenny. I'll do that."

"Okay. Was there anything else?"

"No, no. I'll call you."

With that, Billy flew back to New York.

STEP 2

Five days later, at home in Dallas, Billy started his tape recorder and called the jewelry store. Bruce Litsky answered the phone—Wald was at the dentist—but it was all the same to Billy.

"I wanted to run something by him," he said. "Aw, shit."

"If you want to stop in," Litsky suggested, "you can talk to me about it, Billy."

"Can you talk?"

"Not over this."

"No," agreed Billy, with a touch of impatience. "Can you go to a pay phone?"

Litsky thought this over. "Yup."

"Give me the number."

"Hold on." Litsky came back after a pause. "Billy, you got one your end?"

"Yeah," he said easily. "But I'm way out of state. I can give you an out-of-state number. Doesn't matter."

In fact, it did matter. Litsky had naturally assumed that Billy was calling from a pay phone. If he went on thinking that, he was less likely to be inhibited in what he had to say.

"No, hold on for a second," said Litsky. "I'll tell you the number." He was gone a long time. "Hullo? It's 752-9953. It's now three-twenty. Give me till three-thirty—I'll be there."

"Okay. 'Bye, 'bye."

The fish were swimming vigorously toward the bait.

STEP 3

Feet up on the sofa, with a glass of Irish Cream and the tape recorder running, Billy called Litsky back, ready to strike the hook at the end of his thousand-mile line.

"I don't even know if I can talk to you," he said. "I don't know you that well, and you don't know me that well."

"Which Billy are you?"

"I'm the bookmaker."

"Okay. Now I know who you are."

"I met you the other day."

"The other day you were in the back. Right. Okay."

"I been there several times. I do a few other things. And I ran dry. And I was wondering whether Wald knew where I could reach for something, you know?"

"Ah . . . Possibility."

Billy smiled. "What's your ticket on it?"

"What size units you looking for? Whole ones? Halves? What?"

"No, I'm looking for full keys—if I can get it."

"Ah . . . There's a good possibility."

"Yeah. It's all going out to the West Coast. I got a partner. We can take as much—what happened, my source got busted. Well, he didn't get busted, I think he just packed it in. Can't locate him."

"Ah . . . I can help you out. If I can see you in person. Because I can't discuss this on—"

"No, I understand that," said Billy, heading him off. "But see, if I come in, I want to bring the money and everything else. I don't want to make a trip in because I'm doing something here, you know? I got some other thing coming here."

"Okay. What would your ballpark figure be for?"

Billy laughed. "You tell me what you got. I ain't gonna give you my figure."

"Okay. How about fifty-four?"

"Fifty-four? How many can we move at one time?"

"As much as you've money for."

"Oh, no. There's something wrong." He chuckled in protest, securing the psychological high ground. "I don't go that way. That's crazy, that way. Where we gonna make the exchange? In there?"

"No."

"Okay. I don't wanna talk in the store. What if I came in Friday? Can we do something?"

"Yup. Sure."

"Okay. If it's Friday, I can come in and probably pick up five or six keys if you got it. But let me ask you, will you front me any?"

"The first one I would rather go COD. After that, we can talk about it."

"What if I take five? Can you give me two?"

"You mean you'd pay for three and two on—"

"No, no. I'll pay you. I'll give you two-fifty, that's all I can give you. Can you give me two extra? I only need it for ten days." Sensing some reluctance, Billy moved on smoothly. "Am I going to be able to check each and every one or am I going to take your word?"

"You can do whatever you want to do," said Litsky, swallowing hook, line, and sinker. "I'm not worried about it."

"Okay. That's good. Man, I hope I'm not stepping outa line because—"

"I tell you what," said Litsky soothingly. "Let me talk to my friend tomorrow, okay? If you want to get back to him later on tomorrow afternoon, I'll have a more firm commitment for you."

"Okay. Perfect. I don't wanna make a small move if I can make a big one."

"Okay. Very good."

STEP 4

With Litsky in the bag, Lenny Wald jumped straight in beside him.

"Was it all right to talk?" Billy asked when he called the next day. "He says it was okay. I says, 'Well, you know . . .' "

Wald made reassuring noises. "I'm just surprised you never let me know that—"

"Well, remember the other day? When you wanted to talk to me? And I said maybe, maybe? I didn't know whether I was doing right or wrong, so let me give you a test. If you got, you got. Lemme tell you this, I can use an awful lot."

"All right. I just got a little bit of a problem with how we're going to work things out. I have implants. Having an oral operation on Thursday, and you're first coming in Friday, huh?"

"Yeah. And I'd like to do it and get outa there Friday. I'll have my partner with me. I'll have a stewardess who can pick it up, take it, and run."

Wald grunted. "The only problem," he said, "is I'll have the five pendants that you wanted but I don't have the other two. But in forty-eight hours, once the manufacturers open up after the weekend, I could have the other two most likely."

"Okay. It's not important because I'll pay, you know? Do I have to come in there?"

"Give me a call from around the corner," he said, used to reassuring nervous customers. "We'll have a cup of coffee."

"Perfect. Thank you, baby. 'Bye."

After talking to Jellison and case agent Larry Harrigan, Billy called Lenny back to change the appointment to Saturday. It was now Wednesday, and the Bureau needed the extra day to line up an agent for the role of Billy's partner and to put together a $250,000 flash roll.

STEP 5

On Friday, Billy met Richard Giannotti in the Miami FBI office and liked him on sight. An unassuming young agent with a background in anti-terrorist work, he had never worked a dope case before, and told Billy so up front.

This was a refreshing change. Most agents on meeting Billy for the first time generally felt impelled to assert their status and authority over his superior skill and experience. By the time they sat down with case agent Harrigan and Supervisor Tony Ameroso to work out the details of the bust, there was never a doubt that it would go down Billy's way.

On Saturday morning, he called Lenny Wald from his hotel room to confirm that the deal was on, and arranged to meet him around eleven o'clock at Donut World.

"You'll be alone, right?" said Wald. "Better you come alone."

"Well, you wanna see the money, don'cha?" Billy replied, as if it were all the same to him. "If you wanna see the money, then I gotta bring my partner. You know?"

"Yeah. Okay. See you in a half-hour."

Wald and Litsky were sitting together dunking doughnuts when Billy and Giannotti arrived with the $250,000 in their undercover Cadillac. Wald came out alone and took Billy aside to complain about Giannotti. Billy made soothing noises, introduced his partner as his money man, and sealed an instant friendship by asking Giannotti to show Wald the cash in the trunk.

Suitably reassured, Wald claimed they were $20,000 short, whereupon Billy asked Giannotti if he had any loose change in his pocket, producing about $2,000 from his own. Failing by a long way to make up the difference, Billy assured Wald he would get it to him in ten days at the most.

Now they had to agree on a time and place for delivery. As usual, Billy favored a hotel. That way, the room could be wired in advance for sound and vision and nobody would have to wear a recorder.

Lenny said no.

Lenny wanted Billy and the $250,000 to stay with him while Bruce took Giannotti over to his other store in Pompano to pick up the five kilos.

Billy and Giannotti said no.

Billy suggested the parking lot of a shopping center. The deal was just for openers, he added, getting impatient. If it went down the way he hoped, he was in the market for really substantial loads every week.

"If this goes down right," said Wald, "I can get you any amount you want as often as you like," and Billy could tell it was no idle boast.

Wald then went in and sent out Bruce Litsky. He too took Billy aside to complain about Giannotti, and once more Billy used the healing properties of $250,000 in used bills to bring the two together. He also again proposed a hotel room for the exchange, but Litsky said no. He was already out on bail for a deal that had gone sour in a hotel room.

"Forget hotels," said Billy, when he and Litsky rejoined the others. "We'll do it at Crystal Lakes shopping mall on Sample Road, west of I-95."

They consulted their watches.

"Let's go for one-thirty," Wald said.

•

STEP 6

Wary of a ripoff, Billy and Giannotti went for two o'clock instead, and parked near the Winn-Dixie market. Wald hurried over to meet them, demanding to know why they were late.

They had been there once already, lied Billy, seen no one they knew, and left.

Wald nodded, and told them he would not have been there himself except that the delivery was running late.

"Okay." Billy pretended to look around nervously. "Let's talk in the car." He wanted this on tape.

Wald climbed into the back of the Cadillac. "He'll be here exactly at three-fifteen," he said. "I told him you can't wait that long. That you're going to drive around."

"Yeah," said Billy. "This is a good spot. We'll bounce around. You going to give us a taste? So we can sample that thing?"

"Take a ride together. You don't like it, don't take it."

"As long as you say it, Wald. I'm relying on you."

"If you don't like it, you give it back. But you can't take too much time to do that."

"No, no," said Billy. "If he brings it all in, he takes the money and goes."

"Wait a second," said Giannotti, showing his class. "What about the plane?"

"We'll have to call her." Billy nodded appreciatively.

"I'm sorry to do that to you," said Wald, "but the other guy's alone in the store. I wondered what happened to you guys."

"Well, we get nervous," said Giannotti. "You understand that."

Wald understood very well. "If you didn't get nervous," he said, "you'd make *me* nervous."

"Well, I tell you what. I don't wanna hang around here. We'll come back to this area at three-fifteen."

"How many people are we gonna be dealing with?" asked Billy.

"Nobody. You wouldn't even be dealing with me except I had to come here and tell you."

Billy nodded. "I don't wanna meet a lotta people," he said slowly, going back over their taped conversation. Nobody had even mentioned cocaine. If Wald wasn't coming back, they had to make it clear he was not discussing mashed potato. "Lemme ask you one question. What percentage is it? Any idea?"

"It's the finest," said Wald, sentencing himself to fifteen years. "It's unopened. It's what everybody in the world says is pure. But to the best of my knowledge, when it comes from the other side these days, it's ten percent test. You don't like, you don't take it. I'm told it's pure, but I don't believe anybody that says it's pure."

"Okay, baby." Billy was satisfied. "Talk to you later. And when we come back, I wanna pick up some jewelry, too."

"Now you're talking," said Wald, with about an hour of liberty left.

STEP 7

At three-fifteen precisely, Billy and Giannotti drove up to the I Hop restaurant in the Crystal Lakes shopping mall, and spotted Bruce Litsky waiting outside. Billy got out to talk to him. They would have to wait another ten minutes, Litsky said. The stuff was coming up from Kendall.

"Who's bringing it?" asked Billy suspiciously.

"Two Colombians," Litsky replied. "But they're okay. Don't worry about it."

"Don't worry about it?" Billy looked to heaven to give him

patience. "I told ya—I don't wanna meet nobody else. Didn't I tell ya that?"

He turned back to the car, knowing Litsky would follow. This he also wanted on tape.

"Hey, what happened?" asked Giannotti. "Where d'ya want me to park?"

"Anywhere," said Litsky. "Just park."

Billy fixed him with a stare. "How many guys you bringing here, Bruce?"

Giannotti instantly picked up his cue. "Yeah, you know? What the fuck?"

"Okay, don't worry about it." Litsky looked harassed. "They're just two Colombians, okay? You don't even have to talk to 'em. One of yez want to go and look at the merchandise first?"

Billy declined to change the subject. "Lemme ask ya," he persisted. "How come you're bringing everybody? I don't understand that."

In fact, he was not at all upset at the prospect of taking down Wald's suppliers as well—it was an unexpected bonus—but to stay in character, he was now obliged to go to the very edge of scrubbing the deal.

Litsky grimaced. "No, what happened was, the guy who was supposed to have it up in Palm Beach for me, he got fucked up. They brought him up from Kendall, and that's why it took so much goddamn time. It's the first time they ever fucked up this way. I've been sitting with the other guy, waiting for the guy from Kendall. Now he just met up over at the other store about ten minutes ago. Which is maybe fifteen minutes from here. They should be here any minute."

"In other words, there's gonna be two more guys," said Billy grimly. That was the other problem. The surveillance teams now surrounding the lot would not be expecting anyone else.

"What? Don't worry—"

"I don't wanna meet nobody new."

"Okay," Litsky said. "I'll take the merchandise and I'll bring it in the back of your car, okay? And then you can give me the package I need, and I'll go and take off with them."

"Okay, lemme ask ya—who *are* these guys? Man, I get nervous, you know?"

"Billy, these guys are Colombians," he said, exasperated by all the complications. "They know nothing."

Litsky returned to wait for them outside I Hop, and Billy looked around thoughtfully.

Colombians usually came ready to shoot if anything went wrong, he observed. As he was not carrying a piece himself, at the first hint of trouble Giannotti should go for his gun.

Giannotti sighed. "What gun?" he asked wistfully.

They watched in silence as Litsky went to meet a red Volkswagen that drove onto the lot and parked a few rows away from them. Two men got out to keep watch as Litsky reached in for a brown paper bag, which he carried over to the Cadillac and placed on the backseat beside him.

"Jesus Christ, you're fucking late," breathed Giannotti.

All he had to do now was open the trunk to get the money, and the bust would go down, but Billy was not quite ready. He kept Litsky talking until he made sure the package did indeed contain cocaine, then nodded to Giannotti.

"Where's the money?" Litsky asked helpfully. "In the suitcase or in the office?"

"I'll get it for you," said Giannotti sweetly.

Seconds later, in a wild confusion of squealing brakes and screaming agents, they were hemmed in with guns and undercover cars.

"Didn't surprise *me*," Dave Jellison said later. "I worked with him before. But a lot of guys can't handle Billy's speed and pizzazz. He knows exactly what to do, and he loves making monkeys out of FBI agents. A lot of them don't like to be told how to work a case, but Giannotti had the right attitude. He was an experienced agent but he had never worked dopers before, so he went right along with Billy. What do you think? How do you want to do this? And instead of putting the money in a shiny leather briefcase, they wrapped it up in an old shirt.

"Billy came in Friday, and by Saturday afternoon they had two big dealers, two Colombians, and five kilos of coke."

Looking at an airtight case and perhaps thirty years in a federal penitentiary, Bruce Litsky decided to be helpful. He gave up his suppliers in a spinoff from Billy's bust that led to the indictment of fifty-three people in what the Justice Department described as "the largest cocaine trafficking ring in the nation's history."

In Atlanta alone, thirty defendants were charged with smuggling about five *tons* of cocaine valued at $3.8 billion.

2

Some of Billy Breen's best friends are FBI agents.

He treats them like favorite nephews, with a word of praise here, of genial abuse there, and never hesitates to trade on the "family" connection whenever he wants something. They are "his boys."

How *they* feel about Billy is not always so clear.

Of their patience and affection there is little doubt. It was born of shared experience in hand-to-hand warfare with the bad guys, of the disillusionment that seeps through the trenches of law enforcement like poison gas, of the solidarity that joins those who do the dirty work against those who merely order them to do it.

That is where affection for this ebullient, bullheaded, Boston Irish maverick is sometimes tempered with caution. FBI agents are finally answerable to the Bureau, but Billy is answerable to no one. Where they are often required to act against their instincts or better judgment, Billy is temperamentally incapable of obeying an order he does not agree with.

That is why some of Billy's worst *enemies* are FBI agents.

It is also why the Bureau eventually cut off its nose to spite its face by declaring him "out of control."

He then found out who his friends really were. They were the agents who simply ignored the teletype from headquarters. It means a lot to him that there are still perhaps thirty senior agents in FBI field offices around the country who know who's calling as soon as they hear "Hawiya?"—a greeting so much his trademark that it was registered for years in Miami, Atlanta, New York, Hawaii, and Washington as his official undercover code name. It means a lot because a handful of friends is pretty well all he has to show for twenty-five years of guerrilla warfare against organized crime.

There are no official plaques on Billy's wall to acknowledge his part in choking off the runaway marijuana boom of the 1970s, for instance. Or in helping to solve the crime of the century (the murder of Federal District Judge John Wood and the attempted murder of federal prosecutor James Kerr) in San Antonio, Texas. No citations for leading the FBI through the mobs' national network for stolen goods. Or for cleaning up the mob scene in Cleveland. Or for thwarting an invasion of Haiti. Or for preparing the ground for U.S. Attorney Rudolph Giuliani's show-biz crusade against the New York mobs *after the FBI had turned the case away.*

Billy did not do it for the glory, and he certainly did not do it for the money. At least $10 million in cash, in crumpled, dirty bills, has passed through his hands since 1973, when he settled down in earnest to work with the Bureau, and while he freely admits he lived high on the hog, none of it stuck. He once flew in a Lear jet from Racine, Wisconsin, to Miami with $6 million stuffed into suitcases—and it would not have been hard to persuade the pilot to keep on going.

Since 1973, he has filed reward claims with the IRS for helping to recover cash, property, and other criminal assets totaling perhaps $800 million, and received not a penny. On the contrary, the IRS continues to plague him for back taxes on an estimated income that he never earned, its original demand for $49,000 now standing at over $120,000, what with accrued penalties and interest.

Nor has he ever received a salary or retainer from the FBI. Whenever he brings in a case, the agents assigned to work with him assess its importance and negotiate a fee, which is fine with Billy. On the whole, he prefers to get paid by results. The problem is that, come pay day, the Bureau is usually out to lunch. By Billy's reckoning, Washington owes him around $250,000 in fees, rewards, and expenses (on which he would gladly pay taxes). And that doesn't include the house he lost in Miami after pledging it to mafia loansharks in the case that launched Giuliani's set-piece trials of the New York mobs.

So why does he do it?

Partly because, with Billy, hope triumphs eternally over experience, but mostly because he has nowhere else to go with his cases. He needs the FBI to help him in his private war against crime—or, more accurately, against those who offend his sense of natural justice. No other law-enforcement agency has a broad enough mandate or the necessary manpower and resources.

But that doesn't alter his opinion of the Bureau, based on thirty years' firsthand experience. Like the street agents he works with, he lives in the shadow of a flabby, self-serving empire run on feudal lines from an ivory tower in Washington; a jealous confederation of greater and lesser regional barons, each with his own courtiers and camp followers, who are generally as much concerned to advance their own interests as to round up the bad guys.

As far as Billy is concerned, it's not William C. Breen who's out of control—it's the FBI.

And just who the hell is Billy Breen to knock a government agency that, after the U.S. Supreme Court, is probably the nation's most trusted institution and certainly its last defense against criminal subversion?

Well . . .

"Call William Clifford Breen."

It should have been the proudest moment of his life.

When Billy was ushered into federal court one bright February morning in 1985, it should have been to deliver the most damaging blow ever struck against organized crime. He had seen the Cowboy Palace trial crowning his career with a string of convictions from which the New York mobs could never recover—but instead the FBI had messed up. As usual.

Instead of bringing the mobs to their knees, the Bureau had lost its nerve and pulled the plug at least a month too soon. Instead of fifteen defendants, there should have been fifty—and to make matters worse, Rudolph Giuliani, the U.S. Attorney for the Southern District of New York, had lumped them all together, trying to make one indictment do the work of two or three. Instead of shepherding the whole bunch through to inescapable verdicts of guilty, as he crossed the well of the court Billy had an uncomfortable feeling that *he* was the one on trial.

Two defense attorneys had already suggested as much in their opening statements to the jury.

Lewis Cohen, representing Antonio "Tony Nap" Napoli, a capo in the Genovese family, had claimed that his client was there only because "the government employed a person by the name of William Breen, if he chooses to use that name . . . who is on tapes with Napoli and perhaps will be called as a witness for the government as the devil incarnate." Setting the tone the defense would maintain throughout the trial, Cohen went on to submit "that the proof will show in this case that William Breen . . . is a residual psychopath, and has been so diagnosed, a drunk, a bank robber, a forger, a professional witness . . . an informer for the government."

David Breitbart, representing Jesse "Doc" Hyman, front man for the mobs' loanshark operation, also saw signs of a satanist plot.

"You will find that the government has made deals with the devil himself to justify this investigation," he told the court. "There is a drug known to modern science as Thorazine, the most powerful drug in the world, that quiets elephants and rhinoceri—and their witnesses. You will find that one of their witnesses took fifty milligrams of Thorazine four times a day, this lunatic." Pressing home his attack on William "Thorazine" Breen, Breitbart exhorted the jury to consider "whether or not this case was doomed to success against Jesse David Hyman because the FBI was sucked in by the things that were dredged up from the bowels of the earth."

However quaintly expressed, advance billing of this kind ensured a stir of anticipation when Billy took the stand, although with typically demonic cunning he had chosen to appear as a short, chubby, middle-aged, pink-and-white Irish-American who looked like everybody's idea of a favorite uncle. After swearing to tell the truth, he smiled at the jury uncertainly, as though from a dentist's chair.

Like everybody else in the crowded fifth-floor courtroom on Foley Square, the jurors were already familiar with the outlines of the Cowboy Palace scandal. From the moment the grand jury had handed up its fifty-five-page indictment six months earlier, the media had grasped the importance of a case that showed how the New York mobs had graduated from fracturing working-class kneecaps for defaults on twenty-dollar loans to advancing half a million dollars or more—at between 2 percent and 4 percent *a week*—to supposedly legitimate businessmen.

Adding just the right touch of glamorous sleaze to the story was the fact that a local whizz kid, Thomas Duke, had needed that kind of loan-shark money to fulfill his dream of converting the ballroom of the old Diplomat Hotel on Forty-third Street into the world's glitziest country-and-western discothèque. More-serious commentators had also been impressed by the way representatives of the region's crime families worked together like OPEC oil ministers to manage the supply of black-market loans.

The eight defendants, representing five local crime families, were, in descending order of seniority, Vincent "Jimmy" Rotondo, underboss of New Jersey's DeCavalcante mob and organizer for Local 1814 of the International Longshoremen's Association; Michael Franzese, the Hamlet of organized crime and a capo in the Colombo family;

Benedetto "Benny" Aloi, another Colombo captain; Antonio "Tony Nap" Napoli, a Genovese captain; Carlo Vaccarezza, a member of the Gambino family, co-owner with the Mets' Rusty Staub of Rusty's restaurant at Seventy-third Street and Third Avenue, and occasional driver for John Gotti; Leonard Carl "Lennie" Di Maria and Francesco "Frankie the Hat" Di Stefano, both Gambino soldiers, and Oscar "Al" Albenga, a veteran of the old Lucchese family.

Of the remaining seven "civilians," two were at least as dangerous: Jesse "Doc" Hyman, a Roslyn Estates dentist with a flair for fraud and usury, and Melvin Cooper, his no less enterprising partner in Resource Capital Group, of Lake Success, Long Island.

Unfriendly observers were in the habit of dying around these two. During an earlier investigation into their links with organized crime, one government informant had been found, stabbed and shot, in the trunk of Cooper's Cadillac, and the body of another, stuffed into a sleeping bag, in the trunk of a rental car leased to Doc Hyman. Three months before the trial, Assistant U.S. Attorney Bruce Baird had filed an affidavit in district court about these murders with a motion requesting that the identity of his witnesses be kept secret until they took the stand.

It was a nice thought, but Billy Breen already knew he was under sentence of death. The FBI had told him so—at the same time carefully disowning any responsibility for keeping him alive. And that was okay, too. By now, the number of people who wanted him dead would have half-filled Yankee Stadium.

The remaining five defendants were a mixed bunch: Joseph Biasucci, secretary-treasurer of Teamsters Local 531 in Yonkers, accused of using pension funds to finance illegal loans; Rabbi Chaim Gerlitz, a religious instructor and business tout from Great Neck, Long Island, and three muscle men aspiring to higher office in the New York mobs—Al Albenga, Jr., Stanley Gramovot, and Anthony Capo, Jr.

In the brief silence before Bruce Baird began his direct examination, Billy could feel the dead weight of their stares. Putting them all away for twenty years should have been a formality; the evidence he had amassed against the front men in Resource Capital was overwhelming. But the case against the racketeers behind them was less conclusive, partly because the FBI had pulled out prematurely, and partly because the Bureau's New York office had actually destroyed many of the incriminating tapes that Billy had risked his life to record.

These errors of judgment—to put it charitably—had then been compounded by others in the U.S. Attorney's office. To strengthen the case against the mobsters, the sensible course would have been to convict the front men first and then cut deals to secure their testimony against the others. But instead, Giuliani had elected to try the whole group together, denying himself a chance to augment Billy's testimony, and leaving the case against the more important targets looking less than ironclad.

What Billy had to prove was that Resource Capital Group, in its fancy, glass-walled office building out in Nassau County, had dusted off the traditional con man's bait-and-switch tactics to lure financially hard-pressed businessmen into borrowing mob money at usurious rates of interest. He had to show that suckers like Tommy Duke, drawn in with the promise of legitimate loans, had been told that temporary financing could be arranged at 2 percent or more per week while the necessary paperwork was being drawn up—only to discover later how permanent the mobs' temporary arrangements could be.

In response to Bruce Baird's questions, Billy described how he had come up from Miami to "get over" with the loan sharks, posing as a wheeler-dealer involved with the Provisional Irish Republican Army. Taken into Cowboy Palace by Duke as an "investor," he had subsequently brought in an undercover FBI agent to help him with the investigation, and had persevered with it even after the Bureau took fright and pulled out.

Knowing his views, neither Baird nor the FBI's case agent, Stanley Nye, had been entirely sure how Billy would perform at the trial. Although polite to Baird, Billy had refused to have anything to do with Nye, taking the stand without any of the pretrial coaching customary in cases of this magnitude. The prosecutor's relief was apparent, therefore, as his key witness neared the end of his direct testimony without serious mishap, and mindful of the private investigator who had been digging into Billy's past, Baird concluded by trying to spike the defense's guns.

"Is it a fact, Mr. Breen, that you have been convicted of robbing a bank and robbing a restaurant in Massachusetts in the mid-1960s?"
"Yes, sir."
"Did you serve time in prison in connection with those?"
"Yes, sir."
"About how long?"
"Seven and a half years."
"Now approximately when did you get out of prison after the robbery convictions?"
"1973."
"From that time to the present, have you done some bookmaking?"

"Yes, I have."

"Have you also cooperated with law-enforcement agencies in a number of states?"

"Yes, I have."

"Have you testified in various courts and grand juries?"

"Yes, I have."

Baird hesitated, having left the sorest point until last. "Have you ever been treated for a mental illness?"

"Yes, I have." Billy smiled, as if everybody knew that.

"When did that arise?"

"When did it happen? After I got out of the service in 1948. I used to go to a VA hospital. In 1960, I was confined to the VA hospital in Jamaica Plain in Boston, Massachusetts."

"When were you last actually treated for mental illness."

"1960."

"Have you seen any psychiatrists at all since that time?"

"I saw the psychiatrist at Lewisburg Penitentiary." Billy was not enjoying this, but he knew why Baird was doing it.

"That was when you were in prison between the mid-1960s and 1973?"

"Yes."

Baird nodded, smiled reassuringly, and gathered his papers together. "I have no further questions, Your Honor."

Most reasonable people consider Billy crazy to do what he does, and relays of highly paid defense attorneys have done their best over the years to persuade juries of his mental incompetence. They have not had much luck. For one thing, he has never sought to hide the problems that brought him to his knees as a young man, finding nothing in them to feel ashamed of, and for another, his demeanor on the witness stand is usually so frank, open, and, above all, *sane* that counsel who press this line of questioning more often than not succeed in winning the jury over to *Billy's* side.

He was born on October 27, 1926, in Winchester, Massachusetts, the fourth of nine children to survive Lena Breen's thirteen pregnancies. His father, James Breen, was a truck driver who ran a strict Catholic household on seventeen dollars a week, when he was in work.

A shy, freckled, rather pretty child, though small for his age, young Billy went to Mass every day before school, serving as altar boy or singing in the choir. As soon as he was old enough, he got up even earlier to help the driver of a Whitings Milk truck for six dollars a week, and then did a paper round before going to church. After school he would pick beans on a local farm for a dollar an hour or, out of season, pick over the town dump for rags and old newspapers. On Sundays, dolled up in hand-me-down knickers, argyle stockings, and spats, he would stand outside the church selling copies of *Social Justice*, a radical Catholic weekly.

Not surprisingly, his education suffered. A bright boy, though never academically inclined, he had completed eight years of parochial school and less than two years at Winchester High when the Japanese bombed Pearl Harbor. Dropping out of tenth grade in a burst of patriotic indignation, Billy Breen, just 15, went to work full time in the Charlestown Navy Yard as a shipfitter's helper for twenty-nine cents an hour.

At 16, still weighing only around ninety pounds, he tried to enlist in the navy and was told to come back when he had grown a bit. At 17, now a qualified welder, he tried again, and was ordered to report for boot camp at Sampson Naval Base, Geneva, New York, on the day before his eighteenth birthday.

From there he shipped out to Shoemaker, California, where he volunteered to serve in submarines, the most romantic branch of the service he could think of. Typically, the navy assigned him, as Shipfitter Third Class, to USS *ABSD-6*, part of an Advanced Base Sectional Drydock, and by the time the barge carrying Section Six wallowed out from Tiburon, California, to join a convoy to Guam, Billy's morale had sunk to the bottom. This was *not* how he had seen himself winning the war.

No stranger to muck or discomfort, within a week of arriving on Guam he had forgotten what it felt like to be clean or dry. Cramped to begin with, the crew's living quarters were soon running with filth and infested with rats; the mess halls reeked and steamed, and the brain-curdling din of generators, crane motors, jackhammers, and shrieking metal never stopped.

In endlessly driving rain, Billy's damage-control party slipped and slithered over slimy decks tangled with cables, air hoses, water and welding lines, manhandling jacks, wrestling with stuck bolts and perverse, mangled steel, or else toiled down below half-naked in the half-dark, up to their necks in bilge and grease. Little by little, the days and the work merged into a numb procession of smashed-up ships, their sides torn, shafts twisted, screws buckled, with cranes pecking at them through sprays of golden sparks, and exhausted fitters cursing and cursing.

After six months on Guam, a second Billy Breen was born, around the time of Hiroshima. Hazy about the details after blocking them out for so long, he still backs away almost physically from the memory. He was working on a torpedoed cruiser—he thinks it was the USS *Duluth*—when the ensign in charge ordered him to cut through the plating into a compartment sealed off by watertight doors when the ship was hit.

As the flame of his torch burned through the steel, water began to sluice out, soaking him to the skin, but that was nothing new. It gave off an evil stench, but he was used to that, too.

When the hole he had cut was large enough to put his head through, he took a look inside, In the dim light, the bodies of drowned seamen were breaking up before his eyes. As the water drained from the compartment, so the current shredded the gray, rotten flesh from their bones.

His mind stopped. Unable to move, he just stood and stared as the corpses dissolved in the vile stew and drifted toward the hole he had cut, spilling out over him.

He began to shake. An unspeakable revulsion shriveled his skin. Rasping with panic, his body backed away of its own accord, rejecting the contamination. Jeered at by his buddies, he blundered off the dock, blindly brushing at himself.

Much later, they found him on his bunk, his back turned to the world, staring blankly at the bulkhead.

3

Just before noon on February 11, 1985, open season was declared on Billy Breen in the Cowboy Palace trial.

As always in cases with a large number of defendants, defense counsel had decided among themselves how to conduct the cross-examination of prosecution witnesses. Nothing is better calculated to bore a jury into inattention, or even downright prejudice against the accused, than to have a procession of lawyers trampling over the same ground, making the same points in the same context—particularly when the aim is not so much to dispute matters of fact as to discredit a witness. As Jesse Hyman and Mel Cooper, partners in Resource Capital, were the two defendants who, by general assent, had been most seriously damaged by Billy's testimony, it had fallen to their respective attorneys to organize his character assassination, starting with David Breitbart for Doc Hyman.

An experienced trial lawyer with plenty of mud in his briefcase, he waited until Bruce Baird had taken his seat at the government's table next to Aaron Marcu, the co-prosecutor, and the FBI's case agent Stanley Nye, before leading off predictably with Billy's criminal record.

"Mr. Breen, when was your first conviction?"
"1967."

"When was your last conviction?"

"Last year."

"Between 1967 and 1984, how many times have you been convicted of crimes in federal and state courts?"

"None."

Breitbart consulted his notes. "You have never been convicted?"

"Except the one in 1967. That was state and federal. And in 1984, a federal offense . . ."

First blood to Billy. Knowing they had checked all the way back to his birth certificate, he had decided the best policy was to hide nothing but volunteer nothing. If Breitbart asked the wrong questions, he could hardly expect the right answers.

"How many times have you been convicted of felonies, Mr. Breen, in the state and federal courts?"

"Three times."

"You were convicted of bank robbery?"

"Yes, sir."

"You were arrested for the bank robbery?"

Billy blinked. He could hardly have been convicted without being arrested. "Yes, sir."

"You were out on parole on the bank robbery?"

"No, sir." Another flub.

"You were out on bail on the bank robbery?"

"Yes, sir."

"You were out on bail on the bank robbery and you committed another robbery?"

"Yes, sir."

"You were convicted of that also?"

"Yes, sir."

"You were convicted for drugs?"

Billy hesitated, wondering whether to qualify his answer by explaining how he had been working for the FBI at the time, but decided against it.

"Yes, sir."

"You pleaded guilty in that one?"

"Yes, sir."

"So your history with regard to convictions, just the ones you have mentioned, ranges for your entire adult life—isn't that correct?"

Billy looked at him humorously, eyebrows raised. His first conviction had been at the age of 41. "If you say so," he said, with a touch of condescension. "Yes, sir."

Breitbart was not amused. "You were a police officer for a while?"

"Yes, sir."

"You were dismissed from the police force?"

"No, sir."

"Were there newspaper articles about your being dismissed from the police force?" He looked in his folder, as if ready to produce them.

"No, sir."

"This was the Somerville, Massachusetts, police force?" Breitbart was faltering again.

"Yes, sir."

"You didn't get dismissed?"

"No, sir," he said, already ahead on points.

A different Billy sailed home from Guam. Unassuming, gregarious, and good-natured before, he came back morose, solitary, and belligerent. Racked with headaches, he often found it hard to breathe and was afraid to sleep because of the dreams that lay in wait.

He was enraged with everybody, and in particular with the navy doctors who tried to quiet him down with sedatives. When he was not stumbling about, befuddled by drugs, trying to shake off the nightmare always there in the corner of his eye, he was picking fights or getting drunk to distract himself.

After about a year of this, he and the navy had had enough. On July 10, 1946, Billy was mustered out of the service with $163.23 and advised to report to the Veterans Administration clinic in Boston.

His family hardly recognized him. The jaunty, freckled-face kid who had left home to win the war just twenty-one months earlier had come back a moody, erratic stranger. Still only 19, he looked at least ten years older, and had even changed in physique. A flyweight before, Billy had now moved up to the middleweight division, with a bull neck and shoulders, and arms so heavily muscled they hung away from his sides. Full face, the former choir boy now looked a little like John Garfield in one of his gangster roles.

He was also unemployable. Unable to settle or to take orders from anyone, Billy drifted in and out of at least twenty factory or laboring jobs in the next ten years, his temper taking on a savage edge that frightened *him* as much as it frightened others.

The one stable element in his life was Jeannette Cagnina, a dark pretty girl from the neighboring town of Woburn whom he had known since high school. They were married in 1948, and for a time the role of husband and father seemed to steady him, but after about a year, he took to disappearing without a word, sometimes for days on end, and on returning home would have no recollection of where he had been or what he had done.

It was almost as if he were trying to protect Jeannette from the dark side of his nature—by absenting himself before his demons broke loose. When he left it too late, he would start to abuse her, and several times he saved her from serious harm only by turning his anger against their home and smashing up the furniture instead.

The disappearances grew longer. He came to himself in Wharton, Texas, and found he had been missing for ten weeks. A year later, he turned up in New Orleans. Finally, in 1954, he vanished for seven months and might well have gone for good had Jeannette not managed to trace him to New York. Even so, he failed to recognize her at first, and it took a full year of domestic blackmail before he at last agreed to see a psychiatrist. In May, 1955, ten days before his third daughter was born, Billy reported for treatment to the mental hygiene unit of the VA hospital in Boston, where he was also assessed for a service-related disability pension.

Reporting his findings to the pensions adjudication officer, Dr. Saul C. Holtzman described Billy as a "passive aggressive personality with anxiety features, chronic, moderate—manifested by intermittent impulsive-aggressive outbursts, difficulty in dealing with authority figures, excitability and ineffectiveness under relatively minor stress, periodic hyperapnea [extreme breathlessness], and difficulties in his vocational adjustment."

In Dr. Holtzman's view, this had been brought on by "overseas naval service, including a severe psychic trauma which involved his cutting through a ship's compartment which was filled with the bodies of drowned seamen. . . . He appears to be strongly motivated at this time, and if this motivation continues, it is felt that the prognosis will be good."

Now going on 29, what Billy needed most was peace and quiet—emotional security in a calm, stable, stress-free environment. What he got, as the result of a casual bet in a neighborhood tavern late one night, was a patrolman's job with what was then one of the most corrupt police departments in Massachusetts.

For no reason compelling enough for him to remember it the next morning, Billy backed himself to win two hundred dollars from each of three fellow barflies by scoring higher than they did in a civil-service examination for would-be recruits to the Somerville Police Department. It might just as easily have been an arm-wrestling wager, but by the time he won the bet a few weeks later, he had seen the hand of God at work. After ten years of drifting and looking for a sign, the future had not only taken shape but was due to start at 12:01 A.M., November 18, 1956, when his appointment as permanent patrolman took effect.

To make up for the wasted years, what he brought to the job was no mere inclination toward a career in law enforcement, but a full-blooded commitment of the sort that got Catholic martyrs burned at the stake. Assigned to parking-meter control, he wrote 13,356 tickets in his first three months and had all of Somerville in an uproar.

His formal training as a police officer had consisted of a ride around town with a lieutenant who helped himself to a paper at a corner newsstand, took midmorning coffee and doughnuts at a convenient luncheonette, and broke for lunch at his favorite bar, all without putting his hand in his pocket. Billy was genuinely shocked. In his five years with the department he never took so much as a free stick of gum from a candy store, but he was quickly made aware that helping oneself was a routine police prerogative, accepted by cops and local businessmen alike.

When he refused to join in, his new colleagues looked at him pityingly. Nor did they seem particularly worried when he refused his cut of the payoff from local bookmakers and after-hours joints. He was not the first "idealist" they had had to wear down. It was only when he started going through the files on Sundays after church to "unfix" the tickets he had issued and generally getting underfoot that they began to see him as a problem.

On his way home one night, he found that the door of a liquor store had been left unlocked, and walked around the corner to a nearby police phone to report it. When he returned to the store a few minutes later, two sergeants and six patrolmen were busy clearing the shelves, loading armfuls of bottles into the trunks of their cruisers.

"What the fuck's going on?" he demanded.

They scurried inside for more, ignoring him.

"Hey, what are you doing? Where are you taking that stuff?"

The idea of looters in police uniform was so outrageous that for a moment Billy thought they were removing the stock for safekeeping. But only for a moment.

"Okay," he said, blocking the doorway. "That's enough."

"Get outa my fucking way," panted one of the sergeants, bent over with a case of bourbon, "before I drop this mother on my fucking foot."

Not happy with the odds, Billy tried to be nice. "Come on, Sarge," he said. "Give the guy a break. You're gonna put him outa business."

The sergeant scowled dismissively, still heading Billy's way, the others close behind him. All with their hands full.

"Put it back," Billy said, resting his hand on his gun. "You got enough."

It seemed like a reasonable bet.

They all stopped, as astonished as he had been. They were ready to kill him—he could see it in their faces—but not there. And not for a few bottles of booze.

In the looking-glass world of the Somerville Police Department, incidents like that made him a bad cop. Even those who were privately sympathetic soon refused to work with him or be his partner for fear that the rest might think they were also "untrustworthy." Overnight, Billy found himself virtually ostracized, which suited him fine. His Irish was up. Having annoyed everybody with his virtuoso performance in parking-meter control, he was reassigned to the "penalty box," directing traffic in Union Square—where he continued to annoy everybody by writing a barrel-load of tickets for *moving* violations.

But as relations cooled with his brother officers, so they warmed with the citizens of Somerville. Part of what it meant to him to be the best cop in town was based on the Hollywood/Victor McLaglan image of the lovable, two-fisted Irish patrolman with a smile and a kind word for everybody, one moment helping an old lady across the street, the next, wading joyously into a barroom brawl. Local kids, who would normally start to run as soon as they saw a cop, now came by the penalty box to shoot the breeze, and his particular favorites were even allowed to try their hand at directing traffic. One small boy enjoyed this so much and came so often that he eventually allowed Billy to take him to the local drugstore and have his head cleared of lice.

Pretty soon, people in trouble knew they could count on a sympathetic hearing from the cop in Union Square, which was a revolutionary idea for the citizens of Somerville, who were more accustomed to the police as an occupying army.

Somerville was then the sinkhole of crime in the Northeast, a depressed, depressing township indistinguishable from the rest of Boston's shabby outer sprawl of working-class homes and housing projects except for its form of local government. As the idea of a feudal enclave ran counter to the state's traditionally Democratic ideals, the Irish mobs who lived in and around Somerville and ran the North End of Boston in uneasy alliance with the Angiulo crime family had simply put the police force on the payroll to help keep the neighborhood safe for bookmakers, loan sharks, bank robbers, hijackers, hit men, and other general practitioners of blue-collar crime.

When the summer vacation season came around, Billy was at last given a cruiser and a beat of his own on Lower Broadway, one of the toughest in town. Warned in advance to mind his own business, he decided his first priority would be to improve the traffic flow. The streets were narrow and choked overnight with cars left just anywhere in defiance of the city's alternate side of the street parking ordinance. Had there been a fire or some other disaster, there would have been no way for emergency vehicles to get through.

On his first patrol, he took a good wad of tickets with him and wrote out two hundred before going off duty. The next night he did the same, and the next, and by the time the uproar filtered down from city hall, Billy had personally mailed out over twelve hundred tickets. Back he went to the penalty box.

Reassigned to a cruiser as the summer wore on—and with strict orders to ignore parking offenses—Billy now decided it was time to roust card rooms, crap games, and bookmakers, and the saloon keepers who allowed them to operate on their premises. Once into his stride, he would hit fifteen to twenty joints a night, either closing them up if it was after hours or throwing the bookies into the street. Sometimes, for the sake of variety, he would chase their customers away instead, but always, at the end of each shift, he would pull up a stool in the last joint he reached and order a little Bristol Cream or a Smirnoff and grapefruit. And pay for it.

He was now openly at war with his superiors, partly because their envelopes were getting thinner as a result of his efforts, and partly because, in his capacity of father figure, he was doing his best to obstruct such traditional police privileges in Somerville as beating up handcuffed prisoners in the cells and then driving over to screw their wives. He had come to hate cops who could break into a jewelry store one night, and the next night gun down a civilian for doing the same thing. Or who could pull a drunk from his car and beat him into a bloody mess before getting stoned on free drinks and running every red light on the way home.

Off duty one evening, he took a lady friend to the Rosebud Cafe in Davis Square. They had just settled at their table when there was a tinkling smash of glass outside, and with at least twenty other patrons, Billy stood up to see what was happening. To everybody's astonishment, a dozen uniformed cops, two of them sergeants, were looting a store across the square.

Billy went to the pay phone to report the robbery, hanging up when the desk sergeant asked for his name, and returned to the window to watch the raiding party drive away as though going home from a supermarket. Minutes later, the first cruiser arrived in response to Billy's call, but it was in no particular hurry.

A few weeks later, an off-duty patrolman threw a brick through the window of a Davis Square jeweler's. With the store's alarm blasting away, cruiser after cruiser drove up, lights turning, and one after another their crews went inside to break open the display cabinets and fill their pockets.

Working alone as usual, Billy responded to the radio call from the other side of town and arrived late. When he saw what was going on, he killed his lights and parked out of sight, trying to identify those taking part.

Lying awake that night, still trying to figure out what to do, Billy took a call from one of the officers he had seen in the square. Known to everyone as "Buster," he wanted to know where Billy had been when the radio call came in on the jewelry-store robbery.

Billy hesitated. "Asleep," he said. They had evidently spotted his car.

"Yeah?" There was a short silence while Buster thought this over. "You need anything?"

"Like what?"

"I don't know. Why don't you see us? Why don't you come by the house? We wanna give you something."

Billy snorted. He could guess what they had in mind—money in his pocket or a .38 slug in the back of his head. "Nobody wants to give me nothing," he said flatly. "What's on your fucking mind?"

"Nothing." Again, silence. "You didn't get nothing, that's all. We wanna give you some stuff."

"What d'ya mean? What stuff?"

Buster sighed heavily, made clicking noises, and sounded several times as though he were about to speak before he finally managed, "From the jewelry store. You didn't get none of that shit."

So they *had* seen him. "Save it," Billy said cautiously. "I'll come by in the morning."

To have refused outright would have been to ask for a hit. To go around in daylight would not only be safer but might also give him some hard evidence he could use.

He called at Buster's house around 7:00 A.M., with a .357 in his pocket and a .38 in his waistband. There were four of them, sitting around the kitchen table, and, to judge from the litter of cans and bottles, they had been there all night. Nobody said much. Buster shook about $3,000 worth of gold jewelry into Billy's palm from a small pouch. Billy nodded, put it in his pocket, and left without a word.

He drove straight to the police station and tossed the pouch on the desk of the lieutenant on duty. Waiting to be asked what it was, Billy suddenly realized that the lieutenant already knew. He moved to pick it up again, but the other beat him to it. Dropping the pouch into his open attaché case, the lieutenant snapped the lid shut, got up, and left.

After another bad night, Billy drove over to the Middlesex County Sheriff's office. When the deputy he spoke to heard who he was, he told Billy to wait. He was gone a long time. On his return, Billy took one look at his expression and left.

Next, he tried the district attorney's office, but nobody in authority was prepared to see him unless he first stated his business. When he said it was about police corruption in Somerville, they were all too *busy* to see him.

That left the FBI. Although he had never met a federal agent, Billy shared the traditional reserve of street cops toward the Bureau, and his first encounter with its Boston division did little to change that.

He was interviewed by two agents, who at least heard him out. Making an occasional note, they listened attentively while Billy explained how the Somerville Police Department operated a sanctuary for the Irish gangs and for bookmakers and organized-crime figures affiliated with the Angiulo family, who in turn paid tribute to Raymond Patriarca, the New England mob boss. He told them about the looting of the liquor store and how the cops involved had taken a walk. He described the two most recent robberies by cops in Davis Square and how they had tried to buy him off. He went through his long list of corrupt officers and officials, and the even longer catalog of burglaries, thefts, and payoffs to which he could testify from his own knowledge, including the time when the vice squad, officially on duty and therefore getting paid by the city, had spent an entire shift repainting a bookmaker's premises. He went on an on, dredging up case after case as the two agents looked more and more doubtful.

"What's the matter?" Billy demanded. "Am I going too fast for yez?"

"No, no, Billy," said one of them peaceably. "Nothing like that. I'm just not sure how we can help you. You know how things work in this town. You can't beat the system on your own."

"Jesus, I know *that*. That's why I'm sitting here talking to you."

"Sure, Billy. Sure." The agent pulled at his ear. "But you'll have to bring us something we can use, okay? Something we can make a case and run with."

"You can't use any of the stuff I just give you?" Billy felt stabbed to the heart.

"Well, we can't go out and arrest anybody, if that's what you mean. All we got is your word—which is good enough for me. But a jury needs more. Where's your evidence? You know how these guys cover one another's ass. You must have seen it a hundred times."

"Yeah, but you got enough there to start an investigation." He was pretty close to the edge. He could feel actual tears behind his eyes. "I mean, that's what cops *do*, right? Somebody comes in and tells you about a crime and you go out and investigate?"

"Yeah. If it's a federal violation. Or interstate." They were entirely sympathetic. "We'll talk to the boss, okay? Maybe he'll see it different. But I have to tell you, Billy—from where I sit, this looks like a strictly no-win situation. Bring us a case we can work on and maybe we'll get some of these guys off the street. But if we start messing around with any of this other shit, we're just gonna get you killed, that's all."

Billy grunted. "Don't worry about it," he said. "I already been to the sheriff's office. And the DA."

"Jesus Christ." The agent shook his head. And shook it again. "Goddamit, Billy," he said sadly. "You got more balls than brains."

A few days later, working the 4:00 P.M. to midnight shift, Billy responded to a radio call about a house fire on his route. By the time he arrived, the flames were roaring through the building, and without having to ask either of the officers already at the scene, he knew that another of his nightmares was coming true. He could hear the firetrucks, streets away, trying to force their way through all the illegally parked cars.

There were people in the building, and Billy knew who they were. Half out of his mind, he fancied he saw somebody at an upper window, but the heat was a wall, and forgetting their differences for once, the other officers dragged him back.

Three children died in that fire, one of them the boy with lice in his hair whom Billy had taught to direct traffic in Union Square.

Coming on top of three years' unremitting warfare with the criminal licensees of the Somerville Police Department, and coinciding with the collapse of his marriage, it was too much to take.

Fifteen years after the trauma of Guam, Billy Breen cracked up again.

4

Resuming his cross-examination after lunch, David Breitbart turned his attention to Billy's psychiatric history.

"Mr. Breen, Mr. Baird asked you certain questions about your mental health. And you told him that you had in the past had some psychiatric problems?"

"Yes, I did," agreed Billy.

"But that you are fine now?"

"Yes, I am."

"Was there a period of time, sir, when you were getting Thorazine? Fifty milligrams, four times a day?"

"Yes," he said shortly.

"Was there a period of time when you were getting Mellaril four times a day?"

"Yes." Billy had not understood until now just how thoroughly the defense had done its homework.

"Was that as a result of your having psychiatric episodes?"

"Episodes?" he asked suspiciously.

Breitbart turned to the jury with a superior smile. "Did you get crazy and have to get locked in a padded cell?"

"No." He definitely didn't like this guy.

"Were you ever voluntarily confined to a mental institution?"

"I did it myself. Yes, sir."

"For how long did you have yourself locked up?"

"I went in in 1960. And I escaped in June of 1960."

Breitbart then tried to find out how much Billy knew about the various diagnoses that had been made of his condition in the past and if he had used his medical history to apply to the government *"for a permanent disability as a result of your psychiatric problems."*

"No, sir," said Billy firmly. He had never had to apply for a pension.

Breitbart preserved his patience with an effort. *"Do you have a disability?"* he demanded.

"Yes, I have."

"Do you receive money from the United States government as a result of that disability?"

"Yes, I do."

"Is that a permanent disability?"

"Total and permanent."

"And isn't it a fact, sir, that was based on papers that doctors and lawyers filed for you, that you were permanently and psychiatrically disabled?"

Billy frowned. No lawyers had been involved. There was a lack of precision in these questions that made it difficult to answer yes or no.

"No, sir," he said.

Breitbart invited the court to share his exasperation. *"What is your disability?"* he asked, misunderstanding the reason for Billy's denial.

"A hundred percent disability," said Billy, misunderstanding the misunderstanding.

"Do you have a broken leg?" Breitbart shouted.

"No, sir."

"Do you have a broken arm?"

"No, sir."

Judge Sand came to Breitbart's rescue. *"What is the medical nature of your disability?"* he asked peaceably.

"Psychiatric condition," said Billy, pleased to answer a sensible question at last.

Breitbart went back to his notes. *"When is the last time that you took drugs to treat your psychiatric problem?"*

"In the Lewisburg penitentiary."

"Was it in the Lewisburg penitentiary that you met Wolfram Rieger, the doctor?"

Billy agreed that it was, but Breitbart then got lost in another tangle over whether Billy had seen a letter that Rieger had written *in 1968 to the Veterans Administration when Billy's disability pension was under review. Breitbart showed him a copy to refresh his memory.*

"How many times did you speak to Dr. Rieger?"

"In the penitentiary? Three or four times."

"Was it Dr. Rieger who was giving you the Mellaril?"

"Yes, it was."

"Is it a fact, sir, that you were diagnosed as a borderline paranoid schizophrenic?"

"Like I said, in the past I was a very, very sick man. Today I'm not."

Breitbart sighed. "Is it a fact, sir, that you were diagnosed as a borderline paranoid schizophrenic?" he insisted.

"Yes, sir."

"And at that time, sir, he also did an intelligence test on you—is that right?"

"He did."

"And he said not only are you crazy but you're stupid?"

Billy glanced toward the government table, expecting an objection if only because Rieger's letter had said nothing of the kind, but no one seemed to be listening.

"I can't help that," Billy snapped. "At that time I possibly was. I was a sick man at that time."

"You are not sick anymore?" asked Breitbart, inexplicably throwing away his advantage.

"No, sir," said Billy.

If the fire and Billy's private war with the Somerville Police Department had brought him to the edge of a breakdown, it was libido that pushed him over.

When he and Jeannette finished converting their house on Bromfield Street into a three-family home, they rented the first-floor apartment to Sam De Angelis, a hardworking young man with two full-time jobs, and his wife, Maria, a fast-working young wanton with a weakness for uniforms.

Until then, Billy had been going more or less straight as far as women were concerned, although not for want of opportunity. Partly to distance himself from those who would screw anything they could lure into their cruisers, but mostly because he doted on his three young daughters, he preferred to play the dutiful husband.

Stung by his apparent lack of interest, Maria De Angelis took to greeting him at her door when he came home from work. These were no chance meetings, as he at first supposed. They took place when everyone else was either out or asleep, and on each occasion she wore less than the time before. Finally, after she had appeared on the stairs stark naked, Billy spoke to Jeannette about it.

"You better go down and talk to Maria," he said over breakfast. "She keeps coming on to me, and I don't want nothing to do with her."

"Maria?" Jeannette concluded he was making trouble, as usual. "You're imagining things."

"I'm telling ya. She came out bare-assed. Right in the hallway. Exposing herself."

Jeannette sighed. They didn't talk much these days, which was just as well because when they did it always seemed to end in a blazing row. His moods swung from one violent extreme to another. One day she would be in fear for her own life, and the next she would hide his guns for fear he might kill himself. Too much fear for too long had withered everything between them.

"Yeah, okay," she said, but did nothing.

Maria grew bolder. She started telephoning Billy at the station. Every time the house shook with one of the Breens' epic fights, she would call him the next day to suggest that he leave Jeannette and move in with her. That he *needed* her. That Jeannette didn't know how to look after a *real* man—and not to worry about Sam. She was divorcing him anyway.

One night, after a particularly bitter scrap with Jeannette, Billy agreed to meet Maria downtown. After a few drinks, they adjourned to a motel and fell on each other like sharks in a feeding frenzy. Although no beauty queen, Maria was lustful and proficient. They coupled like demons—in bed, on the floor, in the shower, in the parking lot, and on the backseat halfway home. And when it became obvious that neither could get enough of the other on a part-time basis, she found an apartment for them in the Mystic Avenue Housing Project.

Besotted though he was, however, Billy started to hurt for his daughters as soon as he left home with his suitcase. He returned to Maria in a rage, took her roughly by the throat, and jammed her against the wall.

"All right, bitch," he said, as her eyes opened wide. "You fucked around with Sam, but lemme tell ya. I just left my wife and three kids for you. You fuck around with *me*, and I'm gonna put a beating on yez."

"Oh *yeah*, Billy," she breathed, slipping her hand down the front of his pants.

In a matter of weeks, he knew she was up to something. Maria would drive him to work every day in his three-year-old Cadillac (financed out of his disability pension) and every day the gas tank was empty. So then he kept an eye on the mileage. Sixty miles one day. Ninety the next—and whenever he came home and asked her casually what she had been doing, she would say, "Nothing, honey." And no, she hadn't been anyplace. Hooked on her gymnast's body, Billy was still wondering what to do when war broke out on Winter Hill.

He and Maria were spending the 1961 Labor Day weekend at Salisbury Beach in a cottage owned by Jimmy McGaffigan, whose brother cut Billy's hair in a Somerville barbershop. Having warmed up their act in a couple of bars, Billy and Maria could hardly wait to get back to bed, and were just getting into their stride when the bedroom door burst open.

"Jasus!" said McGaffigan, momentarily distracted by their intricate conjunction. "Billy, you're gonna haveta get the fuck outa here."

Locked together, they stared at him, thunderstruck.

"Aw, c'mon, Billy," McGaffigan moaned, trying not to look too closely. "Will you move it, for Chrissake? I got George downstairs. And he's going crazy."

"What the fuck?" Gorge rising ominously, Billy started to untangle himself. "George who?"

"George McLaughlin, for Chrissake."

Billy reached for his pants. McLaughlin was boss of the Irish mob in Charlestown.

"What's *he* doing here?" he demanded, motioning to Maria to get dressed. "What's going on?"

"Aw, George grabbed the wrong broad, that's all." McGaffigan couldn't take his eyes off her. "You know what he's like. Now they're coming after him, and all hell's gonna break loose. So do yourself a favor. Get lost. I'll come and get you when it's over."

Billy and Maria waited for several hours at a nearby lounge, but McGaffigan never came. Sometime after midnight, Billy decided the weekend was over and they drove back to Somerville.

There was nothing about it in the papers the next day, but when Billy reported for duty, he heard that George McLaughlin had been badly beaten by two of Buddy McLean's hoods from Winter Hill, who had rolled him up in a rug, senseless and bleeding, and dumped him on the highway. His brother, Punchy McLaughlin, had gone to see McLean about it, insisting that he hand over the men responsible, but Buddy had refused to consider it.

Two months later, while working the midnight to 8:00 A.M. shift, Billy was ordered to investigate a shooting on Snow Terrace, where Buddy McLean lived. He drove up, lights out, no siren, to find the area in complete darkness. Gun in hand, he got out of the car and peered around without enthusiasm. The whole neighborhood seemed to be holding its breath.

Alert for the slightest movement, he crept up the street until he came to a parked car with the hood raised. Shining his flashlight inside, he saw five sticks of dynamite with loose wires attached. Some would-be assassin had evidently been disturbed while rigging a bomb. Billy returned to his cruiser to ask for a check on the license plate, and when the dispatcher confirmed that the car belonged to Buddy McLean, Billy marched back to McLean's house and rang the doorbell.

"Waddiya want?" demanded a voice from an upstairs window.

"Who are you?" Billy asked.

"Who wants to know?"

"Patrolman Breen. I got reports of a shooting."

"So?"

"So if you're Buddy McLean, I got something to show ya."

"Yeah? Okay. I'll be right down."

Billy had looked forward to meeting him since joining the department. A loanshark, bookmaker, and hijacker by trade, McLean was a big, colorful, murderous Irishman who liked to stand at the door of the Alibi nightclub in Charlestown and challenge all comers to take him on. Although Billy had no such ambition himself, hard men came from all over Boston to try their luck, and mostly went home by ambulance.

They inspected the dynamite together, and Billy pulled out his notebook.

"Put it away," said McLean. "I'll handle this myself."

The next day, the Boston papers carried the story, along with a picture of Billy looking under the hood of McLean's car. From then on, McLean and the Winter Hill crew acted as though they owed him a favor, which was better than having them hold a grudge, as the McLaughlins found out that same morning. In full view of hundreds of people on their lunchtime break, Bernie McLaughlin, the youngest of the brothers, was gunned down outside a liquor store in Charlestown.

They were the first shots in a war that rumbled on, in and around Boston, for years, thinning out the gangster population, but Billy missed a lot of it. On top of everything else, after his picture appeared in the papers, he began to get death threats from McLaughlin hoods who seemed to think he had saved McLean's life. Billy's invariable response was to offer to meet them at a time and place of their choosing, but it was one more turn of the screw. Sleepless half the night anyhow, he resented being woken up by people wanting to know how he would like to have his balls cut off.

Then there was Maria. He called in sick one night and followed her to the officers' club in the Charlestown naval dockyard. The next morning, when she swore she had not been out, he slapped her around a little until she promised to stay home in the future. He did not believe her, of course, but had to pretend that he did because the only alternative was to kill her.

And then there was Jeannette. He could hardly ignore her when he went over to see his daughters, and she could hardly resist turning the knife in his self-inflicted wound. In the heat of another incandescent row about who was reponsible for what, she hit him with Sergeant Bukowsky.

When word got around that Billy had left home to shack up with Maria, it seemed the sergeant had called on Jeannette to console her. The moment she opened the door, he had dropped his pants, waved hullo with his member, and suggested they might have some fun with it. Unimpressed by this romantic gesture, Jeannette had almost literally closed the door on it, but had taken no further action in order to spare his family. She knew how painful it was, she told Billy, to have an unfaithful husband.

With blood screaming in his ears, Billy went for his gun and she flinched, afraid she had gone too far. But when he put the barrel in his mouth, she clung to his arm like a limpet, and they wrestled each other around the room, sobbing and cursing.

He could have shaken her off if he had used all his strength, but he had been serious enough at the time to make himself sweat when he thought about it afterward. What with the fire, and the whole world against him, he had nowhere to go except the VA hospital—but that, too, turned out to be a mistake. He had forgotten how much he hated psychiatrists.

He did not like the cubicle they put him in. Or the other patients in the group-therapy sessions. Or the military-style procedures he was expected to observe. Every morning they had to stand outside in the hall waiting for the doctors to come around. And so he lied to them or pretended not to hear what they said, even though the headaches and nightmares were destroying his mind. And as they seemed not to care whether he answered them or not, he started to abuse them.

"How you feeling today, Breen?"

"I don't fucking like ya. You know that, don'cha?"

"Yes, but how do you *feel*?"

"You're no fucking good, that's how I feel. Don't like ya. Don't like this place. And you ain't about to fucking keep me here, so don't worry about *that*."

"Well, I'm afraid you're wrong there, Breen. You're going to be here a lo-o-ng, long time—until you get well. So you better get used to it."

"Well, I *ain't* getting used to it. Ain't getting used to you. And I ain't never gonna fucking talk to you again."

Billy would then go into his shell for a few days, until one of the prettier nurses coaxed him out of it. But at the next morning parade he would be even more hostile than the last time, and after several weeks of increasingly erratic behavior, particularly after going home on weekend passes to keep an eye on Maria, he was locked up and reduced to a vegetable on 200 milligrams of Thorazine a day.

"Borderline schizophrenic reaction, paranoid type, manifested by suspiciousness, paranoid ideas, uncontrolled impulsive aggressive behavior, insomnia, and depression," was how Dr. M. D. Reiss diagnosed his condition. Billy's impairment was "severe at the present time, requiring closed ward hospitalization."

The six months Billy spent in the VA hospital were an almost complete blank. To this day, he can recall little about his confinement or about the events leading up to the night of his escape. He had evidently "progressed" to the satisfaction of Dr. Reiss, because the next thing he remembers is leaving the hospital on an escorted trip to Boston Garden for the fights, but he had come back from chemical oblivion with his problems intact. Although wiped out on tranquilizers, some corner of his mind had gone on festering with doubts about Maria. The moment his attendant's back was turned, Billy slipped away in the crowd to telephone the apartment on Mystic Avenue.

A man answered. Billy hung up and stared at the phone for a minute. Then he shook himself like a wet dog, and took a cab to the housing project. But his keys would not open the apartment door. She had changed the locks.

"I know you're in there—open the fucking door," he said, hammering on it with both fists.

He heard scuffling inside, and then silence.

"Maria?" he said calmly, although his voice shook. "Open the door or I'll break the motherfucker down."

"You'll break shit down," a man answered, none too confidently. "Fuck off. Before we call the cops."

Billy wandered away down the hall, looking for inspiration, and came upon a length of two-by-four in a heap of construction materials. Hefting it appreciatively, he went back to the apartment and smashed his way in, his heart pounding with satisfaction now that there was work to do.

Half-naked, screaming and shouting, Maria, a girlfriend, and two sailors retreated before him into the bedroom, where he battered the four of them insensible. He then turned his attention to the apartment, splintering every stick of furniture, wrecking the kitchen, and finally, as an afterthought, poking out all the windows. Tired suddenly, he leaned on his bludgeon and listened to the neighbors chattering like monkeys in the hall and the mournful cries of the Somerville Police Department closing in.

Nobody tried to detain him as he left, but he became more and more worried that he might have killed somebody. From the safety of Boston, he telephoned the Somerville police station to find out.

Sergeant Bukowsky took the call.

More unfinished business. Somehow he stayed coherent enough to tell the sergeant to get over to the Mystic Avenue Project and wait for him. He would be there in fifteen minutes.

Knowing exactly what to expect, Billy returned to Somerville for the second time that night. He stepped out of the cab into a flail of nightsticks and floored three of Bukowsky's reception committee before they beat him to his knees. There were just too many of them. Even so, by the time they reached the station, he had recovered sufficiently to require eight officers to wrestle him into a cell.

The next morning he appeared in Somerville District Court on an array of charges sufficient to get him kicked off the force and put away for years, but then he got lucky. The judge's bagman happened to be there, and for a thousand dollars undertook not merely to represent Billy but to get him off scot-free. And he did. Before allowing Billy to plead, he informed the judge of his client's mental condition and had him remanded to Westboro State Hospital for thirty days' observation. He was then brought back before the court on the *twenty-ninth* day, and as there was no one around to prosecute, the judge dismissed the charges. Without a stain on his character, Billy walked into the station to report for duty.

The chief was not amused. First, he insisted that Billy resign, and when he refused, suspended him. Indefinitely. Whereupon Billy said he would appeal, and demanded a hearing before the mayor, as was his right. If it came to that, he added, he felt sure the media would be interested in what he would have to say about the mayor's "business connections" and the chief's management of the police department.

That afternoon, Billy was called in by Vincent Bertocci, Somerville's city solicitor. A sympathetic and reasonable man, he saw Billy's point of view entirely.

"Look, you'll get your hearing," he said. "But why rock the boat? If you do, the chief will insist on twelve months' suspension at least—and believe me, Billy, after what you did, that's what you'll get. So why don't we handle it this way. If you really want to go back to work, we can settle right now for *six* months. If you promise not to make trouble. Maybe I can even get you your pay."

That was good enough for Billy, who needed a vacation anyway. He accepted the offer and left for Florida to get his head straight.

Six months later, a new Billy Breen returned from Miami to set up house in Medford with a new lady friend, Helen (whom he later married), the same psychological problems as before, and a positively vindictive determination to overcome his enemies by fair means or foul.

Where the old Billy had been a good cop with a bad attitude (when it came to taking orders), the new Billy was a bad cop with a good attitude, in the sense that he no longer much cared about the letter of the law if it got in the way of his cleaning up Somerville. Although outwardly recovered from his breakdown, it had subtly undermined his judgment.

Predictably, he was assigned to Winter Hill and Lower Broadway, the main battlefield in the McLean-McLaughlin war, which was still strewing Boston with corpses. But if the hope was that he might also become a casualty, the department had reckoned without the goodwill of Buddy McLean, who welcomed Billy home to the Winter Hill Cafe, reintroduced him to his crew, and vouched for him with visiting mobsters from out of state. There were many such "tourists," he discovered. Some came to Somerville for sanctuary, some on loansharking, bookmaking, or race-fixing business, and others to recruit mechanics for bank and armored-car robberies, hijackings, or murder hits.

Playing up to expectations, Billy became the perfect stage–Irish cop, complete with half-chewed cigar and blarney enough to stun a horse, but there was no one he could work with. What he needed was someone outside City Hall to whom he could feed the information he was picking up on Winter Hill. Rebuffed once by the FBI, he was not inclined to try again, particularly as McLean had hinted that he had a line into the Bureau's Boston office. That left the state police, who had also failed to impress—until he met John Regan on a hijacking case. But by then Billy was running wild with frustration.

Although outwardly he seemed much as usual, in private he would cry helplessly for hours on end, tormented by voices urging him to goad and harass the bad guys on his route. Night after night he would wade into the criminal population of Lower Broadway, bring in his prisoners—often via the hospital—and watch them go free the next morning when their friends in the department tore up the paperwork. He worked out a scheme for past-posting bookmakers (getting bets down *after* the race result was known). He wagered large sums and refused to cover his losses until there was no one left in town who would take his action—he had stiffed them all. He borrowed money from loan sharks, donated it to the church, and defied their enforcers to collect. He started his own football betting book to infiltrate the gambling syndicate operated by the Angiulo family and demanded a sit-down when one of its loan sharks beat up a client, Uddy Lepo.

As a rule, non-Italians fare badly before mafia tribunals, but Billy had a couple of things going for him, besides the fact that he was laying off his bets with the mob. One was that by now he was widely thought to be under the protection of the Winter Hill gang, and the other was that, for better or worse, he wore a badge. To underline the point, Billy showed up for the meet wearing a civilian jacket over his uniform pants, and with his gun hanging out.

"I'm Billy Breen."

"Yeah. We heardaya." Danny Angiulo looked him over without enthusiasm. "Shit wise-guy cop from Somerville."

"Listen, I don't want no fucking shit. Uddy Lepo is with me. And he don't owe nobody nothing."

"Listen," said Pete Limone, the offending loan shark. "Get outa my face. It's none of your fucking business."

"Oh yeah?" replied Billy. "Well, I'm *making* it my fucking business."

"Oh yeah? And who the fuck are *you*?"

After an hour's debate along these lines, it was finally agreed that if Billy laid off all his numbers with them, he could draw fifteen thousand dollars from Limone if he needed it and tell Uddy he was off the hook.

Without the lifeline to Major John Regan, there is little doubt that Patrolman Billy Breen would soon have been dead and buried, remembered, if at all, as just another crooked cop. But Regan gave him exactly the outlet he needed. Knowing he could never convict anybody of anything through his own corrupt department, Billy could now direct all his crusading zeal into winning the hearts and minds of the McLean mob as Regan's unpaid, unofficial undercover agent, keeping him up to date not only with movements in the Boston underworld but with criminal intelligence of interest to police agencies in half the states of the union.

As McLean's protégé, he hobnobbed with some of the deadliest contract killers in the history of crime. The Bennett brothers, Wimpy, Walter, and Billy, each destined to die during the McLean-Mc-Laughlin war. Joe McDonald, a murderous psychopath who robbed banks. His partner, Jim Simms. Frank Salemme, who told Billy he had committed the notorious Mickey Mouse Lounge murders in Revere. Steve Flemmi. George Kaufman. Jimmy Kearns, whom Billy later put away for the attempted murder of an assistant U.S. attorney in Texas. Murdo Margeson, a conspirator in the same crime. Billy "The Hulk" Kelly, later sentenced to death in Florida for the contract murder of a wealthy citrus grower. Buddy Chrehan. Dick Kadra. Howie Winter, heir apparent to Buddy McLean. "Indian" Joe Barboza, perhaps the most dangerous hit man of them all, who hid out in the Federal Witness Protection Program before being murdered himself.

Preoccupied with their war against the McLaughlins, none of them seemed to mind how much havoc Billy wrought among the lesser fry. They had him down as a rogue cop, and if that was how he got his kicks . . . The more time he spent in the Winter Hill Cafe, the more widely he came to be accepted as an ex officio member of the McLean crew—and, correspondingly, the more clairvoyant the Massachusetts State Police appeared to be.

With Billy's inside information, Regan enjoyed a nonstop run of success, solving or thwarting many of the bank and armored-car robberies, the hijacks, the hits and assorted mayhem that provided the Winter Hill crew with its daily bread. From the start, Regan had agreed never to say a word about Billy to anyone under any circumstances or ever to commit his name to paper. The work was dangerous enough without that. They never met, if they could avoid it, and hardly ever spoke to each other. Usually Billy would call Regan's wife, Rita, from a pay phone to pass on information, and she in turn would call the Winter Hill Cafe or the Harbor Lounge in Lynn to say lunch was ready when Regan wished to talk to *him*.

The first time they broke this rule was very nearly the last.

When Billy reported that a couple of hijacked tractor-trailers loaded with copper were parked by an old warehouse in Somerville, Regan suggested that they bring in the FBI. As a stolen interstate shipment, he said, it was best handled as a federal case. Billy hemmed and hawed but finally agreed to meet with Regan, Special Agent Olin Luxstead, and other agents from the Boston FBI office to tell them what he knew.

From the start, he sensed something wrong. Although Regan had vouched for him (without going into details), they listened with a blend of arrogance, indifference, and skepticism that went straight up his nose. It was only because Billy had no wish to embarrass Regan by seeming uncooperative that he agreed to take a run by the warehouse to make sure the trucks were still there, and if so, to get a description and check the license plates. The agents then gave him a number to call and went away.

Brooding about it afterward, Billy began to wonder why they hadn't checked out the lead for themselves, if they doubted his information. If they felt it was unreliable the first time, why should it be any better the second time? He waited until dark and approached the warehouse with no lights and extreme caution.

The eighteen-wheelers were there all right, but so were at least six cars, parked—apparently for the night—in an area where no one familiar with the neighborhood would expect to find more than their tire tracks the next morning. Without changing speed, Billy made a gentle U-turn, and saw headlights come on behind him as he headed back downtown.

When finally satisfied that he wasn't being followed, he stopped at a pay phone and got Regan out of bed.

"Those motherfuckers set me up," he said. "They tipped off the Hill."

"What do you mean?" Regan asked, half-asleep. "What are you talking about?"

"John, they was waiting for me. A whole bunch of 'em."

Regan digested this in silence. "Did they see you?"

"I dunno. But one thing's for sure—I didn't give *myself* up. And I know you didn't. So who else knew I was going up there?"

The next morning Regan confronted the agents with Billy's story, but they laughed it off.

"He's just making trouble," they said. "How can you trust a crooked cop?"

There was only one way for Billy to find out if his cover was blown. The following night he stopped by the Winter Hill Cafe as though nothing had happened. They seemed to look at him a little longer, were slower to greet him, but that could have been imagination. Then Tommy Blue joined him at the bar and started to talk about copper. Had Billy heard about the trailers parked up by the old First National Stores warehouse?

"Yeah."

Billy was watching the other's hands. Tommy Blue usually carried a hundred-dollar bill in his palm and a longshoreman's hook at the back of his pants. For people distracted by the sight of money, the hundred-dollar bill could be the last thing they saw before the hook bit into their skulls.

"Yeah," Billy said casually. "I heard you talking to Buddy. How the fuck do you move a load like that?"

It was good enough to get him by. They talked for a while and eventually Tommy moved away without showing Billy his hundred-dollar bill. But doubts remained. After that, conversations would peter out as he approached. People would look at him inquiringly instead of taking him into their circle. For several weeks he passed nothing to Regan and worked on rebuilding their confidence, but then the war gave them all something else to think about. Buddy McLean was gunned down by the McLaughlins on the street outside the Winter Hill Cafe, and Howie Winter took command.

Billy saw no immediate problem in this as Howie had always liked him, but in the state of armed emergency that followed the assassination, there were inevitably shifts of relative importance among the Winter Hill hierarchy. Contributing to the unsettled climate was a general probing for personal advantage while the new leadership got its act together, so that even *without* Tommy Blue, shot down in Charlestown, it began to look like a good time for Billy to take another vacation.

What settled it was George Kaufman, who had always seemed friendly before but now deliberately set him up for a hit. He asked Billy over to Wimpy Bennett's lounge and left him alone with Frank Salemme, who had never been a Breen fan and who now, with McLean gone, saw his chance to tidy up.

"I'm gonna fucking kill ya," he told Billy confidentially. "To-night."

Billy chuckled, assessing the odds. He was armed and might take one or two with him, but so what? He put a higher value on his life than that. The whole fucking roomful wouldn't be half enough.

"What's on your mind, Frank?" he asked. "Somebody ticket your car?"

"I don't like cops," he said, puffing whiskey fumes in Billy's face. "I don't like cops who hang around and hear things."

"About *you*, Frank? All I hear is, what a great guy. Always ready to buy a feller a drink, is what *I* hear."

Salemme frowned. This wasn't in the script. "Once a cop, always a cop," he said, trying to get back on track. "I don't like cops who know things."

"All I know is what I hear from Howie," said Billy carefully. "You ask Howie. He'll tell ya."

"Forget Howie," Salemme brushed this aside. "*Fuck* Howie. This is just you and me. And I'm gonna fucking kill ya."

"Fuck *Howie*?" Billy laughed, praying that his stock stood as high with the new leader of the Winter Hill gang as it had with Buddy McLean. "Well, you better fucking call him," he said suddenly turning nasty. "Before you fucking do something stupid."

They glared at each other. Then Salemme ushered him over to the pay phone, dialed the number, and turned away to prevent him from overhearing the conversation. Billy eyed the back of his head. He was tempted, but there were too many people watching. After a muttered exchange, Salemme held out the phone, then tramped furiously back to the bar.

"Yeah, Howie," said Billy, watching the room.

"Get outa there, Billy," said Winter. "You got a serious problem."

Billy got out of the lounge and out of town, without even stopping to inform the Somerville Police Department.

Delighted to hear he had gone AWOL, the chief sent officers around for his badge and gun, but Billy was in Miami, renting a trailer for Helen and their son, Billy, Jr., in the Bel Haven Trailer Court on Seventy-ninth Street. On his return to Medford, he gave Helen some money and a plane ticket, and after seeing them off he reported for duty as usual.

That night, the death-threat calls started again, and after a few chilly days of hanging around the Winter Hill Cafe, Billy decided it was time for a change. He did not *need* a badge to work with Regan. With his disability pension, he did not need the paycheck either. Neither one was worth all the hassle. Once he quit the department, guys like Salemme would probably feel more comfortable with him anyway.

With his mind made up to send in a letter of resignation from Florida, he set off for Miami with bag and baggage—a pretty little nineteen-year-old of Lebanese extraction named Fatima Yezzell—and set her up in an apartment on Seventy-nineth Street, not a mile away from the Bel Haven Trailer Court.

5

With scarcely a dent to show for his attack on Billy's sanity, David Breitbart now decided to expose Billy's criminal record to what he had earlier described as "the blast furnace of truth"—the implacable, revelatory fires of cross-examination. Instead of challenging the evidence connecting his client, Jesse "Doc" Hyman, with the Cowboy Palace affair, he seemed to have pinned everything on exorcising Billy as a demon-perjurer, as though the right abjuration—if only he could find it among his notes—would cause the government's key witness to disappear in a puff of sulfurous smoke, taking his testimony with him.

"Mr. Breen, did you tell someone after you were convicted of the bank robbery, that you had robbed that bank at the behest of Major Regan of the Massachusetts State Police?"

Earlier, Billy would have said no and left Breitbart to find his own way back, but the hamburger he had bolted down for lunch was stuck under his ribs like a marble slab. "I never robbed the bank," he said sourly.

Torpedoed before leaving harbor, Breitbart needed ten questions to get back on course, beginning with, "Were you convicted of the bank robbery?"—to which Billy replied, "Yes, I was"—and ending with, "And you were indicted and convicted of robbing a bank, using force and threats to coerce people to give you money, right?"

Billy took his time. "I believe it was a conspiracy they had me hooked up on," he said mildly.

Breitbart decided to start again. "You know the bank was robbed?" he asked, as though to a backward child.

"I knew it by looking at the newspapers the day afterwards."

"Were you innocent of that bank robbery?"

"Yes."

"Were you innocent?" Breitbart bestowed a knowing smile on the jurors.

"Yes, sir," said Billy, annoyed with Baird for not objecting to all this repetition.

"Now did there come a time when you got out on bail from the bank job?" Breitbart went on.

"Yes, there did."

"Did you go into a bar by the name of Giovanni's and stick a pistol in somebody's ear and rob the place?"

It was another one of those compound yes-or-no questions with a faulty component. "No, sir," said Billy.

"Didn't you make the guy put his head on his arms down on the bar and take the bar?"

"No."

"Did you let the person you were taking the money from see the gun?" Breitbart was getting irritable again.

"Yes," Billy snapped. "And I left the telephone intact and I left the money in the cash register and the money in the safe, so he could call the police immediately after we left."

A shrewder judge of character might have cut him off at the "yes"—and would certainly not have gone on to feed him the cue he wanted.

"You were working for the government on that one?"

"Yes, I was," he agreed. "I was working with Major Regan."

Breitbart nodded. "By the way," he said sarcastically, "you were working for the government at the Cowboy Palace, is that right?"

"Yes, I was." Billy brightened up. It was about time they got to that.

"Now, you had them call Major Regan, right?"

Billy frowned. About Cowboy Palace? "You said that," he replied cautiously. "I didn't."

"I am asking you."

"No, sir."

"Didn't you just say, sir, that you left a note there so that they could call Major Regan?"

"At the Cowboy Palace?"

"No," howled Breitbart.

"That's what you just said."

"Am I going too fast for you, Mr. Breen?"

"No," Billy shouted, and Bruce Baird finally rose to object.

"Just slow it down," Judge Sand admonished Breitbart. "Just a little bit. In your question, 'You left a note so that they could call Major Regan,' who was the 'they'?"

Breitbart ignored this. "Who is Major Regan?" he demanded.

"Major Regan was a major in the Massachusetts Department of Public Safety," replied Billy, correcting the tense. John Regan had died of cancer in 1983.

"Were you an informant for Major Regan when you robbed the bank?"

Billy grunted. There was another one. If he answered yes, the other was sure to twist it into an admission that he had robbed the bank. If he answered no, then Breitbart would say he had not only robbed the bank but had done so without Regan's knowledge.

"Yes, I was," he grumbled.

"Were you an informant for Major Regan when you robbed Giovanni's when you were out on bail from the bank robbery?"

"Yes."

"If you didn't put the pistol in his ear, where did you put the pistol?"

Billy was tempted to reply that he had never put a pistol in John Regan's ear. "I just told him to put his head down, and that's all I told him," he said.

"Well, let me understand first the bank robbery. These two things were pretty much the same time frame, weren't they?"

"Yes." Billy eyed him suspiciously.

"Now, you are telling us, you're telling this jury, that you were working for Major Regan when you robbed the bank, is that right?"

Billy sighed. "That's correct."

"And you were working for Major Regan when you robbed Giovanni's?"

"That's correct."

"And you didn't have to go to jail, is that right?" Breitbart invited the jurors to pay special attention to his answer.

"I would say I didn't have to," Billy said. "If I allowed it to be in open court."

"So you voluntarily chose to go to a federal institution and a state institution, even though you didn't have to?"

"That's correct."

"That's correct?" Breitbart was sure he had him now. "You wanted to do the time?"

"No, sir." They were now entirely at cross-purposes.

"Mr. Breen, isn't it a fact you have been a thief all your life?"

"No, sir." This was getting to be pitiful. "Let me explain why I couldn't go and have Major Regan or the FBI come into court. I had three children in Massachusetts, where the wise guys—that's organized crime, but they weren't Italians—had made a visit to my first wife and told me I better take the medicine and forget anything else. The second one, the woman I lived with, was hurt by the same individuals, and I couldn't do nothing about it. That's why I went to jail."

Once again, Breitbart had lost the upper hand by failing to cut him off. "It is your testimony, sir, that you had a choice? You didn't have to go to jail?"

"I had no choice," Billy insisted.

"You say that the force that was exerted, and the threats that were exerted, were such that you felt you had no choice."

"That's correct."

"Why did you have Major Regan have your time cut?" It was now a rearguard action.

"Major Regan didn't cut the first conviction," said Billy sharply. "I was sentenced under Section 4208 (b), and it was later taken back into court in ninety days, at which time my sentence was adjudged fifteen years."

"Breitbart fumbled through his notes. "So you consented—this makes more sense. You consented to the fifteen, not the twenty-five?"

"I didn't consent to anything," said Billy contemptuously. "It was an order of the court."

"You had a choice?"

"I had no choice . . ."

"In other words, Major Regan never said to you, 'Well, let's take your wife and children and get you out of here because we can protect them'?"

"I was divorced from my wife."

"Your children? He didn't offer to protect them?"

"They offered all kinds of protection. . . ."

But how could he possibly explain how little that meant when you were dealing with a power like the Winter Hill mob?

With time on his hands and money in his pocket, Billy soon made Florida too hot for him.

During his first enforced vacation from Somerville, he had met a crooked cop in Miami named Con O'Reardon, whose sideline was shaking down abortionists and whorehouse keepers. O'Reardon had introduced him to Vivian Walsh, a beautiful detective in charge of security at Burdine's department stores, and almost the first thing Billy did after installing Fatima down the street from Helen was to move in with Vivian.

Not content with this three-ring domestic circus, he proceeded to get his business affairs in a similar tangle, buying into a poker room across the street from where he was living (occasionally) with Fatima, and allowing Vivian to sucker him into a scam she was working at Burdine's with stolen refund vouchers. To complicate matters further, when he discovered that his partners in the poker game were paying off a bunch of killer cops in order to stay in business, he decided to take them all down, O'Reardon included.

Inevitably, it all went wrong. Vivian Walsh cashed several vouchers too many and Billy was arrested as her accomplice, making headlines in the *National Enquirer*. And after sending Fatima back to Massachusetts so that he could move in with O'Reardon and his wife, the better to find out what was going on, the killer cops got wise to what he was up to and pulled him out of a club one night to dispose of the problem.

Billy struggled like a madman. "These guys are gonna kill me," he screamed at the astonished bystanders. "They're taking me to the Everglades to kill me. Call the police."

One of them stuck a gloved hand over his mouth and he bit into it savagely.

"I'm Billy Breen," he yelled, as the writhing mass of bodies hit the sidewalk. "Get the license plate number. They're gonna kill me."

Under a hail of blows about the head and body, he managed to wedge himself across the open door of the car, resisting their increasingly desperate efforts to force him inside, and when some of the onlookers glanced at one another doubtfully, the cops decided to abandon the abduction. Peeling him off the car, they dumped him on the sidewalk, delivered a few parting kicks, and drove off at high speed.

Billy dusted himself down. "Fuck this," he said, and went back to Boston to work with John Regan.

To carry out his mission and survive, Billy had to be accepted as a full-fledged member of the criminal community and to be treated as such by everyone in law enforcement, except for Regan and the few others admitted to the secret. The only way for Billy to pass as one of the Winter Hill mob was to *be* one of them.

Acceptance meant that when somebody on the Hill asked him to do something unlawful he could not—*dared* not—refuse because then he knew about it. And to know about a crime without being involved in it, without sharing the risks, was to be a dangerous loose end, a possible threat to those who *were* involved. In any case, to be a member of the gang implied not just a willingness but a *determination* to take part in its criminal enterprise, so that any refusal to do so was bound to seem suspicious.

"You gotta look bad to look good" is Billy Breen's First Law of Undercover Work, and it applies on both sides of the fence. To protect his cover from the Hill's counter-intelligence agents, Billy's police files *needed* to be stamped "Organized Crime"—just like those on McLean, Winter, Kelly, Margeson, and everybody else from Winter Hill. They needed to be taken at their face value by the FBI, the state police, the Boston police, and every other cop in the country.

Certainly no agent of the FBI was in much doubt about his credentials. Whenever Billy's name cropped up in the files, he was always described as "armed and dangerous." A memorandum circulated by the Boston office, for example, stated that "Breen is a former police officer and, in recent years, has been suspected of being a fingerman in robberies and burglaries." The Tampa office was still less complimentary. After noting his police service, it went on: "He is alleged to have gone bad, and is now considered an armed robber, and he associates with well-known Miami thieves and hoodlums."

Winter Hill was always less confident in its diagnosis. Although meticulously careful in covering his tracks, Billy was still an ex-cop and therefore suspect. It was actually helpful, therefore, when he stood trial in Miami with Vivian Walsh for the Burdine's refund-voucher fraud and the jury found them guilty. The *National Enquirer* story about their arrest had already raised his stock considerably, and their conviction now confirmed him on the Hill as one of the boys.

A prison sentence, on the other hand, would have proved distinctly inconvenient, but luckily the Somerville police chief had planted a fatal flaw in the prosecution's case. In his anxiety to blacken still further the character of his bête noire, he injected so much rankly prejudicial testimony into the record that Billy's conviction was thrown out on appeal.

Although the game he played was appallingly dangerous, Billy found a curious, therapeutic fulfillment in it. (He certainly didn't do it for the money. For the seven years he worked with Regan, he was paid not a penny for all the information he supplied on literally hundreds of crimes, major and minor, committed or intended.) The nightmares that had plagued him since Guam were never far away, but the skills he had acquired in manipulating others also helped him to manipulate himself, to remodel himself, almost. For the first time since Guam, he had a role that fed his self-esteem and a life that made some sort of sense. At least, to *him*.

But it was coming to an end. Early in 1966, while relaxing in Florida with Fatima Yezzell, he met Frank "Doonie" Ryan and two members of Ryan's housebreaking crew from Montreal. As they were evidently mixing pleasure with business—Ryan gave Fatima a cashmere sweater with a mink collar and somebody else's initials on it— Billy fixed them up with Donna and Gayle, two party girls vacationing in Miami from Lynn, Massachusetts, and tipped off a contact in the police department.

Back home, he thought no more about it until Donna and Gayle came to the Harbor Lounge one day to tell him that the Miami police had raided the Canadians' apartment right after Billy's departure. Although Ryan and his companions had managed to escape, they were apparently convinced that Billy had informed on them. Warning the girls strongly against that kind of talk, he again thought no more about it until a few weeks later when Howie Winter called to say that Peter White, a cousin of Frank Ryan's, had shown up on Winter Hill to check Billy out. He had been asking around, wanting to know if he was a stand-up guy.

Howie and Billy had a good chuckle about that, although for Billy it was no laughing matter. Once the question was asked, doubts could remain. With Fatima in tow, he confronted White at the Harbor Lounge and did a good enough job of restoring confidence for White to call Montreal and assure Ryan that Billy was in the clear. By way of apology, they then invited him up to Montreal for a weekend party that tested even Billy's capacity for booze and broads.

A week or so later, Ryan showed up in Somerville with three of his crew: John Aslin, Clifford Piva, and William MacAllister. Loaded with Canadian currency, they scooped up Billy and Fatima, Donna and Gayle, and in three days blew the lot in Boston's nightspots with a recklessness that left Billy stunned (although not so speechless that he failed to advise John Regan that Ryan's housebreaking gang was in town).

When the money finally ran out, they adjourned to the Harbor Lounge for a nightcap, and kept on going until Ryan and Billy were the last two left awake.

"Well, I guess that's it, then," yawned Ryan. "Party's over."

"Listen, you short? You need a few bucks?" Billy reached for his billfold. "Tell me what you need."

"Nah, Billy. That's okay. Soon as we get to a fucking bank, we got plenty of money."

"Ah-hah." None of them looked old enough to rob banks. "Where's this? In Montreal?"

"Yeah. But we'll be back. I like this town. And next time, I wanna stay longer. Maybe we can do something together, you know?"

"Hey. Anytime." They were certainly old enough to go to jail.

"Okay." Ryan looked at him thoughtfully. "Tell you what—why don't you find us an apartment? On the beach, maybe."

"Sure." Sometimes it was almost too easy. "All you gotta do is lemme know when you're coming."

"Okay. And maybe you can rent a car for us."

"Just gimme a call, and you got it."

"How about a garage?"

That definitely meant they were coming back to work. "No problem" said Billy fondly, as wrong as he could possibly be.

He thought no more about it until MacAllister called from Montreal early in August to say they were on their way. Billy then hastily rented an apartment on Revere Beach (from the accountant who fixed the Winter Hill gang's income-tax returns) and got Donna to rent a car for them (as Hertz was unlikely to be impressed by his out-of-date Florida license). The garage he left for MacAllister to find for himself.

With their pockets refilled, Ryan and his party—MacAllister, Piva, and Rene LaChapelle—quickly made themselves at home on Winter Hill. Billy introduced them to everybody, took them to the Sunday-night cookouts at the Harbor Lounge, and as soon as they seemed to be socially on their feet, left them pretty much to their own devices. They were up to no good, but Regan agreed there was no point in making a move until they showed their hand.

Then, on August 26, 1966, the roof fell in.

Billy and Fatima had just arrived for the weekend at the Holiday Inn in Lawrence, some thirty miles north of Boston, and turned on the television to catch the six-o'clock news. Billy was in the bathroom, washing up before dinner, when Fatima suddenly squealed with excitement.

"Look, Billy," she cried. "Come quick. There are your friends."

He put his head around the door in time to see a squad of FBI agents removing Ryan, MacAllister, Piva, and LaChapelle in handcuffs from the Revere Beach apartment. Only hours before, the Canadians had staged an armed robbery at the West Lynn branch of the Essex County Bank & Trust Company, getting away with $49,953.

Billy's first impulse was to head back to Boston, but with the Ryan crew off the streets, it was mission accomplished. So why louse up the weekend? Unless somebody actually reached out to tell him the news, how could anyone be sure he had heard it?

Three days later, Billy appeared at the Winter Hill Cafe acting as though he had just found out—but everybody there behaved as though they had just found *him* out. No, the Canadians didn't need attorneys. They already had the best in town. Howie had seen to that personally. No, Ryan and LaChapelle had *not* made bail. Danny Melinski, Ryan's partner in Montreal, had made off with their money as soon as he heard of their arrest. (Later on, Melinski was to pay dearly for the inconvenience. He was blown to bits in his car while driving down Metropolitan Avenue.) But MacAllister and Piva *had* made bail. And MacAllister was looking for Billy. Why? For informing on them. Like he had in Miami.

Billy flew into a rage of protest and denial, but he could see they were not convinced. It was enough that the question of trust had been raised again. No one was disposed to *do* anything about it— Winter Hill was not directly involved, other than in a collective breach of hospitality—but they clearly intended to freeze him out. They were not even particularly impressed when a squad of FBI agents and state police raided the Winter Hill Cafe on September 1 and arrested Billy for complicity in the bank robbery, although Howie Winter *did* send attorney Joe Balliro downtown afterward to bail him out on a $10,000 bond.

Billy was stunned. It had never occurred to him that the FBI might try to tie him in to the robbery just because he had run around town with the Canadians, or that John Regan would fail to warn him of the danger, but he was now seriously at risk on all sides. On the one hand, MacAllister and many of the Winter Hill gang were making it plain that they regarded his arrest as no more than a routine FBI ploy to protect an informant's identity, and on the other, his defense counsel, Joe Balliro, kept insisting that the U.S. Attorney fully intended to prosecute him as the mastermind behind the robbery. It offended Billy's sense of justice. He had not put a foot wrong, but it was suddenly caught in a trap.

"I know, Billy," said Regan, almost as angry as he was. "It's a bitch. Nobody told me. I only heard about it when they took you in. But they're going to hear from me *now*—don't you worry about that."

"Well, I don't know, John." Billy looked at him doubtfully. "What are you gonna tell 'em? That I've been working against the Hill? Shit. That's gonna get me killed for sure."

"Billy, the Bureau knows how to protect informants. Don't worry about it. Everything'll be in the strictest confidence."

"John, it's *me* you're talking to. I been there. I met these people. You want every motherfucker in Boston to know something? Go tell it to the FBI. In confidence."

Regan grunted. "I know how you feel, Billy. But you're looking at twenty-five years in a federal penitentiary if I don't tell *somebody*."

"Shit." Billy collapsed back in disgust. "Either way, they got me in a trick bag. Even if you get 'em to drop the charges, the Hill's gonna think I cut a deal. And I never been *near* the fucking bank. They never even told me they was gonna rob it."

"I know, Billy. It's rough."

"All I did was find those guys an apartment and let 'em buy me a few drinks. What kind of a case is that?"

A weak one, Regan agreed. He would go to the judge and prosecutor with Special Agent Olin Luxstead as soon as the trial began.

Billy had to be satisfied with that, but the Winter Hill gang was far from satisfied. As most of them saw it, if Billy *had* given up the Canadians, he might also give up people nearer home. Equally, if he had *not* given them up, then he might try to do a deal with the Bureau to get off from the bank job. Either way, the gang needed insurance. With anybody else, a bullet would have been the natural answer, but as a long-standing member of the crew, Billy was entitled to a fair shake. Overruling those who favored the bullet, Howie Winter decided to put him to the test—a test that would not only bind him closer to Winter Hill but give them the leverage required to keep him quiet.

On the night of September 26, still keeping up appearances, Billy took Fatima for a drink at the Winter Hill Cafe and was told that Howie wanted to see him at Pal Joey's across the street. Wishing he had worn a piece, he was shown into the back room, where Winter was waiting with two of his bodyguards. They shook hands, which was a good sign, but nobody offered him a drink, which was a bad sign.

"Bill, you're going on a score tonight," Howie said. It was an order, not an invitation.

"Yeah?" said Billy, already in more trouble than he could handle. "What's the story?"

"The guys'll tell ya. They'll pick you up across the street."

"You mean, right now? Shit, I just came from there."

"Yeah, I know that."

Billy looked for room to stall. "Who are they, these guys? Do I know 'em?"

Howie shook his head. "Don't worry about it. They're good people."

"Okay. But I wish you told me sooner. I ain't exactly dressed for going on a score."

He was wearing a formal shirt, gray slacks, and a highly conspicuous red jacket.

"You're okay." Howie looked him over indifferently. "Just get rid of the coat."

The interview was over.

"Ah—I got Fatima with me," he said.

"Put her in a cab, for Chrissake. Send her home."

"That's a thirty-five-dollar ride."

"Billy, give her the money. They're waiting for you."

"Sure, Howie."

Billy returned to the Winter Hill Cafe, pretty sure that this was some kind of loyalty test. In the men's room, he jotted down John Regan's home number on a piece of paper, and when the cab eventually arrived, he passed it to Fatima with the ten-dollar bills he counted into her hand.

"Call him," he muttered, as he led her across the sidewalk. "Tell him they took me on a score but I don't know where."

He returned to his table to find three men sitting there in longshoremen's clothes: Jimmy McCormick, John Hurley, and William "Silky" Sullivan. They all lived in the neighborhood but Billy had never met them before. They ordered a few beers and fenced around about the job they were going to pull until just after 10:30 P.M. Then McCormick suddenly stood up and said, "Okay, it's time. Let's go."

Their car was parked down the street. Hurley made for the driver's seat, motioning Sullivan to get in beside him. Left with no choice, Billy climbed into the back with McCormick.

Tingling with adrenaline, Billy watched him out of the corner of his eye as they drove away, and sure enough, after a couple of blocks, McCormick reached inside his clothes and started to draw a big service-issue .45 caliber automatic pistol.

Billy struck like a snake. Crushing the other's wrist in his grip, he wrenched the gun free with his other hand.

"Okay, motherfuckers," he yelled. If this *was* a hit, he was going out in company. "This one is *my-an.* I don't like nobody pulling a gun on me unless I got one, too."

"Jesus," McCormick said, rubbing his wrist. "Take it easy, will ya? I was gonna *give* you the fucking piece, for Chrissake."

The other two thought this highly amusing.

"There's no fucking shells in it anyway," McCormick added.

"What's the matter, Billy?" asked Sullivan. "Worried about your health?"

Billy grunted. "Lemme tell ya, you pull a trick like that again and *none* of youse guys won't have *nothing* to worry about. Where the fuck we goin'?"

"Wait and see," said McCormick.

They drove down Route 9 for about forty miles and stopped outside Giovanni's restaurant in Framingham.

"You're shitting me," said Billy. "This it? We come all this way to hit a guinea bar?"

"Put this on," said Hurley. He handed Billy a stocking mask similar to the one McCormick was already pulling over his head, and a pair of white cotton gloves. "Now you and Jimmy go clean 'em out."

Billy shrugged. He had already decided he would have to play along, but at the same time mark a trail a mile wide for John Regan to follow. For a start, he left on his cranberry-red jacket.

McCormick produced another .45 caliber automatic and led the way.

"This is a stickup," he screamed as he burst through the door. "Don't nobody fucking move." To Billy, he sounded hysterical. "Just get your fucking hands up. *Now!* Before I blow your fucking heads off."

He waved Billy around behind the bar and switched off all the lights except for the red emergency signs. Then he started to line up the customers and go through their pockets. Taking his cue from McCormick, Billy showed his gun to the three men who had been serving behind the bar and made them lean on the bar. He patted them down, taking fifty dollars from the one he judged to be the owner of the joint, and emptied the cash register of about six hundred dollars, leaving enough change for someone to call the police on the pay phone.

Next he spotted a safe on the floor, out of McCormick's sight, and passed it by. Then he came upon a private phone, which he also ignored, instead of ripping it off the wall. After that, he could think of nothing to do except watch McCormick, still screeching threats and abuse as he worked through the customers. Getting bored with that, Billy wandered outside to see what the others were doing.

"How much you get?" Hurley asked.

"Who knows? Six, seven hundred?"

"*What?* Shit. They said five or six *thousand.* You get the register?"

"Well, what do *you* think?"

Billy climbed into the car, feeling a bit conspicuous standing out there in his mask.

"Shit. What about the safe?"

"Didn't see one," Billy said cautiously.

"Shit, shit, *shit.*" Hurley pounded the wheel. "Where's Jimmy? What the fuck's he doing?"

"Shaking down the suckers for loose change. But never mind him. What's *Howie* doing—putting me into a two-bit heist like this? He told me you guys were for real."

Hurley and Sullivan exchanged glances, and Billy sat back while they counted the money. It took them about a minute.

"We coulda stayed home and hit a candy store," he said.

Hurley hunched his shoulders, and they were silent for a while. Then Sullivan asked nervously, "What the fuck's he *doing* in there?"

"Who the fuck knows?" Hurley flung open the door. "I'll go get him."

A couple of minutes later, he came out of Giovanni's shooing before him a reluctant McCormick, still shouting abuse at the customers over his shoulder and warning the neighborhood not to follow them or he would blow its fucking head off.

Three miles back along Route 9, they were spotted by two Wellesley policemen, alerted after a telephone call from the restaurant, and although Hurley, who drove hit cars for Winter Hill, managed to outrun them for a few more miles, there was nothing he could do to beat a roadblock at Newton Highlands. The officers seized four automatic pistols and $778 and booked them for armed robbery.

Billy put on a show for the media, cursing and swinging at the TV cameramen, then checked in with Regan from the police station.

"No sweat," Regan said. "Make your bail and relax. Don't talk to anybody. I'll come right over and straighten this out."

He certainly tried, but Billy was now standing in the path of an avalanche. Triggered by nothing more substantial than the for once groundless allegations of a visiting bank robber, the accumulated mass of suspicion, resentment, rancor, and downright hatred that Billy had managed to build up against himself over the years finally toppled over. Regan apart, there was no one in the Somerville establishment, either at City Hall or on Winter Hill, ready to do more than shrug if it buried him. And there was certainly no one in the FBI's Boston field office.

To make matters worse, with the failure he had contrived for the raid on Giovanni's, his position in the gang was more precarious than ever. Far from providing Howie Winter and the others with a hold over Billy to keep him quiet, the robbery appeared to have *increased* the risk that he might give people up in return for a lighter sentence.

Regan had some thoughts about this. On October 14, he staged a high-profile "arrest" of the now notorious Billy Breen in Wellington Circle, Medford, on a phony Florida warrant, and took him in to the Department of Public Safety headquarters in Boston. With dramatic pictures of Billy lashing out with boots and fists at cops, reporters, and cameramen, the story made all the Boston papers and TV news shows, and certainly gave the Hill something new to think about. But, as Regan pointed out, the gang was probably the least of his problems. Unless Billy relaxed his own rules and agreed to play ball with the Bureau, there was not much a state cop could do to influence a federal judge and prosecutor.

After thinking this over for a day or two, showing the flag on Winter Hill, ducking the vengeful MacAllister, and badgering Joe Balliro to prepare his defense, Billy agreed to meet again with Special Agent Olin Luxstead and to give him something big enough to show the feds that he could be of more use to them outside than inside.

As it was no time for half-measures, he gave up Jack Griffith, bank robber, hit man, and Miami Beach karate instructor; Joe McDonald, Winter Hill's leading bank robber and psychopathic killer, and their apprentice, Bobby De Dico. These three had pulled off a hitherto unsolved robbery of the Midway Bank of Tampa.

Billy had known about it because when Griffith heard he was making one of his frequent trips to Florida, he had asked Billy to meet him in Tampa and give him a lift to Miami. This was out of his way, but Griffith had promised to pay three hundred dollars for the ride, which was as good as drawing Billy a picture. To satisfy his curiosity, the first thing Billy did on arriving in Tampa was swagger into his favorite mob tavern, where he learned that McDonald was in town and that there had just been a major bank heist (Q.E.D.).

After listening carefully to all this, Agent Luxstead prepared a statement and asked him to sign it. Billy refused. That was like asking somebody to sign his own death warrant, he explained, more or less politely.

Luxstead shrugged. Without a statement, he said, nobody would act on his information or even take it seriously. Billy had nothing to worry about. The Bureau was always careful to protect its informants.

It was even more careful to protect its agents, retorted Billy. The work was dangerous enough already, without having to expose himself to filing clerks in the pay of Winter Hill. Regan never asked him to sign anything.

Regan wasn't about to send him to jail for twenty-five years, observed Luxstead.

And when Billy violently protested that he had never even set foot in the fucking bank, Luxstead sighed—and stood up to go.

For the first and only time in his life, Billy signed an official statement with his real name, instead of a code name, laying information against major criminal offenders. He knew it was a mistake as he did so, but he felt he had no choice. With the statement in his pocket, Luxstead promised to go with Regan to see the federal and state judges and the federal and state prosecutors to explain Billy's situation. Beyond that, he said, he could offer no guarantees. (He omitted to mention that Billy himself was strongly suspected of being one of the three unidentified robbers of the Midway Bank, and that the U.S. Attorney for Tampa was preparing to indict him with the others.)

Not sure if he had made the situation better or worse, Billy now concentrated on his defense. In the bank robbery case, his Winter Hill attorney, Joe Balliro, reported that some kind of deal was being worked out between the prosecutor, Assistant U.S. Attorney Edward J. Lee, who lived in Somerville, and the smart Boston law firm of Crane, Inker & Oteri, representing the Canadians. It looked like Ryan's crew was going to cop a plea and testify for the government against Billy, setting him up as the mastermind behind the bank job.

"But I wasn't *in* it," said Billy, appalled. He had counted on the truth coming out, on getting affidavits from the Canadians that would clear him, although he knew that would not be easy, with MacAllister still trying to set him up for a hit. "They can't *do* that."

Balliro not only thought they could but that they would be stupid *not* to, and received Billy's instructions to seek the affidavits with tolerant unconcern.

"The government's got a pretty good conspiracy case," he said. "They can prove you rented the apartment. Donna Boras will say you got her to rent them an automobile. They got a witness who says you rented the garage they used."

"Bullshit," Billy bellowed. "MacAllister did that. I don't even know where it's at."

"Well . . ." Balliro studied him critically. "I guess he *does* look a little bit like you. But here's the clincher. They say they got a witness who can put you in the bank *before* the robbery. Changing Canadian money."

"That's a lie." Billy could feel them closing in. "I swear on my life I was never in there. Ask 'em. Ask Ryan. He knows I didn't do it."

Balliro threw up his hands. "Billy, if they cut a deal and say you *did*, then you're cooked. They got you for conspiracy. They got you as an accessory before the fact. You'd be better off pleading guilty."

"Fuck that." He stood up and kicked his chair across the room. "Forget about it."

When word got back to Winter Hill that Billy was in no mood for compromise, Howie Winter ordered the gang to tighten the screws, just in case. Billy's "friend," Jim McGaffigan, called around to see Helen, gave her a couple of slaps, and strongly recommended that if she cared for Billy Jr., she should warn Billy Sr. to keep his mouth shut.

Knowing Billy Sr.'s temper, Helen said nothing about the visit (until years later), packed her bags, and took their son to Florida, but Winter Hill had a long arm. Soon afterward, Jack Griffith stopped by the trailer she had bought as a temporary home and promised to blow them both up in it if she failed to convince Billy to take his lumps like a gentleman.

At about the same time, a deputation from Winter Hill also called on Fatima Yezzell. In their efforts to "persuade" that docile, soft-spoken girl to pass on to Billy a similar message, Howie's hoodlums terrified her so far out of her wits that she never fully recovered and has lived in a nursing home ever since.

For good measure, another team of muscle men visited Billy's first wife, Jeannette, and after complimenting her on the good looks of her three young daughters, suggested that the best way to keep them well and happy was to make certain her ex-husband stood by his shit.

There was nothing Billy could do. He could neither protect them himself nor ask Regan to do so—without as good as confessing to Winter Hill that they had been working together. When the trial began in federal court on December 1 before Judge W. Arthur Garrity, Billy knew he was done for unless Regan and Luxstead could somehow get him off the hook. The prosecutor, Edward Lee, had already refused to consider a deal unless Billy pleaded guilty to at least one of the charges.

"No," he bawled at Luxstead. "That's no good to me. You put me in a frame here. If I cop a plea now and take just a slap, the guys on the Hill'll think I'm giving 'em up. So tell him, go fuck himself. Because I didn't have nothing to do with that job. And you mother-fuckers *know* it."

That left the judge. On the opening day, Ryan, MacAllister, and LaChapelle changed their pleas to guilty, and prosecutor Lee asked that they be held as material witnesses against Billy and Clifford Piva, who has both elected to go to trial. As soon as a jury had been empaneled, the proceedings were adjourned, and Luxstead went with Regan to talk to Judge Garrity in chambers.

"He cut us off," Luxstead told Billy afterward. "Soon as he heard why we wanted to see him. Told us if we had anything relevant to say about you, he wanted the jury to hear it in open court."

Billy looked from one to the other. He was dead. And not really surprised. Now all they had to do was bury him. He was forty years old, and his life was over.

"So you'll have to decide, Billy," Luxstead said.

"Decide what? If I wanna kill my kids?"

"You'll have to decide if that's what you want us to do."

"Fuck off," he said. "Just leave me alone."

He held out for four days, getting louder and louder in his interruptions as the case proceeded, but reserving his wildest out-burst for Mrs. Virginia Rooney, a teller in the Lynn bank, who testified that she had seen him there before the robbery, changing Canadian dollars. In fact, she had seen MacAllister, who was of similar build and appearance.

"Bitch," Billy screamed, like a trapped animal. "Why are you doing this to me? I hope you die of cancer."

Judge Garrity ordered him to be restrained, and adjourned the trial so that Balliro could warn his client against any further disruption.

"Billy, you're making things worse for yourself," Balliro said. "That's all you're doing. While you were yelling and screaming, *I* was watching the jury. And they've made up their minds. You can see it in their faces. They already made up their minds. So what's the point of going on with this? Change your plea and get it over with. Everybody knows you weren't at the robbery, so if you quit now, who knows? Shouldn't be more than five years tops for conspiracy. What do you say?"

On the fourth day, December 8, 1966, lost in the coils of anguish, despair, and hysteria, Billy said yes. And in due course, Judge Garrity sentenced him to the maximum penalty of twenty-five years in a federal penitentiary, subject to confirmation after a psychiatric report from prison doctors at Lewisburg. (The four Canadians each drew fifteen years, with eligibility for parole after six months. A little over two years later, they were back on the street, robbing banks.)

Pumped full of Mellaril to quiet him down, Billy consented to be interviewed twice by psychiatrists, and in between brawling with other inmates, petitioned Judge Garrity for permission to withdraw his guilty plea. Although this was denied, when the marshals returned him to court on April 6, 1967, Judge Garrity evidently felt there were sufficient psychiatric grounds to justify a reduction in Billy's sentence to fifteen years—although not enough, it would seem, to call into question his competence to plead.

Winter Hill and City Hall could now relax. For an ex-cop and suspected informant, *any* term of imprisonment was as good as a death sentence. And a lot less humane.

6

It was not entirely unreasonable for Billy to suspect a plot to kill him. Or rather, *two* plots. On the one hand, City Hall and the federal justice system had rigged (or ignored) enough evidence to convict him of a crime of which he was innocent, knowing that his chances of survival in jail were slim at best. And on the other hand, the Winter Hill gang had seen its chance to eliminate a possible informer by setting him up for a fall, enforcing his silence and letting nature take its course.

With his whole world ranged against him, therefore, was it paranoid to be paranoid? Or was it a necessary condition for survival?

Billy had always been a battler. Although he rarely picked a fight, he even more rarely turned his back on one, and in Somerville, enough had come his way to keep him in shape. He enjoyed the rough and tumble, as long as he won, and when discretion looked to be the better bet, he could always fade away to Florida for a week or a month or until people forgot why they were mad at him. But in prison, nobody forgot. There was no retreat, and when he fought, it was to stay alive.

"Let's go back to a period of time in the sixties, sir," proposed David Breitbart, "where you indicated that you voluntarily felt that you had to go to jail. Remember that?"

"I didn't voluntarily think I had to go to jail," Billy snapped. "I went to jail because I was sentenced to go to jail."

"Was it a horrible experience, sir?"

"Yes, it was."

"You had some very harrowing experiences?"

"That's correct." Where had Doc Hyman found *this guy?*

"Forced you into the psychiatrist's office?"

"Let's say, because I was a former police officer, and the fact that the word got out that I was working with law enforcement, made my time a little tough."

"Is it your testimony at this time, sir, that you were institutionalized in a federal penitentiary and the people in the yard population felt that you were an informant?"

"That's correct." Hadn't he just said *that?*

"And you remained in population for seven years?"

"That's correct. But I did my—" Billy decided to help him out. *"Well, if you want to get to your answer, I did protect myself, yes. I could handle myself. I feared nobody."*

"You don't fear anyone now, do you?"

"No, sir." Not if they kept asking questions like these.

The attacks began in the Charles Street jail even before he was sentenced, before he had grasped what prison meant or the load of time he would have to carry. Trying to get them to recant, he traded punches in the cells with MacAllister and Piva, who still insisted he had informed on them, and almost every day, as word got around that he was an ex-cop, some other inmate would jump him during his exercise periods on the flats.

Then Piva attempted to escape one day while returning from court, and they were all sent to different jails. Billy was transferred to the Dedham House of Correction, where he immediately found himself in worse trouble, first with Pat O'Shea, a hoodlum from Somerville, who denounced him as an informer and swore to kill him the first chance he got; then with a procession of other prisoners with grudges against cops, and finally with the guards, most of them distinguishable from the inmates only by their uniforms. When one of them threw Billy's breakfast into his cell, Billy threw it back in his face. Three of them then threw Billy into the hole, where he went on hunger strike.

It was Billy's last flourish before the weight of Judge Garrity's twenty-five-year sentence crushed his spirit. Assigned under Section 4208 (B) of the Federal Code to Lewisburg Federal Penitentiary for ninety days' observation, he had, until then, failed to grasp what imprisonment meant, but the first slam of his cell door cut as deep as the horror on Guam. There was no escape from his nightmares now, not in women or booze or moving around or filling his days with excitement and risk. He was trapped with his ghosts in a stone labyrinth full of hostile murmurs.

That he had been stripped of any say in the conduct of his own life was almost the least of it. They were animals in here. He had seen them weighing him up like carcass meat, knowing he had been caged up to die. But Billy had never been a *willing* victim. He had already learned to stay out of blind spots in the yard, to be always in view of the guards in the gun tower or on the flats or in the dining hall, to avoid bunched-up lines at meal or movie times, and never knowingly to trespass on the turf of prison gangs and cliques. He also knew how to fight, and from instinct alone, would sell himself dearly. But locked up for the first time in his one-man cell in Lewisburg, listening to the blood thump at his temples, starting up at the strange, faraway echoes and cries that went on through the night, Billy could feel his demons closing in, and had no defense against them.

His cell was windowless, about seven feet by eight, furnished with a steel bed, a metal shelf, a seatless toilet in one corner, and a sink with a sheet of polished metal fixed to the wall above it to serve as a mirror. The only light came from a square fixture above the door. Lights out left him in total darkness.

"Lord have mercy, what am I doing here?" he kept asking the walls, and, "How did this happen to me?"—until he cried himself to sleep.

The injustice cut deepest of all. Billy *believed* in law and order. He had done everything he could to help Regan clean up Somerville, and yet here he was, locked in with the very worst of the scum he had put away.

From his first day in prison to his last, Billy was witness to so many stabbings, rapes, beatings, killings, and suicides, in which the screws made no attempt to intervene if it posed any risk to themselves, that he came to accept the unremitting violence as part of the ordinary daily round of prison life, as unremarkable in its way as office politics to a clerical worker. The level of savagery was numbing to watch and brutalizing to experience, but the last response it evoked in Billy was pity.

"When I went to prison," he said later, "I didn't see any men I would want to see in society. They're all animals. Forget rehabilitation—there's no such thing. Give me a list of every guy that's done heavy time in the joint and I guarantee I can put 'em all back in the penitentiary. They're no good—any of 'em. Sure, they learn something useful. They learn how not to get caught next time. They learn how not to leave witnesses."

Or informers. Billy had to fight almost every day for his right to exist, to exercise in the yard and eat where he pleased in the dining hall. Unable to think of any other way to deal with him, Dr. Wolfram Rieger tried to tranquilize Billy on a regimen of 50 milligrams of Mellaril, four times a day. "It is feared that were he not to receive that medication," Dr. Rieger wrote later, "he could acutely decompensate into a full-blown psychosis."

Although MacAllister was still telling everybody in Lewisburg that Billy was a fink, the arrival in population of Murdo Margeson took some of the pressure off. Then aged around 50, Margeson was one of Winter Hill's senior statesmen, with a lurid record of bank robberies, hijacks, assorted rip-offs, and drug dealing. Having spent most of his adult life in prison, he was widely respected in criminal circles—and he had known Billy since he was a cop hanging out at the Winter Hill Cafe. When Billy told him his troubles, Margeson went to see his tormenters and got them to agree that if Billy kept out of their way, they would not come looking for him.

The relief was only temporary. When the ninety days were up, Billy again refused to allow John Regan to explain his situation in open court, hoping for a miracle, some softening of hearts perhaps, after the psychiatrists' reports. Instead, Judge Garrity resentenced him to fifteen years.

And there was worse to come. On January 29, 1968, at the end of a seven-day trial, he caught an additional seven-to-twenty years in state prison for the robbery of Giovanni's—and because his attorney, Joe Balliro, had allowed the federal case to be tried first, the sentence was to run consecutively instead of concurrently.

The only shred of consolation Billy could find in his situation was that he had begun to meet a better class of gangster. As part of the lip service paid to the pieties of rehabilitation in Lewisburg, he had been required to learn a useful trade. While his fellow convicts had mostly settled for metal bashing or sewing mailbags, Billy had chosen to preside over a chair in the prison barbershop, dispensing regulation haircuts to inmates ignorant or careless of his reputation.

These were often senior mob figures too preoccupied with business and family affairs to pay much attention to prison gossip. What they looked for in a barber was respect, a little light conversation, and a decent haircut, and getting all three from Billy, the prison's aristocracy was soon asking for him by name. In a matter of months, his regular customers included Jimmy Hoffa, former president of the Teamsters International; top mafia hit man Charles Allen; New York big shot Joe Beck; Anthony "Tony Pro" Provenzano, the New Jersey Teamsters boss, and Raymond Patriarca, head of the New England mob, from Providence, Rhode Island.

Although they never talked business in front of him, Billy over-heard a number of heated arguments between Hoffa and Tony Pro, one of them taking Hoffa to the brink of assault before Allen inter-vened. Now in the Federal Witness Protection Program, Allen told the Senate Permanent Committee on Investigations in 1982 that, while in Lewisburg, Hoffa had asked him to kill Frank FitzSimmons, Hoffa's successor as Teamster boss, to clear his way back into office. He also wanted Allen to kill Provenzano, but Tony Pro got in first. According to Allen, Provenzano told him that Hoffa, who vanished without trace in July 1975, had been "ground up in little pieces, shipped to Florida, and dumped in a swamp."

Toward Billy, Hoffa was unfailingly genial. He even gave him a thousand dollars to hire a Philadelphia attorney to argue that Billy had been incompetent to plead in the bank robbery case, citing in evidence his discharge from the navy with a psychological-disability pension.

"If we get a hearing, we can walk Billy on this one," said William Ross Phillips, a jailhouse lawyer and Billy's only real friend in Lewisburg. "Because then the government's gotta *prove* he was com-petent."

"Thanks, but I don't need you to instruct me on procedure," said the attorney.

"No, well . . . The main thing is you mustn't let Billy take the stand. The government's gonna want that, but you gotta say no. If they're gonna turn their shrinks loose on him, we want the court to vacate the sentence first. Then you can ask for bail."

"Nor do I need instruction from you on courtroom tactics, Mr. Phillips."

At the hearing, Billy's new attorney not only allowed him to take the stand but omitted to ask for bail. On the strength of Billy's responses to the questions put to him, the court ruled that he was, and had been, fit to plead, confirmed the fifteen-year sentence, and sent him back to Lewisburg.

Undeterred, Phillips helped Billy file another pro se motion under Section 2255 to vacate his sentence. This time, the case hung fire in district court for almost eight months before a new judge threw it out, but by then Billy had something more serious to worry about. His life.

Although battered and scarred, he had so far held his own in the weekly round of brawls and skirmishes, keeping himself in shape with a little weightlifting and by running at least three miles a day (when not confined to the hole). But with no one around to watch his back, it was only a matter of time before someone got to him with a sneak attack, and that moment arrived one night in cell block H while he was watching television.

Ironically, Billy had gone to some trouble to get assigned to block H because MacAllister and Piva both lived there and he had still not given up hope of getting the Canadians to exonerate him, but when the blow came, it was not from either of them, but from an inmate named Smith, whom Billy hardly knew.

It knocked him out of his chair, scattering his wits sufficiently for Smith to sap his strength with a flurry of kicks and punches before Billy pulled himself together. Reaching under his bunk, he came up with the window pole he kept there in case of emergencies and bounced the iron-shod end off Smith's skull. Smith went down, literally pole-axed, and as Billy went in for the kill, MacAllister, of all people, pulled him off to save him from a homicide charge.

Three days later, Billy was waiting on line in the dining hall when another convict he knew only by sight, a former nightclub bouncer named Fields, started pushing and shoving him from behind. Recognizing this as a deliberate provocation, knowing its purpose and where it would lead, Billy skipped the intermediate stages and floored him with a short right cross to the jaw. But Fields was much bigger than he was, and to neutralize the advantage Billy automatically followed up the punch with his boot. Jailhouse fights were always to maim or kill, and anyone who let up before crippling his opponent was not only in breach of the house rules but unlikely to profit from his magnanimity.

Absorbed in trying to finish Fields off with a well-placed kick, he failed to notice one of the dining-hall guards who had crept up behind him and now jumped on his back. In no doubt that it was a friend of Fields, Billy threw him off so violently that the guard was sent skidding across the floor, crashing into tables and chairs.

"Oh, shit," said Billy, disgusted. Another beating from the hacks. Another thirty days in the hole. Another loss of good time.

That night, locked up in solitary, he waited for them to come with their clubs, but he had made up his mind that he was not going to take another beating. Dumping the guard had been an honest mistake. To defend himself, he broke the sink off the wall for a weapon, and the sight of him at bay in the corner of his cell, wound up to killing pitch, taunting them to come and get him, was enough to deter the goon squad from going in.

He drew thirty days' solitary on half-rations and a bigger dose of Mellaril from Dr. Rieger. It made him feel like a zombie, but he worked off the worst effects with endless sit-ups and press-ups. Hundreds at a time . . . rest . . . then hundreds more.

When his punishment was up, he returned to H block to find

Smith still living in the same open-cubicle dormitory. For days they circled each other like alley cats whenever their paths crossed, until Billy, to show his contempt, finally turned his back on him.

Smith attacked like a madman, determined this time to allow no chance for a comeback. Beaten to his knees, Billy tried to protect his head from Smith's boots, and took savage, full-blooded kicks to the stomach, chest, and groin. With the others urging him on to make the kill, an overconfident Smith now closed in to finish him off, but Billy grabbed his legs and hung on literally for dear life, smothering the attack long enough for his mind to clear. Somehow finding the strength to throw Smith off, and in pain that threatened to burst his mind, he forced his buckling legs to carry him as far as his bunk before he fell down again.

Smith, so far untouched, now made the mistake of not closing in fast enough. As he approached, Billy managed to straighten up with the window pole—nearly fainting as the pit of his stomach seemed to split wide open with the effort—and connected with Smith's head like Mickey Mantle hitting a home run out of Yankee Stadium.

Smith went down, slack-limbed in a spray of blood as though never to get up again, and Billy, split open or not, fought to raise the pole high enough for a blow to make sure he never would.

With no MacAllister around this time, it fell to a guard, attracted by the commotion, to order Billy to put down the pole.

Billy thought about it for an age, and was still undecided when he slowly doubled up from the agony scalding his groin and fell in a heap. The guards then took him back to the hole and Smith to the hospital.

These were not movie fights. Seldom less frequently than once a week since entering the federal prison system, Billy had been forced to defend himself with fists, boots, and any improvised weapon he could lay his hands on. In this world, nobody got up from a punch to the jaw, dabbed at the corner of his mouth, and carried on as if nothing much had happened. A punch to the jaw meant choking on a mouthful of blood and broken teeth. A kick in the stomach could mean a ruptured spleen. In the real world, pain *hurts*.

Smith went to the hospital concussed, with his scalp hanging off, while Billy, doubled up all night in solitary, began to swell and turn black from his knees to his chest. It was not the best thing that could have happened to someone liable to "decompensate into a full-blown psychosis."

To his surprise, he was released early from solitary, and found out why a few hours later. In the middle of the night he was ordered to get his things together, marched down to the yard, and put aboard a bus with a score of other "incorrigibles." With the closure of Alcatraz, the government had decided to house the dregs of the prison system in its Atlanta penitentiary.

Billy did not much care. It would make a change. Although it was a long way from Massachusetts, no one ever came to visit him anyhow, and the climate was better. But any hope of a fresh start faded as soon as he stepped down stiffly from the bus. Assigned to the third tier of C block, a building of individual cells for hard-core offenders serving ten thousand years of prison time among them, Billy had barely reached the first tier before being greeted with wolf whistles, catcalls, and shouts of "Don't check in" and "No cops allowed."

By the time he and the guard reached the second tier, he had had enough.

"Shut up," he wailed, his voice ringing and echoing through the cell block. "Leave me alone, why don'cha? Forget all that shit. I'm in for bank robbery, for Chrissake. Just lemme do my time."

His one hope of surviving in population seemed to be Murdo Margeson, now also serving a federal stretch for bank robbery. Billy met him after work the next day by the iron pile in the yard.

"Sweet Jesus," he said. "Am I glad to see you. What the fuck's going on, Murdo? The minute I get off the fucking bus, everybody acts like they wanna kill me."

He meant it as a joke, but Margeson did not laugh. "That's right," he said. "There's a contract on you."

"On *me*?" Billy stopped in his tracks. "What for? What'd I do?"

Margeson walked on. "You know what you did. Joe McDonald told me."

"Joe McDonald?" That *was* serious. "I never did nothing with Joe. What'd he tell ya?"

"He says you're an FBI informer."

Billy was winded with shock. "Then he's a fucking liar." He began to sweat. "Why's he saying things like that fur? If I'm an informer, why would they put me in here?"

"Don't tell me nothing if it ain't so, Billy. He says he's seen an FBI paper you signed. About the bank job him and Jack Griffith pulled in Tampa. The one they got popped for. So don't gimme no shit."

"It's a setup," he croaked. Fucking Luxstead. Special Agent Olin fucking Luxstead. "I never signed no paper. Shit, what could I tell 'em? I drove Jack to Miami, that's all. That's all I know about the Tampa job. Shit. It don't make sense. You think if I gave 'em Joe and Jack and Bobby, they're gonna say, thanks a lot—here's fifteen years in the can? That's crazy. Some motherfucker's setting me up."

Margeson glanced down at him, his expression unreadable. "Maybe it's MacAllister," he said. "I know he went to see Howie right after he made bail. Said you were real bad. Said you gave 'em up for that bank job."

"Oh yeah," Billy said bitterly. "That makes a lotta sense too, don't it? I mean, *I* got more time than *they* did."

"Yeah." Margeson nodded. "It don't add up right. But watch your step all the same. There's a lotta guys in here'll kill ya just to be on the safe side. You get any problems, come to me."

"Yeah, I will, Murdo. Thanks. I know you'll steer me right."

Fucking Luxstead. Brooding about it that night in his cell, Billy could think of only two ways to explain the leak, outside of some clerk in the Boston FBI office selling information to the Hill. Either Luxstead had deliberately given him up to Howie and the gang, in which case, why had he waited so long? Or else the U.S. Attorney was using the paper Billy had signed for Luxstead as part of the government's case against McDonald and Griffith and had handed it over to their attorneys as disclosure material. Either way, the FBI must have known it would get him killed.

A few weeks later, Billy arrived in Tampa as a co-conspirator in the Midway Bank robbery. He was given a court-appointed attorney and lodged in the county jail with Joe McDonald to await the pleasure of Assistant U.S. Attorney Richard A. Hirsch, whose case appeared to consist of no more than Billy's statement and a few bits of circumstantial evidence.

With a high-priced mob attorney in his corner, McDonald was evidently confident of taking a walk. Whenever he could get within earshot of Billy, in the prison bus or in the courtroom, he would mutter, "Keep your mouth shut," or "Don't talk to the agents"—and his manner made it clear that he held Billy responsible for putting him on the spot.

To underline the warning, Howie Winter sent Fatima Yezzell to Tampa to explain the penalty for defiance. Shocked by her appearance, Billy demanded to know what the Hill had done to her, but she could not tell him. Crying helplessly, she held out a note for him to read.

"Keep your mouth shut." Signed, "Howie."

The case then took another bizarre turn. The charges against McDonald and Billy were dropped, and a third defendant, Dick Kadra, was brought down from Massachusetts to stand trial for a robbery he had had nothing to do with. Billy could only assume that, like him, Kadra had been forced to take the rap for a crime he had not committed because the Hill had threatened his family.

Within hours of his return from Tampa, Billy was jumped by a mob enforcer who seemed happy enough to pick up the contract on his life, until Billy bit through his ear. When this unorthodoxy was brought to the notice of the mob executives who effectively ran the prison, it took all of Margeson's diplomacy at a formal sit-down with the Italians to avert the risk of a *second* contract. Even so, Billy was no sooner off that particular hook than he was snagged by a bigger one.

Jimmy Kearns stood 6 feet 4 inches and weighed around 250 pounds. Then 31, he had been working on his police record since the age of 7, starting as a juvenile with larceny and destruction of private property, moving on to rape and assault at 18, and at 26, graduating from Walpole state prison as a professional hoodlum, with majors in burglary, hijacking, and bank robbery.

Although he took no sides in the McLean-McLaughlin war, he bore the scars on his face of a machine-gun attack that had killed the driver of the car in which he was traveling, an incident that improved his disposition as little as his appearance. When teamed with his friend Billy Kelly, who, at 6 feet 5 inches and 270 pounds, was even bigger, and Murdo Margeson, who was a little smaller but larger in experience, they were Winter Hill's ultimate deterrent.

As a Somerville cop and later as Buddy McLean's protégé, Billy had tried to keep John Regan up to date with their careers, but only when quite sure that the information could never be traced back to him. Now, when it seemed certain that the Hill knew about his statement on the Tampa bank job, almost the last person Billy would have wished to see in Atlanta, apart from McDonald himself, was Jimmy Kearns.

Luckily, he was walking with Margeson when they met. Kearns stared for a moment, then advanced on Billy with such a purposeful air that Margeson stepped quickly between them. Baffled by his intervention, Kearns started to berate Margeson for protecting an FBI informer, and Billy made himself scarce, pausing just long enough to hear Margeson suggest that Billy would never do anything to hurt them.

Later that day, Margeson came to tell Billy that Kearns wanted to see him in the yard. He would not say why, and Billy had to draw what comfort he could from the thought that if Kearns meant to kill him, he was unlikely to do so in front of several hundred witnesses.

They met by the iron pile. Not knowing what to expect, Billy had already picked out the equalizer he would go for if Kearns turned nasty, but after a long, unsettling glare, the other said, "Okay, start walking," and set off briskly across the yard.

"Now get this," he went on, as Billy fell into step beside him. "I am not your friend. You're no fucking good, and I oughta kill ya."

He noticed Billy's involuntary glance up at the guards in the gun tower, and grunted.

"They won't do you no good," he said. "Anytime I wanna reach out for ya, that's it. But Murdo says you're his friend, so I'll put up wit'cha. For now. But watch your step, motherfucker. You get outa line just once, and you're *gone*. Understand?"

"Jimmy, lemme tell ya something—"

"Get away from me," Kearns yelled. "I don't wanna hear *nothing* from you. I don't want nobody to see me wit'cha. I don't want nobody to think you're my friend. Just fuck off."

Billy shrugged and turned away, ready to run if the other came after him. But all Kearns did was shout, loud enough for a hundred cons to hear, "You be careful, you asshole."

Margeson thought he had gotten off lightly. "Just remember one thing," he said. "Don't ever be alone with Jimmy. Not now, not ever. He hates you. I know you never done nothing to him, but he hates ya. And he'll kill ya in a flat second."

In one form or another, death was on Billy's mind for much of the time now. He was dreaming of dead men again and, in his more despondent moments, saw himself among the walking dead, rotting away from the secret injury he had nursed since his fight with Smith in Lewisburg. The black bruising that had spread like ink under the skin of his abdomen from kicks in the stomach and groin had faded very slowly, and slowest of all from the genitals, where a small ulcer had developed that bled constantly and refused to heal.

Always fearful of doctors, and having no faith at all in those who practiced within the prison system, he had kept the injury to himself in the hope that it would eventually go away, but it was getting worse. Unable to delude himself any longer, he asked an inmate who worked in the hospital for some pills or salve. The other promised to find out what was best for a bleeding penis, but came back empty-handed a couple of days later to say that the doctor wanted to see him.

Billy reported for sick call like a condemned man facing the chair. When the doctor shook his head over the injury and said he wanted to run a biopsy, it was no more than Billy expected. Nor was he much surprised when he picked up an infection from the biopsy and was rushed to the hospital with his genitals swollen to twice their size.

From then on, it was all downhill. The doctor decided to operate, and once again the wound became infected. Fed Valium on demand as a painkiller, Billy lay like a corpse on his hospital bed for week after agonizing week while the flesh melted off his bones. Already down twenty pounds to around 160 on admittance, his weight now fell to less than 140 pounds while he waited for the Lord to have mercy.

When Kearns reported for sick call one day and happened to catch sight of him, unkempt, unshaved, and gaunt as a scarecrow, they found themselves in agreement for once.

"Die, you motherfucker," Kearns said.

"Amen," said Billy.

But just as Margeson had kept him alive in population, so two of Billy's barbershop clients, Sam "The Plumber" DeCavalcante, boss of the New Jersey mob, and Gyp DiCarlo, a big wheel in Philadelphia, kept him going in the prison hospital. Both came by daily to stiffen his will to fight, bringing steaks, fruits, and other delicacies to tempt his flagging appetite.

"This is no good, Billy," DiCarlo would say. "They're just letting you die in here. You gotta *do* something. You gotta get somebody working on it. How about your family?"

"Yeah," Billy would say. "How about them?" He had not seen or heard from anybody in years.

But DiCarlo continued to nag and finally took matters into his own hands.

"I got my attorney coming in," he told Billy one day. "I'm gonna get him to help ya. Because you're not gonna just lie there and die in this fucking place. I won't letcha. So think of somebody he can call. Somebody down here, maybe. In Atlanta. A friend or a girlfriend or something. Come on, kid. You gotta beat this thing."

Thinking about old girlfriends that night in one of his increasingly rare periods of lucidity, Billy suddenly remembered Vivian Walsh, who had involved him years before in her Burdine's refund-voucher scam. Her sister Rosalie, who had always been very friendly, lived with her husband, Al Garber, in Atlanta. Billy clung to the thought long enough to tell Gyp DiCarlo's attorney, but it was almost too late.

Sam DeCavalcante issued instructions that Billy was to see his friends alone. Too weak to stand, he was brought in by wheelchair, and the Garbers looked at each other doubtfully. They remembered him as a bouncy, bulky, apple-cheeked Irishman of inexhaustible vitality. It was only after a long hard look that Rosalie Garber finally recognized Billy in the haggard, semi-comatose figure in the chair, and burst into tears. Then into a rage.

She and her husband yelled at the guards to fetch the doctor, then at the doctor to take them to the warden's office, where they yelled some more, and the next morning Billy was taken to Grady Hospital in downtown Atlanta. But he left on a stretcher with a sheet over his face after his family had been notified to come and collect the body.

Billy was in Grady Hospital for eleven weeks, almost until the first anniversary of the biopsy that had gone wrong, and before he eventually pulled through, the family was again invited to make arrangements for his funeral. Besides persistent internal bleeding into the thoracic cavity, he had developed a fistula in his right lung, probably as a result of another kick, and among the medical staff it was anyone's guess as to which would kill him off first.

The fistula was so large that every doctor who examined him advised an immediate operation, but every time he was presented with a consent form, Billy refused to sign. Papers were then drawn up for his wife, Helen, and brother Tom to authorize the operation *without* his consent, but Billy persuaded them to give him ten more days. He had no idea why.

For eight days he prayed hard, and grew weaker. On the ninth day, with the doctors offering little or no hope for his survival unless they acted at once, Billy started to cough during the night, huge shuddering coughs he could not suppress. After bearing the pain for as long as he could, he pressed the bell for help, and when the doctor on duty removed the bandages, he found that Billy had coughed out the catheter in his side.

Without further argument, an emergency operation was ordered—only for Billy to present his doctors with a new problem. On the way to the theater, Billy was wheeled into the X-ray department for a last-minute set of pictures of his fistula to assist the hastily assembled surgical team. But they couldn't find it! The huge suppurating hole in the upper lobe of his right lung had completely and inexplicably disappeared.

There was no doubt in Billy's mind that God had saved him for a purpose. Nor could he doubt what the purpose was. Part revenge—on the corrupt officials and street scum who had brought him to this. And part mission—to bring down every criminal target of opportunity that presented itself. Beyond that, as he wrote in his notes at the time, he felt an obligation to "demonstrate greater appreciation of life; greater tolerance, compassion and concern for others; higher self-esteem; less concern with material goods."

They were not easy virtues to practice in a prison environment. When he was judged fit enough to be moved, Billy was taken back to the penitentiary, and returned to population in just three days, despite his weakened state after nearly twelve months in a hospital bed. On making his first appearance in the dining room, he was accosted by Pat O'Shea, from Somerville, and his cellmate Buddy Cochran, who presented him with a list of items they wanted Billy to buy for them at the commisary.

Showing little "tolerance, compassion and concern for others," Billy told them to fuck off. And when Cochran took a menacing step forward, he swiped at him with his heavy metal tray.

"Breen, you're embarrassing me," screeched O'Shea, and the guards moved in swiftly to prevent a brawl.

A few minutes later, O'Shea came over to demand that Billy meet him down by the barbershop when he had finished eating.

"You got it," said Billy belligerently, as incapable as ever of backing off from a challenge.

"They're setting you up," Margeson observed, when O'Shea rejoined Cochran at the door. "Don't go down there."

"That fag? Shit. They're not putting the arm on *me*."

He was met at the foot of the stairs with a flurry of blows from O'Shea and Cochran, who knocked him down, then started hacking away with their boots at his head and body. Still too weak to put up much of a fight, Billy would almost certainly have died there in the stairwell if a group of convicts coming down from the dining hall had not disturbed them long enough for him to grab at the chance to escape. Stumbling away, he made it as far as the barbershop and collapsed into his chair, knowing he was done for if they followed him in, although he put a razor in his pocket.

The first man through the door turned out to be a guard, attracted by the commotion.

"What happened?" he asked, looking Billy over critically.

Billy peered at himself in the mirror. They had smashed his glasses, but he could see he was bleeding freely from the nose and mouth. Exploring gingerly, he found that most of his teeth were broken. One eye was swollen, the other already turning black. And his side hurt so badly that he had to wonder if they had busted his lung again.

"Nothing," he said.

By the following night, he was on his way to Danbury to finish his federal time, traveling with "Big" Joe Beck, the mafia boss of New York's garment district.

7

Almost from his first day in prison, Billy had made a study of the habits, speech, and attitudes of street people, not just as an aid to survival, but against the day when he would start to exact his revenge. Besides his barbershop clientele, he now had a useful list of major crime figures who had either offered to help him on the outside or from whom he knew he could expect a welcome when he looked them up—people like Jacob Maislich, aka Jack Mace, the master fence who effectively ruled New York's Diamond District; Ali Calabrese, an up-and-coming young hood with West Coast connections who planned to make himself mob boss of Cleveland; and now Joe Beck, who knew everybody who was anybody in East Coast crime and insisted that Billy should call him as soon as he got out, particularly if he had a good connection for Cuban cigars.

But that day seemed as far away as ever. Although Danbury lived up to its reputation as the country club of the federal system—Billy was particularly impressed when he found he could order his breakfast eggs cooked any way he liked—his time there was no more than a relatively peaceful interlude before being turned over to the Commonwealth of Massachusetts to start another seven-to-twenty years in one of the worst prison systems in the country.

After Danbury—even after Atlanta—Billy's arrival in Walpole was like being thrown into a snake pit. Every convict in the prison knew who he was, and when they were not crazed out of their skulls on drugs, they seemed to have been living just for this chance to take a crack at him. Assigned to cell block 4, which housed most of the prison's worst offenders, he quickly discovered that his only allies were Buddy Chrehan, one of Margeson's crew, whose friendship anyone could buy, and two of his co-defendants in the Framingham robbery: Silky Sullivan, now doing life for a murder of which he was innocent (and dying of cancer), and Jimmy McCormick, who *had* committed the murder. The two had staged an armed robbery at South Station, Boston, in which a security guard had been shot dead.

All three warned Billy that he was a marked man, and urged him to pull any strings he could think of to get out of Walpole as fast as he could. Sullivan went further, presenting him with a pair of razor-like shanks that Billy strapped to his thighs. These were a comfort, and so was the can of water Billy kept boiling on his hot plate twenty-four hours a day, but they were of limited value in a prison full of weapons, including guns and even dynamite. If an inmate had money, he could buy anything: drugs, liquor, tobacco, food—even straight sex. When not running his end of the Winter Hill–McLaughlin war in Walpole, George McLaughlin operated a brothel in the prison hospital, busing in Boston prostitutes to service his "patients."

For Billy, the climate was not only hostile but dangerously unpredictable. Inmates were getting stabbed or killed every day, for the most trivial of reasons, and below the surface he could sense much deeper currents of unrest. Blacks against whites. Whites against Hispanics. Irish against Italians, inmates against guards. Now wise in the ways of prison life, Billy could smell riot in the air as unmistakably as the first whiff of smoke from a forest fire. With everybody's hand against him, the guards had only to pull out to save their own necks and he was a dead man.

He reported sick, complaining of breathing difficulties, and in view of his recent medical history was transferred to the better-equipped hospital in Norfolk prison. Just in time. On the day he left Walpole, the worst prison riot in the history of Massachusetts broke out in cell house 4.

But once again, Billy's reputation had preceded him. One of the two convicts in charge of the X-ray room at Norfolk was the Canadian Peter White, cousin of Frank Ryan, Billy's co-defendant in the Lynn bank robbery and author of most of his problems. Although White, doing time for a holdup in Somerville, had to concede that they had probably made a mistake in holding him responsible for the arrest of Ryan and the others—Billy had now served more time for the robbery than had any of the four Canadians who had actually carried it out—

he was not above joining in the popular prison sport of tormenting the odd man out, particularly a former cop.

His first joke was to exchange Billy's X-ray pictures for those of Silky Sullivan, who had also been sent to Norfolk for treatment. As Sullivan's showed a terminal case of lung cancer, Billy's dismay on being told the pictures were his caused great amusement in the prison yard.

White's next coup was hardly less hilarious. Aware of Billy's fastidious personal habits and, in particular, of his aversion to cockroaches, White and his cellmate spend days collecting them in jars and then, one evening while Billy was resting on his bed, released them all at once just inside the door of his cell.

With a howl of blind rage, he grabbed up the length of pipe he kept under the bed for protection and, wincing with distaste as the carpet of roaches crunched underfoot, pursued the Canadians back to their own cell with every intention of cracking their skulls. Although they got there first and locked the door, they could tell from his frenzy that he had not seen the joke. To neutralize a possibly dangerous adversary, they later tried to burn him alive in his cell but got caught in the act.

A sympathetic con named Omar Taylor, whom Billy had known in Florida, now suggested that he try to get into unit 1-2, which was run by a decent, conscientious guard named Ed Reilly. Billy took his advice, and an instant liking to Reilly, who installed him in a cell next door to his first-floor office. That evening, Omar Taylor brought Billy a housewarming present—a fully loaded .38 caliber revolver in a paper bag.

"Take it," he said. "Use it in good health."

Billy thought twice before turning him down. But when Reilly arranged for him to work as an orderly at Medfield State Hospital, Billy knew the end was in sight. Away from the prison all day, he found it easier to keep out of trouble, and suddenly one morning it was all over.

"I kissed the ground and thanked God for allowing me to make it back into the free world," he wrote in his notebook. "I vowed I would fight crime until I died. I'd learned from experts every phase of breaking the law, and I made up my mind to go after the biggest."

In clear breach of his federal and state parole, Billy talked to John Regan about this the very next day, knowing that if he were caught working as an informant, he could be sent back to serve another eight years in the federal system and no less than eighteen years in Massachusetts.

The day after that, he returned to Winter Hill for the first time

since 1966, and learned that Joe McDonald had renewed the contract
on him.

There was no way to beat it except to get out of town. To keep
himself busy while waiting for permission to join Helen in Florida,
he worked a couple of hijack cases with Regan, one of them involving
a truckload of cigarettes stashed in a police captain's garage. Nothing
ever changed much in Somerville.

Once in Miami, Billy twiddled his thumbs for a few days, then
called Regan to see if he could suggest somebody he might work with
down there. Regan consulted his boss, the Massachusetts commis-
sioner of public safety, and called him right back.

"Special Agent Paul Rico," he said.

"Oh, shit," said Billy.

So far, the FBI had brushed him off, treated him like a common
crook, publicly labeled him as an informer, rigged a felony case
against him, and generally done its best to get him killed.

"Have you ever been diagnosed as being a compulsive fabricator?"
asked Breitbart, still looking for a way in.

"No, sir."

"An aggressive personality?"

"That's possible," Billy conceded, not without a hint of pride.
"That could have been my regular diagnosis."

"A violent personality?"

He shrugged. "That's correct." Why split hairs?

"With an extensive drinking problem?"

"No, sir."

That was a new one. Now several hours into his cross-examina-
tion, Breitbart had yet to establish a clear sense of direction. No
sooner would he touch on one subject than some association of ideas
would set him off on another, which in turn would suggest something
else, so that when he did at last return to the original topic, he would
have to ask the same questions again to remind the jury of what had
led up to it in the first place. Like a blind dentist probing for cavities,
he had spent most of the day poking around in Billy's sensitive areas,
inflicting a good deal of discomfort to no apparent purpose.

"You don't have a drinking problem?"

"No, sir," Not unless you counted a weakness for Californian
champagne.

"Did you drink when you were at the Cowboy Palace?"

"I have drank since I have been seventeen years old. No more then
than I do today."

"That is what we are talking about. How much do you drink, Mr.
Breen?"

"Very, very little."

"Well, let us judge that, Mr. Breen. Do you drink a quart a day?"

"No." He was shocked.

"A pint a day?"

"No, sir."

"How much do you drink?"

"Three or four shots—maybe five shots a day."

"Every morning?"

"Never drank in the morning in my life."

This somehow led back to the topic of amnesia and mental health, Billy's resignation from the Somerville P.D. (again), his work for Regan on Winter Hill (again), the mob figures he met in jail, and his necessary departure from Massachusetts to Florida.

"You said that you were robbing banks and robbing restaurants for Major Regan," said Breitbart slyly. "Did the government or the state of Florida give you any criminal activities to engage in?"

"I never told you that I was robbing banks or any establishments for Major Regan," Billy retorted.

"What about in '66 and '67, when you robbed a bank, you told that jury that the major in the Massachusetts State Police was knowledgeable of the fact that you were doing this with a gun?"

"That's absolutely not true," protested Billy, looking around for help. "You're saying it the way you want to say it. That's not the way it happened."

"You were working for him."

"If you want me to describe it, I'll describe it to you."

"No," said Breitbart hastily. "Let's not do that." He changed the subject again. "What did you do for a living in Florida?"

Billy ran a poker game in Miami. Not just for a living but as an engine of retribution.

His pension had been piling up for seven years. His brother Tom had been looking after some money from the sale of the house in Somerville. And he still had what was left of a $52,000 double that had come up at Suffolk Downs before he went inside. It was enough to get started. When Special Agent Paul Rico agreed that gambling was as good a way as any to get into Miami vice, Billy rented a room, spread the word about a new game in town, and the local bad guys lined up like ducks in a row.

But he was never comfortable with Rico, who came from Boston and seemed to know an awful lot of people from Winter Hill. Nor was he much impressed by Rico's dedication to law enforcement. When Billy checked in with a hot tip from the poker game about a Panamanian-registered mother ship cruising offshore with 190,000 pounds of marijuana on board, Rico just shrugged.

"Forget it," he said. "We're not into drugs."

Billy got on better with Tony Ameroso, who later played the sheik in the FBI's Abscam sting, but as far as Billy was concerned, he was just dipping a toe in the water with this low-level stuff. When a two-bit hood could kill you as dead in a 50-dollar deal as a major mob figure in a scam grossing millions, why sell yourself short?

With Ameroso's blessing, he branched out into making book on football games. The poker room remained a valuable source of gossip about who was doing what to whom, but by taking action over the telephone, he figured he could work his way into pretty nearly every wise guy in South Florida, including its principal bookmakers, like Roy Elder, Dougie Stevens, and the Ducketts—Harold, Tommy, and Jimmy—who ran the state's biggest casino crap game in Coral Gables. Through Ameroso, he also started to work with Lieutenant Joe Pierce, of the Broward County Organized Crime Bureau, extending his bookmaking into Fort Lauderdale and Coral Springs and giving up all the other bookmakers he uncovered.

But he was not the only one interested in taking down the state's gambling industry. Early in 1974, Billy was himself raided by a squad from the Metro-Dade County Organized Crime Bureau, led by Sergeant Dave Green. Once over his surprise, Billy was simultaneously flattered to have been targeted by the cop reputed to have the hardest ass in Florida and annoyed with Ameroso for not clearing his operation with the OCB as he had in Broward County. It was only when he started to work with Green that he came to realize just how profoundly a local cop *could* detest the FBI—and that as far as Ameroso was concerned, the feeling was mutual.

Since bookmaking was more of a state than a federal concern, Green now became Billy's Regan surrogate, with Special Agent Dave Jellison taking over from Ameroso to hold a watching brief for the Bureau. Bald, bulky, and amiable, Jellison had a knack for getting along with almost everybody, regardless of what he thought of them privately, and for the next eight years the Breen-Green-Jellison combo played some interesting variations on traditional law-enforcement themes.

The first of them was to develop Billy's football book into a genuinely cost-effective Trojan horse. Three tapped phones were installed in a rented office, and Green assigned a squad of six to eight men to monitor and transcribe tapes, work up cases, and generally take care of the paperwork. In his first week, Billy showed a profit of more than $12,000, and after deducting expenses he meekly handed the balance over to Metro-Dade County in accordance with the ground rules Green had laid down.

In his second week, Billy showed a *loss* of $18,000 after working the Monday night football game, but when he asked for the money to pay off his clients, the cupboard was bare.

"How would *that* look if it came out in court?" Green demanded. "I don't know, you gotta be the dumbest fucking bookie I ever saw. Didn't you lay off the action? I mean, how can you *lose* money when you're making the book?"

"Okay, okay." Billy's professional pride was hurt. "I thought this was a sting. You didn't tell me I gotta run it as a business."

"You think the fucking taxpayer is gonna pick up the tab? Can you cover this or not? Because if you can't, I'm gonna have to pull the wires out and close you down."

"Well, maybe I can borrow it," Billy grumbled. "But lemme tell ya something. If I gotta take the loss, then I'm gonna take the profit. Fucking county can't have it *both* ways. Either it's mine, win or lose, or you can go ahead and pull your fucking wires."

It was too promising an operation to pass up. Green shrugged, and Billy went over to the Pieces of Eight Lounge to borrow $20,000 from a loan shark at 1 percent a week.

A month or so into the football season, Billy was moving as much money in and out as any one-man book in South Florida—upward of $600,000 in a good week. With Jellison, he went on to set up the Ducketts for a successful FBI raid on their Coral Gables crap game; and with Green, moved out to Calder Racetrack to help take down Dougie Stevens and his crew, who were then booking around $1 million a week on South Florida's horse-racing tracks. Billy also had Roy Elder in his sights, along with Joey Covello, Dave Snyder, and Count De Leo—all near-legendary figures among the gambling fraternity—and a client list that included Jamiel Chagra, crown prince of Florida's new multibillion-dollar marijuana aristocracy, and his heir apparent, Bobby Piccolo.

Setting up targets of this caliber was not a problem. With such a high arrest rate among those who did business with Billy, the main worry was protecting his cover. There were just too many "coincidences."

In 1976, to quiet suspicion, Green and Billy hit on the simple though drastic expedient of having him appear before a statewide grand jury looking into Florida racketeering for the first time since the Kefauver hearings. In the 1950s, leading mob figures had moved south to escape attention. Now they fled north for the same reason, but not before task-force investigators subpoenaed (and photographed) every senior wise guy known to have relocated in the state in the previous twenty years, Billy included.

As the task force had hoped, his standing in the criminal community suffered not at all from having to appear before the grand jury with the likes of Meyer Lansky, Sam DeCavalcante, Jerry Catena, Fat Tony Salerno, Doug Stevens, and Vincent Teriarca—especially when he was called twice and took the Fifth Amendment each time. For this he was summarily convicted of contempt of court and locked up for seven weeks in Volusia County jail until the grand jury mandate expired.

To get him off the hook in Broward County, Joe Pierce took him in for bookmaking in Fort Lauderdale, where, by prior arrangement with the court, he entered a plea of nolo contendere and was placed on probation. But there was a price to be paid for this protective coloration. Billy was at home one morning, getting ready for another hard day on the wiretaps, when two Massachusetts state troopers and a corrections' department official came by the house to bust him for parole violations.

It was a doubly unpleasant surprise because he had been assured by the FBI that his federal parole conditions took precedence over the state's requirements. In spite of strong official protests from Special Agent Jellison, Major John Regan, Dave Green, and many other officers, the Massachusetts Parole Board insisted on its pound of flesh. Billy had broken an undertaking not to work with law-enforcement agencies and had to go back to prison.

At this point, a lesser man might have questioned his vocation and given up, seeing little sign of justice in heaven *or* on earth, but Billy was too busy for metaphysical speculation. Every spare moment in jail was spent on the telephone with Helen and with his clerk in an effort to keep the bookmaking business going until he got out. Apart from that, he was not unduly worried. Although technically the board could have locked him up until 1991, he was soon transferred from Walpole to the Dorchester Pre-Release Center, which suggested no more than a year at most.

Seven months later, Jellison and Green threw a party in Miami to welcome him home, and not solely because of what he meant to their careers. To those he could work with, Billy was never hard to like—even if, occasionally, he could be hard to take. Both agreed that as an undercover operator and "catalyst," he had no peer.

"Billy's the best," says Jellison, looking back on their fifteen-year association. "To him it's a challenge, and he does it so fast. He knows exactly what to say to get over. He knows exactly how it's going to go down, and he loves making a monkey out of FBI agents. I'd pass information from Billy to other offices, and they'd respond, 'There's no way that can be true.' And sure enough, a year later they're calling down and saying, 'See if you can find that guy and have him do thus and so.'

"My advice on the phone to these people is always, 'Listen to the guy. He's going to tell you how he does it and he knows what he's talking about, even if it does sound kind of wild. He'll put your man in jail for you.' But to them, it always sounded like he was embellishing everything and making it into a big deal. He wasn't. It *was* a big deal. *He's* a big deal."

Dave Green concurs. Grudgingly. "He's a good bullshitter," he says. "Got a lot of nerve. Doesn't mind going right into something. No, he's good. Very good. Billy does things that normal cops *can't* do. He caused a lot of people to go to jail that we wouldn't have got otherwise."

"By the way," Jellison said, as he dropped Billy off at his door in the small hours after the welcome-home party. "Did I tell you? I'm going to be working over at DEA for a while."

"Yeah? That's too bad." On every side, Billy had heard ugly things about the Drug Enforcement Administration. "But I guess somebody's gotta keep an eye on those people."

Jellison laughed. "Well, that's not exactly why I'm going, Billy," he said. "And I'm pretty sure *they* don't see it that way. But keep your eyes open, okay? You see somebody, or hear about somebody, smuggling or dealing dope, you be sure to let me know."

"You got it, kid," he said. "No problem."

Anything for a friend.

8

"Was Jimmy Kearns a murderer?" Breitbart asked.

Billy nodded. "Yes, sir."

"Did you move drugs with a guy by the name of Piccolo?"

"Yes, sir."

"Did you move drugs with a guy by the name of Chagra?"

"Ah—let me inject something," he said, trying to save them another unnecessary detour, but Breitbart would have none of it.

"Would you please answer my question, Mr. Breen."

Billy shrugged. "Yes, sir."

"Did you know a man by the name of Chagra?"

"Yes, sir."

"Did you move drugs with them?"

"No, sir."

Breitbart referred to his papers. "Did you move drugs with Chagra and Piccolo?"

"No, sir." That was what he had wanted to tell him. Chagra was already out of the picture when he moved in on Piccolo.

"Did you move thousands of pounds of marijuana in Racine, Wisconsin?"

"No, sir." He had got that wrong, too.

"Did you check off-loading sites in Myrtle Beach, South Carolina?"

"Yes, sir."

"Did Chagra and Piccolo ask you to introduce them to someone who could lean on people for you?"

Billy blinked. Lean on people for him? Chagra hadn't been there either, but if he picked up on everything, he would never see Texas again.

"Yes, sir."

"Pursuant to that conversation, did you bring Jimmy Kearns, your friend the killer, down from Boston, Massachusetts?"

"Yes, sir."

"Did he have a meeting with Piccolo in your house?"

"Yes, sir."

"As a result of that meeting, did he get $20,000 in cash?"

"Yes, sir."

"Did he get $25,000 after that?"

"Yes, sir."

Breitbart turned to face the jury. "As a result of getting that $45,000, sir," he said, his manner clearly signaling, Wait till you hear this, "did Mr. Jimmy Kearns kill a United States District Judge in Texas?"

Billy was flabbergasted.

"No, sir," he said

Breitbart was even more shocked than Billy. "Did he plead guilty to the murder?"

"No, sir."

"Did Mr. Kearns tell you that he had killed a Federal District Judge?" Breitbart paged rapidly through his notes.

"No, sir." Billy felt almost sorry for the guy.

There was a pause until the other found his place. "Do you know another man by the name of Kerr?"

"Yes, sir." Now he'd got it right.

"An Assistant United States Attorney?"

"Yes, sir," said Billy kindly. He, too, would have felt a bit shaken after making a mistake like that.

"Did Mr. Kearns attempt to kill an Assistant United States Attorney after receiving that $45,000 in your house?"

"Yes, sir."

"And then Mr. Piccolo came over to you and said, 'Your guy missed. He only shot him a couple of times'? Is that right?"

Wrong again. Piccolo hadn't said that and Kearns hadn't shot Kerr at all, but what the hell? At least Breitbart had the right idea.

"That's correct."

As Jellison said, Billy could never resist a challenge.

After setting up around four hundred arrests, he was getting bored with gambling cases. Although he knew nothing about the narcotics business, he had a way in through Jimmy Chagra, Bobby Piccolo, and the so-called Godfrey Gang, then by far the biggest marijuana-smuggling crew in the Southeast. The problem was that they knew him only as a bookie, and any sudden curiosity about their activities was liable to lead him straight to the Intracoastal Waterway. Face down. Before he could provide Jellison with anything but hearsay, Piccolo had to *recruit* him, and that was going to take time.

Indeed, it took almost a year before "Billy the Bookie" had wormed his way sufficiently into the gang's good graces to be automatically included in the Hollywood-style Roman orgies that filled the social calendar of "The Big House," its $3 million headquarters at the end of Godfrey Road, Coral Springs. Fitted out with all the luxury and glamor of a five-star, Cuban-Arabian motel, it was a custom-built showcase for Jamiel Chagra, who had reached 40 trying to assuage an appetite for women and gambling that only a dope empire could support.

Tall, dark, resourceful, and the youngest of three brothers from El Paso, Texas, he had taken a shine to Billy from their first meeting, when he tried to bet $50,000 on a football game. Billy had clutched his head, staggered back, and replied: "You wanna get paid, don'cha?"—seven little words so charged with tact, independence, and flattery that he won Chagra's endorsement on the spot.

But he needed more than that. More interested in squandering the profits in Las Vegas (where, on one of several junkets, he set Billy up in Caesar's Palace with a $100,000 credit line) than in earning them on the beaches and airstrips of the Southeast, Chagra had delegated most of the gang's operational responsibilities to his executive vice president, Bobby Piccolo, a stocky, 40-year-old juvenile delinquent with a bald head, a lot of gold jewelry, and a coke habit that made his nose bleed.

Like most Sunbelt swingers, Piccolo felt affinities with people rather than affection for them, and he had nothing whatever in common with a heavily bearded, 50-year-old, Boston-Irish book-maker who preferred Buicks to Porsches and did not do drugs. From the start, Billy knew that all he would ever have going for him with Piccolo was usefulness and familiarity.

A further problem was that Piccolo's right-hand man was none other than Peter White, now also known as Peter Mackay, the Canadian bankrobber whom Billy had last seen through a red haze as he chased him through Norfolk State Prison with a length of iron pipe after the cockroach incident. Some years had passed, but it still took a considerable effort on Billy's part to pretend to patch up their differences.

Billy's one disappointment was that by the time he was ready to move, Jimmy Chagra had not only departed for Las Vegas, abdicating as kingpin in favor of Bobby Piccolo, but had already been indicted in Texas on federal racketeering charges. Out on bail, he was said to be drawing a retirement pension of $1 million a load—and the loads were coming in like commuter trains at Grand Central Station.

"Dave, this is the biggest operation you ever saw," Billy told Jellison. "Shit, it's the biggest *I* ever saw. They musta brought in a million pounds since you told me you were going over to DEA. And I'm right in there. Right in the middle of it."

"Well, that's great, Billy. I knew you'd come up with something once I got you thinking about it. They're really going to roll out the red carpet for you over at DEA."

"Fuck that," Billy said. "Ain't never going *near* those people. I'm gonna work this one with you."

"Oh, Billy, I'd like to," said Jellison wistfully. "I surely would. But they won't let us touch narcotics, you know that."

Billy blinked at him uncomprehendingly. "You mean you're not working over there anymore? At DEA?"

"Hell no. That only lasted a few months. I guess I should have told you. I *would* have, if I'd seen you. But I'll put you in with the right people, don't worry about it."

"Are you crazy?" Billy felt crushed. After all that. A whole year's work down the toilet. The goddamn Bureau was doing it to him again. "I'm not talking to nobody over there," he said furiously. "And I don't want *you* talking to 'em neither. They're *bad*. Half those fucking people are on Bobby's payroll."

"Come on, Billy," said Jellison. "Take it easy. I know they got problems, but there are plenty of guys you can trust over there, believe me. I won't steer you wrong."

"No, Dave. Forget about it. I *seen* what they do. Bobby gets all the DEA radio frequencies. He gets printouts. I seen case reports up there—he gets anything he wants. No, you're just gonna get me killed. Forget I even talked to you. I gotta think about this."

He was still thinking about it the following Tuesday when he drove over to The Big House to collect the $8,000 that Piccolo had lost on the Monday night football games. After paying Billy off, Piccolo took him outside for a stroll around the pool.

"Listen," he said confidentially. "You been around, Billy. Who do you know that's real *heavy*? Who do you know who can really *lean* on a guy?"

"Somebody from outa town, you mean."

He *had* to mean that. Piccolo had enough local muscle on the payroll to move Miami several miles inland if he wanted to.

"Yeah," said Piccolo. "Somebody real heavy from outa town. You know somebody like that? I'll tell you why."

"No, you won't." If Piccolo wanted to frighten somebody, that was *his* business. Anybody involved with Piccolo *deserved* to be frightened. "Don't tell me nothing about it. Sure, I know a couple of people. You want me to set up a meet?"

"Yeah," Piccolo said. "Let's make it at *your* house. And like yesterday, okay? Jimmy's coming in tonight, and he's gonna want to know we're on top of this thing."

"Well," said Billy. If Chagra himself was involved, his best bet was to give Murdo Margeson a call. "Lemme see what I can do."

Margeson thought Jimmy Kearns would fit the bill and brought him down from Boston the following weekend to stay with Billy and Helen on Croton Road. It had seemed like a good idea at the time, to get in tighter with Piccolo, but Billy had not bargained on having his worst enemy as a houseguest.

"How much money has this guy got?" Kearns wanted to know.

"They wipe their asses with it," said Billy. "And, Jimmy, leave me outa this. I told Bobby up front and I'm telling you up front—I'll put the both of yez together and that's it. After that, you're on your own. I don't wanna know nothing about it."

Kearns grunted. "What does he want done?"

"I don't know and I don't care. He asked me if I knew somebody real heavy, so I called Murdo. Now it's up to you."

"Okay." Kearns held out his glass to be refilled, and grabbed Billy's wrist as he took it from him. "But remember. Anything goes wrong, I'm holding you responsible."

Billy pulled himself free. "Oh no," he said. "I'm not responsible for nothing. Whatever deal you make, that's your own personal business. Nothing to do with me."

Piccolo drove over on Sunday afternoon with Peter White, who already knew Margeson and Kearns from Winter Hill, and Billy Painter, a tough kid in charge of the gang's off-loaders. Billy hardly had time to pour everybody a drink before Kearns got down to business.

"You want to talk to me?" he asked Piccolo, who had joined Billy behind the bar, as though intimidated by the sheer size of Kearns.

"Yeah, right." He looked at Billy uncertainly.

"Okay, why don't you go talk in the back bedroom," Billy suggested. "Helen'll show you. And take your drinks wit'cha. Here—take the bottle."

He held out the Bushmills for Helen, who gave him a look. She was eager to get back to the kitchen to attend to the Italian dinner she had been slaving over since noon.

They were gone for more than half an hour, reviving Billy's misgivings. If they just had to lean on somebody, what was there to talk about? When they returned at last to the living room, it made him no happier to see that Kearns was actually smiling. With a wink at Margeson, he flipped through a wad of bills that looked like $20,000 at least. Billy refilled their glasses thoughtfully. A down payment like that meant more than a flexing of muscle. That kind of money meant a hit.

Piccolo stayed long enough to eat a meatball and left with Painter, still obviously uncomfortable around Kearns.

Several weeks later, Kearns brought his wife, Catherine—"Rene"—down from Boston with Margeson to join Bobby and Sheree Piccolo, Peter White and his common-law wife, Judy Moeser, Billy and Helen, and a couple of others for dinner at Le Dôme, one of the Godfrey Gang's favorite hangouts in Fort Lauderdale. Between dessert and coffee, Kearns and Piccolo adjourned to the wine cellar, where more money evidently changed hands, but otherwise it seemed to be just a social occasion. Billy relaxed a little, particularly when Piccolo picked up the $3,500 tab.

With the second payment to Kearns, Billy was inclined to think that the contract had been filled, whatever it was, and the whole affair was now behind him, but the moment he saw Piccolo's face the following Tuesday, he knew he was wrong. After settling accounts, they went for another walk by the pool.

"You and your fucking friends," Piccolo grumbled, fumbling in his pocket for a dog-eared newspaper clipping. "Look what that asshole did. I pay the motherfucker forty-five grand for a hit, and what does he do? He fucks up. Fucking misses the sonuvabitch."

Not in his wildest imaginings had Billy dreamed of anything like this. He was used to the megalomania that afflicted successful dopers once they had made more money than they could ever hope to spend, particularly if they were coke heads. He had seen for himself how unimaginable sums of cash could make them feel like gods, beyond reach of the law and mortal man. But it had never for a moment crossed his mind that Jimmy Chagra would get Piccolo to hire Kearns to kill James Kerr, the Assistant U.S. Attorney assigned to prosecute him in San Antonio. Or that Piccolo would agree to do it. But there in his hand was a clipping from the *Dallas Herald* to prove it. On November 21, 1978, they had tried to lop off an arm of the U.S. government.

Kearns had riddled Kerr's car from the back of a van with around twenty shots from a .30 caliber carbine and several shotgun blasts and gotten away without being identified. In a near-miraculous escape, Kerr had spotted a barrel poking out of the van's rear door and ducked down behind the engine bulkhead before Kearns cut loose.

"Now I'm really in trouble," Piccolo was saying. "I got Jimmy on my back because he says I made things worse—now they're *really* gonna get him. And I got your fuck-up friend Kearns telling me I still owe him money. Well, if he thinks I'm gonna pay him for botching the job, he's crazy."

"Bobby, please," said Billy. "Slow down. I don't wanna hear about it. Believe me, you better keep this whole fucking business to yourself. Because if Kearns ever finds out you told me this, we'll both be dead. You understand? Don't tell nobody. That goes for all of yez."

After staying up all night, trying to figure out what to do, Billy called Dave Jellison over to his house.

"Dave," he said, beginning a little speech. "I trust you. You're my contact agent, and I won't talk to nobody else."

"Well, I'm glad you feel that way, Billy."

"Okay. Now I know you don't handle narcotics, but like I told you, the Godfrey Gang is the biggest smuggling crew in this country. And I mean the *biggest*. I've been working 'em for a year, so I know. But I won't go to the DEA with it because I don't trust nobody over there. And that's final. I can't go to the state police with it neither, or Broward County or Metro-Dade—number one, because they're not set up to go outa state, and number two, because these boys spread money around like manure."

"So what are you saying?" Jellison asked. "You telling me you're gonna drop it?"

"Listen, you ask me that yesterday, and the answer is yes."

"Okay." Bringing Billy to the point, he sometimes felt like a midwife with forceps. "But how about today?"

"Today?" Billy set himself up for his announcement. "Dave, suppose I told you I could take these guys down with a federal violation that *wasn't* narcotics. Could you work with me then?"

"Sure. If it's big enough to do the job. What have you got?"

"Dave, this is *giant*. You won't believe what I got here."

"Well, I will when you tell me."

Billy hesitated, then shook his head. "If I tell you now, you'll have to report it, and I just don't have it together yet."

Jellison shook his head, too. "You mean you got me over here to tell me you're not going to tell me something?"

"I just wanna know if you'll work the Piccolo crew if it ain't narcotics, that's all. If I tell ya now, before I got all the pieces together, the Bureau'll just fuck up like they always do. I don't mean *you*, Dave," he added hastily. "I mean those dickheads you work for."

Jellison sighed. "It's really that big, huh?" After working with Billy for several years now, he knew better than to try to insist.

"Yeah. It's that big. And I'll have to work in real close with Piccolo to get it, so please don't fuck me up by talking to the DEA or nothing."

"Okay, Billy. I won't say a word. But if you get yourself busted, or something goes wrong, there won't be a whole lot I can do to help you unless you keep me in the picture. You know that, don't you?"

"Yeah, I know that, Dave. I'll touch base wit'cha every chance I get. Just gimme a couple of months and I'll lay it all out for ya so that not even the Bureau can screw up the case."

Billy was over-optimistic. It took him a couple of years, and even then he had to surface before he had all of it. That was because he fell in love with Brenda Burp, who, perhaps understandably, preferred to be known as Samantha Leonetti. She was his midlife crisis: black-haired, olive-skinned, voluptuous, demanding, socially assured, morally disabled, and ingenious in bed, where she performed with the kind of sadistic detachment common among professional students of the amatory arts.

He met her through Eddie Mode, who ran a sports-tipster service, and who was shacked up in Atlanta with Samantha's twin sister, Linda Burp, aka Linda Holden. Although Linda had become a friend of Helen's, she kept trying to fix Billy up with Samantha behind Helen's back, and after resisting the idea at first, as he had with Maria De Angelis in what now felt like another life, he fell comprehensively from grace in the course of an exhausting weekend at the Hilton Hotel in New York.

9

Once committed to taking down Chagra and Piccolo for the assassination attempt, Billy virtually moved into The Big House on a full-time basis. As an inadvertent conspirator in the San Antonio affair, he met little opposition from the gang in his new capacity and none at all from Piccolo, who put him to work as courier, scout, and general factotum.

Billy's first major assignment took him back thirty years to his navy days in Tiburon, California, where Piccolo intended to land a 30,000-pound shipment of marijuana to service Joe College, his California distributor. For Billy, it was on-the-job training. If he was to get in close enough to build a case against Chagra, Piccolo, and Kearns, he had to make himself indispensable, which meant learning the marijuana business. And here he was, starting at the top, with a perfect overview of the whole operation, from the moment the shrimp boat sailed from Colombia through to the final delivery of the load to Joe College and the multimillion-dollar payoff.

The plan was that the mother ship should come in as close as it dared to a sheltered private beach below a steep cliff—normally a very unpromising site for off-loading and therefore unlikely to be routinely patrolled by the Coast Guard or local police. As the bales were brought ashore in a fleet of flat-bottomed boats, they would be whisked up to the clifftop by portable electric conveyor and loaded straight into two tractor-trailer rigs for final delivery to Joe College's stash houses.

The drivers, Pistol Pete and Freddy, would each have bills of lading and invoices for 30,000 pounds of potatoes and tomatoes. If the Highway Patrol stopped either of them, it would have to unload half the truck before it came upon anything other than innocent vegetables.

Even to Billy's untutored ear, it sounded like a neat, workmanlike plan. He was also impressed by the arithmetic. The expected load of 30,000 pounds of prime Colombian grass was to be delivered offshore at $85 a pound, amounting to a cool $2,550,000. Piccolo then had to pay the off-loaders $750,000 for bringing it ashore; $100,000 each to Pistol Pete and Freddy for taking it to Joe College in their eighteen-wheelers, and $100,000 each to Billy Painter, who had bought and paid for the load in Colombia, Earl and Miles McLennan and Peter White, for supervising the operation, plus another $100,000, give or take a buck, for expenses, including $15,000 for Billy. Piccolo's total outlay, therefore, would be something in the region of $4 million cash.

Against that, he had contracted to sell the load to Joe College at an average price of $275 a pound, for a total of $8.25 million, showing him a clear profit on paper of around $4 million (less the $1 million he had agreed to pay Jimmy Chagra on every shipment).

Except that, after hanging around for weeks, flying Samantha in from the East (for just one day, as it turned out, owing to her other carnal commitments), and generally learning the ropes, Billy took a call one morning from Bobby Piccolo canceling the whole operation. The shrimp boat had been diverted to another landfall. The weather forecast was for strong winds and rough seas, and her captain was not prepared to risk getting caught under the cliffs on a lee shore.

So they all packed up and went home. Piccolo was about $200,000 out of pocket, but with $4 million in prospect, who was counting?

Billy certainly had no complaints. The $15,000 had been the easiest he had ever earned, and he had learned how the business worked. What he needed now was a way to raise his status at The Big House from gofer to partner, and as if reading his mind, Mike Gamboli, one of his biggest betting clients, stopped by the house one night to show him how.

"Hey, Billy," he said, handing over $11,000 to cover his week's losses. "I gotta start picking 'em better than this or you're gonna haveta help me with the tab. Know anybody around here with like a few thousand pounds of weed? And I'm talking about the *good* stuff."

"Well," said Billy. "Funny you should ask . . ."

He called Peter White.

"Sure," White said. "As much as you want."

"Okay. We're looking at five thousand pounds here. What's the ticket on it?"

"To you? Two-sixty a pound. But you better get at least two-ninety for it if you're gonna cut me and Miles in as partners."

"Ah-*hah*! You mean I'm only gonna make ten dollars a pound?"

"*Only*? How much do you want for doin' nothin'? Tell your man he'll haveta take delivery from Michigan Jim in Kalamazoo."

"Okay. That's no problem."

"And we're gonna need to see some front money."

"Right," said Billy, who had no idea how front money worked but was not about to display his ignorance.

He called Mike Gamboli back.

"Hey, Mike," he said. "You can have five thousand pounds from Michigan Jim in Kalamazoo at two-ninety a pound. And it's top of the line."

Gamboli sighed. "Well, that's a little high, but okay."

"Okay. And what about front money?"

Gamboli sighed even harder. "Yeah, yeah. You know Jerry? Hangs out in the poolroom on One hundred twenty-fifth Street? I'll have him stop by your house with half a million when the load's in."

A few days later, Miles McLennan called from The Big House instructing Billy to leave for Kalamazoo to make sure Gamboli and his crew were ready to take delivery, and also to call Margeson, Kearns, and Billy Kelly in Boston to pick up a thousand pounds from the same load.

Yeah, right, said Billy, as if he had known all along that the fearsome three were involved. In fact, it was the first he had heard that payment for the Kerr assassination contract also included half a ton of grass at cost.

His feelings were mixed about this. The less he had to do with Kearns the better he slept nights, but on the other hand, Kearns's continuing connection with Piccolo meant he could work both of them at the same time and possibly incriminate both with the same evidence.

Kearns had been back to the house with Margeson several times since the November attack on the assistant U.S. attorney, and had made no bones about how lousy a deal Billy had gotten him into, but that was just hearsay. In the absence of direct proof, the best course that Billy could see was to bury them all in so many dope violations that, facing fifty years in a federal can, somebody would roll over and testify against the others.

When Billy called Helen from Kalamazoo, she sounded nervous. Mike Gamboli's partner from the poolroom had stopped by. She was sitting in the living room with half a million dollars in two shopping bags. Billy told her to set the alarm and not answer the door to anybody.

To complicate matters, a blizzard was raging across the Midwest. Gamboli's crew, including Danny Mullenberg, his head salesman, arrived on schedule at the Kalamazoo Holiday Inn with his cars and trucks, but Miles McLennan, who was responsible for loading them, called from Ann Arbor to say the shipment was late. Gamboli was not pleased.

He was even more put out when Peter White called in the middle of the night to say that Miles had refused to load Gamboli's vehicles. He would have to use vans, not trucks. Gamboli ground his teeth and sent for two vans, which duly arrived the next day.

Meanwhile, Kearns, Kelly, and Margeson had arrived from Boston in a Winnebago camper, and were, not unnaturally, given priority. When Gamboli heard that he would again have to wait before taking delivery, he sounded off so alarmingly about the half-million reasons for prompt service he had already provided that Billy felt obliged to drive off through the blizzard to Ann Arbor to find out what was going on.

He joined Piccolo, Earl and Miles McLennan, Billy Painter, and Peter White for dinner at the Regency Hotel, and found the climate even chillier than on the road. The load had been smaller than expected, and they were in no mood to put up with squawks from a customer they did not even know. Kearns, Kelly, and Margeson had left for Massachusetts with 1,400 pounds, and Gamboli would get whatever Piccolo could spare as soon as he was good and ready.

Billy drove back through the blizzard.

Luckily, Gamboli had gone by the time he arrived, leaving Danny Mullenberg in charge. And Mullenberg was more interested in buying for himself than for Gamboli. When the two vans were eventually loaded with just 3,800 pounds, and Billy explained that the delivery was unexpectedly short because of the 1,400 pounds now on its way to Massachusetts, Mullenberg almost begged him to phone ahead and ask if Margeson, Kearns, and Kelly would accept $290 a pound for the entire load.

Naturally, they jumped at it. A clear profit of $126,000 for no greater trouble than a round trip from Boston to Kalamazoo made armed robbery obsolete. While Billy stayed out of harm's way in Racine, Wisconsin, trying unsuccessfully to persuade Samantha to join him, Mullenberg picked up the loaded Winnebago in Revere, drove it back to Michigan, stashed the 1,400 pounds, and then headed southeast with the empty camper to Miami, where Billy met him at his house to take delivery of a million dollars in cash.

It was heady stuff for someone whose basic income was a disability pension. But then the bills came in. . . .

Piccolo took $488,000 in payment for Gamboli's 3,800 pounds (to add to the half-million he had already received as front money), plus another $280,000 for the 1,400 pounds supplied to Margeson and Kearns. That left around $230,000. A couple of days later, Margeson and Kearns flew in to collect their $90 a pound profit, and that left a bit over $100,000, of which Miles McLennan and Peter White were in for a third each.

After covering his expenses, Billy was left with around $30,000. It didn't seem right somehow. Particularly when Kearns held *him* responsible for the mess Mullenberg had made inside the Winnebago.

Meanwhile, other loads had been coming in, but it was obvious from the atmosphere at The Big House that things had started to go badly wrong.

A month after Kearns's failure to kill James Kerr, who had been running a federal grand-jury investigation into Jimmy Chagra's affairs, Chagra's older brother Lee was murdered in his San Antonio law office while working on Jimmy's defense. Partly because of this and other distractions, but also because Piccolo was not as good as he thought he was, the Godfrey Gang then lost three successive loads in the space of a few weeks. Nobody told Billy directly about these reverses but he got to hear about them from his attorney, Harold Keefe, whom Piccolo sent in turn to Palm Beach, Boston, and New Orleans to defend the Colombian crews of the three vessels seized by the authorities.

Badly rattled, Piccolo tried to lay the blame for the New Orleans disaster on the McLennans, who vehemently rejected his accusations and virtually resigned from the gang with their friends and associates, leaving Piccolo with no one he could count on but Billy Painter, Peter White, and Doug Ruccio, his brother-in-law.

Except for Billy Breen, of course.

With his revenues off by some $25 million, Piccolo decided to economize by not paying his Colombian connections. They in turn restricted his supplies, and as they ran low, so his regional distributors turned to other importers. Within weeks, Piccolo hardly knew where to turn.

Except to Billy Breen, of course.

On February 26, 1979, Jimmy Chagra was indicted in Midland, Texas, on narcotics conspiracy charges. The case was assigned to the calendar of Federal District Judge John H. Wood, Jr., otherwise known as "Maximum John" for his policy of handing out maximum sentences to drugs offenders, and scheduled for trial on May 29, although it was later put back to July.

Nevertheless, on May 29, as Judge Wood left his San Antonio townhouse and walked to his car, he was shot in the back by an unidentified assassin with a single round from a .240 caliber rifle and pronounced dead on arrival at Northeast Baptist Hospital. Special Agent John C. Lawn, later head of the Drug Enforcement Administration, was brought in to take charge of what then became the FBI's biggest investigation since the Kennedy assassination, but nobody at The Big House seemed particularly worried.

Except for Billy Breen, of course.

If it had even crossed his mind that Chagra was insane enough to go on to a second contract, Billy would have told Dave Jellison what he knew, and the Bureau might then have given Judge Wood a permanent bodyguard after the attempt on Kerr's life. On the other hand, it might not. Prosecutors had been shot at before, but there was no record of anyone in the history of the United States trying to kill the federal district judge about to try him.

Even so, Billy felt implicated—and Piccolo was again the key. If Billy was to set him up for the kind of fall that would make him roll over and testify to all this, he first had to pay out more rope.

"Were you working for the federal government at that time, when you brought a hired assassin in to kill a young assistant?" inquired Breitbart, troweling on the sarcasm.

"Yes, sir," Billy sighed. All he had done, in fact, was make the introduction, knowing nothing about a contract or the target.

"You were." Breitbart felt confident enough to invite the jury to consider Billy's answer. "And when did you tell the government that this man received the $45,000 to kill an Assistant United States Attorney?"

"I told them when I got all the information together, so they could make the case on him."

"Wasn't it five years later? After you were arrested for dope?"

"No, sir." The guy simply hadn't done his homework. "It was only two years later, when I brought the information forward."

"I see. When Chagra and Piccolo told you that Kearns was paid $45,000 to kill the Assistant, you didn't have that information?"

"That was not enough to get a conviction," said Billy. "I know better than that."

"Was it enough to save the life of an Assistant United States Attorney?"

Billy sighed. When he'd first heard about it, the attempt had already been made. And had failed.

"At that time," he said, "I knew he hadn't been shot."

"I see." Breitbart frowned. "And the day after he was shot, did

they show you the pictures in the newspaper of the man being whacked?"

"Three days later." Billy hardly knew where to start to put him straight. "No, he was never whacked. He was—it was an attempted assassination. In Texas."

"What about Judge 'Maximum' John Wood—was he murdered?"

"I have no knowledge of a Maximum Judge getting murdered." Billy was getting tongue-tied with frustration.

"You didn't know about Judge Wood getting murdered?"

"I knew he got murdered," he said. Who didn't? The media had gone to town with it as 'the crime of the century.' "But I had no information as to who did it."

Breitbart turned again to the jury. "When Piccolo and Chagra were charged in the drug case, who was the judge that was prosecuting that case?"

"Er—would you repeat that question?" Billy was too stunned by the suggestion that a judge would prosecute a case, even in Texas, to consider the other, even bigger blunder.

"When Piccolo and Chagra were being prosecuted in Texas," said Breitbart heavily, "who was the judge that was assigned to that case?"

"I have no idea," Billy said. No more Mr. Nice Guy.

"And who was the Assistant United States Attorney?"

"I have no idea."

Breitbart stared. "Didn't you just tell us it was Kerr?"

"You are telling me that Piccolo and Chagra were on trial. They were never on trial together in San Antonio."

"Did Piccolo and Chagra get arrested?" Breitbart demanded, in pain.

"No, sir." Not together, they didn't.

"They didn't get arrested?"

"Positively not." Not together. Not in Texas.

"Didn't they tell you that they wanted somebody to lean on someone?" Breitbart sounded on the verge of losing his reason.

"Positively not."

"Then what was the $45,000 for, to Jimmy Kearns?" he bellowed.

"Jimmy Chagra was not there," Billy shouted back. "Jimmy Chagra was on the lam."

Breitbart took a deep breath and started again.

"Was Piccolo there?"

"Piccolo was there," Billy conceded.

"Was Piccolo the guy that gave him the $45,000?"

"That is correct." Finally.

"When was Judge Wood killed? How long after the $45,000?"

"Six, eight months afterwards."

"Then you do know who Judge Wood is?"

"I didn't say I didn't know who Judge Wood is." Billy was suddenly goaded beyond endurance. "You say that the judge was the one who was trying Piccolo and Chagra. That is not so. They were never on trial together."

Breitbart chose to ignore this. Instead, he picked on the manner of his answer.

"Are you upset now, sir?"

"No, I am not," roared Billy, and the judge winced.

"Mr. Breen," he said gently, "Don't lean so close to the microphone."

"I'm just arguing because he *is* arguing," said Billy. "I am only here to serve justice."

Breitbart smiled. "How many other—" he began, but Bruce Baird was at last on his feet.

"Your Honor," he said, "may the record reflect that Mr. Breitbart is doing his share of shouting as well?"

Judge Sand looked from one to the other and then at the clock.

"The record will reflect that we will take our luncheon recess," he said.

10

If Jimmy Chagra had ever imagined, in his cocaine-induced mega-lomania, that he could dispose of the charges against him by disposing of the judge and prosecutor, the black absurdity of the idea was swiftly brought home to him when he at last went to trial in August 1979, before Judge William S. Sessions, later director of the FBI. He was promptly convicted of having engaged in a continuing criminal enterprise and released on bail of $400,000 to await sentencing.

By then, Billy was hopelessly entangled with Samantha Leonetti and working on a couple of large-scale operations that he figured would earn Piccolo forty years at least. Like the rest of the crew, he had been following Chagra's trial day by day, and as soon as the verdict came in, he flew to Las Vegas with Samantha to find out what everybody planned to do next. Touched by Billy's concern, Chagra opened a $100,000 credit line for him at Caesar's Palace, and made it clear that he had no intention of sticking around for a possible life sentence.

Another reason for Billy's Vegas trip was that he knew Kearns would be there with his wife, "Rene," and he hoped to pump them both for further details of the attempted hit on Kerr. During a drunken visit to the house with Margeson, Kearns had told him that he had taken Rene and their young son, Jimmy Jr., with him to Texas in a rented Winnebago camper to carry out the contract, thus combining business with a family vacation, and in the relaxed atmosphere of the casinos, Billy hoped to put together a few more pieces of the case. To oil the wheels, he tapped the line of credit Chagra had arranged for him and fixed Kearns up with a $10,000 credit of his own.

Kearns lost the lot and more besides in his first night at the tables. In a towering rage, he summoned Billy to his room in the Flamingo Hilton and insisted that he call Piccolo then and there for the money he was still owed for "that fucking job I did for him in Texas."

"I'm not calling nobody," said Billy, caught between extremes of caution and curiosity. "I don't know nothing about that."

"I'm talking about that fucking shooting I did for him in San Antonio," bellowed Kearns. "All the shit I went through—and he *still* owes me five grand. Only now it's *ten*. You tell him that. He made me wait, so now it's *ten* grand."

"*You* tell him," said Billy, edging toward the door. "I told ya up front, this ain't got nothing to do with me."

Kearns tracked him like a man-eating bear. "It was you put me in with that motherfucker," he said nastily. "So you call him. And you tell him I want that fucking money. *Today.*"

Billy called him. And Piccolo told Billy to give Kearns the ten thousand dollars.

"All right." Kearns seemed disappointed. "But I ain't finished yet. I wanna talk to that guy. You set up a meet when you get back."

"Hey, Jimmy," Billy protested. "Will ya leave me out of this? You call him. I dunno what to tell him, do I? It ain't none of my business."

Kearns glowered. "Well, if it ain't none of your business," he said heavily, "maybe I oughta take ya for a little ride in the desert."

"You ain't gonna do shit," Billy muttered, his hand on the door. "I'll see yez later."

He drew the cash from the cage at Caesar's Palace, but before taking it across the street he called Helen to ask Margeson to get Kearns off his back.

On returning to Miami, Billy found Piccolo, White, and the others no more anxious that Chagra should go to jail than Chagra was himself. They were afraid he might do a deal and turn them all in. At a summit meeting in The Big House, they decided that Miles McLennan and his wife, Laura, should return to Vegas with $1 million in cash to see if they could work out some mutually acceptable solution. But paying for all this was getting to be a problem after the succession of lost loads, and Kearns made it no easier when he met Piccolo in Billy's living room a week later and demanded one thousand pounds of grass, free of charge, from every shipment the gang brought in from then on.

Piccolo protested. Kearns got to his feet. Piccolo said he would see what he could do.

Now everybody was mad enough at Billy to kill him: Kearns for getting him involved in a job that had gone wrong, and Piccolo for getting him involved with Kearns. At this point the sensible thing would have been for Billy to shave off his beard and emigrate to Patagonia, but instead he resolved, first, that from then on he would take Samantha with him everywhere (alone, they might kill him on a whim, but to kill her as well would entail advance planning), and second, to set them up in a deal with Jack Corbett, ship's captain and drunkard, of Myrtle Beach, South Carolina.

Piccolo had the connections in Colombia but, after three miss-outs in a row, nowhere safe to bring the loads ashore. Corbett had the landing sites and off-loading crews, or so he told Billy in the Executive Club, North Miami Beach, but no connections in Colombia. As matchmaker, Billy figured he could not only mend a few fences by bringing the two together, but line up another bunch of sitting ducks to take down when the time came, including a local sheriff, whom Corbett claimed to have in his pocket.

Piccolo's attitude improved dramatically when Billy told him what he had in mind. He sent Peter White to meet Corbett, and White was sufficiently impressed by what he heard to set up a private deal with Billy before they reported back. Corbett had quoted a price of $1.2 million for off-loading 60,000 pounds, and $1 million for 50,000 pounds. White now proposed that they add $300,000 to the price without telling Piccolo and split it between them. Why not? agreed Billy, now that they were all friends again.

The next day they set up the deal with Piccolo and Painter at The Big House. Billy, White, and Painter would each receive $100,000 for the job, plus expenses, and after a furious argument, Piccolo also agreed to allow Billy 5,000 pounds at cost—$200 a pound—to sell to Danny Mullenberg in Racine. The rest would go to Michigan Jim in Battle Creek. As for Kearns, Kelly, and Margeson, they could have the 1,000 pounds they had asked for, but at cost, not for free.

"Fine," said Billy. "But don't ask *me* to tell 'em."

The next step was to inspect the landing sites. With $5,000 each from Piccolo for expenses, Billy and White flew up to Myrtle Beach with another $5,000 for Jack Corbett, who drove them and his whiskey bottle out into the country to look at the place he had chosen on a river estuary. White thought it was perfect. All they had to do, he said, was build a platform for the eighteen-wheelers to back up real close to the water.

The next day, Corbett took White on a round of introductions to the off-loading crew. They returned late that afternoon with Johnny

Corbett, Jack's cousin, who was not only sober but clearly the man in charge. Besides providing the boats and labor for bringing the load ashore, he said, they would also supply their own captain, José Clifton, to sail the ship up from Colombia. At which point Jack Corbett unplugged his bottle long enough to ask for more cash.

Piccolo and Painter saw no problems with any of this when Billy and White flew back for a final conference at The Big House. Painter was instructed to give Dogface Christina $300,000 on account for Herman the German to take to Colombia with Doug Ruccio, and they then went to see José Clifton, their new captain. After consulting charts, discussing alternative courses, and sorting out radio codes, Piccolo seemed satisfied that Clifton could handle the job and agreed to pay him $300,000.

Billy then called Mullenberg to settle the details of his own deal. If it came off, he would show a profit of around $425,000 on the sale of the 5,000 pounds Piccolo had promised him—plus the agreed $100,000 for working the load, plus his half of the $300,000 tacked on to the offloading costs. Dazed with higher mathematics, he flew up to Myrtle Beach with Peter White to get everything ready.

Over dinner with Jack Corbett and his girlfriend, Nancy, White spelled out what they were going to need: three rented apartments, each with a phone and stocked with food; four rental cars; state-of-the-art radio equipment and scanners, not only for keeping in touch with Clifton as he sailed up from the Caribbean, but to monitor Customs, Coast Guard, DEA, and local law-enforcement frequencies; enough boats, small and large, to land thirty tons of marijuana as fast as the shore crew could stow the bales in the tractor-trailers, and supplies of lumber sufficient to build a loading platform on the riverbank.

Corbett stayed conscious long enough to make a note of these requirements before collapsing into the arms of his marginally less drunken Nancy, and Billy went up to his room to call Samantha.

Two days later, he sneaked her into the Hilton with strict instructions to keep out of everybody's way until he had a chance to fill her in. The following morning, when the others went off on various errands, he took her to the beach. She was not accustomed to being kept under wraps, and danger signals were flying.

"You're gonna love it," he said earnestly. "We'll stay here a few days, and then we're gonna go to Racine, Wisconsin."

"Racine, Wisconsin?" she said, acid with disbelief. "After Myrtle Beach? Boy, are we living it up! What the hell do people do in Racine, Wisconsin?"

"Count money?" suggested Billy.

She looked at him thoughtfully. "How much money?"

"A lot."

"Do I get some?"

"Fifteen thousand." He had meant to say ten, but what the hell?

She rolled over and looked out to sea. "You wanna put Ombre Solaire on my back?"

Billy had no more trouble with Samantha.

The next day, Jack Corbett came by with a large thirst and the keys to a house and two apartments on the ocean; Pistol Pete checked into the area with his tractor-trailer, and Freddy reported that he was heading down from New Jersey. All the pieces were falling into place. José Clifton and the ship were now due off the Carolinas in about a week.

And so was Hurricane David.

They heard the news on television. Until that moment, their gravy boat had been cruising home serenely; now, suddenly, they could not even be sure it was still afloat. The hurricane was churning toward a Florida landfall at precisely the same speed and on exactly the same course as Piccolo and José Clifton had plotted for the load.

The Corbetts spent all day trying to raise Clifton on the radio, even though the range was extreme and reception so bad they had little hope of picking out a weak signal in the mush of static. Don't worry, they said. Clifton was an experienced skipper. If anybody could ride out a hurricane and bring the shrimper in, it was José.

For two days there was nothing to do but fidget, quarrel, drink, and check the weather forecasts. Then, sober for once, Jack Corbett picked up Clifton's call sign, and after piecing together his broken-up transmissions through the ever-worsening crash of static, reported that the ship was behind schedule but still on course, with its crew of eight Colombians half-paralyzed with fear by the mountainous seas.

As Billy had come to expect with the Godfrey Gang, good news from one quarter was instantly canceled out by bad from another. They had decided that both eighteen-wheelers would load up at the same time, Pistol Pete's to go to Michigan Jim in Battle Creek, and Freddy's to Danny Mullenberg in Racine. But as soon as he arrived, Freddy's refrigerated trailer broke down, and when Jack Corbett finally located a good, used replacement for $8,000, nobody had any money left. Muttering to himself, Piccolo sent Ruccio up with another $10,000, at which point radio contact was again lost with José Clifton at sea.

This time with ominous finality. Hurricane David was now on its final approach, aiming straight for the Carolinas, with Clifton dead in its path.

When Piccolo and Painter arrived in Myrtle Beach to take command, the hurricane was on their heels, and no one had heard from the shrimp boat in three days. To keep up morale, his own included, Piccolo went out to inspect the landing site, of which he approved, and learned through Pistol Pete that the off-loading price had been padded by $300,000, of which he emphatically disapproved.

"What the fuck are you assholes playing at?" he demanded when they all met for dinner at the Hilton hotel's Japanese restaurant. "You think I'm stupid? You think I'm not gonna *know* if you try and clip me behind my back?"

"Nobody's trying to clip ya," yelled Billy, not altogether unhappy with the way things were going. Whatever else might cross Piccolo's mind after this, he would certainly never suspect him of working for the law. "You okayed the price. If we get it done cheaper, that's *our* business."

"The fuck it is," Piccolo retorted warmly. "You guys work for *me*. And this is *my* money we're talking about. That makes it *my* business."

"Hey, keep it down, willya?" said White, looking around nervously. "It's getting to be *everybody's* business."

"Listen, you people wouldn't even *be* here if I didn't set it up for yez," Billy hissed. "Where the fuck does Pistol Pete get off, poking his fucking nose into my business?"

"What business? Ripping me off? Billy, you're fulla shit."

After dinner, as they waited for their cars, a squall of rain lashed out of the darkness.

Daylight returned reluctantly, the sky a ruined cathedral of towering black cumulus lit by shafts of sullen gold. Far below, flat as roller blinds, slate-gray layers of low-level cloud raced in from the ocean with sudden sheets of blinding rain, as if to hide the architecture of Judgment Day from impious eyes.

There was still no word from the boat. And as the steel-colored rollers thundered ashore like range after range of toppling hills, no one but Jack Corbett expected there would be.

Hurricane David was now due to come ashore in a matter of hours, and by mid-afternoon Myrtle Beach was all but deserted. At Piccolo's suggestion, the whole crew had moved into the Hilton, except for Corbett, who refused to leave his radio post in the oceanfront house, convinced still that Clifton was afloat and riding out the storm.

The light went fast as the wind ripped sea and rain into a murk of horizontal driving water that shredded palms, spun cars around, and started stripping roofs. Under a treble clef of drawn-out shrieks and wails, punctuated with startling cracks and bangs as whole structures failed and blew away, a terrible ground bass built up little by little like the rumble of an earthquake, sometimes shaking the hotel to its foundations with solid buffets of wind, like blows from a gloved fist.

At its height, the Hilton's management insisted that all remaining guests evacuate their rooms and assemble in the windowless conference auditorium until the worst was over, and it was then that Samantha Leonetti made her debut with the Godfrey Gang. Piccolo and the others met her coming out of Billy's room as they made their way downstairs.

Although he might have chosen a better moment, Billy watched her inspire just the reaction he wanted. Lust. By morning, his insurance would be in place. Provided the *hotel* was still in place. Even in the conference room the wind could be felt as well as heard, in sharp changes of pressure startling enough to silence conversation.

By dawn, Hurricane David had thrashed inland, breaking up into violent local storms. In Myrtle Beach, the rain had stopped; the ocean was already losing some of its awesome momentum, and emergency crews were out on the flooded streets. To salvage what he could from his own disaster, Piccolo left with Painter and White to find Johnny Corbett, but Billy decided to visit Jack Corbett instead, just in case, by some miracle, José Clifton had lost only radio contact and not the ship as well.

When he rejoined the others at the hotel later in the day, he was glad he had picked the right Corbett. In heavy seas littered with floating wreckage, Johnny had taken them out in a boat to look for the shrimper, with as little success as his cousin's search with the radio scanner.

Not even the presence of Samantha in what Billy considered an unnecessarily provocative outfit could lift the mood at dinner. He took her to bed early with an uneasy feeling that somehow they would manage to hold *him* responsible for the fiasco.

On top of the money he had already laid out, Piccolo still had to pay half the price of the lost load and presumably for the boat as well, as it was unlikely to have been insured for the voyage with Lloyd's of London. There was also the fate of José Clifton and eight Indians to consider, although this clearly weighed less heavily with Piccolo than 60,000 pounds of Colombian gold.

In the morning, the others checked out of the Hilton and returned to their rented apartments to pack. Piccolo was more concerned with pacifying his customers than holding an inquest, but Billy could see one coming. Without him, as he had pointed out, none of them would have been here. Samantha was also giving him a hard time, now that her $15,000 had gone down with the ship. He had been nice about it so far, but was just about to pop her one when the phone rang.

It was Jack Corbett. Still keeping the faith. He had finally made contact with José Clifton, who had been loitering along at a discreet distance behind the hurricane and expected to make a landfall off Myrtle Beach sometime the following evening.

Confident now of a very different reception, Billy drove off to deliver the news in person to Piccolo, Painter, and Ruccio, who went wild when they heard. Piling into their rental cars, they roared off through the littered streets to pick up White before joining Corbett at the house to celebrate. But Corbett had been celebrating already, as well as drowning his sorrows for three days straight, and after trying to raise Clifton again, just to prove he was no hallucination, passed out in a welter of empty bottles. Nobody minded. They were all brothers-in-arms again.

The next day, well before their ship came in, Billy left for Racine with Samantha, having first wrung a promise from Piccolo that he would send extra weight if he could. As soon as the marijuana was safely ashore, the whole crew was set to follow—Freddy, of course, with Danny Mullenberg's load; Billy Painter to weigh it on delivery; White to protect his half-interest in Billy's profits; the Corbetts to collect for the off-loading, and Piccolo because Racine was at a convenient distance from Battle Creek, where he would be supervising Pistol Pete's delivery to Michigan Jim.

In return for the promise of extra weight, Billy also undertook to call Kearns, Kelly, and Margeson to say they could have a Winnebago load of 1,500 pounds instead of 1,000, if they wanted it, but only if they paid cost price—$200 a pound—instead of getting it for free. With a gross profit of around $275,000 in prospect, Margeson was not disposed to argue, and told him they would leave for Racine the next day.

Billy was not entirely happy about these arrangements. Nor was Mullenberg when he called to see Billy and Samantha at the apartment he had found for them on Lake Avenue. A town as small as Racine was going to feel dangerously overcrowded with everybody there, he said. But Samantha, at least, turned from harpie to cooing dove the moment Mullenberg handed over an attaché case containing a down payment of $350,000. When he suggested they go out to eat, she chose to stay behind, preferring its company to theirs.

The next eight days not only completed Billy's training in the marijuana business but put him in a position to testify against some forty violators of state and federal drug and conspiracy laws. When Piccolo called to say the load was short (28,500 pounds instead of the expected 60,000), but that he would be sending up 12,500 pounds anyway (instead of 5,000), Mullenberg went into action, with Billy in close attendance. In the forty-eight hours before Freddy arrived with the load, Mullenberg lined up customers for all of it, starting with Mike Gamboli in Chicago.

At the agreed price of $285 a pound, Mullenberg now owed them $3,562,500. Of this, Piccolo would take $2.5 million (to show a 100 percent return on his investment), leaving something over a million for Billy and White to split between them.

It was a good enough reason for Billy to take an intelligent interest in the next phase of the operation, which was checking the shipment after it had been unloaded into the barn Mullenberg used as his stash. Painter and Mullenberg did this together, bale by bale, tagging each with its exact weight and recording it on their tally sheets. Toward the end, when Painter broke off for a rail or two of coke in the farmhouse, Billy allowed Mullenberg to steal 100 pounds for himself. No one was watching. Freddy had driven off after hosing the marijuana seeds out of his rig.

Despite the snow and a bitter north wind, Billy stayed to watch after Painter and Mullenberg compared sheets and agreed on a total of 12,500 pounds. Mullenberg's foreman, Bruno, then began loading the waiting fleet of cars and vans, starting a separate sheet for each with the name of the customer and the weight, cost, and number of bales. As each driver signed for his load, he was hustled away and the next vehicle would back up into position like clockwork. Billy was hugely impressed. By dawn the barn was almost empty, except for the 1,500 pounds reserved for Kearns, Kelly, and Margeson, now awaiting his call at the Sheraton Motor Inn in Kenosha.

That night, he collected the keys of their Winnebago camper and gave them to Mullenberg, who had driven him over. Billy then felt obliged to stay for dinner, which was not the happiest of meals. Kelly was on a diet, which had not improved his always uncertain temper, and Kearns got dangerously drunk on the most expensive wines in the joint. Having survived through to coffee, Billy was glad to pick up the tab and escape, promising to call as soon as the camper was loaded. In return, they promised to deliver $300,000 to his home in Miami in a week to ten days.

Which brought up the problem of what to do with all the money.

"Listen, doll," said Billy, emptying the $350,000 from Mullenberg's attaché case onto the bed. "We gotta get this outa here before Bobby grabs it. You wanna take it to Atlanta for me?"

"No chance," said Samantha, buffing her nails.

Billy blinked. Until now, she had hardly been able to keep her hands off the money. "I'll *pay* ya," he said.

"I'm not going to Atlanta," she replied indifferently. "I got things to do in New York."

"Okay. So stash it in your apartment—I don't care. I just wanna get it outa here before the crew shows up."

Samantha shrugged. She had begun to disturb him in various ways. For one thing, she seemed never to sleep. Whenever he woke in the night, she was always awake, either pretending to read or staring at him speculatively, as if he had just said something interesting.

"Come on, doll," he said, reaching out for her. "You can wear it under your clothes. And ten grand of it is yours. You earned it."

She brushed his hand off her shoulder. "I'll take a hundred thousand," she said. "That's all. In big bills. And it'll cost you another ten thousand when you come for it."

Billy sighed, and put a quarter of a million back in the attaché case.

As he had expected, they all began to squabble about money as soon as they checked in. When Jack Corbett learned from White that his fee had been slashed from $1.2 million to $750,000 because of the short load, he flew into such a tantrum that Billy ordered them both out of the apartment. Mellowed by a bottle or two, Corbett returned the next day to accept the offer but told his cousin he could get only $75,000, whereupon Johnny had a tantrum and demanded $100,000.

At this point, Danny Mullenberg came by with $200,000, the first in what he promised would be daily installments until the whole load was paid for. Billy thought he should keep this for Piccolo, but then White had a tantrum, insisting that they take $25,000 each for themselves and give the balance to Corbett. As Billy now held an embarrassing $450,000 in cash, he in fact gave Corbett $400,000 on account, which caused Piccolo to have a tantrum on the phone, demanding that he get *his* money first, before anyone else got paid.

Day by day the cash poured in, but Mullenberg was getting edgy. He had warned them from the start—Racine was small enough to notice strangers, and the Godfrey Gang was hardly self-effacing. Piccolo and Painter came and went several times in a chartered Lear-jet, provoking open speculation in town about who they were and what they were up to, and when Jack Corbett staged a spectacular drunken crash-out in the Corner House restaurant, Mullenberg blew the whistle. He insisted that Billy pay off the Corbetts immediately and send them home—which he did, by chartered plane—and that Piccolo call him as soon as he got back.

Fortunately for customer relations, the rest of Piccolo's money was waiting for him when he returned, and after the Lear left Racine for the last time, only Billy and White remained behind. Mullenberg's final payments of around $800,000 belonged to them, less some $20,000 they owed him for cars, the apartments, and various services provided by his crew. Billy packed his share into suitcases, and prevailed on Bruno, Mullenberg's foreman, to drive him home to Miami.

The rest was just tidying up. Margeson appeared at the house a week later to pay for the Winnebago load that had gone to Boston. Billy flew up to New York to collect his money and pay off Samantha. At The Big House, he heard that the Colombians had been paid and that Dogface Christina was satisfied. In fact, they should all have been happy, but nobody was. Helen was short-tempered; Samantha remote, and Piccolo, Painter, and White were giving him funny looks. He could not understand it. Furious with Piccolo anyway for the way he had treated Mullenberg, Billy settled down to write up his notes.

He now had the makings of a federal case that not even the Bureau could ignore. Kearns had told him several times, in front of Helen, that he had attempted to kill Assistant U.S. Attorney James Kerr for a $60,000 fee from Bobby Piccolo. Piccolo had told him several times, in front of witnesses, that he had hired Kearns to do this on Jimmy Chagra's instructions. Jimmy Chagra had confirmed that he had ordered Piccolo to issue the contract, and that he had taken out another one on Judge Wood.

Granted, most of this was hearsay, but Billy also had them locked into a major drugs-racketeering case to which he could testify directly, and which would provide enough leverage to flip any one of them. He had called Dave Jellison a couple of times while it was going on, just to keep him interested, and he was now about ready to turn the whole investigation over to the Bureau. All that would then remain would be for him to guide its agents through the twists and turns of the case, and lead them on to another bunch of defendants in Myrtle Beach and Racine for good measure.

But before Billy was entirely satisfied with his notes, Jimmy Chagra forfeited his $400,000 bail bond in Las Vegas and disappeared as if the desert had swallowed him up.

"Was the Hurricane David a ship?" asked David Breitbart.

A ship? Billy had been on the stand a long time. He was tired. He was also tired of trying to straighten this guy out. A ship?

"Yes, it was."

"Was it a ship that you participated in using to smuggle drugs into the United States?"

"No, I didn't participate in that ship's smuggling. I caught it up in Wisconsin."

"Well, as a result of the Hurricane David bringing illegal thousands of pounds of marijuana into the United States, did you end up with $350,000 in cash?"

"Yes, I did. And I reinvested it in the Piccolo crew. . . ."

Breitbart seemed not to hear. "When you got the $350,000, did you turn that in to agents of the Drug Enforcement Administration?"

"I don't work with the DEA."

"Did you give it to agents of the FBI? Did you ask them to voucher it as evidence?"

"No, I didn't."

"Did you give it to the local authorities in Georgia or South Carolina so they could voucher it as evidence?"

"No, I did not."

"Did you keep it yourself?"

"No," he said patiently. "I put it into the crew."

"And that was the drug crew?" Breitbart prepared to deliver the coup de grace.

"That's right."

"The crew that you knew had murdered a federal judge?" he thundered.

"No," said Billy, infuriatingly. "I didn't know they had murdered a federal judge. But I did know they attempted to assassinate an Assistant United States Attorney—and that I worked on until I got the conviction."

"And you gave them $350,000?" Breitbart invited the jury to share his horror. "How many agents were they able to kill with that?"

"Mr. Breitbart," said Judge Sand, cutting in before Baird could object. "I have asked you not to shout." He looked up at the court-room clock. "All right—we'll call it a day. Tomorrow is a holiday. We will resume at 10:00 A.M. on Wednesday."

11

Like many attorneys, bureaucrats, and public officials who find it easier to cope with stereotypes than with real life, what Breitbart had failed to understand was that in order to pass as a dope dealer among dope dealers, Billy had to deal dope. While it is certainly possible to question his motives, his tactics, and, indeed, his *right* to conduct a private investigation of a major crime, survival in his self-appointed undercover role required him to act as he did and to cope with the consequences, among which were sacks full of money.

Hard as it was for Breitbart, and others, to grasp that in a money-grubbing society, money was *not* Billy's principal concern, the fact is that he could have amassed millions and *still* taken down the army of traffickers he eventually handed over to the authorities.

Although he lived as high on the hog as his constitution would allow, the money was always an embarrassment. He threw it away like confetti. In his cups, he "lent" people huge sums that he completely forgot about by the following morning, and he reinvested what was left in other loads to keep the pot boiling. None of it stuck. The money was a valuable but awkward by-product, like manure in a farmyard. And now that Jimmy Chagra, his principal target, had gone missing, the only way he could cultivate the people who had hidden him was by spreading it around.

Although the Godfrey Gang was a shadow of what it had been in the mid-'70s, Piccolo was still the key. Once turned, he could lock up everybody, Kearns, Kelly, and Margeson included. But there was no way Billy could hang around The Big House socially; his relationship with Piccolo, never very close, was in tatters. To find Chagra and finish off his mission, Billy had to be there on business, and the next item on the agenda was the *Captain Tom*.

Early in November, Peter White called him over to Coral Springs for a summit conference with Piccolo, Painter, and Ruccio. Billy would have gone willingly enough, even if Piccolo and Ruccio had *not* owed his bookmaking business $70,000, but he was even more gratified when they offered to make him a full one-third partner in the Godfrey Gang, along with Peter White, in return for writing off the debt and putting up some front money for the next load. There were two conditions, however. One was that Piccolo would still be boss and give the orders. The other was that Billy straighten out Samantha Leonetti.

"Huh?"

"You know what she's been doing, don'cha?"

Billy's heart sank. He was so infatuated he could hardly bear the thought of her sleeping around.

"She's been calling everybody," Piccolo went on. "Bothering people. Me. Peter. Doug. Everybody. Even Judy—right, Peter? You gotta stop her doing that, Billy. Give her a slap or something."

"Yeah, right." He was so relieved that she hadn't been propositioning the guys he had to work with that he hardly cared what she had said to them.

"I mean, you wanna watch out for that broad. She's crazy. I dunno what you did to her, but she's telling everybody you're no good." Piccolo exchanged a glance with Peter White, who knew all about Billy's problems on Winter Hill. "She says we oughta be careful because you're a snitch. She says you're working for the cops."

Billy's mind went blank for a moment. What could he have done to her? Why would she want to get him killed?

"Yeah," he croaked. It certainly explained the funny looks he had been getting. "That's worth a pretty good slap." He must have been talking in his sleep. "Working for the cops . . ." He laughed furiously. "If I was working for the cops, you'd all be doing thirty years."

"Yeah. Well . . ." Piccolo was impatient to get back to business. "That's what I told Peter. So get rid of her, okay? Before she starts calling the wrong people. Like Jimmy Kearns."

He had a point. If Billy had been himself, he might have taken the advice, but he was past 50, and as moony as a teenager. He was only half-listening when Piccolo went on to say that, as partners, he and White would have to pay their own expenses, and post $100,000 each against the next 60,000-pound load—although he was listening well enough to point out that as they already owed him $70,000, all he had to find was $30,000.

The routine was to be the same as before, except that Jack Corbett was out. José Clifton would be radio man this time for a fee of $350,000. Johnny Corbett would be paid $1 million for offloading the shipment at a new site higher up the river, and as soon as they had settled the details with Dogface and the German, Billy Painter would fly down to Colombia to pick out and mark the bales.

The partners next met in Los Angeles for the 1980 Superbowl. The mood was now calm and confident. The offloading arrangements were all set, and Painter was about to leave for Santa Marta. The countdown had started, but Billy had nothing to do.

"Forget about it," they said, eying Samantha, who had flown in from New York. "Enjoy yourself. Let *us* do the work."

Taking advantage of the warmer climate, Billy learned that it was Miles McLennan and Laura who had spirited Jimmy Chagra away from Las Vegas after he jumped bail. They had been baby-sitting with him and his wife ever since, to begin with in Kansas City and more recently on the road in a Winnebago mobile home. That was useful information, but the friendlier atmosphere worked both ways. After a day or two, Billy became uncomfortably aware that Piccolo and the others were cozying up to Samantha, and that she was a lot less reluctant to accommodate them than he would have wished.

Exploiting his fascination with her, she was, by turn, demanding, capricious, and cruel—but always alert enough for signs of revolt to bring him to heel between the sheets. Soon, he hardly cared if she was trying to undermine him with the others or not, for when Samantha realized he was jealous, she took merciless advantage of it and treated him worse than ever, despite a shower of jewelry, perfume, Gucci bags, and Dunhill lighters. Now she wanted him to pay her rent in New York and take a house in her name in Coral Springs. And Billy *agreed*, pinching himself. He could hardly believe what he was doing.

They stayed on after the others left and lost a little money at Santa Anita Racetrack, but he telephoned White every day to find out if he was needed. He was not. Bored with Los Angeles, he took Samantha to Las Vegas and started calling White from Caesar's Palace.

"Listen," said White, on the fourth day. "If you're getting itchy, why don't you go on up to Racine? Make sure Danny Mullenberg's got his crew together, and rent us a couple of houses, okay?"

"Sure," said Billy, glad to have something to do at last.

The hardest part was getting Samantha to go with him. The

promise of $25,000 finally won her over, and by the end of February, still with no news of the *Captain Tom*, it began to look cheap at the price. Amortized over two months, the cost of her company was down to a mere $1,000 a day (not counting gifts, gambling losses, living expenses, and rash promises).

Early in March, things started to move. White called to say that he and Ruccio were leaving for Myrtle Beach. The shrimper had sailed from Colombia and expected to make a landfall off South Carolina in ten days.

"Great," said Billy. "Fantastic. What's the weather forecast?"

White laughed.

Ten days later, the worst snowstorm in a hundred years was raging across South Carolina, and José Clifton had lost radio contact with the *Captain Tom*.

White's next call was more reassuring. With his radio on the blink, the captain of the shrimper had rowed ashore in heavy seas to report his arrival. It was now snowing harder than ever, but Billy could inform their waiting customers that the off-loading would begin as soon as the sea moderated and visibility improved.

Mullenberg was sympathetic and understanding. Kearns, who had meanwhile checked into the Sheraton Motor Inn in Kenosha with Kelly and Margeson, merely grunted and observed that their Winnebago could hold a lot more than the one thousand pounds they had been promised.

"We can get fifteen hundred pounds in there easy," he said. "Maybe more. So you fix it with Piccolo."

"Yeah," said Kelly. "Billy'll fix it. Even if we gotta pay full price for it. Right, Billy?"

"Right," said Margeson. "He'll look after us, won't you, Billy? He'll get us more."

Billy looked at their eager, shining faces, and his lips went dry.

To celebrate the *Captain Tom*'s arrival, Billy took Samantha to the Corner House restaurant for dinner. With $25,000 almost within reach, her mood had mellowed considerably, and to take advantage of it, Billy decided on an early night. But as he opened the front door of their rented house, he heard the phone ringing, like a harbinger of doom.

It was Peter White.

To help the *Captain Tom* hold its position, the crew had improvised a sheet anchor out of rope and hatch covers, which had promptly wrapped itself around the ship's propellers. She was now drifting helplessly out to sea. He had tried to get Johnny Corbett to start off-loading its thirty-ton cargo of marijuana, but he had refused even to consider it in a force 8 gale and near-zero visibility.

White sounded ready to cry.

"*Jack* Corbett," said Billy urgently. "Talk to him. *He'll* do it."

"No, *you* talk to him," White said. "Last time, I called him a fucking wino. He won't do nothing for me."

But Corbett was willing enough to help when Billy reached him on the phone. Sure, he said. He had a couple of boats he could use. And his friend the sheriff had another one. They'd be happy to give it a try. He was even willing to talk to Peter White, if he was the guy in charge.

In the small hours of the morning, White called Billy again. The crippled ship had drifted out of range.

Billy grunted. He now had some heavy explaining to do.

"What about the crew?"

"Fuck 'em," said White. "I asked Bobby, and he said to hell with it. Leave 'em die."

"He *what*?"

"Well, they're just Indians. And they're all sick and frostbitten anyhow."

"Is that so?" Billy looked at the phone as though to reach in and choke him. "Well, you can tell Johnny Corbett and José Clifton to get their asses out there right now and bring those Indians off, understand?"

"Billy—"

"And don't fucking Billy *me*," he bellowed. "Just do like I tell ya. Or the next time I see any one of yez, *you're* gonna get sicker than they are. In fact, I may just fucking *kill* ya."

"All right, all right."

Now he had to call Kearns, Kelly, and Margeson, who were seriously displeased at the outcome even before Mullenberg held them up another day by returning their Winnebago to the wrong hotel.

"This fucking trip has cost us over two thousand bucks," ranted Kearns. "And you know something? I'm not fucking paying for it."

"Well, why don'cha come to Florida?" Billy suggested. "Make Piccolo pick up the tab."

"Yeah," said Kearns, looking forward to it.

Next, Billy had to send Samantha back to New York with only $2,500 instead of $25,000, and that was even more traumatic.

"I don't *care* if you lost the load," she screeched. "It's not *my* fault if Peter didn't have the guts to make 'em go out and get it. You conned me, you sonuvabitch. You owe me twenty-two thousand five hundred dollars."

And finally, Billy had to cope with a frenzied Piccolo.

"You know what you *did*, you dummy? When you made Peter take those fucking Indians off the boat? I'll tell ya. You cost the three of us a million dollars, that's what you did."

"What the fuck you talking about? They were gonna die out there."

"Good." Piccolo craned his head at him like a rattler. "As long as they were on the boat, the load was *their* responsibility. When you took 'em off, you made it *our* responsibility. You wanna chip in your three hundred and fifty grand now?"

"Fuck you, Bobby," said Billy uneasily. "Get it off the Corbetts. Or José Clifton."

"Huh?"

"You sure those guys didn't rip off the load?"

The more they thought about it, the less sure they became. The Corbetts and Clifton hotly denied doing any such thing, but it would have been easy enough to find the boat again after the crew had been taken off and Peter White had gone home. Adding to Billy's suspicions, when agents of the Drug Enforcement Administration eventually boarded the abandoned vessel, they seized not 60,000 pounds of Colombian gold but only 36,000 pounds, the other 12 tons having unaccountably disappeared in the blizzard.

Piccolo's already shaky Colombian connection now snapped altogether. Suspecting he had been ripped off himself, the Old Man declined to send another load unless $500,000 was posted in Colombia before it sailed and they agreed to a price hike from $85 to $100 a pound. As both conditions were unacceptable, the three partners flew down to Aruba with Billy Painter to talk terms with another Colombian supplier, but *his* price was $125 a pound, and Piccolo refused even to consider it. What was left of the Godfrey Gang returned to Miami in a state of voluntary liquidation.

But it was too soon. The case still needed work. And the only way that Billy could see to keep things going was to hook up with George Mitchell.

Wednesday, the 13th, was David Breitbart's unlucky day. Resuming his cross-examination, he dived straight in at the deep end, only to find that someone had emptied the pool.

"Mr. Breen, on April 19, 1984, did you take the witness stand and testify under oath in the United States District Court for the Western District of Louisiana, Shreveport Division?"

"Yes, I did," agreed Billy.

"At that time, sir, were you asked these questions, and did you give these answers? Mr. Zimmerman—"

"Your Honor, objection." Baird was astonished by so crude a blunder. "He hasn't established any failure of recollection."

Judge Sand upheld the objection, explaining to Breitbart with some severity the restricted circumstances in which he could use Billy's testimony in another case.

Breitbart consulted his notes. "Mr. Breen, do you remember my asking you whether you like to beat up women?"

"Yes, sir."

"You do remember I asked you whether or not you beat up other people?"

"I don't remember that question," said Billy.

"You don't remember being asked, not only did you beat up your wife, but you also beat up other people, and you had to be locked up in a padded room because of it?"

"Yes." He could remember being asked that, but no, he had never beaten up his wife or been locked up for it.

"And you denied that. You said you never beat up anybody. You never beat up a woman, and you never beat up anyone else, is that correct?"

"Yes." He didn't know who the guy was talking about now, and there was a long day ahead.

"You said that under oath?"

"Yes."

"That was a lie, wasn't it?"

"No, sir."

Breitbart smiled confidently. "Isn't it a fact you testified in Louisiana that you beat up your wife and you beat up several other people?"

"No, sir," said Billy stoutly. He had never testified anywhere that he had beaten up his wife.

"On April 19, 1984, sir, in the United States District Court for the Western District of Louisiana in Shreveport, were you asked these questions and did you give these answers? By Mr. Zimmerman, 'Mr. Breen, have you ever suffered—' " He broke off. In midflight this time, he had again noticed that the pool was empty. "Er—that is the wrong question," he muttered, and limped off in a different direction. "Do you also recall telling us on Monday that you never remember waking up in a city married—that you didn't know where you had been for an extended period of time? Do you remember telling us you didn't remember that?"

Billy blinked at him uncomprehendingly. "Waking up married?" He looked around for help.

"Yes, sir."

"Your Honor," said Baird, coming to the rescue. "I don't understand the question. Objection to form."

Breitbart pulled himself together. "Do you remember a certain *series of questions with regard to your amnesia, when I suggested to you that there were periods of time when you woke up and didn't know where you had been for extended periods of time?"*

Billy was with him now. *"There were two occasions,"* he agreed.

"Were you asked this question, and did you give this answer? Question: Mr. Breen, have you ever suffered from amnesia? Answer: If I did, I do not remember it."

The joke had evidently escaped Breitbart, but before Billy could try to explain it to him, Baird was on his feet again.

"Your Honor," he said, *"we haven't established any inconsistent statements, to my knowledge."*

"Sustained," said Judge Sand.

"You don't know what question I am going to read," snapped Breitbart, flat on his face in the dry pool. *"Question: Did you ever tell anyone that you had suffered from amnesia for a couple of years and were kind of just wandering around, not knowing where or who you were? Answer: One time I woke up in another state, wondering how I got there. I do not know what I was doing. I do not remember nothing about it. I was married at the time."*

"Objection," Baird said tiredly.

"It will be stricken," agreed Judge Sand.

Breitbart stared. *"May I know the nature of the objection?"*

"I will take it up with you during the recess," replied the judge, too experienced to risk compromising the trial by humiliating counsel in front of the jury. *"Lack of inconsistency between the witness's testimony and what you have read. Let's move on."*

Breitbart breathed out heavily. *"Mr. Breen, is it a fact that there were periods in your life when you didn't know where you were, and you woke up wandering around in a strange state?"*

"Yes, sir," said Billy, beginning to enjoy this a little.

"That's correct, right?" Breitbart took a deep breath and dived in again. *"In the General Court of Justice, Superior Division, County of Brunswick, State of North Carolina, did you testify under oath, sir?"*

"Yes, I did."

"Were you asked this question and did you give this answer?"

"Your Honor," cried Baird, frankly astounded that Breitbart should repeat the error. *"Again, objection."*

"Mr. Breitbart—" began Judge Sand.

The other cut him off. *"I have already laid the foundation,"* he said despairingly, but the pool was still empty.

"You haven't before this jury," the judge replied, in a tone that brooked no further argument.

Splat! Breitbart rubbed his forehead. *"Do you remember telling us that you never beat up a woman?"*

"On the same subject?" asked Judge Sand.

"Absolutely," said Breitbart. "Do you remember telling us you never beat up a woman?"

That was only part of the question Billy had been asked originally, and the wording was different, but he hadn't the heart to go through it all again. "Yes, I did," he said.

"Do you remember telling us under oath you beat up several other people and as a result of it you were confined?"

"That's not true." He had never been confined for beating up people.

Breitbart shook his head doggedly. "Did you beat up a woman?"

"That's true."

"Did you beat up several other people?"

"Yes, sir."

"As a result of that, were you confined in a mental hospital?"

He had done it again. After setting Billy up, he had gone in for the kill brandishing the wrong end of the stick.

"No, sir," said Billy.

It took six more questions and answers to establish what Breitbart should have known to start with—that Billy had not been confined for beating up Maria De Angelis and the sailors she was entertaining but had escaped from a closed ward at the VA hospital in order to do so.

"What is a closed ward, Mr. Breen?"

"That's a psychiatric ward for the mentally insane—at which time I said I was very sick. Today, I am not. And I wasn't the day of the Resource Capital transaction."

"How about Monday?" Breitbart suggested nastily. "When you said you never beat up anybody. Were you crazy Monday?"

"Your Honor," protested Baird. "Objection. That is not the testinomy."

"Sustained."

"Do you have amnesia with regard to this past Monday?" insisted Breitbart.

"Your Honor, objection."

"Sustained."

Breitbart decided to let it go.

12

After the loss of the *Captain Tom* and Billy's decision to involve George Mitchell with the Godfrey Gang, his career reached take-off speed, flew out of control, and finally crashed through the probability barrier into realms of black comic fantasy uncharted even by the Marx Brothers.

Mitchell was another of those quiet, middle-class, middle-aged, middle managers who ventured into the dope business during the go-go '70s, and after a couple of lucky hits, grew beards, unbuttoned their shirts, and blossomed into cartoon Caligulas.

When they first became friends, after Billy's release from prison, "Mitch" was credit manager at Miami Lincoln Mercury, and his idea of a good time was Friday night at the Playboy Club. By 1980, he was dealing a million Quaaludes a week through a "front" company, Uleta Packaging; landing cocaine and marijuana on airstrips in Baxley, Georgia, with the regularity of a scheduled airline, and generally coming on like J. P. Cornelius Rockefeller.

It was a time and place in which money was a measure of self-esteem and social status, and a lot of money, objective proof of a personal superiority transcending the law or any other such petty consideration. Billy could not stand him anymore, even though Mitch and his girlfriend, Barbara, were like brother and sister to Helen.

It was through Helen that they teamed up again, this time as business associates. Aware of his involvement with the Godfrey Gang, Mitch asked Helen to ask Billy if he was interested in virtually unlimited supplies of high-grade Colombian marijuana—not out of friendship or for old times' sake but for $260 a pound. Importing the stuff faster than his distributors could handle it, he was running out of warehouse space.

With the approval of his "partners," Piccolo and White, Billy decided to check out the operation. He flew up to Jacksonville to meet Mitch's associate in the marijuana trade, Larry Jackson, a good ol' boy from Appling County, who drove him out to Baxley, showed him the airstrips and stash houses, explained the whole setup, and suggested that instead of going through Mitch, they should cut him out and deal with each other directly.

"Looks good to me," said Billy, reporting on his visit. "Larry's got an old soybean farm up a dirt road way out in the country with a couple of five-thousand-foot strips and a stash house. There's another house for the off-loaders to stay in between planes—it's got a peacock in the yard—and there's nobody lives between him and the road except family."

"Well," said Piccolo. "Sounds okay—but with that kinda setup, you gotta be careful. You get a lotta out-of-town cars and trucks and stuff in a place like that and people get nosy."

"Right," agreed Billy. "But Larry took care of that. There's a church just up the highway with a parking lot around back for maybe twenty cars. When the load comes in, they go up to the stash house one at a time and nobody gets to see much."

"What about the law?" asked Peter White.

"The sheriff directs the traffic," said Billy. "Do you believe that? The sheriff of Appling County sends 'em up there. Larry's got him in his pocket. *And* his deputy. He's got the chief of police in Baxley. And he's got a couple of Georgia Bureau of Investigation agents. All on the payroll."

Piccolo looked at White and shrugged. "Okay. You wanna give it a try, Billy, go ahead. But I got something else working, so I'm gonna need Peter here."

"Yeah?" Billy glowered. "What have you got?"

"You'll know when the time comes."

"Okay. But I'm a partner too, remember."

"How can I fucking forget it?" Piccolo said gloomily.

Before Billy could call Mitch, Mitch called him, and after some argument about the price, Billy agreed to take 5,000 pounds at $260 a pound "on front street"—that is, with no money down. He then called Chicago and sold the whole load over the phone for $280 a pound to Mike Gamboli, who said he would leave at once for Way-cross, Georgia, to pick it up.

Stuck for manpower, Billy called Samantha down from New York, and Eddie Mode, her twin sister's boyfriend, from Las Vegas. For $5,000 each, she and Eddie agreed to do all the work while Billy masterminded the operation from his hotel room. As dispatcher, Samantha's job was to send one of Gamboli's fleet of cars and campers from the church parking lot to the stash house every fifteen minutes, and Eddie's to supervise the weighing and loading.

It took them three hours to ship out 3,500 pounds, but everything went according to plan and they returned to the hotel in high spirits. Eddie, in particular, was still chuckling over Mike Gamboli's kid brother, who had been driving one of the cars. As he approached the stash house to get loaded up, he had been so unnerved by the sight of Appling County Sheriff Joe Lightsey in full uniform, sitting there in his cruiser, that he had driven off the dirt road into a field, almost killing a cow.

"Come back here," the sheriff had shouted angrily, running into the field after him. "Where the hell you goin'? The stash house is up there, you asshole."

Two days later, Billy flew to Chicago to pick up the money. Gamboli had only about half of it ready, but even so, $500,000, mostly in twenties, was still too much for him to count. Now wise in the ways of the dope trade, Billy knew that operators of airport baggage X-ray machines could detect bundles of bills in a carry-on suitcase and were under standing orders to ask the owner to open it for inspection. The only safe way to get money aboard, therefore, was to wear it, as the security arch through which all departing passengers had to walk was no more than a metal detector.

Billy accordingly mastered the bandage and compress technique. Starting at the ankles and working up, he encased himself in currency, strapping wads of bills in place with yards of Ace bandage until mummified in money to the neck. He then struggled into long johns a size too small and bandaged himself off at the ankles and wrists in case anything worked loose. Dressed in street clothes several sizes larger than normal, he found he could carry up to $500,000 in this way, but only in winter. Money, he discovered, was a highly efficient form of thermal underwear.

After paying everybody off, Billy was left with a profit of about $50,000 to split with Peter White. Compared with the profits the others were making, it was not a lot to show for the nervous wear and tear, but the bonus for Billy was a new set of targets to take down.

So he did it again.

This time, Pistol Pete delivered the consignment to Racine in his tractor-trailer for $30,000, and a few days later, Billy once more waddled back to Atlanta seriously overweight, with a down payment of half a million dollars in his underwear.

The profit was still small, but when he and Samantha returned to Chicago to pick up the balance of the $1.5 million due, he got lucky at a crap game in Gamboli's house and had to leave in a hurry with about $70,000 stuffed down the front of Samantha's dress. It was not enough to keep her quiet. Several times he woke in the night to find her sizing him up like a cracksman studying a safe.

George Mitchell was not happy with the financial situation either. His marijuana mountain was building up at such a rate that he needed all the customers he could get, cash *or* credit. Before the last of the money was even in for the second load, he was pressing Billy to take a third, but this time he had to refuse. Canadian friends of Peter White and Earl McLennan had come up with a Cuban Communist connection named Diego.

"I'm gonna need a hundred fifty thousand dollars from you toward expenses and the money we gotta post," said Piccolo.

"Yeah," said Billy, who was about broke again, what with living expenses and presents to ward off Samantha's evil eye. "Okay. Gimme a few days."

"And find a shrimper," Piccolo added carelessly. "Big enough for fifty thousand pounds."

"Huh?"

"A shrimper. A *boat*, Billy. They're not gonna *swim* here with it. We're gonna need a boat."

"Right. But why me? I don't know nothing about boats."

"Why you? Because you're a partner. And this time, you fucking *work*."

As it happened, Billy had a friend in the shrimping business named Peggy Rowe. When he hinted at their problem, she put him in touch with her brother Dave, who usually worked out of Savannah, Georgia, but just happened to be down in Key West with *Miss Lynn*, one of their bigger boats. After Peter White pronounced her suitable, Dave Rowe told them he wanted $1 million for the "charter."

"All right," said Piccolo, when the crew met for a planning meeting at the gang's stash house in Fort Lauderdale. "Let's do it. We'll take the load off at the Isaac Light."

"Oh yeah?" Billy looked at him coldly. "When was this discussed?"

"We're discussing it now," said Painter. "There's this guy at the Amity Boatyard. They done it for ten years and never lost a load yet."

"You mean they send boats out to the Isaac Light?"

"Right. They take the load off in international waters and run it right into the yard. Pistol Pete and Freddy, they just sit there and wait for it."

"How about the paperwork?" There was an agricultural checkpoint and weighbridge just beyond Jacksonville, near the state line.

"Simple," said Piccolo. "Once we know how much we got on the boat, we buy a couple of loads of the exact same weight of grapefruit. Then we split our stuff between the two eighteen-wheelers and fill 'em up with the fruit till we got the right weight in each trailer, and dump the rest. Nothing to it. Did it all the time in the old days."

The off-loaders, represented by Charlie and Irving, owners of the Amity Boatyard, hosted the next meeting. The fee for their services was also $1 million, of which $300,000 had to be posted up front. After some perfunctory haggling, for the price was not out of line, Piccolo accepted the tender, and got down to studying charts and compass courses with Captain Chester, a friend of Peter White. They agreed that the return leg of the voyage would take about eleven days, and Irving promised to have his boats standing by ten days after the loaded shrimper sailed for home.

It was now up to Diego. Two days later, he called to say the load was ready. Joey, Piccolo's man in Santa Marta, confirmed that he had picked out 50,000 pounds of the best Colombian gold he had ever laid his one good eye on, and the *Miss Lynn* put to sea from Key West to collect it.

With nothing to do now but wait, Billy called Samantha in New York. As soon as she heard he wanted her to carry money from Racine, she hung up. He called back, and after an expensive long-distance screaming match, she finally agreed to meet him in Atlanta provided he prepaid her ticket. First class. But she was no more amenable face to face in the apartment she shared with her sister on Roswell Road than she had been on the phone. Mocking his big-shot pretensions, she refused even to consider any more penny-ante deals in which she risked everything for a handful of loose change. Never having considered $5,000 in that light before, Billy cooled her out with a promise of $50,000, and normal service was resumed.

The "partners" next met at White's house for a progress report. Piccolo called Rowe's mother, their radio man in Key West, asked for the latest news of the boat, listened in silence, and hung up without a word.

"I shoulda known," he said.

For the third time in a row, a tropical storm had blotted out radio contact.

There was still no news from the boat when Diego called to say that Captain Chester had sailed for home on Friday with a full load.

As it was then Saturday, Piccolo convened a final meeting at the stash house to review the situation. They were all worried by Chester's continuing silence, but when Diego reported that his Colombian associates had again confirmed the time of departure, Piccolo and Dave Rowe, who knew his own ship better than anyone, figured that she should be off the Isaac Light in nine days, even allowing for bad weather.

No problem, said the off-loaders. If she failed to make it the first night, Charlie would have his flotilla spend a second night at the rendezvous. If she still did not show, they would then go to the backup rendezvous for night three. Provided Chester stuck to their prearranged plan, there was no way they could miss him.

A whole week then went by without radio contact with the *Miss Lynn*. To keep busy, Billy sent for Samantha to join him in the Fort Lauderdale Hilton. He was also in daily contact with Helen, to whom George Mitchell had turned after Billy refused his offer of a third load.

"Billy, you better talk to Mitch," she said. "He wants to front some stuff to Murdo and Jimmy Kearns."

"He *what*? He's gotta be crazy."

Billy called him up and told him so. "Mitch, you gotta be crazy. You're gonna get yourself killed."

"Yeah, yeah," he said. "That's easy for you to say. But I got weed coming out of my ass. If you don't want it, I gotta find somebody else who can help me move this shit."

"Mitch, listen to me. You don't understand. These are not marijuana-type people. These are killers. You can't win with these people. You front stuff to them and you're dead. They're not gonna pay you. They'll take the grass and when you go looking for your money, they'll kill you. That's the way they work. Believe me, I *know* these people."

"Yeah. So how come they don't kill *you*?"

"Mitch, that's different. They *know* me. I'm useful to 'em. And Murdo likes Helen. But if they figured they could rip me off for a load—shit, they'd do it in a minute."

"Look, Billy, do me a favor, okay? Just ask 'em. If you can get 'em to pay up front, great. If they don't go for that, and you can get a down payment, that's okay too."

"Mitch, you're not listening. They don't do business that way."

"Well then, I'll just have to take a chance and front 'em a load. I don't have a choice, Billy. I gotta get some of this shit *outa* here— that's all there is to it."

"Mitch, I can't let you do this."

"Billy, I got Murdo's number. If you don't wanna help me, I'll call him myself."

"Okay, okay." Although he owed Mitch nothing, he was not about to feed him to the wolves.

Margeson was ready to leave for Baxley as soon as he heard that Mitchell would front him a load, but Billy told him he would have to wait a few days while he set up the deal. First he had to take care of Piccolo and the *Miss Lynn* shipment.

"They'll come to Baxley for it," he told Mitchell. Everything was suddenly moving much too fast. "You'll give 'em a thousand pounds, understand? That's all. No more'n that or they'll kill ya for sure."

"Okay."

"I'm not kidding, Mitch. Just be a good boy and do like I tell ya."

"Yeah, okay, Billy. Then maybe I should stay out of this. Can you send Eddie Mode and Samantha up there? Maybe *they* can handle it for me."

"Oh, shit." In fact, it was not such a bad idea. "Then put another ten bucks a pound on. That's five grand each. Because, believe me, they ain't gonna do nothing for nothing."

Billy spoke with feeling. Samantha had gone for his throat like a vampire. What about the $25,000 he owed her from last time? What about the $50,000 he had promised her this time? Billy had tried to explain that the money was tied up in the *Miss Lynn*, just as it had been before in the *Captain Tom*, but she was not interested in IOUs.

"Then where is it, this boat?" she demanded. "When's it coming in?"

"Who the fuck knows?" said Billy gloomily.

Nine days after the stash-house meeting, there was still no word from Captain Chester. That night, Piccolo called everybody together again, and after checking the charts, the alternative routes, the weather reports, and the estimated times of arrival, the Amity Boat-yard crew decided that their off-loading flotilla would sail within the hour.

"You wanna call Jimmy Kearns?" Piccolo suggested. "Tell him we may just hit, so get ready to pick up a thousand pounds?"

"Shit," said Billy. "Do we haveta?"

"It's part of the deal. I don't like it any better than you."

"What deal? I didn't make no deal with Kearns."

Piccolo stared. "What the fuck's the matter with you, Billy? The San Antonio deal. The hit on the U.S. attorney. You heard him. You were there. You heard him say he wanted a thousand pounds every move we made, so don't ask me what deal. It's all your fucking fault anyway."

"Bullshit," he said, wishing for the hundredth time he could have worn a recorder. "Kearns fucked up. I don't see why we gotta pay him for fucking up. I told you before, you gotta watch that guy. He's moving in too close."

"I can handle Kearns," Piccolo said uneasily.

"Okay. Then *you* call him."

When Billy had first started out after Chagra and Piccolo, the case had looked no more difficult than walking a high wire over Niagara Falls. What he had not anticipated was getting lost in a fog when only halfway across and that Samantha would then do her best to push him off. She started in on him again as soon as he returned to the hotel, and when he finally escaped by falling asleep, he had to force himself back to wakefulness from one of the worst nightmares he could remember since waiting to die in prison.

"It's not enough you should cheat me out of my money?" screeched Samantha. "It's not enough you should drag me down here so you can play big shot in front of these creeps? Now you gotta keep me awake all night as well, you sonuvabitch?"

"I'm sorry." Billy tried to piece his wits together. "I was having a bad dream."

"*You're* sorry! Well, let me tell you, *I'm* having one, too. And I didn't even get to sleep yet."

Nor did they close their eyes again—or their mouths—until 7:00 A.M., when Billy left to find out if the *Miss Lynn* had come home.

She had not.

"Chester probably slowed her right down to stay out of the storm," said Charlie soothingly, when Piccolo, Painter, White, and Billy descended on the Amity Boatyard like expectant fathers. "I mean, we figured this could happen, right?"

"Nobody heard from him?" Piccolo asked.

"Not a word. But then, if he stayed behind the storm, they probably wouldn't have. Not with the equipment *he's* got." Charlie gave them an encouraging smile. If anything had gone wrong, it sure as hell was not going to be *his* fault. "We just got to sweat it out, that's all. If Chester's on course, my boys'll find him. I told 'em to stay out there until they do."

By early evening, the day felt as long as a week, and Billy had had enough. Unable to stay awake a minute longer, he returned to the Hilton, called Helen in Miami, who sounded funny, quarreled fitfully with Samantha while he got undressed, and fell on the bed.

Samantha had to shake him awake at 4:00 A.M. to answer the phone.

"I'm home," said White. "Get your ass over here." And he hung up before Billy recovered the power of speech.

Preferring to believe that the load had come in, Billy showered and dressed in five minutes, kissed Samantha goodbye, and came back from the door to leave ten thousand dollars on the dresser.

"Stick it," she shrieked, as he left again. "I'll wait for the fifty grand you owe me, you cheapskate."

The moment he saw the faces in White's living room, Billy knew she was in for a long wait.

"What happened?"

White shook his head, and looked at Painter, who turned away. Piccolo smiled with mournful relish.

"You want it from the top? Let's start with Diego. That fuck. He says the boat left Friday, right? That's what they told him down there. But I know these fucking Colombians, so I tell him to call 'em back to make sure. You heard me do that, right?"

"Right."

"Fucking boat left *Sunday*."

"Oh, shit."

"Okay? Now Charlie sends his people out two days early, and surprise, surprise—there's nobody there. So they fuck around off the Isaac Light for a couple of nights, and who do they meet? Not Chester, oh no—although they finally got radio contact. A fucking Bahamian gunboat is who they meet. I mean, do you believe this?"

"Oh, *shit!*"

"Yeah. It's been watching 'em. And here comes a boarding party that wants to know what the fuck they're doing, just hanging around out there. They don't find nothing, but that don't matter. They don't need to. They know what's going on. Finally they tell everybody to piss off—and shadow 'em long enough to make sure they do."

"So where are they now?"

"On their way home. Charlie calls Peter and says we botched the whole job."

"Oh, yeah? Well, he can fucking turn 'em around again," said Billy. "This is the guy that never missed a load, right? He's gonna leave Chester out there with twenty-five tons of grass and no place to go?"

"Out where?" asked Painter scornfully. "Chester acknowledged their signal about the gunboat. The last place in the world he's gonna be is off the Isaac Light."

And Charlie agreed with him when they all started yelling at one another in his office at the Amity Boatyard later that morning.

"Shouting ain't gonna change nothing, Bobby," he said. "I don't know where the fuck he is now, and neither do you. But I can tell you this—Chester is *wild*. His radio's on the blink. He's almost out of food and water. And if he isn't unloaded in the next day or so, he says he's gonna dump the load over the side."

"Holy shit."

They were all awed into silence by the thought of $13 million gently bobbing away out of reach.

"Well, what the fuck are we waiting for?" Billy demanded. "Turn them boats around and go look for him. We're wasting time here."

"Billy, these guys have been out two nights without sleep. Also they're low on gas. I know it's tough, but it's not *their* fault. They gotta come in now. And that's it."

"Charlie, I don't understand," said Billy. "Bobby just told me— he says you're in for like thirty percent of the load. You mean you're just gonna sit on your ass and let Chester toss all that over the side?"

"Get some more boats," said Painter. "And gimme a chart. We know where he was last night. We know how fast he can go. Let's figure out the best place to look."

"Yeah." Piccolo suddenly brightened up. "Do it. And you know what? We'll go out in a plane. So when we spot him, we can guide the boats in."

"That's a great idea," White agreed. "And maybe we can airdrop supplies. Like food and water and stuff."

"Yeah." They were suddenly all excited. "Good. Let's go. Let's do it."

"It's gonna cost you," said Charlie. "We got a lot of water to look at. If I find some more people, they're not gonna do it for free."

"Then pay 'em." With his mind made up, Piccolo was not to be bothered with trifles.

They drove back to the stash house on Forty-second Court, where Piccolo called his pilots to charter a plane at Lantana airport for a sweep search of the waters to the north and northwest of the *Miss Lynn*'s last known position. Painter meanwhile busied himself ordering supplies for an airdrop, and Doug Ruccio went to find Diego, who had some serious explaining to do.

Appalled by the news, Diego could throw no light at all on Chester's delayed departure. A call to Colombia confirmed only that there *had* been a change of sailing time—not why or who was responsible for not telling him about it. When Joey, their hostage in Santa Marta, called later in the day to find out if the load had arrived, Piccolo advised him to duck out as soon as no one was watching.

The first aerial sweep produced a dozen mistaken "sightings" before the plane had to return to Lantana for refueling. In the afternoon, Billy joined White aboard for another try, and they stayed out until the sea changed from crinkled silver to beaten gold and finally to lead as the sun went down. They saw hundreds of boats, but not the *Miss Lynn*.

When they arrived back at the stash house, Piccolo, Painter,

Diego, Dave Rowe, Ruccio, Pistol Pete, and Freddy were hoarse from yelling at one another. Diego's people in Colombia were calling once an hour to demand their money, and just as insistently, Piccolo was telling them once an hour that if the load *had* been lost, it was *their* fault.

Diego was complaining volubly that he could not even cover his hotel bill, winning little sympathy from Painter, who kept telling him they did not pay people to make mistakes.

Dave Rowe was demanding his million dollars. Piccolo had chartered the *Miss Lynn* to pick up a load of marijuana, he said. It wasn't his fault if they had screwed up the off-loading. He still expected to be paid in full.

On the contrary, replied Piccolo. *He* now owed *them* around $10 million. If Rowe and his radio man in Key West had taken the trouble to ensure that the transmitter on board was up to the job, everything would have gone off according to plan and he would have been paid, as agreed, when the load was sold to Michigan Jim.

Doug Ruccio was complaining to anyone who would listen that he was broke and wanted to go home to Massachusetts.

Pistol Pete and Freddy wanted to know what to do with twenty-five tons of fucking grapefruit.

And in the middle of all this, Captain Chester telephoned to say that he had just brought the *Miss Lynn* into her home port of Savannah. He had waited for orders until just before dawn, then dumped the load over the side. . . .

When everybody had gone, the three partners sat around in silence for an hour.

"What'll I tell Kearns?" asked White eventually.

"Fuck Kearns," said Piccolo.

"I'll take care of it," said Billy, who was more worried about what to say to Samantha and whether she had left the $10,000 on the dresser. "I think Mitch has got some for him."

White grunted. "Ask Mitch if he's got some for us, too."

When Samantha heard that her $50,000 had gone the way of the previous $25,000, she harangued Billy with increasing virulence all the way to Jacksonville, where she finally blew up and returned to Atlanta, leaving him and Eddie Mode to go on alone to Waycross to cope with Margeson, Kearns, and Kelly.

Out of sheer impatience the three had arrived a day early and were chafing at the "delay."

"You jumped the gun, Murdo," said Billy. "What can I tell ya? Where's Jimmy?"

"He's coordinating everything," Margeson said. "We got police radios with special crystals in 'em. You know Jimmy. He's sitting up the road there, about a hundred miles, telling everybody what to do. And he's fucking edgy, let me tell ya, just waiting around."

Billy threw up his hands. "Well, you didn't do like I told ya." He was getting too old for this. "How many fucking people have you got anyway?"

"Well, let's see. I got the Buick. Then there's the Winnebago. And a Camaro pick-up, and a couple of other trucks. Billy Kelly's got a car, and so has Jimmy. That oughta be enough."

"Holy shit." They were never going to be satisfied with a thousand pounds.

George Mitchell had other problems, too.

One was the weather. It had been raining without a break for two days, so hard that when Billy and Eddie Mode led Margeson's convoy of vehicles to Larry Jackson's stash house, the dirt road was half washed out and the wipers of their rental car, at double speed, could barely cope with the downpour. Another was the law. The airstrip Jackson had planned to use was under surveillance by the Georgia Bureau of Investigation, and Mitchell was out collecting strobe lights for one of the backup strips.

Billy and Mode left them to it, fearing the worst. To be on the safe side, they also decided to check into a motel instead of returning to the Waycross Holiday Inn, but within an hour of calling the stash house to leave their new number, Margeson telephoned to say they were loaded up and on their way.

"Hey, that's great, Murdo." Billy could hardly believe it. "I knew Mitch'd come through. Tell Jimmy it was worth waiting for."

"Yeah, I'll tell him," said Margeson, in his slow, flat, undertaker's voice. "But you know Jimmy."

"Yeah. Anyway, have a good trip back. And no speeding tickets, okay?"

"No." Margeson chuckled dutifully. "Right."

"How much he give you this time?"

"Oh, around fifty-seven hundred pounds."

Billy swallowed. "Very nice," he said faintly. "How about the money?"

"Two-seventy a pound. That's top dollar, but Jimmy says it's okay."

"Uh-huh." Sure it was okay. *Anything* was okay if you had no intention of paying. "So when are we gonna see it?"

"In about ten days," said Murdo. "I'll bring it down myself."

Only don't hold your breath, was Billy's advice to Mitchell when he reached him on the telephone.

"Man, you don't know what you did," he said. "They'll get three eighty-five a pound for that stuff in Boston. That's like two million dollars. And if you think Murdo's gonna come down here and give you one and a half million of it, then you gotta be crazier than I thought. I told you not to front 'em *nothing*—but if you had to, a thousand pounds, tops. Didn't I tell ya that?"

"Billy—"

"*Didn't* I? You're gonna get us both killed."

"And didn't *I* tell *you*, Billy, I gotta keep the stuff moving? Call 'em up. Tell 'em they'd be *stupid* to rip me off. They can make half a million a week if they wanna come and get it. So why steal? That's just dumb."

"Mitch, they *are* dumb. They *are* stupid. These guys rob banks and kill people. That's all they know. They're not fucking intellectuals like you and me. Once they get their hands on two million dollars—I mean, that's like more money than they ever seen. Believe me, they're not gonna give it back. I told you, these are not marijuana people. They're killers."

"Billy, I can't believe that. These are your *friends*. You introduced 'em to me, so I know you'll make 'em understand. Tell 'em, as soon as I get the money, they can have *ten* thousand pounds. Okay? *Then* see what they say."

"Mitch, you're dreaming."

There was no point in getting mad. They were *all* crazy.

"Trust me. I know these kind of people. And ask Bobby Piccolo if he can use thirteen and a half thousand pounds."

"Okay." That was more like it. "How much?"

"Two sixty a pound. And I want it picked up in an eighteen-wheeler. No more fucking convoys, Billy. They bring down heat every time."

As an importer, Piccolo was not used to paying that kind of money, but after the loss of the *Miss Lynn* shipment, he was in no position to sniff at a profit of twenty-five dollars a pound just for transporting the stuff from Georgia to Michigan. Ten days later, Billy was back in Waycross, with Eddie Mode and a still mutinous Samantha, to supervise the loading of Freddy's eighteen-wheeler. He was not to know it but his career in the dope trade had just exceeded its critical speed and was about to break up in pieces.

"Did you speak to Agent Jellison about the drugs that you were doing with Piccolo and Chagra between '77 and '80?" asked Breitbart.

Billy looked at Baird. He had already answered that. "Yes, I did."

Breitbart smiled scornfully. "Isn't it a fact that you didn't tell any law-enforcement officers anything about that because you wanted to make money?"

"No, sir."

"Do you remember using the expression, 'There's no halo over my head when I want to make money'?"

"Yes, sir."

"Were you asked this question and did you give this answer, again in Georgia, sir. Question: Mr. Breen, had you decided not to tell any law-enforcement officer about your activities at that time? Answer: Yes, sir. Question: Was the reason that you desired to make some money? Answer: Yes, sir. Do you remember being asked that question and giving that answer?"

"Yes, sir."

"Did you?"

Did he what? Remember? *"Yes, sir."*

"And that was about the activities with Jellison?"

"With whom?" He was losing him again.

"Jellison."

"No, sir."

Breitbart looked to be in pain. *"That was not in direct response to a question about whether you spoke to Jellison or didn't speak to Jellison?"*

Billy shook his head groggily. *"Yes, sir."*

"It is correct," said Breitbart, exasperated. *"You couldn't care less whether they killed a United States Attorney—"*

"Your Honor," protested Baird, and Judge Sand nodded. *"I will see Mr. Breitbart and Mr. Baird and the reporter and any other counsel at the side bar."*

He waited until they were all huddled around, out of earshot of the jury, before addressing himself to Breitbart, who had had a terrible morning and saw no immediate sign of improvement.

"How much longer, Mr. Breitbart, do you propose to cross-examine this witness with respect to his mental state or his prior criminal record or matters unrelated to this particular proceeding?"

"I laid the foundation on Monday for all of the prior perjuries which he committed in front of this court," he replied, *"and now I am reading the sworn transcript which lays those out."*

Judge Sand sighed. *"Can I have a response to my question, please? Will the reporter read the question?"*

"Until I am finished, judge," said Breitbart rudely. *"Judge, let me point out—*

"Can you give me an estimate as to how long?" insisted Judge Sand, with ominous politeness.

"I don't think it should take more than an hour, if I get an honest answer. You have seen this witness—"

"I have seen the witness," the judge interrupted, "and the jury has seen this witness."

"But I have seen this witness this morning lie in front of the jury and then, when confronted with prior sworn testimony, change his testimony," Breitbart protested. "It is my duty and obligation to my client and this court to bring that out. He lied on Monday."

Judge Sand was not to be drawn. "You are saying an hour, approximately an hour, if you got responsive answers."

"That is my—as soon as I get direct answers. It would have taken three minutes."

"I will allow that, Mr. Breitbart," said the judge, "on the condition that the questions that are asked are questions which are designed to elicit a response from the witness and are not questions which are asked for their rhetorical impact on the jury."

Breitbart looked shocked. "Is Your Honor suggesting that any question that I have already asked is for that purpose rather than eliciting—"

"Yes," said Judge Sand.

13

Two weeks later, George Mitchell appeared on Billy's doorstep to collect $1,539,000 for the load that Kearns, Kelly, and Margeson had taken to Boston. No one had heard a word from them since their departure from Baxley.

"Didn't I tell ya?" said Billy. "Didn't I *beg* you not to do it? This is just exactly what I told you was gonna happen. And I can't help ya, Mitch. These guys don't listen to me no more than you do."

"Sure they will. They're friends of yours. I mean, I wouldn't even *know* 'em if it wasn't for you."

"Mitch—"

"I told the Colombians that—and you know how they are when they get excited. They want their money. So I told 'em you knew these guys well, and you'd get it for 'em. What else could I do?"

"Oh, *shit!*" said Billy.

He called Margeson in Boston, who said they had run into a little trouble but expected to be there with some money in about five days.

"Oh, *shit!*" said Mitchell.

Then Piccolo called a meeting of his "partners" in Coral Springs to announce that his problems with their original connection in Colombia had been patched up. The coast was now clear for the Amity Boatyard crew to bring in a 50,000-pound load, provided they posted $400,000, supplied a hostage, and made a down payment to

136

Dave Rowe, who would supply another shrimper, the *Miss Mary*, on the same terms as before.

"So if you want in, Billy," said Piccolo, "it's gonna cost you a hundred seventy-five grand."

"Forget it," he said. "I'm flat busted."

"Yeah," said White. "Me too."

"Okay." This evidently came as no surprise because Piccolo had the solution all worked out. "I'll send Billy Painter up in the Lear to get four hundred fifty grand from Michigan Jim."

"Front money?" asked Billy.

"Shit, no. He won't go for that. No, we'll use some of the money he owes Mitch for the load we got from Baxley. We'll use that to finance this deal, and pay everybody back when we get the stuff ashore."

"Well, I dunno." Billy blinked at him thoughtfully. "Mitch is hurting for money. He got nothing from Kearns yet, and if *we* hold him up as well, those fucking Colombians'll kill him and Larry Jackson both."

"Don't let him kid you," said Piccolo, with a scornful smile. "Those fucking Indians need us as much as we need them. Mitch'll get his money in a couple of weeks. You don't know Michigan Jim. Send him a hundred thousand pounds and he'll still cash out in ten days. So don't worry about it."

After the way Mitch had treated him lately, Billy stopped worrying about it. Painter would get the money. Doug Ruccio would fly down to Colombia as the hostage. White would help Piccolo coordinate the operation.

"Okay, what about me?" asked Billy.

The others looked doubtful.

"Ah, listen—why don't you sit this one out?" Piccolo suggested. "We know you got problems."

"Huh?"

"Yeah. You know, problems at home. With Samantha and all that. Why don't you just concentrate on getting everybody's head straight and leave this one to us. You're still in as partner."

Billy frowned painfully from one to the other. "You mean she's been calling you guys again?"

"Has she *ever*!" White laughed. "Every hour on the hour. Bobby. Me. Judy. Helen. Kearns. Mitch. Barbara. Just about everybody you ever met."

"Yeah?" Billy had the sensation of falling stark naked through space.

"What's she—"

He had been about to ask what she had said, and belatedly realized that White had mentioned Helen.

"Same as last time." Piccolo was enjoying his dismay. "We shouldn't trust you. You're gonna rip and run and turn us all in." He laughed. "Good thing we know you better than she does, right?"

Billy cleared his throat noisily. "Yeah."

"I told you a year ago, get rid of that broad before she upsets somebody. But nobody listens to me."

Billy had a bad feeling that she had upset Helen, who had been acting strangely for months. She answered the phone calmly, but when Billy inquired if she'd been getting any funny calls lately—from a woman—there was a brief silence before she blew up in a rage of despair.

Yes, she'd been getting calls. From a woman named Samantha. Every time she and Billy went off together someplace, Samantha would call her every day, sometimes two or three times a day, to fill her in with every detail. What they did to each other in bed. About all the money and presents he gave her. How often he told her he loved her.

"I never said that," Billy protested feebly. "I never did. I love *you*."

"Liar," she spat. "Don't lie to me, Billy. I *heard* you. You called her from my home, and I *heard* you. So don't tell me no lies."

"No, no—you *never* heard me," he shouted, having always taken the greatest possible care to be out of earshot when he called Samantha. "You never heard me because I never said it."

"Billy, I know you did because Mitch wired the phone. I heard all the tapes, so don't try to lie to me. About *anything*."

"Oh, shit. Listen, honey, I'm coming home. We can't—"

"No," she screamed. "No, don't you come here. I got your gun. You come here, I'll kill myself—you hear me? I *mean* it. I'll blow my head off. So don't you come."

"Oh, listen, honey—"

"No, no, no. Don't *call* me that. I know what you've been doing. I know everything about you and her, so don't you ever try to lie to me again."

And she proceeded to tell him what she knew, getting wilder and wilder as she went on, until he was afraid she might shoot herself while she had him on the telephone.

"Oh, baby, why don't you let me come home?" he asked brokenly, feeling old and exhausted. "Lemme try and explain this to you."

"No," she shrieked, so loudly that he pulled the phone away from his ear. "Stay away from me, Billy. Don't you come here."

"Okay, darlin'. Take it easy. Just put the gun down and I'll talk to you later."

He hung up and called the North Miami Police Department. The desk sergeant promised to send somebody over to talk her down, but she refused to open the door and in the end they went away.

Billy let himself in quietly next morning, to find her cleaning the house. Neither one referred to the previous night, and after a while she fixed his breakfast, but he could feel her seething below the surface, like a pot just off the boil. Knowing this state from his own experience, he let her be. Helen had had enough. She would work it through in her own way.

He loved her, and she knew it, but he had never pretended to be faithful. He was as God had made him, and no more ashamed of his appetites than of the shape of his nose. Up front, he had told her what he was like and she had taken him on those terms, knowing he would never change.

Samantha had done this to her. And for no reason that he could see, except to hurt and humiliate. Billy stayed close to the house for a couple of days, encouraging friends to come around, keeping in touch with the progress of the *Miss Mary*, badgering Margeson for money, and waiting for the next blow to fall.

It was a short wait.

Almost catatonic with shock, Barbara Mitchell turned up at the house like an earthquake refugee, clutching a box she wanted them to look after. Mitch and his pilot had been killed in a plane crash at Baxley airport.

Coming on top of everything else, Billy was afraid the news might tip Helen over the edge, but in fact it had the opposite effect. She rallied at once to take care of Barbara, who, though deeply upset, was not so grief-stricken that she forgot to explain about the money and jewelry. She wanted to leave the box with them in case Cuban Mike took everything and left her penniless.

"Who's Cuban Mike?" asked Billy indignantly.

"Mitch's partner," she sobbed. "Mike Delgado. He's trying to get the Colombians off our back."

"Uh-*huh*." Mitchell had never even mentioned Delgado. "I thought Larry Jackson was Mitch's partner."

She nodded, and crumpled into tears again. "That's why he flew up there," she wailed. "To get money from Larry."

"What's he like, this Delgado?"

"Don't mess with him, Billy. He's no good." She accepted another Kleenex from Helen. "Him and his people, they're all bad. Just pay him the money you owe him, or he'll only make *more* trouble."

"What money?"

She stopped sobbing and stared, wet-eyed. "For the Boston load, Billy. And the load you sent to Michigan."

"Honey, I didn't send *nothing* to Michigan. Or Boston, either." His mouth had gone dry. "Mitch asked me if I could help him move some stuff, so we put him in touch with Murdo Margeson. Right, Helen?"

"That's right, darling." She patted Barbara's hand. "I talked to Murdo myself."

"Right," said Billy, who could hardly grasp the size of the fix he was in. "Then Mitch asked me again, so I called Bobby Piccolo in Coral Springs. And that's all I did. It was *Bobby* took the Michigan load, not me. I don't even know where it went. So you tell him that, Barbara. Because *I* don't owe nobody *nothing*."

Barbara shook her pretty little head. "Well, that's not what Mitch told Cuban Mike," she said, dissolving again. "He said *you* took the stuff."

Billy sat back. Under sentence of death. Barbara had no cause to lie. If Mitch *had* told Delgado that, then the guy would now be coming after him for $5 million!

Which was okay, except that about $1.5 million of it was owed by Kearns, Kelly, and Margeson, who had never had any intention of paying up anyway. As soon as they heard the news, any faint chance he might have had of getting at least some of the money would have gone for good. With Mitchell dead, it would be a free load as far as they were concerned.

Nor could he answer for Piccolo. With some $3.5 million at stake, his "partner" might easily see things the same way. In fact, the idea of Mitch's people coming after *Billy* for the money would probably give Piccolo more pleasure than the money itself.

As they were again sharing $10 a pound for each load, Billy called White to urge him to do what he could to expedite payment before the news of Mitch's death reached Michigan. White said he would, but it was only after hanging up that Billy realized he had just given his other "partner" the best possible incentive to join with Piccolo in ripping him off. And not just Piccolo. Kearns, too.

There was only one thing to do. He caught the next flight up to New York. Before he died, he had to straighten out Samantha, who had apparently called Barbara only an hour before the plane crash to tell her that Billy was planning to rip everybody off.

Sensing something in his voice, Samantha refused to meet him at her apartment and suggested instead an eight o'clock date at Maxwell's Plum, then a very public place on Second Avenue.

Billy's first Irish Cream was served at eight on the dot. He knew she would be late. She always was. He also knew that even now, if she had a reasonable explanation for what she had done—or even an *un*reasonable one that he could swallow—he would probably forgive her. And probably hand over the keys of the new Buick Riviera he had bought for her. After all she had done to him, he could only explain it in terms of witchcraft.

By nine o'clock, Billy was on his fifth Irish Cream, and feeling more independent. When he came right down to it, he didn't need nobody. If Samantha figured she had him on a leash, it was time he taught her different. The world was *full* of hookers. And if Piccolo or White or both of them tried to pull anything, well, they'd be sorry. Kearns, too. *And* Delgado, or whatever his name was.

By ten o'clock, Billy had lost count of the Irish Creams. Now he was hungry to see her for a simpler reason—unless she had a real good excuse for standing him up, of course. Unless she came right out and said, Gee, Billy, my apartment caught fire but I got here as soon as I could, he was gonna have to seriously reconsider his position.

Samantha eventually arrived two and a half hours late, cool, unflustered, and unapologetic. When the captain pointed Billy out to her, her eyes passed over him without much interest and appraised the crowd like a pickpocket's as she sauntered toward the table.

"Where the fuck have you been?" he demanded, shouting against the roar of small talk as she pulled out her chair.

"What the fuck are you talking about?" she retorted indifferently, still working the crowd. "You said ten o'clock, right?"

Billy opened his mouth and closed it. He was tired of bickering.

"Why are you calling people?" he asked thickly, not even waiting to offer her a drink. "What are you telling 'em about me?"

"Listen, you don't *own* me, you know." She twisted around in her seat, trying to catch a waiter's eye. "I don't think that's any of your business."

"Don't you talk to me like that," he bellowed, loud enough this time to silence several adjoining tables. "Fucking douche bag."

"Okay, that's *it*, asshole," she screeched, grabbing her purse. "I don't have to take this shit. Not from a scumbag like you."

Billy saw himself reach across the table and take her one-handed by the throat, pinching off the start of a scream. Then he pressed her sideways off the chair, forced her to the floor and put his foot on her neck to hold her down. The love affair was over.

Rasping in a deep breath, she started to shriek like a factory whistle, and two men got up uncertainly from a nearby table.

"Now, now," said Billy, not so drunk that anybody was going to catch him sitting down. "Just a little private problem. Let's all behave real nice."

"*Nice?*" They looked at each other in amazement.

Billy could not stop to argue. Samantha had taken advantage of the diversion to scramble to her feet, grab her purse, and bolt for the second-floor powder room. He lumbered off after her like a tank chasing a cottontail, barging into people and spilling their drinks, stumbled up the stairs, and crashed through the door in hot pursuit.

Ladies adjusting their bras or makeup froze, squealed, or giggled, according to their outlook and state of undress, but Samantha had nowhere to go. As Billy closed on her, he saw fear in her face for the first time, hesitated in frustration, and instead of wringing her neck like a chicken's, dropped her with a short right cross to the jaw.

Suddenly sober, he backed out, apologizing profusely, to find a heavyweight deputation waiting for him on the stairs.

"Okay, fellers," he said, adjusting his glasses. "Nothing to worry about. Little domestic dispute, that's all. You know how it is. All over now, so just let me pass."

Nobody moved.

"Now I don't want no trouble," he said, putting his hand to his armpit, although he had nothing there but deodorant. "Just step aside and nobody'll get hurt."

They parted like the Red Sea for Moses, but on reaching the street he could hear sirens homing in from all directions. As he turned the corner, the first cruiser appeared on the avenue, lights turning, and when he passed by in a cab on his way to the airport a few minutes later, there were five police cars and a paddy wagon outside.

The position in Miami had not improved in his absence. Besides Barbara and Cuban Mike Delgado, George's brother Jack Mitchell and another partner, Mark, had also come forward to stake their claims to the millions Billy "owed." It was all they could talk about at George's funeral—that and what had happened to the quarter of a million dollars on board the plane when it crashed. Only half that amount had been reported by the sheriff's deputies first at the scene. One of them was said to have rolled George's corpse off the rest and, finding the bills soaked with blood and body fluids, had taken them home literally to "launder" the money in her washing machine.

For as long as he could convince them that there was still a chance of getting the money, Billy figured he was reasonably safe from his "creditors," but the day after the funeral, Kearns, Kelly, and Margeson put paid even to that slender hope. They showed up without warning in Miami, not with $1.5 million, but with some cock-and-bull story about getting ripped off. Trapped whichever way he turned, Billy went to see if any money was coming through from Michigan Jim.

While he was gone, Kearns embellished the story for Helen. He had personally cut the throat of one of the two guys who did it, he said, but there was no money and therefore no chance of paying for the 5,700 pounds they had picked up in Baxley. They had come down to explain this to George Mitchell and to set up another deal so they could pay everything off with the profits from the next load.

Helen did not believe a word of it, of course, but it hardly mattered. To keep them away from Barbara, she felt obliged to break the news that George was dead.

As Billy had feared, Kearns lit up like a kid at a birthday treat. After much laughing and joking, Margeson announced that as far as they were concerned, the debt was canceled. Just because some Cuban geek had come outa the woodwork claiming to be Mitchell's partner didn't make no difference. Anybody could *say* that. The only guy they had dealt with was Mitchell, and with him gone, it was a free load.

"No, Murdo—you can't *do* this," said the diminutive Helen, to around nine hundred pounds of the deadliest contract killers in the annals of crime. "This is not right. You should pay the money to his wife."

Margeson looked at the others doubtfully. "Maybe I'll go over to Barbara's with Helen. Explain things to her."

"The fuck you will," said Kearns. "Let *Billy* do it. We don't have the money. We're not gonna pay, and that's *it*."

Having finally met Delgado and some of his crew, Billy preferred not to relay the message in precisely those terms. Instead, he told Barbara and Delgado that he was going to Michigan to get them some money from Piccolo. Painter had called, providentially, to say that Michigan Jim had just left $170,000 with him as a first installment and the rest of the $3.5 million should soon be rolling in.

But as soon as he checked into the Hyatt Regency in Dearborn and called Painter's room, Billy sensed that something funny was going on. No, Michigan Jim had not actually delivered the $170,000 yet, Painter said, but there was no need to worry. It was like money in the bank.

Hemmed in by bank robbers, Billy was not reassured. Michigan Jim was Piccolo's man—Billy had never met him. And there was nothing he could do to speed things up except bitch about the delay to Painter and anybody else he could raise on the telephone. Either come up with the money, he insisted, decibels rising each time, or return the fucking merchandise.

After several days of this, Painter called to say that the *Miss Mary* had hit and he had to go weigh the stuff at the Amity Boatyard.

"Hey, wait a minute," Billy bellowed. "What about the fucking money? You better gimme Michigan Jim's number."

"No, it's okay," said Painter. "I talked to him this morning. Just sit tight. He'll call you as soon as he gets in."

Billy stared at the phone in disbelief. Then he slammed it down, checked his Derringer pistol to make sure it was loaded, and went to Painter's room for a showdown. Only to find that Painter had checked out an hour earlier and had presumably called from the airport.

That was Tuesday.

By Sunday morning, when Painter returned with Piccolo and White and checked in to one of the hotel's penthouse suites, Billy was fit for a straitjacket. He had heard nothing from Michigan Jim, and would not even have known that the others were in town but for a call from Freddy to say he had just parked in Battle Creek with a 28,000-pound load from the *Miss Mary*, and what should he do now?

Billy got through to the penthouse and ordered everybody down to his room, adding that he had just heard from Freddy.

"Okay," Piccolo said, pushing past him as he opened the door, with Painter and White close behind. "What's all the fucking mystery? First, I gotta call Freddy."

"No, you *don't* gotta call him," said Billy nastily. "First you talk to *me*. Where's my fucking money?"

"What money? For that shit you sent up from Baxley?" Piccolo sniffed. "From now on, get samples first."

"Why? What's wrong with it?"

"Nothing. If you like pig shit. It's no fucking good, that's what's wrong with it. Takes time to sell garbage like that."

"You see it? *Did ya?* That was top-grade Colombian. But I'm not gonna argue wit' yez. If Michigan Jim don't want it, get it back."

"Get it *back*? What the fuck you talking about?"

"Freddy's going back empty. Tell Michigan Jim to call the stuff in if he can't sell it, and Freddy can take it to Baxley. Okay? Either gimme the money or gimme the stuff."

"Come on, Billy," said Piccolo. "Relax. It's all over the street, for Chrissake. How the fuck can he call it in? You'll get your money, but you gotta be patient. Now gimme Freddy's number."

Billy was sorely tempted to hang him out to dry, but that would have stranded Freddy, and he had no beef with him. They would all go down together soon enough. He gave them the number, insisting that they call from the room, and listened in silence as Painter told Freddy to "sit still"—they would leave the hotel at 6:00 P.M. to meet him.

"No, you're not," said Billy, when he hung up. "Nobody's going no place until I see some money."

"Billy, I don't *have* any fucking money," said Piccolo. "Michigan Jim has your money. I dunno what you think *I* can do."

"You can *call* Michigan Jim, that's what. Right now. I wanna talk to him. I wanna see all the money he's took so far. And I wanna do that before any of you cocksuckers leave this hotel."

Piccolo dialed the number grimly and, after a few pleasantries, put Billy on the line. Affable, friendly, and inadequately briefed in advance, Michigan Jim confirmed that the Baxley load had been hard to sell, but said he now had around $1.2 million on hand, in addition to the $450,000 he had already given Painter to finance the *Miss Mary* shipment. He also promised to bring it around to the hotel that evening at six o'clock when he stopped by to pick up Piccolo and the others.

"He says he's got a million-two," said a much-relieved Billy, putting down the phone.

"May be," said Piccolo. "But not for you. What you got coming is a hundred and eighty thousand. Like as a down payment."

"*What?*" Billy screwed up his face in anguish. "What's *with* you people? You think I'm just gonna roll over and let you rip me off?"

"Nobody's ripping you off, Billy."

"You think I'm just gonna stand still and let Cuban Mike wipe me and Helen out while you fuck around with *my* money?"

"Billy—" Piccolo gave up with an exasperated shrug. "Just be here at six, okay?"

As he turned to go, Billy nipped into the closet and came out with his Derringer. The three of them froze.

"I guess Samantha was right," Piccolo said uneasily, backing up against the wall. "You *are* a flake."

Billy controlled himself with an effort. Then he changed his mind and took a swipe at Piccolo's head.

"What else did she tell ya?" he asked. And when the other hesitated, he jammed the muzzle under his nose.

"Nothing," said Piccolo hastily. "Same as always. You're gonna rip us off and turn us in. I warned you about that broad."

"Rip *you* off!" Billy grunted. "For what you're doing to me and Helen, I oughta fucking kill the three of yez."

"Billy, you'll get your money," White said. "Freddy's got twenty-eight thousand pounds out there for Michigan Jim, and you're a partner—you're in for a third of that. So put the gun away before you do something stupid. Soon as he cashes out, we can pay off everybody."

"That's right," said Piccolo. "That's seven million-plus waiting for us. All you gotta do is stall for a little bit."

"Well, waddiya *think* I been doing?" Billy howled, lowering the gun nevertheless. "Plus Jimmy Kearns stiffing 'em for fifty-seven hundred pounds—shit, these guys are *wild*. And I'm in the middle.

They're holding me up for five million. If I try and stall Delgado with a stinking hundred and eighty thousand, he's gonna kill me for sure. Then he'll kill *you*. So I gotta have that million-two. Right now."

"Billy, we *spent* it already," Painter said. "You agreed to that. You agreed we'd use the Baxley load to finance the *Miss Mary*. I flew up here and got the money, remember?"

"Right. You got four hundred fifty grand. Now there's another million on the table, and I *need* it."

"Billy, we *all* need it," said Piccolo soothingly. "We owe the off-loaders. We owe Dave Rowe front money for the boat—he didn't even get paid the first time. We owe the fucking Colombians. I mean, shit, if you think *you* got problems, how about Doug Ruccio? He's sitting down there with a gun up his ass waiting for us to pay for this shit. We all got problems, Billy. So do the best you can. Payday's coming."

He nodded to the others, and they eased themselves cautiously off the wall.

"Call Jimmy Kearns, why don'cha?" Piccolo went on, covering their retreat to the door. "Tell him you got something else going. Tell him, if they want a piece of it, they better pay their bills first."

Billy snorted. "He says they were ripped off."

Piccolo laughed heartily, and ushered his colleagues out. "Just be here at six," he said.

Billy drove home with $180,000. Before leaving Dearborn, he even called Boston, as Piccolo had suggested, to see if Kearns might have had a change of heart about paying Barbara and Cuban Mike, but Margeson just laughed. He sounded even more amused when Billy explained how bad a spot he and Helen were now in because of them, how he had pulled a gun on Piccolo, Painter, and White because they, too, were ripping him off. How could he pay Barbara and Cuban Mike, he complained, if nobody paid *him*?

"Don't worry about it," Margeson said. "We're flying down there tonight. They give you any trouble, we'll drive over and spray 'em for ya."

"Oh, shit," said Billy, who had to go back because of Helen. Whichever way he looked at it, his life was now totally out of control, on course to a crack-up of epic proportions.

For a start, the $180,000 proved more of an irritant than a palliative, as he had known it would.

"Mike Delgado and his people want to talk to you," said Barbara Mitchell, when he called her about it. "They've been waiting for you to get back. And they're pretty upset."

"Okay. I'm *here*. When do they wanna talk?"

"Tomorrow night. At your house."

"Okay. How many?"

"I don't know, Billy. What's the difference? We're coming over."

"Fine," he said. "Bring as many as you like."

After brooding about it most of the night, Billy called Dave Green. He was still not quite ready to turn everything over to the FBI, although Piccolo, Kearns, and Samantha had pretty well closed out his options.

"What do you want me to do?" asked Green.

"Bring iron," said Billy.

He distributed his collection of firearms around the living room, parking two .38s behind the bar, from which he could command a view of the whole room, and a pair of .45s under the cushions of the big couch, in case things went sour during the sit-down. When Dave Green arrived in his truck at four o'clock, Billy sat him on the couch with his gun in his hat.

Then they waited.

It got dark.

Eventually they heard cars arriving, but nothing happened. After a while, Helen said she would look through the drapes to see what they were doing, and as Billy told her to sit down, the door bell rang.

"Okay." He nodded to Green. "Just act natural, and let *me* handle it. Go let 'em in, Helen. They won't hurt you. They seen you at Barbara's."

"Well, I sure hope you're right," she said.

It was like opening a sluice gate. The door banged back, and fourteen men tramped in with their hands in their pockets or armpits, leaving her face to face with Barbara Mitchell, who brought up the rear.

"Okay, gimme your guns," shouted Mike Delgado, at the head of his army. "Shut the lights off. Everybody up against the wall."

Billy was affronted. Apart from anything else, it was *his* house, and this was no way for a guest to behave. Already behind the bar, he waited long enough to make sure everybody was inside and then started shouting himself. With a .38 in each hand.

"All right," he yelled. "Motherfuckers. Get your hands on your head, and don't nobody move."

The .38 in his right hand was aimed unwaveringly at Delgado's face, not six feet away. Billy was rather hoping that Green would now produce *his* weapon, too, but he looked as stunned as everyone else.

"*Do* it," snarled Billy, and Delgado clutched convulsively at his head with both hands. As his followers followed suit, rather more reluctantly, a couple of Ingram submachine guns fell out from under their owners' jackets and clunked to the floor.

"All right." Billy was feeling quite pleased with himself. It was just like the old days. "Now here's what you're gonna do. You're gonna keep your hands on your head and back outa the door, understand?"

They understood.

"Okay. Then get the fuck outa here. One at a time," he bellowed, as a jam developed in the doorway. "But not you, Mike. *Or* Barbara. You go sit on the couch. The rest of yez get in your cars and don't move. Anybody comes back, Mike here's the first one who gets it, understand?"

They understood.

When Helen closed the door behind the last of them, Billy put his guns away, came out from behind the bar, walked over to Delgado, and looked down at him, smiling.

"Don't you ever come in my fucking house like that again," he said amiably, holding out his hand. "That is a no-no."

Delgado's shoulder bag was at his feet, and Billy felt sure he had a gun in it, but when the other hesitantly accepted his offered handshake, he decided to let him keep it.

"Barbara, why don't you take the armchair?" he suggested. She was sitting on one of the .45s. "You'll be more comfortable."

"No, I'm okay, Billy," she said. "I wanna sit with Mike."

He let that go, too, knowing he held the initiative for once. In fact, he felt better than he had in months, particularly when he saw that Green was sweating. After introducing him to Delgado as one of his boys, he fixed everybody a drink, explaining calmly as he did so, like one businessman to another, how he had warned Mitch—in front of Barbara—that it was madness to give any marijuana to Kearns, Kelly, and Margeson unless they paid for it "on Front Street." As Barbara could hardly deny this, Delgado shifted his ground and demanded that Billy give him their telephone numbers and home addresses so that he could go with his men to collect the money himself.

Billy chuckled. "Forget it," he said.

The idea of sending an undersized Cuban, with his gold chain and *numero uno* medallion, to take on the Boston trio was appealing, but just as appalling was the thought of what the three might do if he started handing out their addresses to potential assassins.

"No, they'll eat you alive."

And he told them the story of how the Florida Highway Patrol had once pulled Kearns and Kelly over to search their car. They had started a fight with eight troopers, who were eventually forced to let Kelly go in order to cope with Kearns. Having finally managed to wrestle him into the back of a cruiser, they had then had to stand back helplessly while he wrecked the car, kicking off the rear doors.

"So you better leave 'em to me," Billy said. "I'll get you the money if I can, but you gotta be patient."

"Don't tell *me*, be patient," said Delgado. "Tell the Colombians. It's *their* money they stole. If you don't tell me where these guys are at, you don't gimme no choice. I gotta hold *you* responsible."

The phone rang, and Billy motioned impatiently to Helen to take it while he started in on the whole thing again.

The call was from Murdo Margeson. "You mean, you got the fuckers *there*?" he demanded. "In your house?"

"Yes, that's right, Murdo," Helen said, emphasizing his name so that Billy would pick up on it. "And they want their money."

"All right," Margeson said grimly. "Hold 'em there. We'll take care of those cocksuckers once and for all."

"*Murdo!*" she gasped. "You *can't!*"

"No, it's okay—we'll kill 'em on the lawn," he said, thinking she was worried about her shag-pile rugs. "Give us twenty minutes."

"No, listen, Murdo, please." Helen beckoned Billy over frantically. "No, no. Wait, Murdo. Talk to Billy first. *Please* . . ."

Billy managed to convince him that a bloodbath in front of the neighbors was not the tidiest of solutions, but he was left in no doubt that the only question in Margeson's mind was where and when, not if. Billy rejoined the others, shaking his head.

"This could be a very bad war," he said. "This could bring down a lotta heat."

"No," said Delgado. "We kill 'em all quick. Nobody rips off number one. We gotta teach people."

"Listen, a lotta heat is bad for business. And you need money, right? I got a better idea."

Over Helen's objections, he told Barbara to go wait in her car, and fixed Delgado another drink. With thirteen heavily armed Cubans on the street outside his house; with four professional killers armed with automatic weapons less than twenty minutes away (Margeson had let slip that their equally lethal associate, Hobart Willis, was also in town), and with Piccolo, Painter, and White scheming to dump him the first chance they got, it was no longer a question of tactics but of strategic redeployment.

And so he wove a little fantasy, invoking the soft, persuasive blarney of his ancestors to lull Delgado's suspicions and tickle his cupidity. Mitch had owned another plane, he said, and before he died he had made it over to him. Nobody knew this, not even Barbara, but the time had come to use it. Instead of losing money in a war that no one could win, why not get rich first and *then* get even?

"I gotta strip up in Georgia where we can land the plane," he said. "A nice, quiet spot run by real friendly people. I got sources for the grass. I got customers for the grass. I got *everything*. Except a partner to help me run the operation. That's why I been waiting to talk to you. I'm through with Piccolo and that bunch. I'm through with Kearns and *his* crew. Soon as I get your money out, Mike, we're in business for ourselves, and fuck everybody else."

He worked on Delgado for fifteen minutes, then walked him to the door with an arm about his shoulders.

"Sleep on it," he said. "Then come back tomorrow and tell me if you think we can do a little business together, okay?"

"Okay, Billy. Then I give you my answer."

"Fine. And we don't need Barbara, neither. I mean, it's up to you, but there ain't nothing *she* can do." Except blow his story out of the water. "Do we need another mouth to feed?"

"No. Right. Fuck her."

"Good boy." Billy tightened his grip into a hug at the door. "And listen, Mike. This is my *home*, so don't you bring nobody over here unless I ask you. You tell your guys to stay outa the neighborhood. Because if I see one roll by the house, he's gonna get another hole in his ass."

He laughed. Delgado laughed. They shook hands.

"Okay, I'll see you tomorrow." Billy eased him outside and closed the door.

"Shit," said Dave Green. "You're crazy, you know that? Why'd you draw down on those people? You almost got us killed."

Billy stared, speechless for once.

"He just beat 'em to it, that's all," Helen said proudly. As soon as the last car drove away, she went to their bedroom to pack.

"Shit," said Green. "My truck's out there. They got my number. They got the number off my truck."

Billy was suddenly depressed. "You should worry." Helen had put a lot into this house. "If they got *my* number, I'm the one that's in trouble."

"But what am I gonna do about the truck?"

"Well, I'll tell ya," Billy said patiently. "You're gonna put Helen in it, and you're gonna drive her up to Virginia to stay with her mother."

To this day, Dave Green still wonders how they got away with it.

"I didn't think we were going to come out of that one," he says. "That scene is still in my head. I'm sitting there with a gun under a pillow and the Cubans are there with their hands in their little fag bags. It was bad. It was tough. There was an Irish mafia involved, the worst bunch of killers you ever saw. There were these Cuban people, who used to hang people upside down by their feet and hit them in the head with sledgehammers to kill them, or torture them to death.

And these two crews were against each other, with us in the middle. I've asked Billy a lot of times since then, 'Have you ever thought how close we come to getting it?' "

They waited around in the dark until after midnight, wondering if they had enough money. Billy had cashed in the balance of his credit account at Caesar's Palace for $77,000, but that was hardly enough to finance a new life. Then he remembered the box Barbara had left with them, which turned out to contain over $100,000 in cash and a lot of expensive jewelry. As they could hardly leave it behind, he gave Helen enough money from the box to tide her over for a few weeks, watched her ride off in Green's truck on her way to Virginia, and stowed the rest in the trunk of the Riviera he had bought for Samantha.

Goodbye, Florida.

And just in time. A few days later, Peter White was invited to meet his old friend Hobart Willis at a Fort Lauderdale hotel. When he entered the room, Kearns, Kelly, Margeson, and Willis ordered him at gunpoint to telephone Painter and get him over there as well. Next, they made him call Piccolo, who was away for the weekend in Massachusetts. Unless he flew back right away with $500,000, said Kearns, White and Painter would be killed immediately, and Piccolo as soon as they caught up with him.

When Piccolo arrived with the money, the whole party left for Battle Creek, where the Boston crew seized Michigan Jim's stash house and confiscated the bulk of the 28,000-pound load from the *Miss Mary*, plus what remained of the 13,500 pounds from Baxley, shipping the whole lot back east in an eighteen-wheeler.

It was the end of an era.

After the slapdash, extravagant, curiously innocent days of the Godfrey Gang, Piccolo, Painter, and White now had to dance to the grittier tune of Kearns, Kelly, Margeson, and Judy Moeser, Peter White's common-law wife, who, finding she had more in common with Kearns, had masterminded the takeover from the inside.

The only other active member of the gang was Doug Ruccio, languishing in Colombia as human collateral for $1 million. "Doug *who*?" said Kearns, when Piccolo reminded him of the debt.

All Billy could do was step off the juggernaut.

"In 1980, sir, did you put away a thousand pounds of marijuana for Jimmy Kearns?" asked Breitbart.

"Yes, I did. In Wisconsin."

"And this was in an attempt to bring him to justice, right?"

"This was one way to know that Jimmy Kearns was promised a thousand pounds from Bobby Piccolo for his attempted assassination *of an Assistant United States Attorney," said Billy stoutly. "And the only way I could get that further evidence is to take that marijuana to Racine, Wisconsin, and give Jimmy Kearns a thousand pounds of grass on orders of Bobby Piccolo."*

It was not the answer Breitbart wanted. "But isn't it a fact, sir, that you just testified five minutes ago that you were in that transaction just to make money?"

"Oh, Your Honor, objection," said Baird. "That is not the testimony."

"That's exactly what the testimony is," Breitbart retorted angrily.

"Overruled," said Judge Sand.

Breitbart thanked him with a nod. "Isn't it a fact that it's from that same trial in North Carolina—"

"You have asked a question," observed the judge. "There has been no answer to it."

"Fine. Isn't it a fact sir—"

"Would you repeat the question, sir?" asked Billy, confused with all this to-ing and fro-ing.

"The question was, didn't you just tell us, not five minutes ago, that you were in this marijuana thing because there was no halo on your head and you wanted to make money?"

"Did I say that in this courtroom?" Billy looked around again for help.

"Yes, you did, sir. Five minutes ago."

Both Baird and the judge started to interrupt, and Breitbart saw his error. Once again, he took Billy through his answers in the North Carolina court. "Were you asked those questions and did you give those answers?" he repeated.

"That was in the case in North Carolina," said Billy. "Not in this courtroom."

"It wasn't in the case in this courtroom?" Breitbart seemed as lost as he was.

"You asked me if it was in this courtroom that you asked that question, and I said, 'No, sir.' It was in a case in North Carolina."

Breitbart stared. "In the case in North Carolina, were you asked a question about whether or not you had a halo on your head when it came to making money?"

It was one of those times when Billy felt almost sorry for the guy. "There is no halo on my head," he said kindly.

14

No halo, certainly—but no horns either.

So far, as a "catalyst," Billy had received not a penny from the FBI or any other agency for taking down a small army of major and minor criminals. Since settling in Florida, he had lived off his undercover roles, finding the free-spending style of a bookie and marijuana dealer entirely congenial, and had used whatever was left over to finance his two-year penetration of the Godfrey Gang. When he sat down with Special Agent Dave Jellison to review his adventures in the dope trade, the tally of violators to be locked up came to well over a hundred—at a cost to the taxpayer of precisely nothing. He had made the bookies and dopers pay for their own elimination.

But the end of his self-financing undercover role also meant an end to his undercover income, and his relationship with the Bureau changed accordingly. Until now, it had been guarded and mainly social. Although he had kept Jellison more or less in the picture, in no sense had Billy been *authorized* to participate in the Godfrey Gang's activities. All Jellison knew was that Billy was trying to put together one or more narcotics-conspiracy cases as a means of cracking a more important case, and knowing Billy, he had been prepared to wait.

Once Billy had laid it all out in Jellison's living room, however, everything changed. It was one thing to work *with* the Bureau as an independent citizen waging a private war on crime, and quite another to work *for* the Bureau preparing cases for trial. No longer free to act as he pleased and to tell agents as much or as little as he chose, Billy now had to toe the bureaucratic line and obey orders.

But there was still time for one last insult to his better judgment. As a refugee from Miami, with all of the United States to choose from, he set out in the Riviera for Atlanta, even though Eddie Mode had warned him after the incident at Maxwell's Plum that Samantha had bought herself a .357 Magnum. On arrival, he checked into the Howard Johnson's Motel on Roswell Road, not far from the apartment complex where she lived with her sister, Linda, who answered the phone when he called.

No, Samantha was there but she didn't want to see him or talk to him. No, if he so much as set foot in the building, they would call the police. No, she would *not* have dinner with him, not after the way he'd behaved. He should go away and leave them alone.

She hung up, and Billy ordered another drink.

An hour or two later, he called again to *insist* that Linda have dinner with him. She hung up.

After reconsidering his position from the standpoint of a new bottle, he called back and asked her to put Samantha on. She hung up.

He finished the bottle. As she was obviously playing hard to get, he called again, and when she again refused to go to dinner, lost his temper.

"You bish," he shouted, amazed by the precision of his elocution. "You're 'sbad as your fucking shister. Tell her I'm comin' over."

"Now don't you do that, Billy. I already called the police."

"I don' care who the fuck you call. All I did was give her a little slap, thash all. And grab her by the throat. Thash all I did."

"Billy, I'm gonna call 'em again, you hear? You stay away from here."

"Don't tell me what to do, bish. *I'll* tell *you* what I'm gonna do. I'm gonna come over there and I'm gonna fucking *bite* your fucking throat. Thash what I'm gonna do."

She hung up.

He brooded on the injustice and inequities of life until after midnight. Then he got in the Riviera and drove over to give it to Samantha. But as soon as he entered the grounds of their apartment building, he was stopped at gunpoint by a small army of Fulton County cops, who booked him for drunk driving and threw him in the tank.

So far, so routine. But while Billy was sleeping it off, they found Barbara Mitchell's money and jewelry in the trunk of the car, and in his pocket the keys to a safe deposit box he had rented earlier to hold the $77,000 from Caesar's Palace. Beginning to wonder how big a fish they had caught, the arresting officers called the Atlanta FBI office, and at 6:30 A.M. Special Agent Arthur Krinsky arrived at the police station.

He inspected the car, the money, and the jewelry, diagnosed a dope trafficker, and, without consulting anybody or waking Billy up to explain himself, called the Internal Revenue Service. It was another two hours, after a befuddled and bewildered Billy had been shaken out of his alcoholic stupor to be photographed and fingerprinted, before Krinsky talked to Dave Jellison, at Billy's insistence, and realized what he had done.

"I wanna see my attorney," Billy enunciated, with immense care.

"You don't need an attorney," said Krinsky having now checked him out with several other agents and with Major John Regan in Massachusetts, all of whom had urged him to keep the IRS away from Billy, at least until he had sobered up. "*I'm* an attorney. *I'll* take care of you."

Billy blinked at him. He was not as drunk as *that*. He called Harold Keefe in Miami, who said he would send in his Atlanta associate, Darryl Cohen.

"You didn't have to do that," Krinsky said, trying to keep Billy awake with Coca-Cola. "I'm going upstairs now and I'll have all the charges against you dropped."

Billy nodded off as soon as he left. When he woke up again, Cohen was there, insisting that he should say nothing to anybody. Krinsky was furious.

"He doesn't *need* an attorney," he said. "I have personally made arrangements to have the charges dropped. You can check on that."

Confused by all these comings and goings, Billy took a nap.

"You see?" said Krinsky, when Cohen returned. "There's nothing to do. So now you can leave."

"Not without my client," said Cohen. "And why are you so anxious to get rid of me? Is there somebody else who's interested in Breen?"

Billy could hear them arguing, but he was too preoccupied with his headache to pay much attention until Krinsky mentioned the IRS.

"Mr. Breen," said Cohen, "I have to leave in a minute to attend to another matter. As far as I can see you are free to go. So I strongly advise you not to talk to anybody. Including the IRS."

That suited Billy just fine.

"There's no *need* for that," Krinsky shouted. "They're not interested in Billy. They just want to talk to him about the girls, that's all."

"Listen," Billy whimpered. "Don't shout. *Please*. I need medication. Will somebody get me some medication?"

They ignored him.

The moment Cohen left, Krinsky propelled Billy into a room where two men in suits were waiting. When they identified themselves as IRS agents, Billy staggered out again, shouting after Krinsky that he wanted Cohen there before he talked to them.

"Look, I told you—*I'm* an attorney," Krinsky said soothingly, leading him back like a lamb to the slaughter. "If you need me, I'll be right here. Just tell them about Samantha and Linda, that's all they want to know."

"Yes, tell us about the sisters," said the agents. "And make it good. We'll get right on it and bury 'em."

Even with a brain of red-hot cement, Billy knew it was a mistake, but the chance to get back at the girls for landing him in this mess was hard to resist. So he made it good. After explaining their role as money handlers in his recent excursions into the marijuana trade, he said he had paid Samantha a total of about $75,000. When they seemed unimpressed, he asked the agents how much they *needed* to bury her—$150,000? $200,000?

But as the conversation went on, he dimly perceived through the alcoholic fog that they were not really interested in the girls at all. Their questions kept coming back to him and the money *he* had handled. And when one of them finally reached into his pocket and produced the printed text of the *Miranda* warning against self-incrimination, Billy blundered out of the room again, hollering for Krinsky, who was nowhere to be found.

He managed to raise Cohen and Dave Jellison on the phone, however, and as there were still no charges against him, they urged him to leave at once, before he did himself any more damage. But that was easier said than done. The IRS had impounded his car (registered in Samantha's name), the money and jewelry (about which he had told the agents a number of stories as well as the truth), and the keys to the safe deposit box (containing money that, strictly speaking, he owed to Caesar's Palace).

When he finally ran Krinsky to earth in the late afternoon, he was given five hundred dollars, his briefcase, and the keys to the car. He was also given to understand that he was now registered as a source in the Atlanta office of the FBI, with Arthur Krinsky as his contact agent. Too tired and depressed to argue, he went away to nurse his hangover in peace.

Meanwhile, Dave Jellison had been mulling over Billy's two-year haul. At the federal level, there were the makings of a solid narcotics conspiracy and continuing criminal enterprise (RICO) case against Chagra, Piccolo, Painter, White, Judy Moeser, and the rest of the Godfrey Gang, right down to the truck drivers. Plus a similar, overlapping case against Kearns, Kelly, Margeson, and their Boston associates. Plus a similar, overlapping case against Cuban Mike Delgado, Barbara Mitchell, and the rest of the late George Mitchell's crew. Plus a similar, overlapping case against Larry Jackson, his off-loaders, and the corrupt law-enforcement officers in Appling County. And, most important of all, a conspiracy to murder and attempted murder charges against Chagra, Piccolo, White, Kearns, Margeson, and possibly others involved in the attempted assassination of Assistant U.S. Attorney James Kerr.

At state level, the list of possible defendants was even longer, and threatened to get out of hand as Billy kept adding names to it. Besides those already caught in the federal net, there were the Corbetts, the boat captains, the off-loading crews, and the corrupt officials at Myrtle Beach; the management and off loaders of the Amity Boatyard in Fort Lauderdale, plus the owners and captains of the shrimp boats; the distribution networks operated by Michigan Jim, Danny Mullenberg, and Mike Gamboli and their crews in Michigan, Ohio, and Wisconsin, and a host of minor and major characters Billy had met along the way, including Eddie Mode, Linda Holden, and Samantha Leonetti.

"This is going to take a bit of sorting out," Dave Jellison told him, contending for the law-enforcement understatement of 1981.

To lighten the load a little, Billy gave the Amity Boatyard pinch to his friend Lieutenant Joe Pierce, of Broward County, thereby knocking out by far the most efficient marijuana off-loading crew then operating on the eastern seaboard. The raid also spared Billy the need to blow his cover by appearing as a witness, for Pierce caught the boatyard operators with fourteen tons of Colombian gold on the premises.

The question of Billy's safety, once it became generally known that he was willing to testify, and of immunity from prosecution at the state level, was beginning to concern Jellison, but Billy was too busy trying to put the pieces of his life back together to worry much about the more distant future. Almost everyone he knew was out to kill him, or *would* be as soon as they learned he had dropped the boom; Samantha had broken his middle-aged heart; her sadistic phone calls had brought Helen to her knees; they had been driven out of Miami, and now had to start over again in a place where nobody knew them, and he was almost flat broke. What he did *not* need, on top of all that, was some scrawny college kid with FBI credentials pulling the Bureau's same old we-know-better-than-you shit.

The most immediate problem was to find a new home in another state. Having no particular preference, except for a warm climate, Billy was wide open to yet another of those improbable factors that always seemed to determine the course of his life at crucial moments, and it duly appeared on cue in the person of John Charles ("Butch") Piazza III.

Billy had lent Mrs. Piazza five thousand dollars while her husband was in the joint serving a moderate twelve-year stretch for a major cocaine-smuggling bust. In return for his testimony against Meyer Lansky in another matter, the government was now letting Piazza out after an even more moderate forty-two months and putting him into the Federal Witness Protection Program.

"They're gonna set him up in Dallas," said Jellison. "How d'you feel about Texas?"

Billy shrugged. "Will I like it any better with Piazza in it?"

"Maybe. And it's not Piazza anymore. It's Petracelli now. He gets a new ID, a new life—the whole bit. Courtesy the U.S. government."

"Ah-*hah!* Plus a new start as a doper, right?"

"Could be." Jellison never had to draw Billy a picture. "And if you want to try Dallas," he added casually, "I can probably get the U.S. marshal's service to move you both together."

Billy nodded. "Dallas is a nice town," he conceded.

"Yeah. Plus it's your best shot at collecting the five grand he owes you."

That settled it. In the absence of a better idea, Texas won the day. With Piazza standing guard at the door with a .45, Special Agent Dave Jellison, Sergeant Dave Green, and a U.S. marshal helped Billy load his worldly goods into a U-Haul truck, which Green and Piazza's father-in-law then drove across country to the house Billy had rented north of Dallas.

But it was to be many months before he could spend much time with Helen in their new home. Jellison was busy setting up meetings with other agents around the country to parcel out the casework, and clutching at Billy's coattails to claim him for Atlanta was Special Agent Arthur Krinsky. . . .

The key meeting was with agents of the FBI's San Antonio office. Getting nowhere with the attempted murder of AUSA James Kerr, they had left the case on the back burner to concentrate on the Judge Wood killing. Now, nearly two years later, the FBI was not much closer to an arrest than it had been to start with. Without a murder weapon or an eyewitness to the shooting, the federal grand jury had nothing to go on but circumstantial evidence and a few unreliable informants.

Billy's inside account of the attempt on Kerr's life was about the most promising lead they had been offered, but it was greeted with qualified rapture by Special Agent Ron Iden and his colleagues. In fact, they did not believe him. It was only after Jellison had vouched for him and he passed a polygraph test that they began to take Billy seriously.

Then they tried to blame *him* for Judge Wood's death. If he had come forward in the beginning, they said, they might have been able to crack the case and the judge would still be alive. Bullshit, said Billy. Already disgruntled by his reception, which was eerily reminiscent of his earlier experiences with the Boston FBI office, and, unlike the Bureau, having had no reason to suppose that anyone other than Kerr was in danger, he told them what he had told Jellison: that had he gone to them in the beginning, the Bureau would still have had to work through him—and would probably have fucked the whole thing up, if this was the way they handled a sensitive case. After that, they got down to business.

With no indictments pending against him, Billy was offered immunity from prosecution; protection for himself and his family within the Federal Witness Protection Program, if he wanted it, and a payment of $125,000 for his services in securing the arrest and conviction of those involved in the attempted murder of James Kerr. In the presence of Dave Jellison, Ron Iden, and other agents of the San Antonio office, Billy formally accepted these terms.

The Bureau also agreed to Billy's strategy. Now that he had identified those responsible, the investigating agents were in much the same situation as they were with the Judge Wood killing—they knew who had done it but had little or no admissible evidence. What they needed was for one of the lesser conspirators to roll over and testify against the others, and the best way to make that happen was to keep jamming them up with jail time for narcotics violations until somebody hollered uncle. Piccolo, preferably. Billy had often heard him say he would never serve a day inside.

With the Kerr case taking precedence, Billy gave the agents all his handwritten notes on the activities of the Godfrey Gang, the Kearns, Kelly, and Margeson crew, and the Mitchell, Jackson, and Delgado partnership, leaving it to Iden to sort out who would prosecute whom for what in federal or state courts. There were complications, however. Iden, on behalf of the FBI's San Antonio office, was interested in Billy's narcotics cases only to the extent that they helped with the Kerr/Wood affair, while Special Agent Roger McLaughlin, on behalf of the Savannah office, was interested only in perfecting those cases as an end in itself. Whenever these aims were in conflict, Billy was inevitably caught in the middle. More serious still, there were indications that state prosecutors, notably Donald W. Stephens, the assistant attorney general of North Carolina, were preparing to move against *him* as a co-defendant.

"When I got up there," Billy recalls, "Don Stephens—he's a judge now—he says, 'Well, we're gonna indict you.' I says, 'Great. After I give you all the evidence, you're gonna make a case against *me*.' 'Well,' he says, 'you were working with 'em.' 'I didn't say I *wasn't* working with 'em,' I says. 'I infiltrated this whole crew. I worked with Dave Jellison.' But for a time there, after I refused to go with the DEA, I wasn't reporting to nobody. I couldn't. And that gave 'em the opening. I didn't lie about any of it. If I lied, then these guys don't belong in jail. I ran it by 'em exactly as it went. So then Ron Iden comes up and says, 'You can't indict him. We got an agreement with him.' And Stephens says, 'That's federal. This is state.' Small-minded people. That's always been my problem."

And they were not finished yet. Billy's next meeting was in Wisconsin to assist federal and state authorities in framing charges against Mike Gamboli, Danny Mullenberg, Michigan Jim, their respective distribution crews, and various local wholesalers whom Billy had visited in Kalamazoo, Kenosha, Grand Rapids, Racine, and Chicago. For several days, he ran around with FBI agent Tom Cauthens, identifying the stash houses and other places he had visited, but he was excluded from the conference of federal and state law-enforcement agencies that met to consider the cases he had brought them.

"You got no friends in there, Billy," said Special Agent Arthur Krinsky when he came out of the meeting.

"I got none out here either," he said, walking away.

As it turned out, they were both right. After much haggling, protests, threats, blandishments, and interagency squabbling, Assistant Attorney General Donald Stephens of North Carolina eventually offered Billy a deal, take it or leave it, on August 12, 1981. In exchange for his "full cooperation and truthful testimony," he would be charged in North Carolina with one count of felonious conspiracy to possess marijuana from the *Captain Tom*, and in Milwaukee, Wisconsin, with one federal felony count in connection with the Hurricane David case. No other state or federal charges would be brought against him, and the "prosecuting authorities promise to recommend to the State of Massachusetts that any remaining sentence in that state, upon which you are now on parole, *NOT* be activated and that your parole *NOT* be revoked."

Billy huffed and puffed, hollered, complained, telephoned everybody concerned, wrote angry letters, got drunk, kicked himself for not salting away a million or two before pulling the plug, and finally accepted their terms. Jellison, Iden, and McLaughlin had tried their best, and seemed to think that the chances of a prison sentence were fairly remote, but the FBI had done it again. Apart from those three, agents appeared to *resent* his showing them the way. As in Boston, they seemed at least as eager to humiliate *him* as to lock up the bad guys.

As Billy saw it, his two-year extravaganza was justified to the extent that Jellison, in the presence of Sergeant Dave Green, had asked him to widen his scope from gambling and bookmaking to take in the dope trade as well. As a result of his efforts, federal and state agencies were now in a position to take down three major trafficking groups with associates all over the country, to prosecute around 125 defendants, and to seize assets worth many millions of dollars. He had also opened up the Kerr/Wood cases for them in San Antonio and provided the Bureau with a bonanza of criminal intelligence.

And what was his reward? A possible five years in the can. For "crimes" they would not even have *known* about unless he had told them.

"Hey, it's not *my* fault, Billy," said Special Agent Arthur Krinsky.

"Sure it's your fault," he yelled. "You're my contact agent. Every fucking thing is your fault. The IRS is your fault."

That at least was true.

"Where did you get the money?" asked Breitbart. "The $200,000 that was seized from you by the IRS on January 7, 1981, in Atlanta, Georgia?"

"That money was placed in my house by Barbara Mitchell," replied Billy. "George Mitchell and another fellow were dope dealers. Their plane went down in Baxley, Georgia. There was an investigation came down—"

"You have answered the question," interrupted Judge Sand. "That was the source of the money."

"Did you make $300,000 on the Hurricane David deal?" Breitbart continued.

"Yes, I did. And I reinvested it in the Piccolo—"

"You were a third partner in the Captain Tom?*"*

"Yes, sir."

"How much did you make on that one?"

"Nothing."

"Did you give $75,000 in presents to Linda Holden in 1980?"

"Yes, I did." It was out before he could catch himself. The truth was more complicated than that.

"Did you tell the IRS agents you had done that?"

"The IRS agents—that's how they duped me. Because it probably wasn't $75,000."

"Mr. Breen," said Judge Sand patiently. *"Will you look at me, please? Mr. Breitbart is trying to ask questions which you can answer yes or no. Just answer the questions 'yes' or 'no' or 'I can't answer that yes or no.'"*

"I have no objection to him answering in narrative form," said Breitbart helpfully.

"I have," the judge replied.

Breitbart sniffed. *"Did you tell the IRS that you had given $75,000 in money and presents to Linda Holden in 1980?"*

"I have to answer yes or no? Yes, sir."

"That is what got Agent Krinsky to your presence for the first time, isn't it?"

An accurate answer would have been no, but Billy could see what he meant. *"Yes, sir.*

"And he responded to the station house where you were sitting with your box keys and your money and your jewelry?"

"I don't know when he got there, or if that was there or not."

"You were pretty drunk that day?"

"I had a few drinks." Billy grinned ruefully. *"I was on a pretty good toot."*

"Did you meet Agent Jellison as a result of that, or did you know him?"

"I knew him before that." The guy didn't even listen to his own questions, never mind the answers.

"Did you ask Krinsky to call Jellison?"

"Yes, I did."

"Did you meet Special Agent Jack Fishman of the—"

"Yes, I did."

"And did you meet Agent John A. Truluck?"

"Yes, I did." Although his name was actually William R. Truluck, and they were both agents of the IRS.

"Were you highly agitated that day?"

"Yes, I was."

"Were you obsessive about women?"

Before Billy could think how to answer that curious question, Bruce Baird protested and Judge Sand sustained his objection.

"Were you hung over?" asked Breitbart, turning to a less controversial weakness.

"Yes, sir."

"Did they grab your money? Seize it?"

"Yes, sir."

Having seized the money, the IRS seemed less intent on seizing Billy, but its interest in him never quite flickered out after that, flaring up at irregular intervals, rather like herpes, and just about as welcome. Nor did anything in his subsequent association with Krinsky cause him to revise his bleary first impression of inexperience coupled with obsessive self-regard.

As Krinsky came to understand how central a figure Billy was in the chain of federal and state prosecutions now pending across the country, and how effortlessly prolific he could be in setting up targets wherever he went, the deeper his hooks sunk in. But for Billy, the fun had gone out of it. Having to sit down and go over and over the same old thing while squads of agents verified every last detail was simply a bore.

But the motivation was still there, and so was the realization that time was running short—not just in the sense that any 55-year-old could understand, but in the knowledge that when he was eventually obliged to testify as a government witness against Kearns, Piccolo, and the rest, his undercover career would be finished. Agents and prosecutors still had a long way to go before bringing his massive haul of offenders to trial, but at the most optimistic estimate, Billy had about three years left to wreak his particular brand of justice on the criminal community before the government blew his cover.

He stayed depressed for about a week, taking stock. But then it was time to go back to work, time for a third-act finale that would confound his critics, captivate the girls, and leave everybody gasping at his daring and ingenuity. In the time he had left, he would hack such a trail through the jungle of crime that the Bureau would need a task force to keep up with him, and in years to come, people would mention his name in the same breath as Dick Tracy.

15

The only good thing Special Agent Art Krinsky did for Billy was to introduce him to Sergeant Wesley Derrick of the Atlanta Police Department.

If Billy was as close to a cartoon caricature of a Boston Irishman as real life can get, then Derrick was his southern counterpart, with a magnolia-and-grits drawl, a laid-back devotion to the pleasure principle, and an approach to law enforcement for which the authors of police manuals made little or no provision. They were soulmates.

"So he asks me if I'll assist him in cleaning up Atlanta," Billy remembers. "And I says, 'Wes, it'd be a great pleasure. Where do I start?' 'Well,' he says, 'I'm trying to clean up the escort services. This here's a convention city, and we got problems with 'em clipping delegates from out of town.' I says, 'Don't worry about it. How many are we gonna pop?' He says, 'Now hold on a minute. How we gonna do this?' 'Well, I'll tell ya,'' I says. 'We're gonna get two rooms someplace and have them come to us. I'll be in one room, and you'll be in the holding room. I'll call 'em and give 'em all my business cards and credit cards—whatever they need—and when they come to me, I'll qualify 'em, then you come in and finish it off,' And that's what we did. Many a night we wrastled five, ten—as many as we could get.

"Coupla times we held back. 'Wes, this is a gorgeous little thing,'

164

I says. 'Oh God, I can't do it to this one. Wes, I'm gonna ask you to give me a break with this one. I'm gonna take her to Vegas.' "

Her name was Cheryl Cole. She liked to use cocaine, and as their acquaintance ripened over the next several weeks, she told Billy all about her connections in Atlanta and Vegas. She also knew Samantha Leonetti, which gave him an extra incentive.

With nowhere to go with the case except to his contact agent, he called in Krinsky, who in turn called in Drug Enforcement Administration agents Donald Augustine and Chuck Crane. Billy had met them before—reluctantly—and having little choice in the matter, agreed to finish off the case for a fee of $5,000.

He called Cheryl Cole and told her to get him some coke.

"Come on up to my apartment, honey," she said. "I got plenty right here. All you want."

A raiding party went instead. Cheryl Cole and three of her associates were arrested, tried, and convicted. The DEA seized five kilos of cocaine, $265,000 in cash, and two cars. And Billy was not paid a penny of the $5,000 he had been promised by the two DEA agents and their supervisor in the presence of his FBI contact agent, Arthur Krinsky. Or even his expenses.

It just confirmed his already jaundiced view of the DEA. He was not even surprised when Krinsky, who had gone along on the raid, told him that he had answered the phone in Cole's apartment after her arrest and an unknown caller had warned him to get everybody out as the feds were coming.

"Didn't I tell ya?" said Billy. "Nobody else knew about it. Only the DEA. So don't ask me to work with those people no more. You can't trust 'em. I told you that last time."

A few months earlier, Billy had taken a cab to the airport on his way home to Dallas and, as usual, wiled away the journey in conversation with the driver, a hotshot named Monroe Morgan. Before the ride was over, Morgan was boasting of his heavyweight connections for marijuana and cocaine, and when Billy paid him off, they exchanged not only vows of undying friendship but also telephone numbers.

"I'll call ya when I know I'm gonna make my next trip," Billy said.

"Yeah," said Morgan. "And then maybe you and me and this guy I know, maybe we can do a little business."

"Right." Billy beamed. "Yeah. Why not? I'll bring my partner along and maybe we can put some kind of a deal together."

He had figured on taking Krinsky with him, but Krinsky insisted on introducing him to Augustine and Crane. After flatly refusing to work with them, he allowed himself to be persuaded when their supervisor authorized a payment of $5,000. (Billy was so broke at that point, thanks to Krinsky's IRS friends, that he hardly knew where his next bottle of California champagne was coming from.) He agreed to introduce Augustine as his partner to Morgan and Morgan's supplier, Donald Watts, and ride herd on the deal until the case was airtight.

This he did. Morgan and Watts were duly arrested, tried, and convicted. The DEA seized a lot of cocaine, guns, cars, and nearly $300,000 in cash. And Billy was not paid a penny of the $5,000 he had been promised. Or even his expenses.

Naturally he was annoyed, but not really disheartened because he had never expected anything better from the DEA, or from Krinsky either. But he was seriously disappointed with the FBI. Living in Dallas and working with Iden in San Antonio, McLaughlin in Savannah, Krinsky in Atlanta, and occasionally with Jellison in Miami, Billy was alarmed at the way his travel, telephone, and subsistence expenses were mounting up. The Bureau also owed him payments for services which, when not specifically agreed in advance, were left to the discretion of the agents concerned.

With Krinsky, however, it never seemed to work out quite right. In a typical week, Billy's expenses would amount to perhaps $1,500, which he would itemize, sign, and turn in along with the appropriate vouchers and receipts. In due course, he would receive a $1,500 payment, divided, typically, into Services $800, Expenses $700.

"Hey, what the fuck's this?" he demanded, the first time it happened. "You're paying me with my own money. I already *spent* the fifteen hundred."

"Sorry, Billy," said Krinsky, "but this is how we do it. Some of what you claimed was disallowed."

"Disallowed? Shit. If I get busy here, I'm gonna go broke trying to pay you what you owe me."

Although officially he had turned over the Piccolo/Kearns investigation to the Bureau, Billy was still working the case, alongside Cole, Morgan, and other local diversions. For one thing, to drop completely out of the picture after so much hollering and screaming about the rip-off of "his" marijuana from Baxley and Michigan would set people wondering, and for another, until the government got its act together, empaneled grand juries, and attended to all the other ramifications of a huge and complex web of cases, he could at least help keep track of the principal defendants. By telephone.

To find out what the Boston crew was up to, Billy taped a call to Murdo Margeson, and pretended to believe him when Margeson denied taking over from Piccolo and seizing the load in Michigan Jim's stash house.

"You say you didn't get it, right? Then Bobby got it. And kept the three and a half million for my fucking stuff."

"He's not doing some things right," Margeson agreed. "It was a drop in the bucket, what I got. I can't follow him around every day and keep track of everything. But I'm concerned now with this new thing, you know?"

"I gotta go in and see him. 'Cause he tells me you guys got it all."

"What, your stuff? It's an easy way out to say that. If I got it all, I'd be settled. I'd be practically retired, if it's what you said it was."

"Well, I wish you had it," said Billy, "because if I think you had it, I think you'd give me something."

"Fine. I would. I'm not a fucking greedy guy. . . . Let's drop it now till I get back down there."

Billy had no intention of being within a hundred miles of Kearns, Kelly, or Margeson ever again if he could help it, and he had a hunch that Piccolo might already be feeling the same way about his new "partners." At any rate, Billy felt it was worth a shot at flipping him even at this early stage. If he could somehow talk Piccolo into becoming a government witness, it would not only save everybody, himself included, a heap of trouble, but get the whole crew off the streets in a matter of months, rather than years. With luck, a cooperating Piccolo might even spare him the necessity of having to testify and thus prolong his undercover career indefinitely.

"Lemme ask you a question," he said, catching him at the Fort Lauderdale stash house. "Have you been fair with me?"

"Have *I* been fair with *you*?" Piccolo laughed scornfully. "One hundred percent. *You've* been unfair with *me*. I put you somewhere, and you fucking took advantage of me, Billy. I haven't taken advantage of *you*."

"How in the fuck did I take advantage of *you*? Where am I now? Where is my house?"

"Well, how do *I* know?"

"You're *home*, Bobby."

"I'm *home*? Are you kidding me? I'm on my way to the fucking can shortly, pal."

"Is it *that* bad?"

Piccolo made mocking noises.

"Bobby, let me say this much. You think I'm gonna sit down and take a loss like this? You must think I'm fucking crazy if you think I'm going to take the loss. If you'da introduced me to Michigan Jim, let me handle it the way it was supposed to be . . ."

"He didn't want to meet you."

"I don't give a fuck. It's my fucking stuff—how can he not want to meet me?"

"*Your* stuff, *my* man."

"You're responsible for the fucking stuff, then."

"*They* took it," Piccolo said flatly, meaning Kearns, Kelly, and Margeson. "*You* lost it. You're the one that's responsible."

"Bobby, *I* didn't lose nothing. They were coming down on you before that. Ask 'em. Believe me what I'm telling you."

"You, me, and Peter'll sit down and figure it out. I don't got the stuff. You don't got the stuff."

"Bobby, I only want what I gave *you*. I didn't give it to them. If they took it, or somebody else, that is not my problem. My problem is I gave it to you, you gave it to Michigan Jim, right? That's what I want back."

"If you want to fucking get this thing settled, let's get it settled," said Piccolo, turning up the volume. "If you wanna be a fucking gentleman and swallow your fucking pride—"

"What pride can I swallow?" Billy demanded, matching him decibel for decibel.

"You were trying to fucking beat everybody, get everybody beaten."

"Was that fucking stuff mine or wasn't it?"

"Who the fuck knows whose it was?"

"Oh, you give a fuck whose it was. It was *my-un*. I gave it to you to fucking sell, didn't I? Did I give it to you? Hold it. Did I give it to you to sell? Whose the fuck's stuff *is* it? That was *my-un*."

Piccolo gave up the unequal struggle. "And after all the screaming," he said, "we ain't got anywhere."

"Well, how much money are you going to give me? I need some fucking money, Bobby."

"Meet you Wednesday."

"Bobby, give me fifty thousand. At least hold me over."

"When do you wanna make it?"

"Call me Thursday morning."

"Whenever you want Thursday. Don't call my house. The fucking line is tapped."

"Will you do me a favor? I'm busted."

Piccolo sighed. "Oh, Billy. I tell ya—you fucking amaze me. I'll call you Friday morning."

"Good. That's a better time. Call me Friday morning."

"I ain't gonna say nothing to you but hullo. That means I'll be at the Ionosphere at four o'clock on Friday afternoon."

"Okay . . . I heard you're working," said Billy, trying to slip one under his guard.

"I hope so," said Piccolo. "It's in the process."

"You told me you weren't."

"I want to sit down and talk to you so we can get this fucking thing straight. Stop all this aggravation."

"Bobby, bring me at least fifty thousand."

"Fine," said Piccolo. "Four o'clock."

It was a nice try, combining greed, rage, and anguish in plausible proportions, but Piccolo did not bring the fifty thousand or even keep the appointment. Between the call and the meeting, he and Margeson evidently realized that Billy could not believe *both* of them, and that by pretending he did, he could only be playing some game of his own.

So they sent a hit man instead.

Knowing his adversaries, Billy was not unduly surprised when nobody showed at four o'clock, but Krinsky could hardly hide his disappointment. At five o'clock, one of the stakeout agents came over to sit at Billy's table.

"He's obviously not coming," she said, checking her watch.

Billy eyed her sourly. "It's going-home time, is it?"

"Now wait a minute," she began, but broke off as Rebecca Esposito, a waitress friend of Billy's who liked to wear shoes in bed, approached with her tray.

"Billy, some guy just offered one of the girls fifty bucks to point you out," she murmured, wiping off the table. "I thought you'd want to know."

"Did she do it?"

"No."

"Thank you, Rebecca. I'll take care of her later."

"What's going on, Billy?" asked the agent, as Rebecca moved on to the next table.

"You heard her," he said. "Get the fuck away from me. We got heat."

She looked blank.

"Oh, for Chrissake," he said irritably. "They're looking to take a shot at me. Will you kindly give me some fucking room?"

No sooner had she left, wide-eyed, than the Ionosphere started paging Billy Breen. He surveyed the room, glass in hand, watching for signs of interest.

"Then," as he tells it, "Krinsky comes over and he says to me, 'You got a phone call, Billy.' So I said, 'Well, go and see who it is.' And he *does*."

Years later, he still cries with laughter to think of it.

"He goes to find out who's calling me, and I see this sharp-looking sonuvabitch get up and head out. I don't have nothing on me, but the agents, they don't know what's going on, so it's up to me. I follow the guy out on to the concourse and tackle him. Meanwhile, Krinsky comes off the phone. 'Where is he? Where is he?' And the other agents tell him I went out the door.

"By now I got the guy cornered. 'Take a good look, motherfucker,' I says to him. '*I'm* Billy Breen.' And I'm just ready to slam into him when Krinsky comes up and says, 'What are you doing here, Billy?' And he turns to the guy and says, 'I'm his attorney.' So the guy looks from me to him like we're both nuts, and slides off in the crowd. Nobody stops him. They didn't question the guy. Didn't lock him up. Nothing. 'Oh, man,' I says. I mean, I met some dumb fucking people in my life but this is the coup de grace."

Although he drew blank that time, the Ionosphere Club was always one of Billy's happier hunting grounds. In late August 1981, he flew up to Savannah to testify for Assistant U.S. Attorney Fred Kramer before the federal grand jury investigating recent events in Appling County. On the way back, while waiting in the airport club for his Dallas connection, Billy struck up a conversation with a fellow traveler, Jim Lewis, who painted such a luridly entrancing picture of Johnson City, Tennessee, as a gamblers' paradise that Billy could hardly wait to find out if his story was true.

It was. For ten years the FBI had been trying to get a handle on the casino and bookmaking operations of Don T. Anderson, of Kingsport, Tennessee, widely known throughout the state as "the Godfather of Sullivan County," and still more widely credited with having corrupted (in ascending order of importance, operationally speaking) a U.S. senator and congressman, key state legislators, agents of the Tennessee Bureau of Investigation, and the Sullivan County sheriff, along with several of his deputies. Anderson was also rumored to have a key to the back door of the governor's mansion, and to have successfully bribed a jury to beat the only criminal charges so far brought against him. In 1978, Billy learned, the FBI had drawn the attention of state authorities to Anderson's activities, but it might as well have saved its breath.

"Oh, come *on*," said Billy, who had never even heard of Johnson City until now. "*I'll* get him for you."

After checking with the Bureau's offices in Miami, San Antonio, Savannah, and Atlanta, Special Agent Steve Buttolph and his colleagues in Johnson City thought it might be worth a try. And as somebody with Anderson's connections was likely to be familiar with the name and face of every Justice Department employee in the state, Special Agent Jerry Forrester was drafted in from the Bureau's Miami office to work with Billy undercover.

On the strength of ten minutes' casual conversation at Atlanta airport, Jim Lewis proceeded to vouch for them everywhere in Johnson City. Even Billy was surprised. To snare an experienced wheeler-dealer with interesting bank connections he would normally have allocated half an hour at least. But Lewis not only introduced them to several local bookies, including Anderson, he even stood guarantor for their bets—which was just as well, for on his first weekend in town Billy staked twenty thousand dollars.

He had no authorization to do this or any way of paying up if he lost, but as far as Billy was concerned, first impressions were everything. If he was going to get over with Anderson, as big a bookie as he had ever come across, it could only be as a high-roller. To reinforce that image, he rented a Lincoln Town Car, bought some new clothes, and left an indelible mark on Johnson City's leading restaurant, Superwheels, with his champagne appetites and 25-percent-tipping policy.

On a limited budget and bound by the Bureau's strict accounting procedures, case agents Steve Buttolph and Lonnie Smith tried to call Billy to order, but found themselves at a disadvantage when he actually *won* twenty thousand dollars on his first series of bets. More than that, his Barnum & Bailey approach to law enforcement also created the opening that had eluded the Bureau for years when Anderson actually *invited* Billy into his illegal blackjack casino to collect his winnings.

With a belated twinge of caution, Jim Lewis viewed Forrester's arrival with some suspicion. While driving through the glorious countryside of Sullivan County, Forrester happened to comment on a particularly pretty string of small lakes, and Lewis grunted.

"If you're not who you say you are, buddy," he said, "you could find yourself *in* one of 'em."

"Hey, Jerry," said Billy. "Can you swim?"

It was not a retort that would have sprung readily to the lips of the average FBI undercover agent. Lewis laughed, his associates in the car relaxed, and the moment passed. But it was not forgotten. Billy used it a few days later to sink his hook deeper. After discussing a plan to launder Billy's "illegal earnings" through Lewis's banking connections, Billy told his host that Jerry Forrester liked the idea but wanted to punch Lewis in the mouth for embarrassing him the first time they met by threatening to throw him in the lake.

"Hey, listen, I'm sorry," said Lewis. "I didn't mean—"

"Don't apologize to *me*," Billy interrupted. "Apologize to Jerry when he gets in tomorrow."

And Lewis did. Not only that, he invited them home with him to catch their own trout for supper in his private lake, and swore several times that he would do everything in his power to help them set up the bingo-parlor-and-flea-market operation that Billy had in mind for Johnson City.

Don Anderson also liked the idea when they explained it to him at the casino. They stayed for a couple of hours on their first visit, with Billy pumping so hard that at one point Forrester poked him to go easy. Feeling irresistible by now, and fairly certain that the dealer, Ron Nelson, had seen him do it, Billy rounded on Forrester and, to everybody's astonishment, yelled, "Don't ever do that to me again."

Nobody, except Forrester, knew what he meant, but one thing was again certain: no undercover cop ever behaved like *that*. Anderson paid Billy his winnings, chiseling him out of a couple of thousand, which Billy let pass in the interests of goodwill, and when they left, Anderson and Nelson saw them to the door.

Steve Buttolph agreed it was a good night's work. The following day was even better. To probe Jim Lewis's bank connections, and also to encourage general confidence in their solvency, Billy spent most of the morning making $500 look like $140,000. First, he divided about four hundred $1 bills into eight separate stacks, topped with a $10 or $20 bill, and held each together with rubber bands. Then he laid the local newspaper in the bottom of his attaché case, carefully arranged two of the hotel's towels on top of it, and covered them with a shopping bag. When the eight stacks of bills went in, they came neatly to the lip of the case, and after strapping them together with Scotch tape, the $140,000 illusion was complete.

The money was supposed to be the first consignment of cash to be washed by Jim Lewis's banker friend in Mountainview, although Billy obviously had no intention of parting with it. At the last moment, he or Forrester intended to make some excuse to postpone the delivery, but when Lewis called Mountainview from his office, the banker played straight into Billy's hands by suggesting they come up the following week.

"Dammit," said Billy. "I made a special trip to the lady who looks after my money and picked up a hundred forty grand. I got it right outside in the car."

"Jesus, Billy," said Forrester peevishly. "Will you cut it out? Are you crazy? Don't go telling people you're carrying all that cash with you."

Billy glared. "Jim, come out to the car," he said. "I wanna show you something."

"No, no, Billy. Stop it," Forrester protested. "You don't have to show him anything."

"No, that's right," Lewis said. "I don't have to see it."

"Jerry, don't you tell me what to do," Billy said dangerously, ignoring Lewis. "If I wanna show somebody something, I'm gonna do it. Just get on out there and open up the car."

He shepherded both of them out to the parking lot, Forrester protesting all the way and Lewis pretending not to care if he saw the money or not.

"For the last time, Billy," said Forrester, "I don't think you should do this. With all due respect, Jim. I mean, I don't know you that well, but—"

"Jerry, will you shut up?" Billy yelled. "How many more times have I gotta tell ya? *You* work for *me*, right?"

"Yeah, but—"

"Then do like I say. Open the fucking door."

Muttering to himself, Forrester threw open the rear door and Billy dived in. Unsnapping the catches of his attaché case, he gave Lewis a good look inside, watched his eyes widen, and snapped it shut again, confident that Lewis had seen enough to convince his banker friend, and anyone else who asked, that they were on the level.

Billy and Forrester perfected their double act that night at Anderson's casino. Arriving after dinner with a couple of girls supplied by the management, they dropped about thirty-five hundred dollars between them before the joint closed. By then the two were completely at home there, accepted by everyone, and adding names to their target list whenever they stopped losing money long enough to chat with Anderson or Ron Nelson or Red Garland, who picked up the cards for Nelson and negotiated the chips and cash.

Around fifty people, most of them local business and professional men, some with, some without, wives or girlfriends, were in and out of the joint in the course of the evening, with no more than eight playing blackjack at any one time. With a house limit of $300 a hand, between $1,500 and $2,000 was wagered on every game, five hours a night, five nights a week.

To Billy's experienced eye, the action was rigged to produce an average weekly profit for the house of between $50,000 and $100,000, and perhaps double that at peak times, but even so, it was small potatoes next to Anderson's bookmaking business. Although Billy could not yet put a figure on it, the operation was among the biggest and best organized he had come across—and he had made a lifelong study of the subject. Even more remarkable, Anderson had been running the business more or less out in the open for thirty years, as calmly as if he had a license.

With other cases to attend to, Billy and Forrester now had to break away for a week, but this was to be expected of free-wheeling entrepreneurs with their fingers in a dozen pies and, if anything, made them all the more welcome when they joined Don Anderson and his party for dinner at Superwheels on their first night back.

Seated next to Anderson, Billy complained about having plenty of money but not being able to show it. Anderson allowed that he had the same problem, and gave him the names of two vice presidents in the Tri-State Bank of Bristol who could wash it for him.

"I'm only giving up one percent," said Billy cautiously.

"You talk to them about it," Anderson replied. "I'll introduce you and then you're on your own."

"Well, maybe when we get back from the islands," said Billy, preparing him for their next absence. "Gotta little business to take care of first."

They talked marijuana for a while, with Anderson visibly warming to him as one man of the world to another, and when Billy eventually insisted on picking up the tab for dinner, they parted like brothers.

A pattern was now established. Billy and Forrester would arrive for two or three days, still ostensibly spotting locations for their bingo parlor and flea market; they would visit the casino, dine once or twice with Don Anderson, who now saw himself as a future partner, running a keno game alongside the bingo, and thereby fit a few more names and pieces of evidence into the overall picture before flying out again to work on other cases.

In this way, they unearthed Steve Skaggs, who ran a down-market blackjack game for Anderson in the local Amvets post; they tempted Anderson into boasting before witnesses of the protection his operation enjoyed from the Sullivan County Sheriff's Department, agents of the Tennessee Bureau of Investigation, and others; they located his property and other assets for possible seizure by the IRS; they established that he and his five principal lieutenants held IRS gambling stamps, which meant they could be tried at the federal level only on racketeering and tax-evasion charges; they continued to add to their list of accommodating bankers, businessmen, attorneys, and other Anderson associates prepared to fix "the system" any way they wanted it; and in between visits, Billy kept the pot boiling by calling in (and tape recording) football bets from all over the country.

By Christmas 1981, he had wagered over half a million dollars with Anderson, generating a lot of tricky paperwork and a few sleepless nights for his budget-conscious case agent Steve Buttolph and IRS agent Tony Deaton.

By Christmas 1981, Billy had also generated a good deal of paperwork for Special Agent Ron Iden in the San Antonio case. Within days of his accepting the deal worked out by Assistant Attorney General Donald Stephens of North Carolina, warrants were issued in Brunswick County, North Carolina, for the arrest of Kearns, Kelly, and Margeson. All three made bail in Boston pending extradition from Massachusetts and, with the ease of constant practice, vanished.

"What's the *matter* with all of yez?" Billy howled, when the news filtered through. "I tell ya who did it. I set 'em up for ya. I walk you through the whole fucking thing, and what happens? They post some loose change and blow town."

"It was in municipal court, Billy," Iden said soothingly. "Nothing we could do. And the bond was a hundred thousand dollars."

"That don't mean nothing. Their attorneys own the bail-bond company. This is *Boston*, Ron. Maybe they put up five percent. Maybe five thousand dollars. Shit, they just ripped Piccolo off for *millions*. You ain't never gonna find 'em now."

"No, we'll get 'em, I guarantee you. But you got to remember, Billy, this is a big case with a lot of defendants. We can't watch 'em all."

"Ron, Ron. I known the Bureau too long. They fumbled it. Kearns was the *shooter*, for Chrissake. They shoulda had somebody watch him. Somebody in the Boston office shoulda given up his volleyball time and watched him."

"Billy—"

"Ron, you coulda held 'em. Believe me. I know for a fact they're wanted for dope in Plymouth County. Billy Kelly's wanted in Florida for murder. You gotta understand, Ron—everybody I give you, they're all pros. And if you guys don't get your act together, you're gonna blow the whole thing."

"Billy, we'll get 'em, okay?"

"Yeah. Maybe. If I find 'em for ya . . ."

(Billy's scorn for Boston's bail-bonding arrangements turned out to be amply justified. The $100,000 bonds for Kearns and Kelly had been written by Allied Fidelity Insurance Company for a fee of only $1,500, or 1.5 percent instead of the usual 10 percent. Stranger yet, when the court ordered the forfeiture of the $200,000, the attorney general for the Commonwealth of Massachusetts settled for a mere $2,500, elevating an eyebrow or two among even the most jaundiced of Bostonians.)

Also within days of accepting the Stephens deal, Billy testified before the federal grand jury in Savannah against Larry Jackson and his crew in Appling County. Nobody looked like getting away there. Special Agents Roger McLaughlin and Phil Dennis, working with Assistant U.S. Attorney Fred Kramer, had such a firm grip on the case that Billy tried to persuade them to indict Kearns, Kelly, Margeson, and the Piccolo crew as well. Still at odds with San Antonio on questions of jurisdiction, McLaughlin, for one, would have liked to, but they already had eighteen defendants, including five former law-enforcement officers, lined up for conspiracy to violate the RICO

statute. A dozen more would have made the trial impossibly complicated.

As it was, it went very smoothly. Jackson and his associates were
indicted at the end of October, convicted in U.S. District Court,
Brunswick, in December, and sentenced in January—Larry Jackson
and his accomplice, Joe Lightsey, the former sheriff of Appling
County, each drawing exemplary sentences of forty-five years' imprisonment.

On the whole, Billy did not enjoy his debut as a government
witness. There was satisfaction in knowing that he had helped clean
up police corruption in Baxley and at the county level—always of
greater importance to him than marijuana trafficking—but in court
he was playing in somebody else's game, and he was never much of a
team player. He belonged on the streets, on his own, playing by his
own rules.

Remembering how the Bureau had let Kearns, Kelly, and Mar-
geon slip through its fingers, Billy insisted on going along with the
FBI raiding party when the time came to arrest the Piccolo crew.

"I couldn't let 'em screw it up," he said, "after I'd put it all
together for 'em. I don't care how they look at it, the Kerr case was
dead. I gave 'em the whole story. Who did it. Who paid for it.
Everybody involved. And after that I stayed on it. My phone bills
were like five hundred bucks a month, checking people. I went to
Florida. I went to Vegas. I followed Chagra's trail all over the country.
I gave 'em such a lesson in FBI work that they could not accept it.

"So now the pinches are going down on the Piccolo crew. Iden's
got an army of agents with him, including Dave Jellison, and they're
at the Holiday Inn at Coral Springs. But nobody knows what to do.
They're like a bunch of blind mice—just stumbling over everything.
We go to Peter White's house. They've been watching it but they don't
know if he's in there or not, and some big shot has told 'em there'll
be no kicking down doors unless they're positive somebody's home.

" 'What makes you think he's in there?' Iden says to me. 'He's *in*
there,' I says. 'Just gimme the phone. I'll show you how to flush him
out. I'll show you how to do *everything* if you just step back for me.
I'm gonna call the house and say I'm the pool man.' But then I give
the phone to Dave. 'Better than that,' I says, '*you* call him. He knows
my voice and so does Judy.' So Dave says he wants to talk to the man
of the house about servicing his pool, and Judy calls out, 'Pierre, it's
the pool man.' Soon as he gets on the phone, Iden says, 'Hit the
house,' but Peter smells it and hangs up. They catch him around the
back, coming out the window.

"Now it's Bobby Piccolo's turn, only they go to the wrong house.
I mean, can you believe it? Hadn't lived there for six months. So I

take 'em to his new place, and I says, 'Now be careful. You got twins in there, and little Bobby.' Those are his kids. 'Oh,' says Iden. 'Well, you didn't tell us that.'

" 'Oh, Dave,' I says. 'I'm getting a fucking headache.' "

Billy's depression deepened when Peter White and Judy Moeser skipped the country.

"Ron," he said, "we *need* those two. It was Peter told Piccolo to talk to me about getting somebody heavy down from Massachusetts. He knew I was in tight with Murdo Margeson."

"Yeah, Billy, I know. I know."

"Judy was in on that, too. And after she cozied up to Kearns, who the hell knows what else he told her? You gotta get 'em back, Ron."

"Yeah, Billy, I know. I know."

The FBI eventually located them in the Dominican Republic, where White had turned his hand to money laundering. Deported to San Juan, Puerto Rico, he was arrested there on a federal warrant for parole violations and flown back for questioning in the Kerr case and to catch a crushing load of jail time from Billy's marijuana cases.

Judy Moeser, however, proved a tougher proposition than any mere bank robber. When agents attempted to force her onto a flight from Santo Domingo, the captain of the aircraft refused to allow them aboard with a prisoner in handcuffs.

"So what are they gonna do? They gotta take the cuffs off, right?" Billy almost choked with glee. "Soon as they take off the cuffs, Judy strips right off, right down to bare, bollocky bare-ass, in front of everybody in the airport. Now, not just the captain but the police, the militia, come to her rescue and they chase the agents right out of the country.

"But she's a bad girl and involved in a lot of stuff, so when they get home they go through the whole routine of getting extradition papers from the Justice Department, the State Department, and the this-and-that department. Then they go down again for another try, only she's moved. And not only that, while they were gone, she's married a Dominican. She's a Dominican citizen now, and they can't touch her."

Billy had nothing against Iden, who tried always to treat him fairly, was genuinely worried about his prospects in Wisconsin and North Carolina, and was plainly embarrassed when the Bureau reneged on its promised reward of $125,000. Still without an indictment three years after the murder attempt on Kerr, and two and a half years since the Judge Wood killing, the FBI's San Antonio office had so many difficult considerations to juggle with that it was bound to drop some, and to worry about dropping more.

Billy's approach was more carefree. When Piccolo failed to crack under his first two convictions, Billy cheerfully urged Iden to hit him again.

" 'Don't stop,' I told him. 'What is *wrong*? You guys got the power. Keep going with it. Try 'em again.' So they says, 'Where else can you go with them?' And I says, 'I'll go down to Louisiana.' Piccolo and his guys lost a load down there near New Orleans, but nobody pinned it on 'em.

"I let Krinsky go with me—as stupid a move as I ever made because I almost got hurt. He made me sign use immunity. I said, 'For what? I'm bringing this case. You people don't have this case.' 'Just a formality,' he says. A formality? Another one? Like the formality I signed for Luxstead up in Massachusetts that nearly got me killed? Anyway, I got 'em indicted down there, and that did it.

"In the end, I testified at three different trials. Bobby Piccolo got more time. Painter got more time. The truck drivers caught more time. Everybody got more time. And Bobby cracked, just like I always knew he would. It was all over. With Bobby cooperating, they had the Kerr case locked up. They already had Jimmy Chagra. All they had to do now was find Kearns, Kelly, and Margeson. Before they found *me*."

Although he had done everything that was asked of him, and more, the FBI's San Antonio office at first refused to pay him anything at all. It was only after Ron Iden risked his promotion prospects by making a fuss that Billy was grudgingly awarded fifty thousand dollars, take it or leave it—less than half what the Bureau had promised. In consequence, his opinion of the FBI, never very high, descended to the unprintable, but on the other hand, his opinion of FBI agents, never very high, rose appreciably (with certain loudly advertised exceptions).

Billy's relations with the federal government continued to fascinate David Breitbart, although the precise significance of the IRS agents' seizure of Barbara Mitchell's $200,000 continued to elude him.

"Did they make a jeopardy assessment against you for that money?" he asked.

"Yes, sir."

"Wasn't the assessment based on the fact that you told them that you had given Linda Holden $75,000 in 1980?"

"It was based upon the fact that Jack Fishman told me to tell them any amount they wanted so they could go after the girls, Linda Holden and Samantha Leonetti. And I fabricated the story for them because that's what he wanted me to do."

It was a damaging admission, and not even true. All Billy had done was exaggerate the amount he had paid her. He was getting tired.

"In other words," suggested Breitbart, gratefully seizing the opening, "if a federal agent of the United States government asks you to fabricate a story so it will help you make a case, you are willing to do that?"

"No, sir."

"Didn't you just say you fabricated a case against Linda?"

"Yes, sir."

"You lied about the amount of money because Agent Fishman asked you?"

"He told me, 'Tell me anything you want. We will go after the girls.' "

"How many times have agents of the United States government asked you to lie?"

"There has never been an FBI agent or a regular law-enforcement agency ever asked me to lie."

"Why did you lie for Agent Truluck and Agent Fishman?"

"Because I was a little upset, and I was still drunk when I talked to them."

"And would it be fair to say, sir, that if a federal agent asked you to lie, you will do it?"

"No, sir."

"Then why did you do it in '81?"

"That was not a federal agent," Billy spluttered. "He was an IRS agent. There is a complete difference. Are you talking about an FBI agent or any organized crime law-enforcement officer? I would not lie for him."

"Well, will you give us a list of the agencies you will *lie* for?" asked Breitbart silkily.

"None."

"Well, you lied for the IRS."

"That was—I was duped into it."

"Someone as smart as yourself?"

Billy had to give him that one. "Oh, you can be smart and still fall down," he said wearily.

16

There are two kinds of agents in Billy's book: good agents and bad agents.

Bad agents are concerned only with themselves and their careers. They can be found in heavy concentrations at the supervisor level and above, and in the gym during working hours. There is nothing to be done about bad agents except avoid, ignore, or abuse them.

Good agents, on the other hand, come in two varieties: company men and kindred spirits. Company men, also heavily represented at the supervisor level and above, stand in the same relation to the Bureau as priests to the Catholic Church. For them, the public and national interest is the same as the Bureau's interest. The director is therefore infallible even when he is wrong, and things are important, or not, to the extent that they serve the FBI's purpose.

The one thing they have in common with bad agents, although for different reasons, is that they often describe Billy as being "hard to control" or even "out of control"—the idea of control reflecting their bedrock presumption that the Bureau always knows best.

Kindred spirits take precisely the opposite view. Bureaucrats *never* know best. More than anything in the world, kindred spirits enjoy using the power and facilities of the Bureau to knock bad guys off their perch, this taking priority, if necessary, over official policy or even the precise letter of the law. Half their skill lies in bending the system to serve their sense of natural justice—and half the pleasure is keeping their bosses at bay until the time comes for them to ratify a fait accompli and sign their expenses. For kindred spirits, the only acceptable measure of efficiency is how much damage has been inflicted on the criminal community.

In Sullivan County, Tennessee, it began to look like a lot. After the frustrations of dealing with company men in San Antonio, to return to his kindred spirits in Johnson City was always a relief. Gambling and bookmaking had never ranked as major crimes in Billy's estimation, but rather as useful starting points for more serious investigations. Don Anderson was an important target, to him as to the federal government, not as a bookmaker but because he had corrupted the machinery of Tennessee justice to the point where state law officers refused to act against him even when the local U.S. attorney referred the case to them for prosecution.

Billy kept things going as long as he could, but on February 26, 1982, he and Special Agent Jerry Forrester paid their final undercover visit to Anderson's blackjack casino. Knowing that a federal raiding party would close it down at midnight, they drank champagne and took a last sentimental turn at the table, where Forrester immediately started to win big.

"At about five minutes to midnight," he recalls, "Billy comes over and tells me to cash in. There was no budget for this job so the only way he could cover himself was by keeping whatever he made betting football or playing blackjack. Not officially, of course, but I'd generally be looking the other way when it happened. Anyway, he was supposed to get all the money we won on the last night, so he says, 'Come on. You gotta get off the table.' 'Why?' I says. 'I got time for a couple more hands yet.' 'No, no,' he says. 'Not with those Johnny come-quicks outside you don't. Pick it up and get off the table.' 'Well, okay, then—just one more,' I tell him, because I'm really on a streak.

"Sure enough, they hit the place early, right in the middle of the deal, and the money's all out on the table. So Billy drops it on the floor and puts his foot on it, cursing me out like a camel driver. But it's no good because the guys slam us up against the wall along with everybody else, and right away they see it. Now it's evidence, right? See, we got busted, too. That was part of the plan. To protect our cover.

" 'It's all your fault,' he yells at me. 'You shoulda done like I told ya. You people are all the same. None of you fuckers ever *listen* to me.'

"People hear me talk about him and they say, 'Aw, he couldn't have done that,' or 'He couldn't have done this,' but Billy can do *anything*. As a source, I'd rate him as the best—even if he *did* almost get us killed ten times. The Bureau *should* have listened to him more. It *should* have treated him better, because what Billy promises he delivers. I'd work with him again anytime, anyplace."

Following the raid, a federal grand jury indicted Anderson for racketeering and tax evasion, and his five principal lieutenants with one count each of racketeering. Billy was disappointed that no corruption charges were brought against the law-enforcement officers who had allowed Anderson to operate so openly for thirty years, and that no attempt was made to follow up all the other leads he had turned over to the Bureau on money washing, banking abuses, interstate dealing in counterfeit jeans, and so on—all of which he considered more serious than bookmaking or bilking the IRS—but he accepted the U.S. attorney's assurance that knocking out Anderson would go a long way toward cleaning up Sullivan County.

The case that Billy and Forrester had built against him was airtight, so unassailable that all six defendants pled guilty, sparing them both the need to testify. At the end of an investigation into Tennessee's illegal gambling, begun in 1978 and now completed at a reported cost of half a million dollars in public funds, federal justice had triumphed again.

Except that sixteen months unaccountably slipped by after Anderson's indictment before he and his associates at last appeared in Knoxville's federal district court for sentencing. And all this time seemed somehow to have undermined the importance of the government's case as far as Judge Robert L. Taylor was concerned. While noting that Anderson had "operated wide open in Sullivan County without any interference from law enforcement," and that he admitted owing the IRS, $558,000 in taxes on an illegal bookmaking income of $18.5 million, the judge sentenced him to a fine of $5,000 and one year's imprisonment for tax evasion, and eighteen months' probation for racketeering. (The maximum penalties available were $100,000 and three years' imprisonment for the income-tax charge, and $20,000 and five years' imprisonment for racketeering.)

So that no lingering doubt should remain as to what he thought of "the Godfather" of Tennessee's illegal gambling industry, Judge Taylor went on to sentence each of Anderson's three closest lieutenants, Ron Nelson, Red Garland, and Steve Skaggs, to a $100 fine and twelve months' probation.

Even the Tennessee press was surprised.

"Ridiculously lenient sentences handed down earlier this week by U.S. District Judge Robert Taylor will do about as much as the efforts of Sheriff Mike Gardner to halt illegal gambling in the county," concluded an editorial in *The Kingsport Times-News.* "And that, in a word, is nothing. The judge's action, and Mr. Gardner's continuing inaction, are insults to law-abiding citizens. . . . If Mr. Gardner and his deputies spent as much time and money raiding gambling parlors as massage parlors, Federal officials could turn their attention elsewhere."

Billy already had.

Soon after his release from prison, John Regan had put him in touch with the Regional Organized Crime Information Center, based in Memphis, Tennessee, and under its auspices Billy had undertaken a number of special assignments around the country. Now its assistant director, Jim Hobbs, called to find out if he would be interested in working in Texas with the Greater Dallas Organized Crime Task force.

Billy was very interested.

With Piazza/Petracelli to get him started, Texas had already opened up for Billy like Hiawatha's happy hunting ground, with limitless vistas of human larceny spread out in all directions. Just getting a pool dug in his backyard, for instance, had plugged Billy into the Dallas network for bookmaking, narcotics, prostitution, stolen goods, and illegal arms dealing.

The pool contractor, Jeff Coleman, was an engaging young man who hated to be left out of anything, who contrived to be hard-driving and laid-back at the same time, and who never stood a chance. After beating him out of the cost of the pool in a crap game, Billy took Coleman over, in spite of his objections, with a view to keeping him out of jail while he moved in on his connections, one of which helped Billy save the Judge Wood assassination case in San Antonio.

After almost three years of increasingly desperate investigation by hundreds of FBI agents at a cost of over $10 million, the government had finally cobbled together a murder and conspiracy-to-murder case against Jimmy Chagra, hit man Charles Harrelson, their respective wives, and Joe Chagra, Jimmy's brother and occasional attorney. Where not circumstantial in character, the evidence consisted mainly of dubious, and probably inadmissible, "confessions" by Harrelson, later recanted; ambiguous conversations between Jimmy Chagra and an FBI "plant" recorded in Chagra's prison cell, and bugged conversations between Jimmy and Joe Chagra that were probably privileged, as between client and attorney. Worst of all, Harrelson had an alibi witness putting him far from the scene at the time Judge Wood was shot and killed outside his home in San Antonio.

Without this witness, there was a reasonable chance of securing a conviction. With him, there was little or no point in going to trial.

While the case was stuck fast at this point, Billy and Jeff Coleman got to talking one day with the bikers hanging out in a motorcycle shop run by a Dallas bookmaker. One of them had just been forced to cancel a long-awaited trip to Mexico, he told them.

"Yeah?" said Billy, perennially interested in lowlife connections with dope-producing countries. "Tough shit. What happened?"

The other shrugged. "Aw, Billy T, my partner, stuck his dick in the wringer," he said. "He's maybe got to go and testify in San Antonio."

"Too bad. He in trouble?"

"Hell, no. Could be a lot of money in it for him."

Billy's antenna twitched. "You mean he's gonna get paid? To testify?"

"Sure. If he gets the guy off. He's an alibi witness. Happens all the time."

"Yeah, right, right. Sounds like he got himself a pretty good deal."

"Yeah," agreed Coleman. "I could use a piece of something like that myself."

"Yeah, how about that?" said Billy. "Maybe he can use a couple more alibi witnesses, this guy. What's his name?"

"Haroldson? I dunno. Something like that. Anyhow, he can use all the help he can get. They claim he killed some judge over there."

"Well, there's another good reason to help the guy out," said Coleman.

"Right," purred Billy. "Maybe we can get Billy T to introduce us."

"Naw," said the biker. "Anyone gets a piece of this, it's *me*. But I don't think Billy T ever met the guy."

Special Agent Ron Iden was very happy to hear of this conversation. Shortly afterward, two agents came to Dallas to warn Billy T of the penalties for perjury, and soon after that, on April 15, 1982, Jimmy Chagra and Charles Harrelson were indicted for murder.

It was a promising start for Billy's unwilling assistant.

"Jeff Coleman is the kinda guy you can straighten out," he says. "I like to think I'm a pretty good judge of character, even though his is at the bottom of the heap. So I said, 'Fred, we're gonna take a chance with Jeff. Let's work with him. He's a little wacky, but he's clean.'"

Fred was Fred Cochran, a senior agent of the Texas Department of Public Safety, and a kindred spirit. They met when the ROCIC (Regional Organized Crime Information Center) hooked Billy up with the Greater Dallas Organized Crime Task Force, which had just decided to blitz local bookmakers—around fifteen hundred of them, thanks to their low priority as police targets. Believed to be handling at least $150 million a *week* in bets, virtually out in the open, they were now also getting into cocaine trafficking, fencing stolen property, fraud, money laundering, and various other varieties of white-collar crime.

"Oh, yeah," said Billy to the Task Force Coordinator. "Sure, I'll take care of that for you. Me and Fred can handle it. But first you gotta help me nail this guy Piazza."

He had been working the case with Lloyd Hough, of the Dade County Organized Crime Bureau in Miami, who, like Jellison and Billy, had known from the start that Piazza's new life as Petracelli in the Federal Witness Protection Program meant a new career as a drug trafficker. Linked with at least a dozen murders in South Florida before his conviction for cocaine smuggling, Piazza had lived the dream life of a Miami playboy, with a string of race horses, several palatial homes, his own golf driving range, and a Lamborghini for a shopping cart.

After his arrest, he boasted of having made $100 million from operating one of the biggest and most ruthless drug crews in the Southeast, but served only forty-two months in prison, buying his way out by agreeing to testify against anybody accused of anything, including Meyer Lansky, although his story of lunching with the mobs' elder statesman in 1974 to discuss the legalization of casino gambling in Miami Beach was never corroborated.

Billy, for one, could see no reason why Lansky would wish even to piss on Piazza, but that was the government's business. The Justice Department might have wiped his slate clean, but Billy knew Piazza could never exchange his Arabian Nights life style for a split-level tract house in the suburbs of Dallas. And anyway, Piazza owed him money.

While Hough kept tabs on him during his frequent trips to Florida, Billy spent hours watching his house from a clump of trees across the street or parked discreetly near the office in which Carol Piazza answered the phone and otherwise attended to her husband's unspecified business activities. It was the best he could do. There was no way he could get in on their act because the Piazzas knew of his FBI connections.

But routine surveillance, even with an unwilling Jeff Coleman to help him, was not Billy's favorite occupation, and he was glad to turn the job over to the task force as soon as he and Lloyd Hough had pieced enough together to suggest that Piazza was on the verge of something big. And big it turned out to be when, acting on Billy's early warning, federal authorities were, for once, able to *prevent* a serious crime rather than sort out the corpses afterward.

Tracked one last time to Florida, where he was met by Steve Pearson, another convicted trafficker, Piazza was arrested at Pearson's home in Miramar by a raiding party from the then–Vice

President Bush's Task Force. In the house, agents found a stolen police radio; a scanner programmed to monitor "secret" law-enforcement frequencies; portable landing-strip strobe lights; aviation charts covering South America, the Caribbean, and South Florida; four hundred gallons of aviation fuel; military fatigues; bush hats fitted with mosquito netting, and a load of insect repellent.

The intention of Piazza and Pearson to mount an airborne commando-style drugs expedition to Central or South America was clear. So, too, was their determination to avoid rip-offs and/or arrest. There were forty guns of all types in the house, including a fully automatic AR-15 rifle, fitted with a silencer. Not only that, many of the guns were loaded with Teflon-coated bullets, designed to pierce government-issue bulletproof vests.

Both men were charged with violations of the Federal Gun Control Act, possession of automatic weapons and silencers, and possession of firearms by a convicted felon. Goodbye Piazza/Petracelli.

Hello, Dallas bookmakers. After taking down hundreds of their colleagues in Florida, and fresh from dismantling Don Anderson's operation in Tennessee, Billy was probably better qualified than anyone to tackle the problem in Texas, but whereas in Florida he had had nine cops and an FBI agent to help him, and in Johnson City, eight FBI agents, plus assistance from the IRS and the Tennessee Bureau of Investigation, in Texas he was given Fred Cochran and thirty-five hundred dollars.

"You're *kidding*," Billy said to Dallas Police Sergeant John T. Williams, responsible for running the task-force operation. "Thirty-five hundred? That's unreal. We'll bet more than that on one game with one bookie. Plus we gotta set up in a nice apartment someplace, rent a limo, flash a few bucks around the bars and nightspots a little bit. . . . Shit, you can't be serious."

"Reckon I am, Billy," Williams said. "That's all the money I can get for it. Plus expenses, of course."

"Oh, man. That's no good. I mean, we gotta take down *fifty* of these guys if you wanna make a dent in this thing."

"Yeah, I know, Billy. I'm sorry, but that's how it is." Knowing his man, Williams then added slyly, "So if you wanna back off, I want you to know I'll understand."

Billy glowered. "Just don't let nobody get in my way, John," he said. "And don't push me neither. I'm gonna stay with this thing until I *get* you fifty. I got bookmakers we can bet up to fifty grand. But if I gotta get 'em with a lousy thirty-five hundred, then watch how I do it."

He did it by changing his name and occupation to Billy Clyde Walker, international arms dealer; renting a swanky two-bedroom apartment in Spring Valley; hitting town in a rented Lincoln Continental with his partner Fred Collins, aka Cochran, and using his local "associate" Jeff Coleman, who was into guns as well as swimming pools, to fix them up with a couple of local bookmakers so they could bet a few dollars on football games. Coleman was none too keen to extend this service, but, knowing how much Billy now knew about him, he could hardly refuse.

Starting small—necessarily—Billy and Cochran kept themselves afloat by picking football games in which they could bet both teams to win (with different bookmakers!), so that at worst they would more or less break even. But with Billy's feel for football, which seemed to pay off only when he was working a law-enforcement sting and never for himself, they quickly drew ahead. Within a month, they were betting up to twenty-five thousand dollars a weekend, and Coleman's four or five bookie friends had been joined as targets by a dozen more.

"We got lucky," Billy recalls. "I'd bet one way with one guy, another way with another guy, and try to catch a point off line, and maybe catch a middle or something so we'd have plenty to play with. Ultimately, we ran it up to close on eighty thousand a week, and the guys in the task force couldn't believe it. Me and Fred were out on the town every night drinking champagne. And Jeff Coleman was getting madder and madder with me because I kept pushing him all the time. 'Come on, I know you're into guns,' I'd say to him. 'Get me some gun dealers.'

"That was our business—guns and cocaine. Fred and me wanted to show those people, the bookies, that we were *bad* motherfuckers. One night we were out with Coleman drinking up pretty good and showing our guns to some guys at the Inn of the Tower—I don't even remember who they were now—but I know we told Coleman to take a walk. He's already pissed off at me because I've been leaning on him all evening to get me a dope dealer—like, as an act of contrition—and now he tells Cochran he's had enough of my shit. He's gonna fucking blow me to pieces. And Fred says, 'Oh, okay. Go ahead.'

"So Jeff goes home, gets this bomb out of his safe, drives back, and puts it under the front seat of the Lincoln Continental. Fred's sitting there behind the wheel, waiting for me, and just watches him do it. Doesn't say a word. Finally I come out and get in the car beside Fred and we drive off. Like me, he's got a real snootful, but holds it like a gentleman. Me, I can't wait to get to the bathroom. I start squirming around, and Fred says, 'Don't do that. You're sitting on a bomb.' Like he's telling me I got a crumb on my lip. So I take a look. And I *am*."

This is one of Billy's favorite stories, and anyone who doubts the truth of it can ask Fred Cochran for confirmation (although he insists Billy was too drunk to remember the details), or Jeff Coleman, who recalled the incident clearly when reminded of it.

"Yeah, I got it out of the safe and I stuck it under the seat."

"Fred let you do that, huh?" said Billy.

"Yep."

Billy laughed uproariously. "Why did Fred let you do that fur?"

"We was all drinking," said Coleman, and Billy laughed even louder.

Besides the bomb, as a result of Billy's pressure that night, Coleman also gave him Vito, the cocaine dealer he had asked for, thereby thwarting an armed invasion of Haiti.

The firm of Walker & Collins had put on such a convincing show that, besides winning the hearts and minds of bookmakers, it was soon having to fend off propositions from buyers and sellers in the illegal arms trade. Much to his sorrow, Cochran had to refuse a consignment of ten thousand stolen .45 caliber semi-automatic pistols for want of money and manpower to pursue the offer, and to keep their cover story going without actually doing any business in guns, he often had to improvise wildly. Would-be customers or suppliers were reluctantly turned away because they were too small for them to handle profitably or too big for them to handle efficiently or because they were fresh out of Cobra gunships. But Vito was different.

Vito called from New York, where he had an office in the Empire State Building, as agent for a group of Haitian exiles in Florida who were planning their own Bay of Pigs to overthrow the repressive regime of "Baby Doc" Duvalier. They were interested in buying a thousand M-16 automatic rifles, phosphorus bombs, TOW missiles, machine guns, and other equipment, but they were having trouble converting Haitian money into U.S. dollars. They were working on that in Switzerland, but meanwhile would Billy be interested in bartering weapons for coke?

Billy was very interested indeed. But he could foresee problems when it came to the exchange of merchandise. He told Vito he would be glad to supply the weapons his clients needed, but to keep the bookkeeping straight, he would prefer to handle the deal as two separate transactions. First, he would buy the coke at the going rate, and then Vito could use the money to buy the arms. No doubt scenting an extra commission, Vito readily agreed, and Billy called the FBI to find out if it was interested in a five-kilo coke deal with political overtones.

"Oh, come on, Billy," said Krinsky. "Cut it out. We're kind of busy right now."

As there was no way of handling the case in Dallas without upsetting the bookie-busting program, Billy had to deal with Vito in New York, but he had never worked there before. To line up a suitably high-level contact in the New York Police Department, he called Peter Gallagher, a friend of John Regan's in the Massachusetts Strike Force, who said he knew just the man: Lieutenant Jack Ferguson, with the Intelligence Division of the NYPD. He promised to speak to Ferguson right away, brief him on Billy's credentials, and have him stand by for Billy's call.

Ferguson was another kindred spirit.

"Hey, kid," he said. "You want me to put my ass on the line and I don't even know you."

"Your ass is safe with me, Jack," said Billy.

"Well, you come highly recommended, so I guess it's okay. What's this all about?"

Billy told him. He also told him he wanted to do it on Thursday because he was rather busy.

"*Thurs*day?" Ferguson laughed. "Come on, Billy. You gotta give me time to get you open as an informant. When are you coming in?"

"Thursday," said Billy. "We'll take him down Thursday night and do the paperwork Friday morning before I fly back to Dallas. Lemme call Vito now. I'll set it all up and come back to you."

He turned on his tape recorder and telephoned Vito in his office.

"Billy? I been waiting your call."

"You're a tough man to reach," he said. "Listen, that price is a little bit too high."

"I got something better also."

"What kind of a price are you talking now?"

"Sixty."

"Sixty?"

"For you, right?"

"Right. Can I get four at one time? I got the cash. We'll use two rooms in any hotel you want to use. But I want to make one transaction. I'm gonna have somebody with me because on account of that much money, you know? But you won't see him. He'll be in the other room. And these people wanna have a little taste."

"No problem," purred Vito. "I wouldn't let you do it without doing that."

"What percentage is it, Vito?"

"Oh, beautiful. Top, top. Eighty, eighty-five."

"Okay, now here's what I want to do. Follow my instructions now. I want to set it up for Thursday of this week. And I'm not gonna call you no more till I get there."

"Listen, I'm ready. I am *ready*."

"Okay, I want to do it all at one time. I don't want to go to your office. I don't want to see nobody. I want everything done at one spot."

"That's it. Listen, I am ready. I am waiting for you."

"Okay. You can bring somebody with you if you have to."

"Don't worry about that. I don't have to do that. I know what I'm doing."

"You know what you're doing?" Billy shook his head. They had never even met. "Okay. I'll have the money and everything ready. I don't wanna have to make a lot of changes."

"It's *you*," said Vito. "Only. Billy, I'm ready."

Lieutenant Ferguson was ready, too. When Billy checked in on Thursday afternoon, he was agreeably surprised to find everything set up. As Vito had left the choice of hotel to Billy, Ferguson had taken three adjoining rooms in the Hyatt on Forty-second Street: one for himself and his recording equipment; Billy's room, hooked up with hidden cameras and microphones; and a third room, also wired, in which Billy's "partner," a police undercover agent, would wait to receive his "taste" of Vito's merchandise before handing over a quarter of a million in cash.

"Please," said Ferguson. "I'm way out on a limb here. Don't fuck up."

There was nothing like an implied slight to his competence to spur Billy into pushing his luck. When Vito called up from the lobby, Billy went down in the elevator to fetch him. Standard practice. Waiting in a hotel room with a lot of money for a doper he had never met before could prove unhealthy if the guy forgot to mention he had brought a couple of friends with machine guns. But if Vito had a rip-off in mind, he hardly needed any help. He was bigger even than Kearns or Kelly. Billy's hand disappeared into his when they greeted each other, and the elevator settled an inch as he stepped inside.

Safely back in his room, Billy introduced him to the police undercover agent posing as his partner, fixed Vito a drink, and fenced around with a little preliminary small talk, trying to draw him out about his Haitian clients and giving Ferguson a chance to adjust his recording levels before they got down to business. But as soon as Vito produced his package, Billy could see it was much too small to contain four kilos.

"What the fuck's this?" he demanded, puffing himself up and turning red. "What the fuck you trying to pull here?"

"Me?" Vito was astounded by his sudden fury. "Nothing. You said your man wanted a taste so I brought a key."

"Yeah? Well, you just blew the whole deal," bellowed Billy, picturing the consternation in the next room. "I told you how this had to go down. All at one time. One shot. No changes. So take it back and fuck off."

"You don't want it?"

"You can stick it up your ass." He got up to show him the door.

"Hey, Billy, take it easy," said the undercover agent uneasily. "He misunderstood you, that's all. No big deal. Vito can leave that one here while he goes for the other three. Right, Vito?"

"Well, I—"

"Vito, you told me four keys," Billy ranted on. "I brought cash for four keys. Either come up with the four or don't waste my fucking time."

"Hey, I'll get it, man. But you gotta understand—"

"No, Vito. *You* gotta understand. Either you got the four or you got nothing to say to me. Go show him the money."

"Billy, I got it, I got the four, okay?"

"Then where is it? What the fuck's wrong with you? You wanna see the money? Show him the money."

After Vito had seen the money, Billy let him go, and waited for the others to join him.

"You sonuvabitch," said Ferguson amiably. "Suppose he doesn't come back."

"Relax. You got a tail on him, don'cha? You got the tapes?" Billy poured himself another drink. "This way, he'll lead you right to the stash. Then he'll come back with the four. Don't worry about it."

"He didn't even *want* to see the money," said his "partner."

"Didn't haveta," Billy said complacently, and they left him to it.

After a couple of hours with no word from anybody, he began to wonder, but then Ferguson called from the lobby.

"Come on down and have a drink, Billy," he said. "It's all over."

They had followed Vito to his stash on Staten Island, allowed him to leave with the four kilos before raiding the place, and then arrested him in the hotel as he was getting into the elevator.

The next morning, Ferguson took Billy downtown, opened him as a NYPD source under the code name of Paul Revere, paid him four thousand dollars, and put him on a plane. By late afternoon, Billy was back in Dallas calling a new batch of bookies for their line on the weekend games. And for once, Jeff Coleman was glad to see him. Bomb or no bomb, in recognition of his part in setting up the Haitian bust, Billy gave him half the reward, the other half just about covering his expenses. It was the kind of operation he most enjoyed: short, sharp, and surgically precise.

Although Ferguson was not much interested in Haitian politics, the exiles plotting to overthrow Duvalier were set back severely by the arrest of their arms-purchasing agent and the still more serious loss of four kilos of near-pure cocaine. Before they could replace either one, word filtered through to the FBI that Florida's Haitian refugees were up to something, and that Billy was somehow involved. Weeks after Vito's arrest, the Bureau's office in Miami called him down to explain what he knew to Special Agent Tom Dowd and other interested parties.

His round-trip air fare to Miami, hotel bill, meals, taxis, and incidentals amounted to a little over $750. When he asked for reimbursement in Miami, the FBI office advised him that the paperwork had been sent to his contact agent in Atlanta, Art Krinsky. When he asked Krinsky for the money—many times—he was told, many times, that the Miami office should have paid him while he was there. In the end, he received nothing from either office, but he was getting used to that.

He was also getting used to having the plug pulled on hugely successful undercover operations for want of a few dollars. After three months' work with Fred Cochran in Dallas, they had assembled enough evidence to arrest twenty-seven bookmakers, were betting around $80,000 a week to snare more, and owed their victims about $140,000, which they had no intention of paying. Billy reckoned he could stiff them for about three more weeks before the roof fell in, by which time he hoped to corral about fifty defendants in all. But then Sergeant John T. Williams called him at home.

"Billy, I'm going to break it to you the way it was given to me," he said. "Fred's boss, Captain McWhorter, threw a shitting fit when we told him what we planned to do. There's a ten-thousand-dollar limit on it, and that's it. They're gonna bet football games Friday evening—Fred's gonna get in and bet whatever he can, and that's the way they're gonna go with it. McWhorter is against taking a shot at them with Fred because he's afraid that Fred'll get hurt if they come to collect. I think you've done a fantastic job, Billy, but that's the way they told me it's gonna have to be."

Billy bit his tongue. It wasn't Williams's fault.

"John," he said, "I got bookmakers we can bet up to fifty thousand—guys who lay off in Vegas. I got guys like Jimmy Cole, who runs the Inn of the Tower. He's Dallas manager for Caesar's Palace—in Vegas *and* Lake Tahoe—and they say, 'Let's throw the rag in'? John, I'm confused. I don't understand these people."

"I know, Billy. I told him. If we had the money, you could bring out twice as many. but he says he's worried about Fred."

"Well, he can probably tell Fred what to do but he can't tell *me* what to do. I'll take a shot and just get outa town with 'em. Because the only person that can get hurt in this whole thing is *me*. . . . The weight comes back on *me*."

"That's why I called you at home," Williams said earnestly. "We want to give you a head start. Get your money from these people and then get going. Get to where you're not going to be in jeopardy. That's my feeling on it, Billy. I want to try to take care of you."

It was not only frustrating but dangerous. After the task force pulled the plug, at least two contracts were put out on Billy Clyde Walker and Fred Collins, although the bookmakers concerned were quick to change their minds when Collins paid them a visit to explain who he really was. As for Billy, there were now so many people looking to kill him, a couple more hardly made much difference.

For Helen's peace of mind, as he was away so much, he had the latest in laser alarm systems installed, and was glad he did when someone started shooting out the streetlight in front of his house. Every time the tube was replaced, the unknown marksman would shoot it out again, which made Billy particularly circumspect in his comings and goings after dark. Even during the day, his antennae would tingle at the sight of an unattended van on his quiet, residential dead-end street, but he was not about to relocate again.

As soon as warrants could be issued, six teams of officers from the Texas Department of Public Safety, the Organized Crime Task Force, the IRS, and the Dallas County Sheriff's Department harvested the pick of Billy's crop, arresting twenty-seven bookmakers and seizing their records. The cases against them were open and shut, but when they appeared in state court, all twenty-seven either took a walk or were slapped on the wrist with a small fine and probation.

"They were really doing some talking out there," Sergeant Williams told the Dallas press, echoing the time-worn complaint of cops who break their backs to catch violators of the law only to have the courts throw them back in the pool. "It's just a shame the cases didn't get prosecuted better."

Fred Cochran thought so, too. "The operation was a total success because of Mr. Breen's expertise and tireless work," he wrote in his report. "I personally can take very little credit for the operation since I simply followed the leads furnished by Mr. Breen."

Mr. Breen thought Fred Cochran was pretty good, too, but by then he was off on another tack. Through Lloyd Hough, his friend in the Metro-Dade Organized Crime Bureau, he had been teaching narcotics undercover tactics to groups of law-enforcement officers in Miami. And Lloyd Hough had recently introduced him to Maury Joseph, con man, smart ass, and all-around fink. . . .

"How long did you know Maury Joseph prior to August of 1982?" *asked David Breitbart, addressing himself at last to the substance of* *Billy's testimony against his client, Jesse "Doc" Hyman.*

"About two months."

"Did Joseph suggest to you that you get involved with Tom Duke in the financing of a nightclub called the Cowboy Palace?"

"In the beginning?"

"Did Joseph suggest to you that you get involved—"

"No, sir," said Billy wearily.

"Then how did you find out about the Cowboy Palace?"

"Maury Joseph brought me to New York," he explained carefully. *"He told me there were shylocks in New York, and in fact he bought me a new suit, put me on a first-class ticket, picked me up in a limousine, drove me to the St. Moritz Hotel. The next day I still hadn't heard or seen any shylocks. He met me in the morning for breakfast, at which time he took me to the Diplomat Hotel, and where Tom Duke was attempting to open the Cowboy Palace."*

As that seemed clear enough, Breitbart veered off to ask Billy about the sources of Duke's finance for the club, and after one or two questions along those lines, digressed again to consider Duke's personal habits.

"Did you have a feeling after working with Tom Duke that he was putting a lot of the money he borrowed for Cowboy Palace up his nose?"

"No, sir," said Billy. *"He was wasting it staying at the St. Moritz and on limousines."*

"He was wasting a great deal of money, is that right?"

"Yes."

"Did you encourage him to waste the money?"

"No, sir."

"You wanted the Cowboy Palace to open?"

"Yes, sir."

"You said that many times?"

"Yes, sir."

"That is so the Cowboy Palace would net $12 million a year?"

"If the Cowboy Palace had went a little longer," said Billy flatly, *"we would have 50 defendants instead of the twelve or fifteen we have now."*

And that was the truth, the whole truth, and nothing but the truth.

17

When not on the move—and Billy clocked 300,000 air miles in 1982—there were still old ghosts to trouble him beyond the reach of sleep at 3:00 A.M. or 4:00. He was not an introspective man by nature, but he would lie awake then and sometimes ask himself if he knew what he was doing, and had he gotten it right—questions that never occurred to him during the day.

He could feel his years now. Fifty-six of them. It had been a hard road from Guam, but he had survived—and with few regrets. Not even regrets. Second-guessing himself, Billy could see a few things now that he might have handled differently, a few temptations he might have resisted—even a few he wished he had *not* resisted—but that was unimportant. It had been a hard road, but where was it leading?

Sometimes, at 3:00 A.M. or 4:00, he could feel the lack of a destination, of movement toward some particular objective that would pull everything together and make sense of it. And that was frustrating because he knew the elements were all there, within reach.

Since declaring war on the bad guys, he had lifted some notable scalps. If he did nothing more, to have broken up the Dixie mafia by introducing Kearns, Kelly, and Margeson into the Sunbelt marijuana business like pike into a carp pool and then turning them into fugitives was no small triumph. What was missing was proof of any lasting damage to the *institutions* of organized crime. If he had an ambition left, it was to shoot the piano, not the player.

The FBI was the key to that. And the problem there was that, while Billy knew he needed the Bureau, the Bureau had yet to realize how much it needed him. Some agents, the kindred spirits, understood what it took to do this kind of work. The rest—midlevel management in particular—did not. With his neck stuck out in a roomful of bad guys, Billy could not afford to be patient and understanding with people who let him down. But at 3:00 A.M. or 4:00, he could sometimes bring himself to make allowances.

An agent's badge and credentials are backed by the virtually limitless resources of the federal government. Theoretically, nothing within the Bureau's criminal jurisdiction can stand against it, and that knowledge is both a weapon and a shield for its agents in the field (as well as a cause of considerable irritation among state and local cops). For agents behind a desk, however, it can also be a potent source of self-importance. From behind a desk, it is all too easy to confuse status with ability and, more critically, to identify personal ambition with the *Bureau*'s best interests.

Worse yet, in a huge, sprawling bureaucracy like the FBI, even the best professional managers are likely to concern themselves more with the smooth running of the machine than with the purpose and function of the machine. For graduates in law, accounting, and business administration who have never made an arrest in their lives, management concepts like "cluster theory" and "program purity" can hardly fail to take precedence over the untidy business of actually busting crooks inconsiderate enough to engage in more than one kind of crime and having no regard for the territorial integrity of the Bureau's divisional offices.

Unless real life is prepared to fit into their organizational charts or translate into double-entry bookkeeping, bureaucrats are not really interested in real life. And in the FBI's well-oiled machine, Billy Breen was pure grit.

Even so, he *needed* it. When he learned from Lloyd Hough that Maury Joseph could put him among the mob's loan sharks in New York City, he knew right away that, while here was a chance to crown his career by dismantling part of the basic structure of organized crime, he could never manage it without the Bureau behind him. He also knew, from past experience, that he could not always rely on it to see things *his* way, and being also wary of Maury Joseph, he tried to put any such large ambition out of his mind. He would go to New York to see if he could stiff some greaseball shylock for fifty thousand dollars to get the IRS off his back in Atlanta.

Maury Joseph had turned out to be a severe disappointment. Bright, smooth, personable, and a compulsive double-dealer even when it was against his own interest, he had won Billy over at first with a flattering deference to his wider experience and tantalizing glimpses of the Caribbean drug-trafficking network to which he was connected. Seeing all kinds of possibilities in taking him on, Billy arranged for Joseph to be opened as a source by the U.S. Customs Bureau, knowing that he already worked as an informant for Dade County and the FBI, so that they could share the rewards on offer for the interception of narcotics smugglers.

Six times in as many weeks Joseph called Billy from Jamaica or the Bahamas with details of inbound shipments; six times Billy passed the information to Customs, and six times the boats off-loaded at different places and times from those that Joseph had given him. The seventh call was to propose that they deliberately let the next one through in order to share in the profits, whereupon Billy ordered him back to Miami and arranged for Customs to close him out as an informant. He also brought Joseph's unreliability to the attention of the Miami FBI office, where he was registered under the code name Lone Ranger, but nobody seemed to care.

Joseph's next proposition, relayed through Lloyd Hough, concerned the mob-connected loan sharks. Joseph knew Billy as Billy Clyde Walker, a wealthy Irishman and property owner, and it turned out that this had more to do with their expense-paid trip to New York than Billy's prowess as an undercover operator. Wearing the new Adolfo suit that Joseph had bought him at a bust-out warehouse in Little Havana, and soaking up the privileges of first-class air travel, Billy tried to pump him during the flight for some idea of what he was getting into, but Joseph was not to be drawn, even into explaining his own role in the affair. To punish him for his reticence, after they checked into the St. Moritz hotel on Central Park South, Billy took him to Smith & Wollensky, where he ran up a three-hundred-dollar tab for lobster, steak, and champagne, which Joseph paid for in cash.

Something funny was going on.

Although dying to sleep off a skinful, Billy kept himself awake for half an hour after going up to his room, then went downstairs again and took a cab to the Hyatt Hotel on Forty-second Street, where he checked in under another name, leaving an early-morning wake-up call so that he could get back to the St. Moritz in time for breakfast. If Joseph was setting him up, then at least he would not be caught napping. And although nothing in his room appeared to have been disturbed when he returned, Billy's suspicions deepened again over coffee and croissants at Oscar's when he could still get nothing out of Joseph but double-talk.

Then the limousine that had brought them in from La Guardia reappeared to pick them up after breakfast. As Joseph had already missed out on better places for a hit than midtown Manhattan in the rush hour, Billy allowed himself to be taken for a ride, and had barely made himself comfortable before it was over. He followed Joseph out of the car and into the lobby of the Diplomat Hotel on Forty-third Street, just west of Sixth Avenue.

"This where they operate?" he asked doubtfully, waiting for the elevator. "The shylocks?"

"Yeah." Joseph laughed. "Yeah, you could say that."

They got out on the mezzanine floor, where he ushered Billy through a door marked COWBOY PALACE into a bedlam of hammering, sawing, shouting, and ringing telephones. The grand ballroom of the hotel, which might once have served as a set for a Fred Astaire movie, was being remodeled as the world's biggest country-and-western nightclub and discothèque, to designs apparently inspired by Pizza Hut.

Billy was impressed, although he refused to show it. He had a headache. He resented the mystery. He felt at a disadvantage. When Joseph steered him into a back office hung with pictures of movie stars and introduced him to a smooth-looking kid named Tom Duke, he was as prickly as a hedgehog.

"Heard a lot about you, Billy Clyde," said Duke, waving him to a chair. "Sit down."

About to sit, Billy stood up again.

"Hey, kid," he said. "Forget giving me orders, okay? Don't tell me what to do. Just tell me what the fuck I'm doing here."

Duke studied him for a moment, and decided not to take offense.

"Maury said you were the kind of guy who likes to get right to the point. Now I see what he means."

"Yeah, well, let's get hoofing with it. Sonuvabitch has been stalling me for two days. What's on your mind?"

Duke reminded Billy of an insurance salesman. And the best way to deal with one of those was to pressure the guy as he made his pitch, keep him off balance, break up his rhythm.

"Well, I'll tell you, Mr. Walker—"

"Billy Clyde."

"Billy Clyde. My problem is getting more money to finish remodeling this place. Most of it's done but there's still a lot of fitting out and furnishing to take care of, and I want to open before Christmas."

"Yeah? So?"

"So Maury says you're a wealthy man, Billy Clyde."

"Then Maury's wrong. And just Billy's enough."

"Okay, just Billy. But you own property, don't you?"

Billy looked at him suspiciously. "What's it to you?"

"Well, that could be the answer. All you've got to do is post your property as collateral. Then I can borrow on it and get this place finished. There's no risk. You'd still own the property. Or if you like, I'll buy it from you when the time comes, at *your* price. It's up to you."

"Wait a minute," said Billy. "You're losing me. Not so fast."

Duke smiled. "Well, basically it's very simple. If you sign the property over to me, I'll get a high appraisal on it, borrow against it, and then buy it from you at the appraised price when it's all over."

"No, no." Billy shook his aching head. "Something's wrong. I'm not gonna give you my property, Tommy. That's crazy. What's in it for me?"

"What's in it for you? A big fat profit, that's what. I'll be buying your property for more than it's worth."

"Yeah, listen to him, Billy," urged Joseph. "You can't go wrong."

"Maury, please," Billy said.

He was trying to spot the flaw. He knew where he was with guys who robbed banks or sold dope or handled stolen goods, but Duke was obviously one of these hotshot kids who could shuffle paper and turn it into money without hardly leaving the office. If this was on the level, he could maybe pay off the IRS with legitimate dollars.

"Okay. I got four pieces of property we can talk about," he said cautiously. "One is in Florida, with an IRS lien on it. One is in Dallas, and another one in Virginia. All family homes. Then there's a bar and lounge I got in West Covina, out in California."

"Uh-huh. How much is *that* worth?"

"Well . . ." Billy thought fast. "With the apartments up above, I guess around a million. Say nine-fifty."

"Uh-huh." Duke's boyish charm glazed over thoughtfully. "Can we do that one first?"

"No," said Billy. "First, I wanna see how this works. If I decide to get into it, we'll start with the place in Virginia." He had bought the house for Helen's mother. "And I can tell ya right now," he added, thinking of what they would say if they knew, "my wife is never gonna sign no papers unless it's done with attorneys. In a bank."

Duke chuckled sympathetically. "Don't worry about it, Billy. I'll handle that. We can have the documents notarized right here in the office and fix 'em up any way we want. Nothing can happen to your property. I got a title company takes care of that stuff. You can reconvey it back or whatever you like. How much do you think this Virginia place is worth?"

"Oh, fifty, maybe fifty-five thousand."

"Okay. Then we'll get it appraised for like ninety-five thousand. You'll make it over to me and I'll pay you thirty-five thousand up front out of the money I borrow against it and the rest with postdated checks. How's that?"

"Well . . ." Billy looked from Duke to Joseph and back to Duke. If the kid was on the level, this could be the answer. "I'll have to talk to my attorney."

"Sure." Duke could hardly have been more understanding. "Talk to him about those other properties, too."

"Yeah, well, let's see how we make out with this one. You get this money from a bank or what?"

"No, I got a finance company out on the island. Resource Capital. Excuse me." Breaking off as his receptionist put her head around the door, he followed her outside.

"Well, what do you think?" asked Joseph.

"I thought we were gonna take down a bunch of greaseball shylocks," Billy said. "What the fuck's going on?"

"You couldn't be closer," said Joseph. "Just do like Tommy tells you."

Billy did like Tommy told him.

When he flew back to New York a week later, the inflated appraisal of his Virginia property was already on Duke's desk. All that remained was a little more creative paperwork, a pinch of forgery, and they would be ready to cook the books at Resource Capital Group.

"Fine," said Billy. "First I talk to Resource Capital. Then we sign the papers."

The following day, Angelo drove them out to Long Island in the limousine, which Duke kept on permanent twenty-four-hour standby. No slouch himself at living it up, Billy was beginning to understand why Duke was strapped for cash. With an apartment in the St. Moritz, his basic expenses had to be five thousand dollars a week.

It also became clear that Duke's financial backers were less than impressed by his standard of living. After he and Billy had been kept waiting for half an hour in the reception area of Resource Capital's glass-walled headquarters in Lake Success, Billy walked over to the receptionist, who had already parried several requests to remind her employers that they were there, and patted her cheek.

"Hey, sweetie," he said. "Do me a favor. Tell those motherfuckers to get their asses out here or I'm gonna start kicking the doors in, okay?"

Evidently accustomed to relaying expressions of client impatience, she interpreted the message into her telephone, and moments later Billy was being introduced to Jesse "Doc" Hyman and Mel

Cooper, partners in Resource Capital; Al Albenga, Sr., and Al Albenga, Jr., mafia handymen, and a number of other muscular executives whose names he failed to catch. They were breathless and
irritable. As far as he could make out, they had just come from
beating up a client.

"Who the fuck do you think you are?" Billy demanded, jutting his
face into Hyman's. "You *never* make me wait."

"Oh, for Chrissake," said Cooper, turning to Duke as Hyman
recoiled. "Tommy, take him into the conference room and cool him
off, will ya? I had enough fucking aggravation for one day."

Business meetings at Resource Capital tended to be one-sided
affairs, with Cooper and Hyman informing their clients of what had
been decided while a floating caucus of sharp-suited observers wandered in and out in powerful auras of aftershave to make sure that no
liberties were taken with their employers' money. Discussion was
generally limited to allowing borrowers an opportunity to take it or
leave it.

The main item on the agenda for Tommy Duke's meeting was to
negotiate a further loan, using Billy's Virginia property as collateral.

"Okay, so what's the story?" asked Billy belligerently.

"All right, here's what we're gonna do for you, Tommy," Cooper
said, ignoring him. "We'll go fifty grand on that. At two percent. But
we're gonna want more stock, okay? Not a lot. Like another six
shares."

Duke shook his head, but said, "Yeah, Mel. Okay."

"And just so you don't get in over your head with the payments
before you get open," Cooper continued, "we'll take ten weeks' vig
off the top. Then you don't have to worry about it."

Billy looked at Duke expectantly, awaiting an explosion of protest,
but to his astonishment, the other just sighed and scribbled something on his pad, scoring it out immediately.

"Then there's the air conditioners," Cooper went on. "The guy
says he still didn't get paid yet. And that's after we worked out a
special deal for you. Now that ain't right, Tommy. So we'll take it
offa this one, okay? That's eighteen thousand, right?"

Duke nodded, and threw down his ballpoint. Billy gaped. They
were down to twenty-two thousand dollars, and still not a word from
the boy wonder.

"Okay. Then we got thirteen-fifty for the attorneys, and that's it."
Cooper did a quick calculation. "I make that twenty thousand six-
fifty you got coming, right?"

Duke sighed and shrugged.

"Okay." Cooper turned to Hyman. "Give the man his check, Doc."

Hyman opened a large corporate checkbook with a flourish and wrote out several Sterling National Bank checks while they all watched in silence. He then passed them to Cooper, who scrutinized each one before handing it on to Al Albenga, Jr.

"Okay, you cash these for him," Cooper said grandly. "And don't you charge him more than ten percent, you hear? He'll give you your money tomorrow, Tommy."

"*What?*" Billy felt he owed it to Duke to put a word in. For eighteen thousand dollars, the kid now owed them fifty thousand at 2 percent a week. "Here, gimme the fucking checks. I'll cash 'em myself. Tommy, you don't have to sit here and take that kinda shit. It's a fucking rip-off."

"Billy." Duke shook his head. "Stay out of this. It's none of your business."

The others were looking at Billy as though this was sound advice.

He whistled in disbelief. "Well, I gotta hand it to you, Doc," he told Hyman. "You got some operation going here, lemme tell ya. You and me oughta talk a little business."

Hyman looked him over. "Sure. What's on your mind, Billy?"

"In private."

Hyman continued to size him up. "Okay. We'll use my office."

Without consciously concluding that a middle-class dentist with a legitimate six-figure income potential was probably working the rackets because he got a bigger charge out of mixing with wise guys than with orthodontic patients, Billy came on to Dr. Jesse Hyman like a one-man Winter Hill Gang. There was nothing he hadn't done in his whirlwind career of wheeling, dealing, and stealing. He told Doc about "Buddy's," his mythical million-dollar lounge in West Covina. He dropped names. He hinted at investment opportunities and a network of associates who could handle anything. Did Hyman ever come into any—er—contraband? Like stocks, for instance? Or credit cards?

Funny he should say that, Hyman said. They'd just recently had to burn a bundle of securities because he couldn't unload them. Billy groaned in sympathy. But how about diamonds, Hyman wanted to know. They had a load of hot stones worth around $6 million—him, Mel Cooper, and a guy out in Cleveland named Curly Montana. Nobody messed with Curly. He was connected. If Billy was serious, if he wanted to see what he could do with the stones, Hyman would send his driver around to Billy's hotel in the morning with a gemologist's report.

Yeah, Billy said. Yeah, you do that.

They enjoyed their talk so much that they both snarled at Tommy Duke when he broke in to remind Billy that they had a dinner date at Rusty's. Billy wrung Doc's hand warmly, wished Mel Cooper his best, and tore into Duke as soon as he joined him in the limousine.

"What the fuck was that?"

Duke sighed, and pressed the button that raised the driver's partition.

"I told you to let *me* do the talking, Billy," he said. "Those are bad people."

"So am I bad people," howled Billy. "You take my property. They say, 'Here's fifty thousand on it.' I let you do the talking, and right away we're down to eighteen thousand. How the fuck you gonna pay me thirty-five thousand if you only got eighteen?"

"Billy, you don't understand. I need *cash*. I don't give a fuck how much I owe. I'm into those guys for like half a million already, and I couldn't care less. Whatever it takes to get the place finished, that's what I've got to have. If it costs ten or twelve thousand a week, fine—but I have to find the cash to cover that. Until I get Cowboy Palace open. Then I'll be taking a million a week, and this'll look like what it is. Chicken shit."

"Yeah, but suppose you *don't* find the cash, Tommy. Things could get a little hot."

"Not really." He looked out the window. "Mel and Doc get the money from some heavy people, but it's their responsibility. Anything goes wrong, *they're* the ones that get hit."

"You kidding me?" The kid might know about high finance, but when it came to mobsters he was talking to an expert. "Who we dealing with here? Who's putting up the money? The Gambinos?"

"Who knows? Doc's friend is Mike Franzese."

"Uh-*huh*." Franzese was a rising young capo in the Colombo family. "How about this Albenga—the older guy?"

Duke shrugged. "Somebody told me he ran with the Lucchese mob, but I don't pay much attention to all that mafia shit. Mel and Doc hang out with a whole bunch of wise guys. You know Jimmy Rotondo? He's supposed to be big in New Jersey."

"Yeah, he's big," Billy said. Rotondo was Sam DeCavalcante's underboss. "So it's everybody, right? They all get a slice of the pie."

"They're businessmen, Billy. I don't care how many gangsters I have to deal with. Soon as I get the place open, there'll be more than enough to go around."

"Yeah. Fine. But how about *now?*" Billy hugged himself internally. This was it. This was the big one. "How about my thirty-five thousand?"

"You'll get your money, Billy. I got other people, too. You'll see. In fact, you'll see tonight."

"Okay. But next time let *me* cash the checks. I'll do it for nothing."

Duke laughed. "You pay those in, Billy, and nothing is all you'll get. That's street money. They don't keep that in banks."

Back at Cowboy Palace, Billy presented Duke with a draft agreement drawn up by an attorney he had picked out of the Yellow Pages to protect his interests in the Virginia property. Briefly, it stipulated that Duke would buy the place for $95,000, with $35,000 down (plus two postdated checks for $5,000 each) and the balance in fifty weekly installments of $1,000, starting in two months; that he would not encumber it while the agreement remained in force without Billy's permission, and that Billy would receive 7 percent of the stock in Duke's company, to be held in escrow.

With a few trifling changes, Duke signed the document as though it were of no consequence (as, indeed, it turned out to be); Billy signed the papers making the property over to Duke; Duke forged Helen Breen's signature to the deed before having it witnessed and notarized, and they then adjourned for dinner at Rusty's Restaurant, on Third Avenue at Seventy-third Street. There they were joined by Maury Joseph, who, it now appeared, was not only an old friend of Duke's but also his principal fund-raiser, and two of Duke's other "partners," Butch Gorgone and Charlie Diverna, who, like Billy, were also putting up assets for Duke to exploit in his hunger for cash.

They seemed like nice kids (except for Joseph, who was neither), but Billy found it hard to connect with them. There was no shared experience to draw on, nothing solid to get hold of. When he reached out, trying to be friendly, they squirmed through his grasp, like Jell-O. Even speaking the same language, they meant different things; their self-satisfied banter was full of insider allusions that meant nothing to Billy. He felt more at ease with Carlo Vaccarezza, manager and co-owner of the restaurant with Rusty Staub, of the New York Mets.

Here, at least, was character (if most of it bad). A made man in the Gambino family, who later became better known as chauffeur and bodyguard to John Gotti than as a restaurateur, Vaccarezza combined an interest in Resource Capital's loan shark operation with cocaine trafficking and sports bookmaking. This gave them plenty to talk about, but for Billy it proved an expensive conversation. To cultivate their acquaintance, he insisted that Vaccarezza take his football bets from then on, only to discover that the house rules stipulated a "dime" minimum wager (one thousand dollars).

This was to cost him plenty before the case was over, but his first big problem was getting it started. Convinced, now that he had seen how Resource Capital worked, that he held the key to an undercover investigation that could dismantle one of New York's most lucrative rackets and decimate the city's organized-crime families, Billy could hardly wait to get on a plane to Las Vegas and explain what he had to his friend Special Agent Joe Gersky. Knowing nobody in the FBI's New York divisional office, he was eager to check in there with the best possible introduction so as to waste no time trying to get past underlings to somebody who would appreciate the magnitude of what he had to offer.

"Looks like you got yourself a live one," Gersky agreed, after Billy told him all about it. "Get your ass back there and talk to my friend Jerry Lang. I'll give him a call, so he expects you, but I'll let *you* tell him the story. Jerry's a good agent, and he'll give you a fair shake."

Billy took the next flight back to New York, checked into the Hyatt at Grand Central Station ($165 a night), and called Special Agent Jerry Lang.

"Yeah, Joe called me from Vegas," Lang said, "and I sure wish I could help you, Billy. He says you got something big."

"Big ain't the word," said Billy. "This could be *giant.*"

"Wouldn't you know? I just got transferred to Connecticut. I'm in here clearing my desk. But I tell you what. You want to fill me in a little bit? If I know what it's about, I'll talk to some people here and get somebody to call you right back."

Having little choice, Billy told him what he had. Like Gersky, Lang was impressed. Don't go away, he said. Just wait by the phone.

Billy waited until the next day. Then he called downtown again, and after being passed around for a while, explained his problem to Special Agent Bob Matthews.

"Gee, I can't imagine what happened, Billy," Matthews said. "You want to tell me about it? I'll ask around and come back to you."

Billy told him about it, waited all day, and telephoned again, to be told that Matthews was working on it. Finally, three days after Billy's original call to Lang, Matthews called him back.

"You might as well go home, kid," he said kindly. "Nobody here knows any of the people you're talking about, or heard about Cowboy Palace. They don't see any criminal violations either, so you might as well forget about it. But thanks for your trouble, okay?"

"Fine," said Billy. "And fuck you, too."

He put in a call to Lieutenant Jack Ferguson of the New York Police Department's Intelligence Division, who immediately opened file #239 Cow Palace Investigation, Informant #322 "Paul Revere." The following morning, Detective Fred Elfine was assigned to the case and Billy took him into Cowboy Palace to start work.

"This here's my bodyguard," Billy told Duke. "He's with the Provisional IRA, so those greaseballs better not mess with him."

He was up and running with potentially the greatest undercover case in the history of organized crime.

To set the seal on it, he called Special Agent Rick Bakken in Las Vegas about the $6 million in stolen diamonds that Hyman, Cooper, and Curly Montana were trying to move, and sent him the gemologist's report.

"Looks like you may have hit lucky," Bakken said when he called back.

"Yeah? They're for real?"

"Oh, yes. Do this right, Billy, and you could just be looking at a six-hundred-thousand-dollar reward. How does that grab you?"

"Right where it tickles the most, Rick." For a rare moment, Billy was speechless before the inscrutable workings of providence. "How we gonna handle this? New York don't want it, so if I can get these guys to deliver in Vegas, we could take 'em down there."

"Well, Billy, that'd be great, if you can do it. There's a federal grand jury sitting right now in L.A. and we could take it to them."

"Fine. I wouldn't want to give *these* fucks the satisfaction."

"I know, Billy. I don't understand that at all. But if you need any help, there's a guy named Hanley in the Brooklyn/Queens office. I'll give him a call—just in case you need to talk to somebody. He's a good friend of mine."

"Listen, just make sure they spell my name right on the check."

Bakken chuckled. "Go get 'em, tiger."

Billy was happy for several days. Then early one morning he answered a knock at his hotel-room door and in walked Special Agent Art Krinsky.

"Surprise, surprise," he said, and for the second time in a week, Billy was struck dumb by the wantonness of fate.

"Helen told me you were in New York," Krinsky went on, detecting a certain lack of delight in Billy's manner. "I called you at home to say I was going to be in Manhattan on temporary duty, so when I heard you were here, I figured I might as well tell you in person."

Billy grunted unhelpfully, but the other sat down anyway.

"She also told me you were working on something big," he said.

If Billy had gone to bed earlier or had had his breakfast, he would probably have denied this, or at least played it down. Caught with too little sleep before his first cup of coffee, he not only agreed that he was, but explained exactly *how* big, and how far he had gone with it. Warming to his theme, he went on to suggest that the FBI's New York office would not recognize a major case if it bit them in the leg; that he preferred working with "good honest cops" than with agents who seemed more interested in chiseling him out of what they owed him than getting results, and that if he never worked with the Bureau again, it would be too soon. He then invited Krinsky to leave and went back to bed.

Two days later, Krinsky tried again, this time in company with FBI Supervisor Damon Taylor and Special Agents Dennis Madulla, Rick Sutter, and Walt Stowe, all from the Manhattan office. They were taking over the case, Taylor announced.

"You're not taking over shit," said Billy.

"I'm afraid you've no choice, Billy," Krinsky said. "It's been decided."

"Yeah? Well, *I* decided I won't work wit' yez. So get out of my room. I'm doing this with the NYPD."

"Take it easy, Billy. I went to see Ferguson. Told him you were my man in Atlanta. He agrees we got first call on you. He's ready to turn the case over to us."

"Yeah, well, I'm not." It was a bad blow. "I don't even wanna talk to yez, so you might as well fuck off."

Taylor frowned. "And you might as well be reasonable," he said. "Because we're in, Breen, whether you like it or not."

"Okay." Billy really did not like this little motherfucker. "Fine. You're in. Be my guest. But I'm going home, okay? I mean, *I* got in there undercover. *I* met all the people—but never mind. It's all yours."

He yanked open the door of the closet, but Taylor got in his way.

"You know I could charge you with obstruction of justice," he said.

After some heavy breathing, Billy unbunched his knuckles. "Will somebody get this idiot out of my room?" he asked plaintively.

They argued for an hour. They offered him $10,000, plus expenses, and he laughed. He had spent more than that already, he said. Not to mention pledging a piece of property worth $55,000 to find out how the Resource Capital shylocks worked their bait-and-switch scams. At this point, Taylor produced a letter for him to sign.

"What's this?"

"It's a waiver," Taylor said. "It says the Bureau is not responsible for your property. Sign there at the bottom."

"I'm not signing no paper," howled Billy. "What's the matter with you people? First you don't want the case, and tell me to go home. Then you *do* want it, but you're not responsible. I mean, gimme a break, will ya? Just get outa here. Leave me alone."

Stowe and Madulla then tried to persuade him to sign, urging him to trust them, and Billy almost choked. Recovering his breath, he began to tick off some of the reasons why he could never trust the Bureau, starting in Massachusetts, and when he again flatly refused to work with them, Krinsky had a muttered colloquy with Taylor, who shrugged and led his troops away.

The following morning, Krinsky tried again. He returned with

Walt Stowe, the only agent who had made any sense to Billy the night before, and after all manner of grumbles and protestations, he allowed them to take him to lunch. Behind all the storm and bluster, he knew as well as they did that in the end he would have to give way. There was nowhere else to take the case, and to have abandoned it at this point might well have meant abandoning his mother-in-law's house as well.

By dessert, he was ready to be persuaded. And when, for the first time in their association, Krinsky picked up the check, Billy finally agreed to work Cowboy Palace with Walt Stowe. But nobody else. Not Krinsky, not Taylor . . .

"Just you and me, Walt," he said. "We'll do it ourselves. No case agent or nothing. I don't wanna meet nobody."

"Well, on Sunday you're going to have to meet my wife," replied Stowe, "because we've got paperwork to do. We've got to show probable cause to get wires into Cowboy Palace and Resource Capital."

As for the $6 million in stolen diamonds, Supervisor Damon Taylor subsequently ordered Billy not to take the case to Las Vegas.

"You can't stop me," Billy said, but he was wrong.

The Las Vegas office declined to act on his information and closed the file. The Manhattan office did nothing more about it either and the case died.

"Mr. Brain, Breen—whatever it is," said Breitbart, digging deeper into Billy's role in Cowboy Palace, "did Agent Taylor tell you that if you wished to continue your relationship with the FBI, any criminal activity that you were involved in would have to be approved by the FBI and the United States Attorney's office in the Southern District of New York?"

"Never read it to me," he said flatly, familiar with the standard warning given to all FBI sources.

"Did he tell you that your activities must be in conformance and pursuant to Attorney General guidelines?"

"No, sir. Let me say my conversation with Damon Taylor was very short and sweet. When he pulled out a piece of paper and said, 'Sign this. The FBI is not responsible for your property,' I says, 'Goodbye.' "

"Did he tell you that the FBI does not sanction the possession of any illegal weapon or solicitation of any violent actions on your part?"

Billy was not quite sure what that meant.

"I never had a weapon," he said cautiously, which was true in the sense that he had never carried one on his person. But with gun-toting wise guys in and out all the time, he had kept a .38 concealed

in the pedestal of the conference-room table at Cowboy Palace in case of emergency.

"Did he tell you that if you wished to continue your relationship with the FBI in connection with the investigation of the Cowboy Palace that financial benefits from your participation could not and would not be sanctioned by the FBI?"

"He never told me that, no, sir." Not even Damon Taylor was as long-winded as that.

"Well, take a look at this document, sir," said Breitbart, holding out what appeared to be an FBI report of interview. "See if it refreshes your recollection with regard to the FBI talking to you on October 31."

"I will look at it," Billy said hesitantly. "I have never—he has never talked to me that way. No, sir."

Not for the first time, he found himself at a disadvantage as a result of his refusal to work with case agent Stanley Nye in the usual pretrial review of case documents.

"Take a look at it," urged Breitbart.

"Anything that is on there—I had very little conversation with Damon Taylor." Billy could see himself getting cornered into calling Taylor a liar.

"Look at it," Breitbart insisted.

"I don't care what this document says," said Billy stubbornly. "Damon Taylor had one conversation with me in the beginning, when Walt Stowe came in, and another in October—"

"LOOK AT IT," shouted Breitbart.

"Mr. Breen," said Judge Sand. "The sole question before you now is whether that refreshes your recollection of that conversation having taken place."

"This conversation—" Billy began, still trying to explain that he had locked horns twice with Damon Taylor and they were talking about the wrong occasion.

"Sir," the judge said firmly. "Does that refresh your recollection, yes or no?"

"No, sir."

Judge Sand nodded. "Next question."

Breitbart grimaced. "Did you know that if you were working as an informant for the FBI you could not make money?"

"There was no money to be made. Especially at the Cowboy Palace, because I already lost a piece of property."

"You went into it to make money, didn't you?"

"Absolutely not. I went in to pay $49,000. . . . I was told there was a shylock up in New York City, that I could get $50,000. I owed

$49,000 to the IRS, and I was going to sell the first piece of property for that money. So I could pay the IRS."

"You believed Maury Joseph?" jeered Breitbart. "A smart guy like you?"

"What's your name?" Billy barked.

The other blinked. "You've forgotten already?"

"I have. Like you forgot my name. You said, 'Breen, Brain, whatever it is.' "

"All right," Judge Sand said patiently.

"Mr. Breen, did you believe Maury Joseph?" repeated Breitbart.

"I never believed Maury Joseph or Tommy Duke."

18

Even so, Billy pledged his Texas house to show Special Agent Walt Stowe how Resource Capital operated.

This was Billy's first real exposure to money manipulation, and by the time he had learned enough about business finance to see through Duke's fancy real-estate jargon, he was in too deep to extract himself gracefully. That was Billy's mistake, born of inexperience with tricky paperwork and larcenous yuppies. Duke's mistake, born of inexperience with street-wise operators of the old school, was to imagine that a fine-spun web of deceitful patter would serve to keep an "investor" of that sort in check. Billy's "bodyguard" Fred Elfine, of the Provisional IRA, had scarcely been replaced by his IRA "accountant" Walt Johnson, aka Special Agent Walt Stowe, before Billy was swaggering around Cowboy Palace dishing out orders, riding herd on Duke's mob-connected suppliers and contractors, and generally acting as though he owned the place.

Contrary to what he had been told originally, the FBI *did* have files on Doc Hyman and Mel Cooper, which made it all the more remarkable that the New York office should have turned Billy away without first checking its own records. It was only when Stowe uncovered the earlier reports that he saw the true potential of the case, with Billy already on the inside, and pressed for permission to work it.

If it had been anyone but Stowe, Billy would probably have gone home, property or no property. Too loyal to the Bureau to be a true kindred spirit, and yet too resourceful an operator to be a true company man, Stowe was the ideal candidate for the job, particularly as he had to double up as case agent and take care of the paperwork as well. In fact, Billy's only complaint about his new partner was that Stowe's general workload kept him out of Cowboy Palace too long and too frequently, but he was in no position to carp, for he too was away as often as not, either testifying somewhere against the Piccolo crew or working on the Kerr/Wood case in San Antonio or rolling up bookies in Dallas or taking down dopers in Fort Lauderdale.

When he *was* in town, he would put in a full day at Cowboy Palace, starting around 9:30 A.M., often before Duke himself put in an appearance, and sometimes finishing as late as 3:00 the next morning. To begin with, his aim was simply to identify mob-linked figures among Duke's visitors, to log the comings and goings of Hyman, Cooper, and other "executives" in Resource Capital, and to make notes of meetings he managed to muscle his way into or of conversations he was not supposed to overhear. But as he got to know Duke's associates better, he also began to take the initiative, engineering pretexts to call them on the telephone with his tape recorder running and lure them into compromising admissions.

Prominent in the rogues' gallery he and Stowe compiled in this way, in addition to those already identified at Resource Capital, was Benedetto Aloi, of Queens, a capo in the Colombo family; Tommy Pecora, of the Jersey mob; Tony Napoli, a capo in the Genovese family; Jimmy Rotondo, number two to Sam "The Plumber" De-Cavalcante; Curly Montana, linked with contract murders in Cleveland and Chicago, and a procession of "salesmen" from mob-linked suppliers of meat, provisions, liquor, linen, fruit and vegetables, and most other catering necessities.

Most significant of all, perhaps, was Resource Capital's link with Michael Franzese, the young, college-educated capo in the Colombo family who was thought to have served as the model for Michael Corleone in Mario Puzo's *The Godfather* and who typified, for many, the new breed of yuppie mobster coming in off the streets to the corporate boardroom. Billy established the connection one Monday night by following Doc Hyman and Mel Cooper to the Casablanca, in Syosset, Long Island. Every Monday night, Franzese took over the restaurant to entertain his cronies and business associates. By invitation only.

It was dangerous work. Two previous government sources, passing information on Hyman and Cooper in connection with other crimes, had been savagely murdered, and on two separate occasions a potential witness against their associate Carlo Vaccarezza had been knocked down and killed by a tow truck running a red light. All that stood between Billy and something similar was the fragile discretion of Maury Joseph, who, as Billy well knew, was always open to any reasonable offer, and Tommy Duke's ever-more-precarious calculations of advantage.

From a security angle, Billy was least worried by Duke, whom he had grown almost to like, in spite of his interminable cleverness and extravagance with other people's money. So far unaware of the double role Billy was playing in Cowboy Palace, Duke made no secret of how he had been drawn into dealing with Resource Capital or of his confidence in beating Hyman and Cooper at their own game. Unable to raise the capital he needed from conventional sources, he had swallowed their bait-and-switch tactics with his eyes open, or so he claimed, and accepted the offer of a $440,000 loan without collateral as cynically as it was put forward.

As expected, this had been followed up immediately with a second agreement covering short-term "interim" financing while the long-term arrangement was being "negotiated." These "emergency" loans, of course, had to be collateralized with stock and pledged properties in view of the commercial risk, and were rather more expensive than conventional finance: 2 percent per *week*! With other little extras, this added up to weekly juice payments of around $12,000, and a powerful incentive to forge documents and signatures.

Having missed a couple of payments before Billy arrived on the scene, Duke had not only been physically threatened by the younger Albenga but punished by having his juice extracted in advance, which explained Duke's meek acceptance of Cooper's terms at the closing Billy attended. Another new rule was that before any cash was handed over, less 10 percent for check cashing, suppliers and workmen hired by Doc Hyman for Cowboy Palace had to be paid first.

Billy's sympathy for Duke was muted, however, by his own difficulty in collecting the payments due on his property. The first was to have been paid the day after their meeting at Resource Capital, but Duke stalled and stalled until one morning at Cowboy Palace, Billy realized that Duke had paid off Corky Pecora, the carpet man, with *his* money.

"No," he yelped, yanking up the newly laid carpet.

Pecora gaped. "What are you *doin'*?" he gasped, unable to credit such anarchy.

Slightly taken aback himself, Billy looked around for support and beckoned to John Johnson, boss of Duke's all-black squad of security guards, with whom he had already reached an understanding.

"You ain't laying no more carpet in here, Corky," he said. "Not till I get this straightened out." And he went to find Duke, confident that no more carpet *would* be laid until he told the guards it was okay.

In his first day in Cowboy Palace with Walt Stowe, Billy had taken Johnson aside for a little talk.

"Look, I'm one of the owners," he had told him, "and I don't want any problems. I know you guys don't get along too well with Italians, but you do with the Irish. It's different in Boston. We're the IRA. Any trouble and you're gonna see the IRA *in* here."

"Oh, no," Johnson had said. "No, no, no. You won't have no trouble. Who needs problems? I don't need problems."

"Right. Then you won't have none. But you're on *my* side if any shit comes down."

"Gotcha."

Johnson had then brought in one of his men, a tough young ex-Marine, and told him to watch Billy's back at all times whenever he came to Cowboy Palace. Following instructions, the guard was just outside the door, watching, when Duke stalled Billy again. The money had finally come through, he conceded, but it was in his strongbox back at the hotel. He would bring it to Gallagher's when they met for dinner that night.

At Gallagher's that night, with Maury Joseph and Butch Gorgone, Duke told Billy it was too dangerous to carry that kind of money around. He would have it for him at the St. Moritz after dinner. They then tried to drink Billy under the table, or at least into forgetting what Duke had promised, but drunk as he was, Billy could still remember he was broke, what with living in one hotel and sleeping in another, and flying in and out of New York all the time. When they left the restaurant, he swung Duke up against the wall and considered him gravely, nose to nose.

"I want my money, Tommy," he said with perfect clarity, and Duke sighed.

The ever-faithful Angelo and his limo (both belonging to Tony "Tony Nap" Napoli, Billy had discovered) drove them back to the St. Moritz, where Duke removed a package from his safe deposit box, trying to screen the rest of its contents with his body but not quickly enough to prevent Billy from seeing that it was full of money.

"Thank you, Tommy," he said, swaying gently as he accepted the package. Although tempted to rip it open, he knew he was drunk enough to fumble the money all over the floor, and so disdained the discourtesy. "Thank you, gentlemen," he added, acknowledging the others, "and good night."

His thanks and farewells were both premature. When he counted the money—several times—in his room, it amounted to just seven thousand dollars. Now very sober indeed, he rode the elevator up to Duke's floor and kicked at his door until he opened it.

"Where's my money, Tommy?" he asked gently, pushing him back inside. "And don't you say *nothing*," he went on, rounding on Butch Gorgone, who was sitting at the window and seemed about to answer for him. "Don't you say one word to me, Butch, unless you got wings. Because you're just liable to fly right out that fucking window. I want my money, Tommy. And I want it *now*."

"Billy, there *is* no more money," said Duke, boyishly frank. "You saw me. I had to pay some of the guys to keep working."

"Tommy, you got a boxful of money downstairs," he said. "I saw it myself. Just gimme my money for my property."

"Billy, it's late. I'm tired. Aren't *you* tired?" Duke yawned in his face to show how tired he was. "I've had it. Don't make me go down again. Take that until tomorrow. I'll give you the rest in the morning."

By the time they had gone around the course again, they were all yawning. Sooner than drop where he stood, Billy made a few more belligerent noises and teetered back to his room. But not to sleep. His instinct for survival was still srong enough to get him around to the Helmsley before he keeled over for the night.

All he forgot to do was leave a wake-up call. By the time he resurfaced, Duke was nowhere to be found, and Billy had barely enough time to catch his flight to Dallas for a meeting that had almost slipped his mind.

On returning to New York a few days later, he found Duke in deeper trouble than ever. With the weekly vig payments now approaching fourteen thousand dollars, Hyman and Cooper had put Anthony Capo, Jr., into Cowboy Palace to watch out for their interests. Related to Jimmy Rotondo, he was the kind of petulant, ambitious young hood guaranteed to get straight up Billy's nose. Like a near-grown puppy challenging the pack leader, he questioned Billy's presence in Cowboy Palace as soon as they met, and after backing him off with a flea in his ear, Billy suddenly found himself not so much gunning for Duke as rooting for Duke.

But for this confrontation he might never have considered pledging a second piece of property. With Maury Joseph backing him up, Duke now offered to pay $180,000 for Billy's Dallas home, against a true valuation of $150,000, plus the balance of the $35,000 down payment overdue on the Virginia property.

For the second time, Billy allowed himself to be persuaded. He had a contract drawn up to cover the deal, which Duke signed as readily as he had signed the first one, and later admitted cheerfully, in the presence of Special Agent Walt Stowe, that he had forged all the papers required on the property when placing it as collateral with Resource Capital. Concluding the matter in a shower of post-dated checks and gilt-edged promises, he then allowed Billy to advise him on how to deal with Capo and Capo's bosses at Resource Capital.

This took the form of post-alcoholic suggestion. After getting Duke and Charlie Diverna very drunk at Studio 54, Billy fixed them with a solemn gaze and made Duke repeat after him, "I'm not paying any more money to Cooper or Hyman or anyone else."

"No, no, Tommy—that's no good," Billy said. "I can't hear you. You gotta make it *count*. You don't wanna pay no more juice till you're open, right?"

"Right."

"And when you're open, you'll pay 'em catch-up money, plus anything they want, right?"

"Right. Anything. Anything they want, I'll pay 'em."

"Okay. Then grab my hand and hold on. Scream after me—and I mean *scream*, Tommy—*I'm not paying any more money to Cooper and Hyman.*"

"*I'm not paying any more money to Cooper and Hyman,*" screamed Duke obediently.

"That's better. When Mel Cooper comes tomorrow morning with Doc Hyman, what are you gonna tell 'em, Tommy?"

"*I'm not paying you any more money,*" screamed Duke.

"Okay. You got it."

Just to be sure, Billy made him scream it again at regular intervals for the rest of the evening.

The following morning, as soon as Cooper and Hyman arrived at Cowboy Palace, Duke said he was not paying them any more money, and Capo gave him a slap that almost removed his head from his shoulders.

Having anticipated something of the sort, Billy caught the whole incident on tape (Walt Stowe had impressed upon him the legal requirement to show wherever possible that menace and violence were being used in the collection of unlawful debts). And while neither he nor Stowe had been present, the slap nevertheless constituted a clear threat to Billy's authority as part owner of Cowboy Palace, not to mention his standing in Duke's eyes. After a series of heavy phone calls, a round-table meet was set for Rusty's Restaurant that night to thrash out the whole situation.

The guest list comprised Hyman, Cooper, the two Albengas, Anthony Capo, Jr., Billy, Walt Stowe, Duke, Maury Joseph, and Charlie Diverna, while the uninvited guests included several carloads of FBI agents deployed around the restaurant with enough firepower to destroy the Upper East Side.

Wearing a Nagra body recorder, Billy did his best to steer the discussion the way he wanted it to go, although this was far from easy with so many prima donnas at the table. At the trial, the tape he made that evening probably inflicted more damage on the defendants than any of the other 119 tapes admitted as evidence. It was October 27, his fifty-sixth birthday, and an odd way to celebrate.

The Albengas were the first members of the Resource Capital team to arrive, and Billy seized the chance, as one street guy to another, to see if he could win Al, Sr., over to conceding what was right and thereby gain a little leverage. They agreed that it was not right to humiliate Duke the way they always did by making him kick his heels for hours whenever they sent for him.

"They're fucking around," said Albenga. "There's another deal that comes in . . . if Mel can make three cents more somewhere else, Tommy's gonna wait five hours. That's all."

"Al, somebody should straighten these guys out," Stowe suggested.

"Nobody can. Nobody can."

"Lemme ask you a question," said Billy. "When *he* has his money coming, and it's vig or anything else—"

"He's paranoid," Albenga agreed. "You're right, a hundred percent."

"If he has vig money coming, when does he want it? What time?"

"On the minute. I can't argue wit' ya."

"I have nothing more to say," said Billy, although that was not quite true. The idea was to lead the Resource Capital team into laying their whole scam out on tape in their own undeniable words.

"You're right," repeated Albenga. "I'm not disagreeing wit' ya. . . . I think that you should concentrate on going forward, and iron everything out. Once and for all."

"You know how they're gonna go forward?" Billy said. "I'm gonna tell ya how they *gotta* go forward. You're gonna give the guy money to go forward. And they're not gonna jerk him. They're not gonna do what Anthony did with him today, because it's not right. You know what they're doing to him? Let me tell ya what they're doing to him."

"They're grinding him out," said Albenga, who knew better than Billy what they were doing to Duke. "And it's not important money. You'll never accomplish nothing that way."

"He can't get done."

"I know that."

"They're taking it all," Billy said. "They're giving him a little bit and taking it all. Am I right or wrong?"

Albenga acknowledged that he was right, and proceeded to put still more distance between himself and the principals of Resource Capital by agreeing eventually with Stowe that they were trying to kick Duke down so that he could not pay.

"Now is that fair?" asked Stowe. "Is that decent?"

"In their philosophy, it's decent," Albenga said flatly.

"Then we're talk . . . Al, we're talking to the wrong guy, 'cuz we're all in agreement," said Stowe.

That was getting too cozy. "You don't understand," Albenga said, back-pedaling in case they got the wrong idea. "I'm telling you the way they are. They're tough to do business with. And they play a game of poker."

Billy tried to steer everybody away from the sensitive issue of loyalty, but Stowe persisted.

"What you're telling us," he suggested, "is that we're doing business with the wrong people."

"Unfortunately," agreed Albenga. "Hey, listen—if you could wipe yourself out, good. Fine. There's no hard feelings."

"Al, let me ask you—" Billy began, making a last-ditch try to change the subject before they lost his goodwill entirely.

It was too late. "Is there anyplace else you could go?" Albenga demanded. "Let's talk realistically."

Maury Joseph then blew the whole thing. "Come on, Al," he said, evidently feeling that his competence as Duke's financial adviser had been called into question. "You got a fucking hundred percent secured interest. Come on, this is *me* you're talking to, Al. I grew up on the street."

"So why don't you go get it?" Albenga demanded heatedly.

With Billy vainly trying to intervene, Joseph insisted six times that alternative sources of finance were available, and six times Albenga suggested he should "go get it."

"Al, let me ask you something," said Billy, but Albenga was furious.

"No, wait a minute," he snarled. "The man says he can go out and replace it."

"Why don't you . . . Al, why don't you sit there and . . . and . . ."

"I know what it is to go out and get money," Joseph said loftily.

"No, man," groaned Billy. "You're gonna create a monster."

"The stage the club's in right now," said Duke, speaking up for himself at last, "I get offers every day. Three months ago, no. You know? But we're also four days away from opening, and I don't need all this extra bullshit. I would like to see it finished first."

"If I felt the way you do," Albenga said, "I would go out and get the money. Say, 'Here, fellers. Here's what I owe you. Thanks and goodbye.' "

"If I felt the way *you* do," Joseph said recklessly, "I'd go around kissing everybody's ass and sucking everybody's prick."

Even Billy was silenced.

"Oh, no," Albenga said, after a pause. "No, no, no. I don't suck prick. I don't kiss anybody's ass."

"No, no, no," said Billy appalled. "No, no, no, no, no."

"See, you say the wrong thing," Albenga went on, ominously calm.

"Well, I—I'm only giving it back to you, pal." Joseph tried to laugh it off. "I ask you a question. You answer me straight. What would you do if it was *your* kid *Duke* slapped?"

"If it was *my* kid?"

"Yeah."

"I'd call you on it."

"That's it," said Joseph. "Case is closed."

He was wrong. Billy tried to get in again, but Albenga waved him off.

"Hold it," he said. "You want the answer? Go get a gun and kill Anthony."

Now they were all talking at once, but Albenga was not to be silenced.

"You're asking me what I would do, my friend? That's what *I* would do if anybody hit my fucking son. I'd kill 'em. Waddiya think of that?" Everybody tried to tell him what they thought of it but he ignored them. "Okay? You do the same thing. I'm giving you the okay. You got the balls to do it, then do it. If not—"

"Al, Al," said Billy.

"—you gonna get smacked again. All right? That's what you do."

"Al, sit down," Billy said. "Sit down."

"No, I'm giving 'em the green light. Go ahead and do it. Want me to bring the kid over here?" With the others, he had just noticed Capo at the door with Doc Hyman and Mel Cooper. "You want me to bring him, I'll bring him here to the table."

"Hey, Al, c'mon," said Stowe.

"If I was gonna go down to his level," Duke said unconvincingly, "I would have hit him back, wouldn't I?"

When the rest of the Resource Capital team approached the table, Duke, Joseph, and Diverna got up to leave, in protest at Capo's presence. Billy made a token attempt to persuade them to stay, but in fact their departure made it that much easier for him to steer the discussion into more productive channels once they had all calmed down a little.

"The bottom line is, we gotta get the joint open," said Stowe, trying to get everybody talking about the same subject. Billy was busy complaining to Doc Hyman about being made to wait for hours before anybody saw them, and Cooper was simultaneously explaining Capo's role in Cowboy Palace.

"Listen to me," Hyman began.

"If you want what's coming to ya," Billy was saying, "you guys gotta treat him right. Before you get your money, you gotta realize—"

"You don't understand something," said Hyman.

"—it's gotta open."

Hyman tried again. "We wanna . . . We went—"

"Got to open."

"—we went to a lotta people."

"We want it worse than anybody," Cooper said.

"We're on the hook to a lotta people for this money," said Hyman.

"That's what I'm saying," Albenga chipped in, on behalf of those people. "That you don't know the extent of what's going on there."

"We gotta answer to them," agreed Hyman.

"I understand," Stowe said, every inch the IRA accountant. "I understand that."

"And another thing," Albenga went on. "Between us, Bill, he deserved a crack in the face today."

"That's not so," said Billy virtuously, having engineered the whole incident.

"Al, he's under a lotta pressure," Stowe said.

"Believe me," Albenga said. "He was forgiven three or four times already because of the place."

This brought them back to Capo, his role at Cowboy Palace, and an earlier incident in which he had slapped one of the suppliers for demanding payment.

"He thinks—he, he thinks that I'm not gonna be there no more," Capo said, doing a fair imitation of the young Marlon Brando.

"Huh?" said Billy.

"Tommy. He thinks I'm not gonna be there."

"He's right," Billy said. "You're not gonna be there. You're not gonna be there."

"Hey, Anthony," Stowe said soothingly. "You didn't get on his good side, man."

Billy held up a hand. "Lemme . . . lemme tell ya—*no*body's gonna be there."

Capo ignored him. "Good side? I don't haveta get on his good side. I don't give a *fuck* about his good side."

"Lemme tell ya, Doc," said Billy, turning to Hyman. "Nobody's gonna be there. Nobody's gonna beat ya—I'll make sure you get the money. Nobody's gonna beat ya, but nobody has to be there. Lemme tell ya what happened. No, no—I gotta tell ya, and I'm not saying this because the kid's a nice kid. But he thinks—he says to the guy with the glass, 'I'll bust 'em on the wall before ya take 'em out.' "

"That's right," agreed Capo.

"No, no. That's not how you handle it."

Capo looked him over insolently. "Are you telling the story?"

"That's . . ." Billy bit down on his temper. "But you don't handle things that way."

"Number one," said Capo, "number one, you're not telling me how to handle things."

"Ah, Anthony, I have nothing more to say. I will tell you, it's *my* money. I'm gonna tell ya whether you like it or you don't like it."

"When—when the guy says you're gonna . . . when the guy says— is unreasonable and says, 'Well, I'm not gonna wait for my money,' what are ya gonna do?"

"I'm not even interested, Anthony."

"When the guy—when the guy . . ."

"Anthony," said Billy wearily.

". . . when the guys say to ya—when the guy says to ya . . ."

"Anthony, I'm not interested."

". . . when the guy says to ya, uh, 'Even if you give me the money, I'm not—I'm taking the mirrors off the wall . . .' "

"The guy was looking for his money," said Stowe, still playing the voice of reason. "Just like everybody's looking for his money."

"Everybody's uptight," Albenga agreed. "It's pressure. People owe you money, you get excited."

"You've got the picture. You gotta handle a guy easy when he's like that. Am I right, Al?"

Albenga shrugged. "Plus the same token—Billy, let me interject one thing—if a cocksucker came in over there to shoot somebody, he'd be the first guy to put his body up in front."

Capo nodded solemnly."No one wants—no one wants to believe that."

"That's for *sure*," Albenga added. "You understand?"

"Yeah, Al," said Billy, "but—"

"That's something you can't buy, that kinda loyalty."

"I know that, Al, but—"

"That's for sure. You understand?"

Capo stirred again. "No one wants—he don't want to believe that."

"Al, that's not—"

"So you can't buy that loyalty. You understand?"

"Al, he's loyal to you and Doc and Mel," said Billy. "Is he loyal to Tommy? Tommy got slapped."

"But he came in with a bad attitude the last two days."

"No, Al. I was there. I watch everything. Tommy didn't have a bad attitude."

"He came in with a bad attitude. Bitching about how they kept him waiting, and that kinda stupid stuff."

"And understandably so, Al," said Stowe the peacemaker. "You know? Just from what I saw last week, okay?"

"You don't have a bad attitude."

"No, I don't have a bad attitude. I *had* a bad attitude. You know I sat there for three hours?"

"So what?" Doc Hyman demanded. "You think it's so easy to raise this kinda money? You think it's easy on a place that's not open? That's been mismanaged? That there's a Chapter Seven lawsuit? That has an eviction on the—on the rent?"

"Right," boomed Albenga. "That kid lives it up on like four thousand a week. He's fooling around with the joint for a year."

"Okay?" Hyman asked. "You think it's easy finding money for him to piss away like that?"

"That leaves—that means he's pissed away two hundred thousand dollars," said Albenga. "It's simple. It's mathematics."

"Well, wait a minute," Stowe began, but Hyman was bursting. with righteous indignation.

"And you gotta remember," he said, "we're not—we got money from people who don't go for that shit."

Cooper nodded emphatically. "You're looking at a hundred people behind this table, and they don't take shit from nobody."

"These are people who can blow your fucking head off," Doc Hyman said.

Billy's Nagra tape of the sit-down at Rusty's, backed up by Special Agent Walt Stowe's testimony as a participating witness, would probably have been enough in itself to secure the convictions of Hyman, Cooper, Albenga, Sr., Capo, and other defendants at Resource Capital, but Billy was now fired up to get at the "hundred people behind this table" who could "blow your fucking head off." But they presented a special problem, as he and Stowe discovered the following day.

Around two in the afternoon, Billy happened to be passing through the lobby of the Diplomat when he saw a group of soberly dressed "family" men climbing out of two stretch limos at the curb. As it seemed unlikely that they were there for any other purpose than to check on their investment, Billy waited long enough to identify

Vincent "Jimmy" Rotondo, walking with a cane, as the leader of a deputation that included a number of other familiar faces before scooting upstairs for a word with Stowe.

"Sorry to do this to you, Walt," he said, "but we got company. Rotondo's coming in with a couple of old-timers who are gonna know me from the joint. Plus another guy I worked in Florida. If they see me, it's gonna blow the case."

"Okay." Stowe thought for a moment. "Still no sign of Tommy, right?"

"Nah. Musta blown his brains out on coke last night. No, it looks like it's down to you, Walt."

"Okay. Then I'll head 'em off in the ballroom before they come up here. But call Damon Taylor for me, will you? Tell him I need some backup real fast. Then you duck out. I can handle the rest."

"Sure, Walt. Hey, and listen—tell Rotondo you're my man from the IRA. Then they won't give you no trouble."

The mythical IRA connection, coupled with Billy's repeated observation to all and sundry that one call to the Hibernian Society would be enough to get a dozen 250-pound Micks around to Cowboy Palace in minutes, continued to work its magic. While severely displeased with the absent Duke, Rotondo's family gathering was affability itself with Stowe, once he explained who he was. After he had shown them around, all agreed that it was in everybody's interest to get the club open as quickly as possible and put an end to all the aggravation and disrespect.

Billy did not agree. He had gotten it into his head from the start that he had at all costs to prevent Cowboy Palace from opening, at least until the investigation was complete, or else the mob shylocks supplying Resource Capital with its funds would fade into the background again, out of reach.

This was not a comfortable view to take. The latest twist in his financial arrangements with Duke was yet another worthless agreement, to add to the mounting pile of dud checks and dishonored contracts, this time specifying that all previous commitments would be met as soon as the club was open, and that in addition he would receive a hundred thousand dollars a year for as long as it remained open. Contrary to his own interests, therefore, and without even telling Stowe, Billy embarked on a campaign of sabotage. Whenever Duke was confident enough to set a target date for the opening, Billy would find some way to wipe it off the calendar.

Mysteriously malfunctioning fire extinguishers ruined most of the drapes one night. Another night, a rogue rhinoceros apparently blundered into the men's room and reduced most of the fixtures to rubble before blundering out again. And as if that were not bad enough, sheer carelessness with welding rods put the elevators out of action for several days.

But Hyman and Cooper were still the most effective brake on progress. By bleeding Duke of cash, interfering in his decisions, and getting underfoot in his dealings with suppliers, they had closed out most of the shortcuts to completion still open to him. Unable to buy his way out of trouble or shop where he pleased for essential work and supplies, he had grown ever more off-handed and cynical, arriving later and leaving earlier. To Billy's eye, he was also showing unmistakable signs of consoling himself with coke.

The day after he had left Stowe to deal with Rotondo and his deputation of heavies, it was Billy's turn to find himself alone in charge of the office when Hyman, Cooper, the Albengas, and Capo arrived to tighten the screws still further.

He met them in the hallway, hollering.

"Why did you bring *him* fur?" he demanded, jerking his head at Capo. "Didn't I tell ya? I don't want nobody in here, putting their hands on people."

"Come on, Billy," Hyman said, pushing past him toward the back office. "Anthony's with me. Walt's with you. Why make trouble?"

"Trouble? *Me?*" Weaving in and out and getting in the way, he tried to block their progress toward the door. "Lemme tell ya something—there'll be no more putting hands on anybody. You wanna put your hands on somebody, put your hands on *me*."

Capo looked at him, seriously considering the invitation, and Billy threw open the door Cooper had just closed behind them to make sure John Johnson, the security boss, was standing by with the ex-Marine.

"Hear what I'm telling ya, Anthony?" he said, a little happier with the odds. "You're a cocky little motherfucker. One of these times you're gonna put your hands on the wrong person and you're gonna get your hands busted. And put the fucking phone down, Mel," he yelled, switching targets. "You got no right coming in here using my phones. I don't do that in *your* office. Don't do it in mine."

"You can't talk to me like that," said Capo, with a sideways glance through the door.

"You want I should bring 'em in? I'm talking to *you*, Anthony. And I'm telling ya, you're not gonna do nothing. Doc, will ya get your hands outa that fucking desk? This is a private office. That's none of your fucking business. Just get over there, do your talking, and then get the fuck outa here."

"He can't talk to me like that," said Capo, the weight of the insult beginning to register, but Albenga, Sr., patted his arm.

"Billy don't mean it," he said tolerantly. "He's got the hump this morning. What's the matter, Billy? Not getting enough?"

"Maybe getting too *much*," Cooper suggested, and they both laughed.

"Yeah." Billy threw himself into Duke's chair behind the desk. "Too much bullshit. Too much of *you* guys. So do me a favor. Stay outa the fucking joint, okay? Don't come in here no more."

"Hey, Billy," said Hyman. "You forgot something. We own a bigger piece of this than you do. So be nice. We just wanna straighten the kid out, get the place open, and start seeing some money back, that's all."

"Oh, that's good—that's very good," he grumbled, cooling off reluctantly. "I mean, *you're* the assholes screwed everything up in the first place. And what are you gonna do now? Break his legs? That'll *really* keep him on schedule, right?"

Doc Hyman thought it would speed things up if he brought in his own union plumbers, electricians, and painters to finish the job.

"Forget it—I got that under control," lied Billy, again in an oddly ambiguous situation.

Technically, as a creditor and part owner of Cowboy Palace, he had more in common with Hyman and Cooper than with Duke, and yet he felt impelled to fight Duke's corner. If anybody was going to mess things up, deliberately or not, it was going to be *him*, not Resource Capital. At the same time, it was *Duke* who was compromising his properties, not Hyman and Cooper, and so while they and their associates remained his principal target, Duke was his principal problem.

It was not only confusing but could lead to mistakes. He had realized almost at once that if he had agreed to Hyman's suggestion, he might well have added a half-dozen crooked union bosses to the target list.

When the meeting finally fizzled out, Billy rode uptown to the St. Moritz with Maury Joseph to find Duke. Getting no answer from his room, Billy had the St. Moritz security men force open the door, only to find Duke in a state of high elation, part of it pharmaceutical and part on account of a new loan he had just negotiated over the telephone with Carlo Vaccarezza at Rusty's Restaurant. He was to get fifteen thousand dollars from Lenny Di Maria and "Frankie the Hat" Di Stefano at 3 percent a week.

"Oh, *man*," groaned Billy.

They argued for half an hour. Joseph then returned downtown to Cowboy Palace for a meeting with a disbarred attorney and several mob acquaintances to plan an alternative strategy; Duke and Charlie

Diverna headed uptown to check out a new discotheque, and Billy went to bed early.

Unaccustomed to so much sleep, he also got up early, and with Walt Stowe, arrived with the hired help at Cowboy Palace. Joseph was already there, looking as though he had spent the night on the sofa, and they went through to the inner office with the idea of calling Duke at the St. Moritz to get him out of bed. From the pall of stale cigar smoke and the litter of spilled ashtrays and abandoned drinks, Joseph had evidently held his late-night meeting in there. The desk was covered with balled-up scraps of paper, and as Billy dialed the number, he saw one with his name on it. In Maury Joseph's handwriting. He hung up and reached for it.

"Billy Clyde Walker is Bill Breen," he read. "Bill Breen is an agent working for the FBI. Bill Breen is self-centered. Bill Breen is an alcoholic. Bill Breen is an egotist. Bill Breen brought Walt Johnson into Cowboy Palace. Walt Johnson is an FBI agent," and so on.

Billy handed the paper to Stowe without a word and marched to the door.

"Maury," he called politely. "Will you come in here a minute, please?"

As soon as Joseph came within reach, Billy's temper exploded. Grabbing him by the lapels, he dragged him inside, kicked the door shut behind them, slammed him against the wall, and measured him for a blow that would turn his face inside out.

"No, no, no," said Stowe. "Don't hit him." With their cover blown, he now had to go by the book, although he swung Joseph around no more tenderly than Billy had done. "Watch the door, Billy. Don't let anybody in."

Joseph ungummed his lips, and groaned. This was no way to treat a hangover.

"What the fuck's wrong with you guys?" he muttered. His eyes, alert as a reptile's, suggested he knew already.

"You write this?" Stowe demanded, waving the paper under his nose.

The other shrugged. He could hardly deny his own handwriting.

"Why? Why did you do it?"

"Why?" Joseph flared up feebly. "Because I've had it with Billy, that's why. I'm sick of him hanging around here all the time, telling people what to do."

Stowe fended Billy off. "Who saw this? Who'd you show it to?"

"Nobody. I was doodling, that's all. While the other guys were talking. How do *I* know who saw it? Probably nobody saw it."

"What guys?"

Joseph started to turn away, but Stowe pushed him back against the wall. "*What* guys?" he insisted.

"Guys," said Joseph. "Just guys. Guys who came to the meeting."

"He means wise guys," said Billy. "You wanna take a walk around outside, Walt? While me and Maury talk this thing over?"

"No, no, Billy. I'm taking this creep downtown. And you better come, too. I'll wait while you get your stuff."

"Not a chance, Walt." There was too much at stake. Not to mention his home and his mother-in-law's house.

"Billy." With Maury Joseph listening, Stowe was hampered in his argument. "Don't go stubborn on me, Billy. You *can't* stay here. Not now."

"I got unfinished business, Walt," he said. "I'm not going. So do us both a favor. Get that sleazeball outa here before I puke on his shoes."

Walt Stowe was instructed not to return to Cowboy Palace, and for his own safety was subsequently transferred to Washington. Over the next two days he spoke to Billy several times, trying to persuade him to get out before he got whacked, but Billy's Irish was up.

Two days later, Special Agents Stowe, Krinsky, and Dennis Madulla arrived at the Hyatt to take him downtown to the FBI's Manhattan office at 26 Federal Plaza. He was met there by Supervisor Damon Taylor, who informed him that the Bureau had confirmed intelligence reports that a contract was out on his life.

"No doubt about it," Taylor said. "You'll have to leave town tonight. My agents will check your stuff out of the hotel and take you to the airport."

Billy looked him over incredulously. "You brought me all the way downtown to tell me *that*?"

"You knew?" Taylor frowned.

"Billy, if you stick around, you're going to get hit," said Krinsky. "Be sensible. Go on home."

If Billy had had his doubts before, there were none now.

"You people are fucking cuckoo," he said, looking at Stowe, who should have known better. "I got a dozen contracts on me in ten states. It don't mean nothin'. I *like* to feel wanted."

"Yeah, Billy, but this is different," Stowe said. "You know who we're talking about. They don't kid around, these guys."

"Neither do I, Walt. And I don't hide."

"Billy, I'm out. It's over. What's the point?"

"*Over*? What are you talking about? It's just getting interesting. I'll work it bare-assed if I haveta."

"Billy, you can't go back in there alone," Krinsky said. "I can't let you do that."

"Walt, do I have to talk to this idiot? Where the fuck d'ya think I've been for two days?"

"All right, Breen." Taylor handed him a typewritten statement. "Read this and sign it."

"What is it?"

"It's a waiver. We've warned you of the danger. We advise you to get out of town. If you won't take our advice, it's on your own head. The Bureau can't be responsible for your safety."

"Well, that figures," Billy said contemptuously. He was almost amused, but not quite. "First, you're not responsible for my property. Now you're not responsible for me."

"Not unless you leave town tonight," Taylor agreed.

"Well, I didn't sign then, and I ain't signing now." Very deliberately, Billy tore the paper in half and dropped it at his feet. "I ain't leaving New York, and I ain't leaving this case. I don't care if Walt comes back or not, I'm gonna work these motherfuckers to the fucking dying end."

"Did you put up your property in exchange for an interest in the Cowboy Palace?" asked Breitbart.

"It could never open," said Billy. "I knew it couldn't get open."

"Sir," Judge Sand said wearily.

"No, sir," said Billy, contrite.

"And did you get ten percent of the Cowboy Palace?" Breitbart persisted.

"Did I get ten percent of it?" Billy had never considered the transaction in that light before.

"Were you given a piece of paper and a contract with Tom Duke which indicated that you had a proprietary interest, an equity interest, in the Cowboy Palace?"

"Yes, sir."

"And in addition to that, did you tell him that you wanted $1,000 or $2,000 or $3,000 a week for a long period of time? As long as it was open?"

"Tom Duke gave me phony checks for that period of time," said Billy, confused.

Judge Sand again tried to put him back on the rails. "The question, sir—Mr. Reporter, read the question back. Don't argue with counsel," he went on. "Just answer the question." He waited while the court reporter read back the question. "Now the question is, did you say that to Tom Duke?"

"He offered it to me," Billy said.

"Did you sign a contract with Duke?" Breitbart demanded.

"Did I sign—no, sir."

Triumphant at last, Breitbart now asked Billy to identify one of the prosecution's own exhibits, a contract with Duke that Billy had signed. But the problem with this was that it related, not to the Virginia house, but to the Dallas property. When Billy tried to tell him, the other would have none of it.

"Did you enter into an agreement with Tom Duke?" he insisted.

"Yes, I did," agreed Billy resignedly.

" 'Duke will deliver to Breen,' " said Breitbart, quoting from the document, " 'ten percent of the corporation, 312 West 91st Street Corporation, to be held in escrow.' "

"Yes, sir."

"Did you by that contract get the right to have yourself or an accountant of your choice to inspect all the books?"

"There were no books."

Judge Sand leaned forward. "The question is—"

"Yes, sir," said Billy meekly. "Excuse me."

"Did Duke agree to represent you as an owner of the Cowboy Palace?"

"Yes, sir."

"And did he tell you that the purchase price for the property was $215,000, payable in the following manner: $65,000 at the execution of the contract and six consecutive checks made weekly in the amount of $1,500, commencing September 1, 1982, and running for a period of six months, ending February 1, 1983?"

"That's what the contract says," agreed Billy, too tired to check the other's arithmetic. "I never got no money."

"And you were supposed to get $3,000 a week after that?"

"Yes, sir."

"Now you did enter into such a contract, is that correct?"

"Yes, sir."

"And you remember it now that you look at it?"

Billy gave it one more try. "That is not the original contract that I drew up."

Breitbart brushed this aside impatiently. "We are talking about the terms that we just discussed verbally."

"Yes, sir."

"You were going to make money if the Cowboy Palace made money?"

"No, sir."

Breitbart reeled away in frustration.

"You put up your Virginia property?" he shouted.

"Yes, sir."

"How much was that worth?"

"$50,000. They got an appraisal for $85,000."

"Who got an appraisal?"

"They got an appraisal."

"WHO?" thundered Breitbart.

Bruce Baird rose at last to defend his witness. "May we have the questions in a civilized tone?" he suggested coldly.

Breitbart glared. "How did he get an appraisal for $85,000 on a $50,000 property?"

"He was pretty good with a pen and paper," said Billy, and several jurors tittered.

"And in your presence, he represented that the $50,000 piece of property was worth $85,000?"

"All I was getting was $50,000," Billy said. "Exactly what I paid for the property."

"Listen to the question," Judge Sand said sharply. "Mr. Reporter, read the question back, and answer the question, Mr. Breen."

Billy listened as it was read back, but Breitbart cut in before he could answer.

"And you were supposed to get $65,000 for that on the date of closing, weren't you?"

Billy shrugged helplessly. It wasn't his fault if the guy kept making a mess of his brief. "I was supposed to get $50,000," he repeated.

"Mr. Breen," said Breitbart, with an effort. "Take a look at the contract and see whether or not in fact you were supposed to make $15,000 immediately, as soon as the contract was signed."

"Objection to the form of the question," said Baird, but Billy was not interested in technicalities.

"He is asking about the wrong property," he said wearily. "You are wrong. This is not the property in Virginia."

Breitbart stared, then looked again at the contract. "Were you supposed to get $65,000?" he repeated, still not perceiving his error.

"Off of a $215,000 piece of property," Billy explained.

Breitbart examined it once more. "There are two pieces of property?"

Billy nodded. "Which one?" he asked, prepared to discuss either.

"Is this the one that you changed the deed on?"

"Your Honor," said Baird, not displeased with the way things were going. "May Mr. Breitbart return to the lectern, and may the questions be put in the proper form? He is not refreshing his recollection."

"Yes," said Judge Sand, with a reproving nod.

"There was another piece of property, right?" asked Breitbart, struggling to regroup.

"Yes, sir."

"What happened with that one?"

"Same thing as happened to the first one."

"You never intended to put up any property here, did you?"

Billy could make no sense of that at all. "My property was placed, yes. It was."

"But you meant to scam everybody, didn't you?"

"No, sir," he said, with a touch of contempt.

"You went in there to steal money?"

"No, sir." It was pitiful.

19

Walt Stowe agreed that Cowboy Palace had been botched.

"They would have been better off if they had left me alone for another month or so," he told Billy, just before the trial. "If they'd let you and me keep running with those guys. Even though Maury Joseph did the best he could to put us in the trick bag."

"All I want is a conviction up there, Walt. I'd hate to go through this here and not get a conviction. I brought it in after they refused it. Now I've taken it in again after they killed it. The fucking New York City Division stinks."

"There are some good people up there, Billy. The problem is it's a big, big office, and so much stuff slips between the cracks that I don't know what the answer is. If they had left me alone and left me in that thing, it could have gone a lot further. But they were getting scared."

"I don't think anybody woulda killed us," Billy said. "They'd look and say, 'Well, who is this guy?' And I'd say, 'The IRA. You want fucking problems? We'll give you problems.' "

Stowe laughed. "You know, I'm convinced that story kept us from getting hurt. I think they would have killed me that day, but they were a little bit concerned about who we were and how crazy we were. That one day they came up there with about eight or nine guys?"

"I think going into Cowboy Palace made you street-wise," Billy said fondly. "You could never get a better lesson in crime fighting than Cowboy Palace."

"You're absolutely right. That did a lot for me. . . . The case was badly mishandled, Billy, but it still turned out to be a good case. The big thing was hanging up Jesse Hyman. That really has been a big deal for us."

But Billy was not to be consoled. The mishandling of what should have been his greatest case was all the more frustrating because his reputation had never stood higher. Agents in a dozen states—even in the New York Division—were lining up for his services, and the other cases he was working at the same time as Cowboy Palace were going off like clockwork.

Supervisor George Dyer, for instance, no sooner heard that Damon Taylor had pulled the plug on Walt Stowe than he asked Billy if he knew a way into Jacob Maislich, better known as Jack Mace, king of New York's Diamond District and America's master fence.

"Oh, yeah," said Billy. "No problem. I know Jack. We were in the joint together. You gimme an agent I can teach to work with me undercover and I'll get him in there for ya"—which is how he teamed up in Operation NYCON with a young man who really *was* in a different class as an FBI agent, particularly under cover. He was Vincent Wincelowicz, also known as Frank Kohler, and they worked together like pepper and salt.

Set up behind a dummy corporation, Investment Capital SA, with offices at 575 Madison Avenue, NYCON was a Group 1 undercover operation aimed at high-level con artists, swindlers, and white-collar thieves, but until Billy joined forces with Wincelowicz and case agent Dale Hackbart, results had fallen sadly short of ambition.

One reason for this was management's lack of enthusiasm. George Dyer's boss, assistant coordinator Fred Verinder, had inherited NYCON along with the office furniture, and, having no proprietary stake in its outcome or seeing much scope for glory, seemed content simply to let matters run their course. A second, related reason was that the team lacked the heavyweight experience and connections required to take on the canniest, most self-protective of all professional criminals.

Dale Hackbart, who could have passed anywhere as a bank vice president (and *did* before Billy was through with him), was a dedicated, knowledgeable, imaginative agent with a well-organized intelligence more than capable of handling the most intricate of cases. Vincent Wincelowicz was a tough, highly motivated street agent with an intuitive flair for undercover work and a sense of proportion which suggested that he could not only "get over" with targeted criminals but live to testify against them. But they were both stalled for want of the high-level openings needed to make NYCON work. Like Dyer, who had written the program with Special Agent Al Steineker, they knew whom they wanted to bust but could not get near enough to do it. Until Billy went to the Diamond District.

Familiar with Mace's habits, he waited until after lunch before arriving on Forty-seventh Street to comb through the bedlam of people and traffic. With no sign of Mace in the eddies of sidewalk trading, he patrolled back and forth from Fifth Avenue to Sixth, trawling the booths and stores until his feet hurt. Only when he was about ready to give up for the day did he finally catch sight of Mace through the window of number 52, concluding a deal with three men in wise-guy suits.

With the gods on his side, Billy waited for him to come out.

"Hey, Jack," he cried. "Jack Mace. Remember me?"

Mace shook his hand warmly, remembering him at once from the Atlanta penitentiary and Walpole State Prison, although he could not recall the name. As that was a considerable plus, Billy forgave him freely.

"Bill Murphy," he said. "But call me Murphy. It's just plain Murphy to my friends."

"Yeah. Sorry, Murphy. Now I remember. Must be getting old or something."

"You?" Mace had to be nudging seventy. "Listen, you don't look a day over forty. And if you think *you* got a problem with names, Jack, forget about it."

Billy was already into his pitch. What he needed more than anything, he said, was a good set of ID papers.

"Yeah? Well, now you come to the right department," Mace said, happy to make amends. "What do you need, Murphy?"

"Well," said Billy. "A good driver's license. Social security. Plastic. You know. Anything."

"No plastic. My guy just got busted. But social security, birth certificate, driver's license—those are easy. What do you want? A New York license? A Jersey license? If you wanna go to Georgia, I got a friend in Augusta can get you a legit Georgia license for a hundred and fifty bucks. Wait there a minute while I get rid of this stuff."

Mace crossed the street and went into number 31, returning almost at once without the three loaded shopping bags he had acquired from the wise guys.

"So what are you into now, Murphy?" he asked amiably, steering Billy into the Burger Restaurant for a cup of coffee. Billy showed him his Rolex.

"Oh, yeah," Mace said, counterfeit watches being a specialty of his. "I got all kinds of lumpies."

"Hey, that's not a lumpy. That's real."

"Yeah, *I* know that and *you* know that, but who else is gonna know? Tell me what you want. Rolex? Cartier? Longines? Any kind of lumpy you want. Real nice quality."

"And real nice prices, right?"

"Listen. Diamond-face Rolex, seventy-five bucks. Okay? Other kinds, sixty bucks. You know how to move 'em, it's like I'm handing you money."

"Oh, I can move 'em," said Billy, still fishing. "And I'll take a few. But right now I'm looking to make some *big* money. I'm looking for paper, you know? Like traveler's checks. Stuff like that."

"How about money orders? American Express. Unsigned. Can you handle those?"

"Try me. How much?"

"Shoot. I just turned down a deal on six hundred thousand dollars' worth. Guy out on furlough from Trenton. Says he can steal the machines, too. But I tell ya what I *do* got. Well, no. I don't. I gave 'em to a guy to move, but I can put the two of yez in touch. Krugerrands. Gold Krugerrands. You interested in those? They look real good, but the gold content ain't quite right. He'd probably sell you the die for making 'em as well, if you want."

"Well, yeah. That sounds good, Jack. But I still like paper. How about Treasury notes? You get that kinda stuff?"

Mace laughed. "That's how I got forty years. But I can find you some, sure. Can you really do anything on those?"

"Positively," Billy said. "I got a foreign banker."

"Hey. No kidding. Well, lemme see what I can do. We'll talk about this later."

"Okay. And if we're talking big money here, I'd like to bring my partner next time—if that's all right with you, Jack. He's a good kid. You'll like him."

"Sure, sure. Why not? You say he's okay, he's okay. And we're talking like sixteen to twenty-two percent for the stuff. Somewhere in there."

"For like how much?"

"How much you want?"

They talked for two hours.

"You're shitting me," said Dyer, when Billy reported in. "What do you mean, you got Jack Mace? You mean you found him, right?"

"Yeah, I found him. I found him and I got him. I got counterfeit watches, counterfeit gold coin, stolen money orders, traveler's checks, airline tickets, stocks, bonds, securities. I got phony ID papers, driver's licenses, passports. I got guns. I got bootleg videos and first-run movies. I got boxes for bilking the phone company. I got hijack truckloads of all kindsa merchandise. I got pills. I got coke. I got diamonds, paintings, and all kindsa works of art. I got shylocking. I got everything. Everything big that goes down has gotta go through Jack Mace. I got every kinda crime there is, plus a bunch of his connections. I got him tied in to the New England mob with Patriarca. I got him with direct lines into Paulie Castellano, Matty Ionello, Fat Tony Salerno, and John Gotti. And I got him ready to meet my partner next time I go to see him, so you better get me that kid Vinny what's-his-name."

"Wincelowicz."

"Yeah, that's the one. But first I gotta go to Atlanta to get the fucking IRS off my back."

To this day, George Dyer finds it hard to understand how anybody can get into a target so fast and come out with so much in so short a time.

"Takes an exceptional person," he says. "I never saw anybody else who could go into a city cold and next day write the book on it. Who's doing what, when, where, and how. Billy was the greatest, and I'm glad he's going to Quantico now and trying to pass it on."

Recovering from his astonishment, Dyer decided to send Wincelowicz down to join Billy in Atlanta so that they would lose no time in getting their act together. And having tried to say Vincent Wincelowicz a few times, the first thing Billy worked on was getting his new partner used to being Frank Kohler.

The next thing was to sever the connection with Art Krinsky. Coached by the NYCON team, he composed a letter to the special agent in charge of the Atlanta office.

"Due to the increasing difficulties I am incurring in Atlanta, both financial and personal," he wrote, "I believe I can be of limited or no use in this area. Due to the personal threats upon my life, and threats of harm to my family, I have no desire or belief that I will ever reside in the Atlanta area. Special Agent Krinsky is fully aware of these threats and my finances. For those reasons, I have requested S.A. Krinsky to close my file, to no avail . . .

"I informed S.A. Krinsky in the past and present that I had gone deeply into debt as he was unable to repay me for my expenses I paid out of my pocket. I had to wait for reimbursement of $6,600 that I personally used in the Johnson City, Tennessee, case for over seven months."

Billy then went on to list twelve other occasions when Krinsky had failed to reimburse him for expenses or to secure rewards or payments promised by the FBI and other government agencies, including the $125,000 agreed with Ron Iden for his work on the Judge Wood/James Kerr cases.

"I have been without funds, and have used my 100 percent disability VA check and have had to borrow large sums of money from friends and associates in order to do work for the FBI. . . . I have received little if any payment for my services. . . . So as a result of the above problems and other reasons I will not mention at this time, I do not want to continue being a source for Agent Krinsky or the Atlanta office. . . ."

Bowing to his wishes, Lawrence York, Special Agent in Charge of the Atlanta office, duly closed the file on Hawiya. As he did so, the NYCON team gleefully opened Billy as New York source NY 20376 C "Hawiya" and took him to dinner at the Playboy Club to decide how he was to get paid.

"Don't worry about it," Al Steineker said. "I already talked to George. We can probably get you five grand a month. Plus expenses."

"Ah-*hah!*" said Billy. The idea of a paycheck coming in as regularly as the bills had a certain charm, but the others looked doubtful.

"You know how many targets he's lined up already?" Dale Hackbart shook his head. "He'd make a lot more case by case."

"Yeah," said Wincelowicz. "Dale's right. Leave it to us, Billy. We'll put a value on what you do, case by case, and pay you out of the informants' fund. You'll do better that way."

Billy beamed. "Sound good to me," he said cheerfully. "And you know what? To get things rolling, I'll give you Mace for free."

When the agents then insisted on picking up the tab for the evening, he did allow himself briefly to wonder if perhaps a new day had dawned after all, although he had yet to see any of the ten thousand dollars plus expenses promised by Supervisor Damon Taylor.

Meanwhile, back at the ranch, the Cowboy Palace outfit under Tom Duke was considering a change of tactics. Sinking fast under the weight of his weekly vig payments to Resource Capital, Duke had turned to Tony Napoli as a possible source for refinancing the whole project—and Napoli was interested, not least because Duke already owed him seventy thousand dollars for limousines. They agreed to meet for dinner to discuss the possibilities, and Duke begged Billy to go with him, for moral, physical, and financial support. Napoli was thinking about buying the Cowboy Palace lease, he said, and Billy, with his properties, was the key to everything.

But Billy at this point was as much concerned for his life as for his properties. He had to assume after the note incident that Maury Joseph had told all the wise guys involved with Cowboy Palace that Billy was working for the government. For those disposed to believe him, the subsequent disappearance of his "IRA accountant" might tend to confirm it.

On the other hand, Joseph was widely known as a devious son of a bitch, and Billy's continued, unruffled presence around Cowboy Palace could equally be taken to confirm that Joseph was lying as usual. It was an even-money gamble. Given that his properties *were* at risk—Duke had Xerox copies of the deeds that he proposed to give to Napoli at dinner—and given that Napoli was one of his prime mob targets, Billy shrugged, and stuck his head into the lion's mouth.

It turned out to be an agreeable experience. Napoli was a big, affable Italian in his midforties with exceptionally large teeth and the inner assurance that came from being a capo in the Genovese family with two or three generations of made men in his bloodlines. Polite but visibly unimpressed by Tom Duke, he tended to address his more serious remarks to Billy, as from one street-wise operator to another. Duke might have the nimbleness and charm of a junk-bond salesman but they had the power and the property.

Napoli was plainly intrigued by the idea of taking over from Resource Capital in Cowboy Palace, but if Duke had hoped to play one crime family off against another, he quickly learned that the New York mobs complied with a code of business practice that made Wall Street look like a thieves' kitchen. A change of funding and the recovery of Billy's properties could be done only with the consent of all concerned, said Napoli. And as more than one family was involved, this would entail some tricky diplomacy and probably a ruling by the commission.

"You know something?" Duke said. "I added it up today. I paid those guys like two hundred eighty grand in interest already. Can you believe that?"

"Sure," said Napoli. "I believe it. It's stupid."

"I mean, in six months? Who can live with that?"

"Nobody. You're right. It don't make sense."

"See, this way, he's *never* gonna get open," Billy said happily, another major mob figure now squarely in his sights.

"I know that. And it's gotta open."

"Right."

"Mulberry Street needs the place. Money owed must be paid back, and when it's open, the families are looking for a third off the top."

Duke sucked his teeth ruefully. "Yeah. Well, Mel and Doc, they've already got a piece of the door, the hat-check concession, and the vending machines."

"I know that," Napoli said. "But we can work something out. We gotta hire the right people for the door and all positions where money is involved. I had a lot of calls since I took an interest, and that's good. If Billy goes along with what I got in mind, maybe I can set up a deal we can *all* live with."

Billy was more than happy to go along. It had been too dangerous to wear a body recorder at dinner, but after that he took to phoning Napoli almost every day and recording their conversations. As he was already doing the same with Hyman, Cooper, Duke, Vaccarezza, and the rest, and calling from Dallas, Miami, Atlanta, or wherever else he happened to be, he soon had a suitcase full of tapes and phone bills of five hundred dollars a month.

Having left him to work the main mob targets alone, the least the FBI could do, he felt, was to pick up the tab. But with a perversity that left him gasping, Supervisor Walt Smith, who had taken over the responsibility for Cowboy Palace from Damon Taylor, not only declined to pay Billy's bills but was almost equally reluctant to accept the incriminating tapes. He was even less keen on the idea of Billy talking to Napoli face to face. When Billy reported on their conversation over dinner and his standing invitation to sit in on Napoli's Brooklyn crap game, Smith ordered him not to go, which naturally ensured that he went.

By Christmas Eve, Billy and Napoli were calling the shots at Cowboy Palace. Napoli had cleared the decks to some extent by persuading Carlo Vaccarezza's shylocks to bow out of the picture with their seventeen thousand dollars at three percent a week, but had uncovered a serious problem with the so-called lease on the ballroom of the Diplomat. The owner of the hotel knew nothing about it! As far as he was concerned, as long as Duke paid the rent, he was free to improve the property as much as he pleased.

"Looks to me like Resource worked a deal with Butch and Maury to establish that lease, and it was just a piece of paper all the while," Napoli told Billy, on one of the better tapes. "To try and put pressure on you and Tommy to get more money together. You understand?"

"All right."

"The owner wouldn't accept two cents from nobody. He wouldn't perform a new lease. That lease was not performed by the owner but they had his name in there."

"Yeah."

"It was a piece of paper. A scam. Performed by Maury and Resources. So you could be enticed to sign the papers for the properties. So they could have more cash."

That was bad enough, but there was an even worse problem over the liquor license. Duke did not have one, and the existing license was about to expire in a welter of lawsuits between the owner of the hotel and the previous licensee. In Napoli's opinion, the prospects of a new one being issued in the absence of a lease and in the middle of litigation were fairly remote, but he had an answer for this, too.

"I told Tom, 'I might be able to talk to the owner, and you could rent it certain nights of the week.' All right? You wouldn't need a liquor license. You rent it like for, um, private parties, and the caterer comes in and uses *his* license for that particular night."

"Oh, yeah."

"See, I got caterers that could come in with their licenses at what they call a temporary night. And, ah, we use the word *benefit*. You know what I mean?" Napoli laughed. "Oh, you understand what I mean."

"Yeah, yeah, yeah."

"We use the word *benefit* that, uh, we're gonna—some money is donated to certain charities, organizations, and the publicity would be for a charity-raising thing."

"Right."

"A benefit. And we put the priest on the premises. And we give him so much money to go home with."

Billy laughed. "You have a priest to put on there?"

"We got about ten of 'em. You know? I got a few rabbis, too."

"Oh, yeah?"

"Yeah."

"Good boy."

"Put 'em on the premises and we give, 'Here, you take, uh, five hundred. Now go home.' You know? If these guys get five hundred, they're happy. They put it in their, in their collection box."

"Right."

"So, in other words, that's how it's done. Ya get—ya advertise a good band. Ya advertise a disco for the night, and a private caterer comes in. Of course, these things I'm telling ya—I haven't gone through the whole rundown with Tom yet."

"Right."

"So if he does receive any money on Monday, he's to come right to me, and he's going to send you the five-o immediately."

"But—"

"Before any of it else is touched."

On the Monday Napoli referred to, Duke was due to meet with Resource Capital to pledge Billy's last piece of real estate, the Miami house he had vacated a year earlier after his confrontation with Cuban Mike Delgado. Although he had nothing but a pile of worthless checks to show for the two previous transactions, Billy had managed to preserve his title to the Virginia and Dallas properties despite Duke's manipulations of the deeds, and with Napoli holding the reins, Billy felt he now had a better chance of getting the fifty thousand dollars that he still needed for the IRS. It was also the only way to keep Napoli in the game, for he clearly had no intention of risking any of his own money. While Billy's properties underwrote virtually the whole investment in Cowboy Palace, Napoli could wheel and deal with impunity.

"See, if Tom forfeits," he told Billy a week later in another taped call, "well, then Doc will process the properties to get enough money to pay back the street people who gave him the money to give to Tom."

"Right. Well, what about 804? Didn't they give him money?"

Billy already knew perfectly well that Local 804 of the International Teamsters Union was an important source of funds for Hyman and Cooper, but he wanted the FBI to hear it on tape.

"Well, 804 *is* Jim," said Napoli, unwittingly torpedoing Vincent Joseph "Jimmy" Rotondo, underboss of the New Jersey mob.

"Oh. Oh, okay."

"Eight-oh-four is Jim."

"Right."

"So now, uh, 804 has reserve money, which is a part of Teamsters, and Jim is able to okay that, you see."

Napoli went on to say that he also had a meeting scheduled for the same Monday to find out exactly where Rotondo stood in all this.

"The man has to say what his position is. What he intends to do in the future."

"Right," Billy said happily. A couple more tapes like this and both these guys were dead in the water.

"Does he want a clear payoff?"

"Right."

"How much does he want?"

"Right."

"See, I'll have those answers for you after Monday."

When Billy returned to New York at the weekend to collect the fifty thousand dollars he thought he had coming from Duke's meeting at Resource Capital, he learned from Napoli that Jimmy Rotondo had already called all the interested families together at his Brooklyn social club on First Avenue at Thirty-third Street. Unable to reach any final decisions, they had adjourned the meeting until that night. Meanwhile, Rotondo had endorsed the loan Hyman and Cooper proposed to make on Billy's Miami house, even though it meant taking second position to the IRS, which already had a lien on the property.

But endorsing it did not necessarily mean making the money available. After completing the paperwork, Duke and Billy left to meet Napoli in Bamonte's restaurant with no more than Doc Hyman's assurance that a check was in the works. They both complained about this when Napoli eventually joined them, but he had graver matters on his mind. Although "beneficial," his meeting had again been adjourned until 3:00 A.M. so that mob figures senior to Rotondo, Franzese, and himself could attend.

"In the meantime, no one sleeps," he said.

It appeared that Mel Cooper and Doc Hyman had a serious problem. The feeling was that Mike Franzese had no right lending money to Resource Capital for Cowboy Palace when Rotondo was already involved. Later that evening, speaking to Billy privately on the telephone, Napoli looked forward to the day when they could drop Duke and his cronies altogether and run Cowboy Palace between them.

There was still no sign of the money when Billy went to see Duke on the following Monday evening. (In a gesture to placate his mob creditors, Duke had moved out of the St. Moritz into the apartment building where Carlo Vaccarezza lived, at 401 East Eightieth Street.) Having come up empty too often to feel surprised or even particularly annoyed, Billy telephoned Vaccarezza upstairs to place a "dime" bet (one thousand dollars) on Miami to win that night over Buffalo and settled down to watch the game on TV. But they were barely into the first period before Napoli called to say he was sending his driver to bring Duke and Billy to Brooklyn.

He met them at an Italian bakery on Metropolitan Avenue and, when satisfied that they had not been followed, took them on to his social club at Leonard and Metropolitan, where a table was being set up in the back room for a crap game. He wanted to discuss ways and means of keeping Tom Duke alive, literally as well as figuratively. One of the possibilities was to buy out Resource Capital, but as they had talked about this before, and as Napoli clearly wanted to work on Duke for reasons of his own, Billy asked if he could join the others in the back room.

"Sure," said Napoli, misreading boredom for tact. "Be my guest. But it ain't no big deal, Billy. It's a hundred-dollar-limit game."

"That's okay, Tony," he said. "I can use the practice."

It was Billy's lucky night. Miami beat Buffalo 27 to 10, which meant Vaccarezza owed him money, and after an hour with the dice, he was up twelve hundred dollars. When Napoli took them to dinner at Wessin's Steak House an hour after that, Billy was still about five hundred ahead, but gave most of it away in tips. Admiring his style, Napoli went to the phone and ordered a call girl for Billy as a present.

But Billy by now was catatonically drunk. When he surfaced the next morning, he was surprised to find himself back in Duke's apartment. After a quart of black coffee, he vaguely remembered

Napoli's gift, but had no recollection of whether he had taken advantage of it or of where he had gone with her after leaving the restaurant.

Of little or no importance next to the calamity of his hangover, it suddenly became significant when Napoli called that afternoon to warn Billy to get out of town. It seemed that an hour after they had sat down to dinner, the police had raided two of Napoli's crap games, including the one at the social club, and busted everybody. They had later picked Napoli up as well, and even as he spoke, a squad was sitting outside his house, waiting to arrest him on additional charges.

"It was that fucking broad I gave ya," he said. "She's a snitch. One of the cops told me."

"No shit," said Billy, who could have done without this complication. "She didn't hear nothing, did she? I didn't say nothing to her."

"Come on, Billy. How the fuck would *you* know? You were too fucking drunk to get in the car."

"Yeah," he conceded. "That's true. I don't even remember getting my pants off."

"Well, don't worry about it. I'll take care of the bitch. I already took care of the guy that sent her."

Billy cranked his wits painfully into gear, trying to remember where she lived. "You mean she fingered the games from hearing us talk?" Napoli's limo driver would know because he had taken them there.

"Yeah. No. I don't know," Napoli said irritably. "That's not why I called. Listen, if I send Neil over with the limo, can you give him a couple of thousand? I can't go home yet, not with the cops outside, and they're watching everybody."

"Sure, Tony. No problem. I'll give him whatever I got on me."

"Thanks, pal. And listen, stay outa Brooklyn until this thing cools off. Blow town for a coupla weeks. Just in case."

Doing his best to think about this advice, Billy wondered if Napoli was trying to get him out of the way for some other reason, perhaps while he reorganized Cowboy Palace for the mobs, but he gave Napoli's driver fifteen hundred dollars, which was all he could spare, and then drove around for the rest of the day with Special Agents Walt Stowe and Vinnie Wincelowicz in a vain attempt to track down the call girl before anybody else did.

After that, Billy spoke to Napoli once or twice more on the telephone but never saw him again until they met in court a year later.

"Lucky I made those tapes," Billy said to Dale Hackbart, his NYCON case agent. "The ones with Tony talking about Jimmy Rotondo and Local 804 and all that stuff. Without my tapes, you wouldn't have no case against the guy."

"Yeah. The tapes . . ." Hackbart hesitated. "Billy, you better talk to Walt Smith."

With half the office tied up transcribing Billy's tapes, Supervisor Walt Smith had ordered his agents to accept no more. An unspecified number had even been destroyed without being transcribed. Billy actually saw agents throwing his cassettes against a wall.

"Have you ever said that FBI agents are incompetent?" asked *Breitbart.*

Billy hesitated. "Let me say, FBI agents—there may be one or two. But not the FBI agency, because I believe it is one of the greatest organizations in the United States that we have for law enforcement. There may be one or two that don't step in line."

"How about Damon Taylor?"

Billy hesitated longer. "Damon Taylor and I have a personality conflict."

"Did you ever scream at him?"

"I scream at him? Yes, I probably have."

"Did you ever throw him out of your room?"

"No. But I asked him to leave."

"I see." Breitbart referred to his notes. "Did you ever say that Stanley Nye was incompetent and a fool?"

"I had nothing to do with Stanley Nye," said Billy, covering up.

"Didn't there come a time when you were told that Stanley Nye was taking over the case?"

"Let me tell you . . . I got into an argument with Stanley Nye like I would get into an argument with you."

"You and I have never had an argument," said Breitbart, letting him off the ropes.

"No," agreed Billy. It was like taking candy from a baby. "I think you are a nice guy."

"Thank you. Did you think that Assistant United States Attorney Kerr was a nice guy?"

"Positively."

"And Judge Wood? Did you think he was a nice guy?"

"Positively."

Even Breitbart could see this was getting him nowhere. "Now, did you ever say Stanley Nye is a fool?"

Billy looked across to where Nye was sitting at the government table with Baird and Aaron Marcu, but they were busy with their papers.

"Probably I did."

"Did you say that he doesn't know how to handle a case like this?"

"I never knew Stanley Nye when the case was going on." He just hated to give Breitbart the satisfaction.

"I asked you a question as to whether or not you said those things."

"Yes, I did."

"Did you say that he doesn't know anything about real estate?"

"This was not a real estate transaction," he said, back on the ropes. "If it was straight real estate—"

"The question," Judge Sand reminded him, "was 'Did you say that Stanley Nye didn't know anything about real estate?' "

"Let me object on relevance grounds," Baird said hopefully, but he was overruled.

"Yes, I probably did," agreed Billy.

"Did you say he didn't know anything about mortgages or closings?"

"That's correct."

"Did you say that he was totally incompetent to handle this case?"

"No, sir." As far as he could recall, he had never gone as far as that. "Did you say that—" Breitbart broke off, out of ammunition. "Did you know Agent Stowe?"

"Positively. One of the finest agents I have ever met." No chance for anybody to drive a wedge there.

"And he's crazy about you?"

"Just ask questions, please," Judge Sand said sharply.

20

Nobody in NYCON quite believed what Billy had told them until he took Vinnie Wincelowicz to meet Jack Mace at booth 8, 52 West Forty-seventh Street.

"This kid here's my partner, Frank Kohler," he said, not making too big a thing of it. "He just got out of Auburn state prison, and he's not as dumb as he looks. Frank, say hello to Jack."

Mace sized him up unhurriedly, smiled, put his arm around Kohler's shoulders as though he had known him for years, and steered them across the street to his office at 31 West Forty-seventh to talk a little business.

It was as easy as that. When they reported back to Investment Capital SA a couple of hours later, Wincelowicz wore the slightly puzzled air of a Klondike prospector whose pick had just wedged in a vein of pure gold. Laid out before them was the entire panorama of organized crime in America, with Jack Mace at their elbow, as guide, mentor, and friend, to point out the landmarks.

Wincelowicz made Billy take him back the next day, just to be sure he had not dreamed it. They found Mace in the Burger Restaurant with a man he introduced as Marty Riff, his connection for airline tickets. When Riff left to wait at booth 8, Mace showed them a list of several hundred validated Pan Am and American Airlines tickets that they could have for half price. Billy slipped Wincelowicz a thousand dollars so that he could buy some. They also bought a few Rolex "lumpies," ordered some blank New York State drivers' licenses, and discussed a consignment of stolen securities that Mace assured them was on the way.

When they reported back, Supervisor George Dyer was pleased with their progress but foresaw a problem. For one thing, NYCON's remit was white-collar crime, and some of the stuff they were lining up had to do with organized crime or property crime, for which other squads were responsible. For another thing, a lot of the leads they had uncovered would take them into the territory of other FBI divisional offices. He could not see Assistant Coordinators Fred Verinder or Julian J. Perez agreeing to out-of-town excursions that brought no obvious benefit, kudos or statistics to the Manhattan office.

Billy and Wincelowicz thought he was crazy.

Billy had no patience with company men anyway, and Wincelowicz, though wise beyond his years in the ways of street people, was too green an agent to pay much attention to Bureau politics. He was still under the impression that the FBI had a duty to apprehend criminals regardless of geography. His credentials said nothing about collecting evidence of crime in New York but of crime against the United States—and Jack Mace seemed willing to instruct him in many of its more important aspects.

It was almost as though, near the end of his career, Mace had found a long-lost son and was eager to show him the inheritance that would one day be his. When Billy was around, Mace still treated him as the senior partner, but by the beginning of 1983, after they had made three or four joint visits a week to the Diamond District for a month or more, Mace had begun to ask not for Billy but for Frank Kohler when he called the undercover number.

Billy was genuinely pleased. Dyer had put the training of agents high on the list of Billy's duties with NYCON, and nobody could ask for more sensational progress than this. Wincelowicz was a natural—all Billy had expected and rarely found in an FBI agent—and not the least of his assets was that he had come to the Bureau later than most, with his values formed and some practical experience of life behind him.

On January 4, 1983, Mace called "Frankie" at Investment Capital SA and asked them both to come to Forty-seventh Street. He had something for them. Mindful of Dyer's reservations, Billy started off by asking Mace if he could get them a $200,000 Treasury note, and was treated to a lengthy discourse on how to exploit securities that belonged to other people without actually stealing them. An old school buddy of Mace's, now a senior executive at Bache, could, for a fee of $10,000, "loan" out securities held by his brokerage house, provided they were replaced in time for the regular six-month audit.

Billy promised to think about it, but said that he preferred to buy stuff outright, which brought Mace to the point of his call. His friend with the counterfeit Krugerrands had a hundred of them, priced at $20 each, and $10,000 in unsigned Cook's traveler's checks, for which he wanted 35 cents on the dollar. He was also prepared to sell the Krugerrand die, if they were interested, for $10,000.

"Oh, yeah," said Billy. "We're interested. Right, Frank?"

"Oh, yeah," agreed Wincelowicz. "We're interested all right."

"Okay. Wait here while I set it up," Mace said. "Then we'll go see what he's got."

Frank Caggiano met them in the lobby of 49 West Forty-seventh Street and took them up to an apartment on the eighth floor, where he showed them the Krugerrands, the Krugerrand die, the stolen traveler's checks, blank New York and New Jersey driver's licenses, social security cards, and birth certificates. Jack Mace beamed, Wincelowicz fingered everything incredulously, and Billy made Caggiano an offer he could only refuse.

"What the fuck is this?" Caggiano demanded, glaring at Mace. "I thought you guys were coming to buy this stuff. Now you want to bargain with me?"

He started to gather everything up, but Wincelowicz shook his head at Billy in mock reproof and said he would take it at the price agreed.

"Well, you can't blame a guy for trying," Billy said amiably, and chatted with Mace while Wincelowicz counted out a down payment of $2,500.

Two days later, they were back to complete the transaction, although permission to spend $10,000 for the Krugerrand die had been refused for reasons of "program purity." (Unwilling to allow a fraud to continue that could already have milked millions from its victims, case agent Dale Hackbart then turned for the money to the South African consulate in New York, which seemed rather more anxious to protect the American public than the government in Washington.) Mace met them at the Burger Restaurant with his friend and associate Elmer Dudley, who dealt mainly in guns and drugs and was on his way home to Augusta, Georgia.

After Dudley left for the airport, Billy handed over $14,000 and sent Wincelowicz with Mace to collect the merchandise: a hundred phony Krugerrands ($2,000); the Krugerrand die ($10,000); a fat bundle of Chinese and Japanese currency ($3,000); two blank driver's licenses, one from New York and one from New Jersey ($400); a blank birth certificate ($300); a social security card ($200); and $840-worth of counterfeit Rolex watches. They then arranged to meet Mace later for dinner, and returned to 575 Madison Avenue, where Wincelowicz turned their purchases over to Dale Hackbart for safekeeping, although not before Wincelowicz, mistrusting the gleam in Billy's eye, had carved his initials and the date on each of the Krugerrands.

"What the hell are you doing?" Billy demanded, catching him at work with his jackknife. "How can I use 'em like that?"

"We can't *use* this stuff, Billy. It's evidence."

"Frank, I want to put one on a chain. As a souvenir."

"Uh-uh. It'd turn your neck green."

Over dinner, Mace complained that Frank was not spending enough time on Forty-seventh Street.

"You're never there when I need you," he said. "Murphy, he's always moving around—I can't reach him either—and this way you're missing a lotta good stuff. Guy comes in with something, he wants to cut a deal right away. I can't put him on hold. Where d'ya live, Frank?"

"Me? Queens. But I can always drive in and—"

"No, no. Queens? Forget about it. I tell you what I'm gonna do. I'm gonna get you an apartment on the street. Right across from where I'm at. I'll keep a key, but you can live there. That way I'll have you on call. What d'ya say?"

"Well . . ." Wincelowicz looked to Billy for support. "Sounds good to me."

It sounded good to Billy, too. As far as he knew, no agency—federal, state, or local—had ever mounted a successful undercover operation in the Diamond District, let alone had an undercover agent installed there and vouched for by the country's leading fence.

"You wanna do it, go ahead," he said indifferently. "Pay attention to Jack and maybe you'll learn something useful."

They learned something useful the very next day, when they went to Forty-seventh Street to collect another batch of phony Rolex watches. Over coffee in the Burger Restaurant, Mace told them he had lined up a hundred thousand dollars in traveler's checks and for the first time spoke of a cocaine connection with the best stuff in the city. From the hints he gave them, and the name he had dropped so frequently in other contexts, Billy had no doubt that Mace was referring to his friend Fat Tony Salerno, consigliere of the Genovese family, and a by-now traditional target of the Bureau's.

Not sure how they stood on narcotics, Billy switched the conversation to electronic gadgets for swindling the telephone company, one of which he had ordered from Mace's friend Freddy for four hundred dollars. Anything else they bought from a source of his, he added, would in future attract a commission, a thoughtful touch that

Mace appreciated, and which reminded him that he had not yet
taught them how to beat the phones by dialing the right sequence of
numbers.

Billy wrote them down carefully. His long-distance phone bills
were keeping him poor, he said. In the coming week, he expected to
be in Dallas and then on to Los Angeles.

"Yeah? Well, when you get to L.A., you better talk to my friend
Jimmy Chypres," said Mace. "He can help you with the phones. He
can help you with anything. Every month he gets a list of numbers
you can use to charge your calls to General Motors or Exxon or some
other big corporation. I mean, Jimmy's something else. Any type of
scheme you can think of, he's a master. I'll give you his number. No,
I'll do better than that. I'll give you his number and tell him you're
gonna call."

"Oh, yeah,' said Wincelowicz. "We'll give him a call, Jack. Don't
worry about it."

Mace beamed. "And listen, I talked to the landlady. About the
apartment? You're all set."

The rent was $650 a month, cash, which Wincelowicz had to pay
in person to Joe Gentile, aka Joey Lane, the other major fence in the
Diamond District who ran his operation from the back of the first
floor of 55 West Forth-seventh Street. The first time they met, he said:

"Yeah, Frankie. You're with Jack, right?"

"Right."

"Yeah. Well, we took care of you. We hooked your gas line up with
another apartment, so you're okay for gas. And don't worry about the
electricity either. We cut the meter out."

"Gee, thanks," said Special Agent Vincent Wincelowicz.

"Well, I know you got a problem getting home. Jack told me. You
want we should do something with the phone?"

"No, no," he said hastily, wondering how he was going to explain
all these fringe benefits to middle management. "No, that's all right.
I'll take care of my own phone."

Once installed in the apartment, Wincelowicz had to keep up
appearances. Every day a couple of FBI supply clerks would deliver a
truckload of paper or office equipment or electronic gear to the
apartment, and the next day, a couple more would come in a rented
truck to take it away again. After a few weeks of this, Billy and
Wincelowicz became known on the street as guys who would deal in
anything, and day by day Frank Kohler's association with Mace grew
closer and more filial. The two would stand talking on the sidewalk
for hours, Mace with his hand on Frankie's shoulder, introducing
him to everybody and passing on the accumulated wisdom of a
lifetime.

"Don't buy nothing, Frankie, unless you already got a place to lay it off. What do you want to sit around holding something for? Number one, it's dangerous. Number two, you already spent your money and you're not earning nothing from it."

And again: "You wanna do a deal, and you're gonna make a lotta money, but it's a little risky? Okay, do it on a holiday. The feds don't work on a holiday. Or after five o'clock. Or on a rainy day. Or on a Friday afternoon in the summer."

Mace belonged to a vanishing breed of professional crooks who could never really retire because they worked for the impure joy of "getting over," of beating the system. Beyond a certain point, money was unimportant, except as a symbol of success. If the challenge was strong enough, they would go anywhere to make a dime. Being similarly motivated, Billy understood this perfectly, but for Wincelowicz it meant dumping a lot of preconceived ideas.

"We sat around one night talking about different ways of scamming things," Wincelowicz recalled later. "Their whole idea was to get over. Over on the cops, over on their wives—didn't matter. That was the whole thing. Getting over.

"One of the guys was at the airport, and he saw these change-making machines, where you put the dollar in and get quarters out. And he says, 'There's gotta be a way to beat this.' So he Scotch-taped two dollar bills together end to end, one face up and the other face down. When he inserted the first dollar bill the correct way up, the quarters dropped out. But then the machine would reject the second dollar bill taped to it and both dollar bills would come back. He said he walked around the airport and did that until his pockets were so full of quarters they were pulling his pants down. And this was a guy who used to carry a hundred thousand dollars with him all the time in case a deal came up. He wasn't doing it for the money. He was doing it for the sheer sensual pleasure of beating the system."

Before the winter was out, Jack Mace's wife died. Wincelowicz was not entirely sure they had ever been legally married, but they had certainly been together a long time. Invited to the funeral, he drove for ten hours to Rochester through a blinding snowstorm to join New York's aristocracy of crime for a burial that could not take place because the ground was too hard, and then drove ten hours back again through the same blizzard.

A day or two later, when they met on the street, Mace suggested that Wincelowicz share his apartment, all but saying in so many words that he was ready to retire and hand over the running of his business to the younger man. Wincelowicz gently declined, not because he undervalued the chance of penetrating to the inner sanctum of the nation's trade in stolen goods but because he still had to report to 26 Federal Plaza from time to time, and needed a little privacy if he was to wear a body recorder every day.

Mace took his refusal philosophically, soon persuaded that a young man with an eye for the girls needed an apartment of his own, but he was less inclined to take no for an answer when Fat Tony Salerno invited him and Frankie down to his place in Florida for a couple of weeks soon after the funeral. Wincelowicz was more than willing to go.

"If I get over with Salerno," he said, "if I get in as Jack's boy, I can go from there and get over with anybody you want in organized crime. Anybody at all. In six months, we could have a hundred cases. Narcotics. Property crimes. Labor racketeering. Loan-sharking. You name it. And all of 'em major LCN figures."

Forget it, said the Bureau. Too risky. And anyway, what did any of this have to do with NYCON and white-collar crime?

"But I'll be Salerno's house guest," Wincelowicz protested. "It's social, not business. Business comes later. Once I get in there, I can work any kind of crime you want. Nobody ever got over at this level before."

No, said the Bureau. Stay away from Salerno. Fat Tony belonged to the narcotics squad or the organized crime squad. If they needed help, they would ask for it. How would Wincelowicz feel if one of their guys muscled in on Forty-seventh Street and tried to tell him how to work Jack Mace?

"But that's unreal," he protested. "*I* can get in with Salerno. *They* can't."

Their attention would be drawn to his report, said the Bureau. But until further orders, Wincelowicz was there to work white-collar crime for George Dyer and NYCON, and that was it.

Mace was puzzled and hurt when Wincelowicz made his excuses, but his mob friends had already decided to plug the gap in his domestic life by fixing him up with Annie Schwartz, widow of Carmine "Lillo" Galante, boss of the Bonanno family until shot dead over lunch in Greenwich Village.

Although the NYCON team mourned the wasted opportunity, Mace's sojourn in Florida at least gave them a chance to catch their collective breath. In addition to the case files on Mace himself and his Diamond District associates, about twenty more had been opened on his more important out-of-town sources and connections. If any or all of these were to be developed, only Billy and Wincelowicz could do it, for Mace had to vouch for them personally. There was no way in which New York could simply pass the files to the appropriate FBI office for action. If the Bureau was to take down his nationwide network, it had to set up a three-man mini task force—Billy, Wincelowicz and Dale Hackbart (to take care of the paperwork, purse strings and liaison with local offices and prosecutors)—and turn it loose to follow the trail wherever it led.

George Dyer was willing, but his boss, Assistant Coordinator Fred Verinder, could see no percentage in it for the New York office. On the other hand, he could see no reasonable pretext for blocking it, either. Soon after New Year's, the NYCON road company left for Atlanta with all the guilty elation of high-school seniors unexpectedly let out of class, unaware at the time that they were pioneering one of the more promising ways of freeing the Bureau from its generally arthritic approach to organized crime.

After collecting evidence against two major distributors of bootleg videotapes in Atlanta, the team rented a bright red Lincoln Town Car and drove to Augusta, where local agents wired Wincelowicz up with a recorder, taped to his chest, for a prearranged meeting with Elmer Dudley at a car dealer's showrooms on the edge of town. Dudley was sitting in the office talking to somebody when Billy and Wincelowicz drove up, but gave them a wave to show that he had seen them arrive.

"Okay, Frank," said Billy. "Turn it on. Let's make sure the thing's working."

"Yeah. Good idea." Wincelowicz switched on the body recorder— and they both heard a funny squeaking noise. *Eee-er. Eee-er. Eee-er.*

"What the fuck's that?"

"I think it's the Nagra," Wincelowicz said, trying to press his ear against it. *Eee-er. Eee-er.* The agents had taped the machine so tightly to his chest that the spools were scraping against the plastic casing.

"Well, you can't wear *that*," said Billy, with a hasty glance at Dudley, who was getting ready to come out and join them.

"I *know*," muttered Wincelowicz, frantically unbuttoning his shirt to unhitch the wires. *Eee-er. Eee-er.*

"Come on, Frank. Stop messing around. Take the thing *off*, will ya?"

"Okay, okay, okay." *Eee-er. Eee-er.* The tapes holding it in position seemed to have bonded themselves to his skin.

"Goddamit, Frank—he's coming," Billy said urgently. *Eee-er. Eee-er.* Reaching over, he grabbed the recorder and ripped it off.

"Aaaaargh," Wincelowicz said. With all the chest hair hanging from it, the Nagra looked like a dead cat.

Billy stuffed it under his seat. "Hey, Elmer," he said, greeting Dudley through the car window. "Hawiya?"

Dudley was fine. Arranging his huge bulk in the back of the Lincoln, he wanted to know why Frankie was crying. Frankie said he was allergic to Billy, and they all laughed. They talked about dope and guns, and as soon as he felt at ease, Dudley invited them over to his apartment, where his girlfriend, Sheba, was sitting on the couch slicing seeds out of marijuana and rolling joints. She was delighted to see them.

"Hey, fellers," she said. "Get out of your things. He'p yourself to a beer. I'm sure glad you came by 'cos now we're gonna *par*-ty."

"Oh, yeah," said Billy, peeling off his jacket. "Yeah."

"So you just sit down and take the weight off your feet and I'm gonna call my friend," she went on. "I'm gonna call her right now. I'm gonna tell her to get right on over here and we're really gonna *pa-a-ar*-ty."

Wincelowicz scowled. After watching Dudley eat at their first meeting in New York, he had marked it down as arguably the most disgusting thing he had ever witnessed. The idea of watching Dudley, who had to weigh in at around 350 pounds, indulge in any form of sexual activity was utterly unthinkable.

"No, come on, Billy. We've got things to do," he said. "Let's get on with it."

"Aw, relax." Billy was edging up on Sheba. "Have a beer. Make yourself comfortable. Why are you always so—so . . . Come on. We're gonna be here for a while, so take off your jacket. Do like the lady says. She wants us to *par*-ty. Right, darling?"

Sheba giggled. Wincelowicz glowered. It had to be ninety-five degrees in the apartment. He was wearing a hat, and a big leather jacket that he could not take off without exposing the wires still taped to his arms and torso.

"All right, gimme the keys," he said. At least if he went down to the car, he would have a chance to get rid of the wires.

"What?"

"The keys. Gimme the keys. I want to go down and get something out of the car."

"Okay. Go ahead. I ain't got 'em."

"What do you mean, you ain't got 'em? *I* ain't got 'em."

"Sure, you do. Unless Elmer's got 'em. You got 'em, Elmer?"

"No, I ain't got 'em."

"Well, Elmer ain't got 'em," said Billy, returning his attention to Sheba. "Let's see if *you* got 'em, honey."

Wincelowicz borrowed a coat hanger and went downstairs to see if he could open the car with it. The keys, he noticed, were still in the ignition. After fifteen minutes he had managed to get the wires and his jacket off, but the Lincoln, fitted with the latest antitheft locks, was still defying his every effort to break in. It was a shame. The car was brand new, without a scratch on it.

"You got a hammer?" he asked Dudley when he went back upstairs. "I'm gonna have to break a window."

Billy was sitting in the corner of the couch with a Budweiser in one hand and Sheba in the other, although she continued to roll marijuana cigarettes with impressive speed and dexterity.

"You don't have to do that, Frank," he said. "Let's stay the night. We can get somebody to open it tomorrow."

"Billy, we're going to Savannah," Wincelowicz said grimly. "Soon as we finish our business with Elmer."

"Why? What's the hurry?" asked Dudley, feeding Sheba a couple of Quaaludes. "You can stay. I got plenty of room."

"Yeah, he's got *plenty* of room," agreed Billy. "We'll go tomorrow."

"Fine. You do what you want, Billy. But *I'm* going to Savannah." Wincelowicz turned to Dudley. "How about that hammer? You got one?"

Dudley had a better idea. He sent for a friend of his who stole cars for a living, but he took one look at the Lincoln, shook his head, and drove away again. Dudley fetched the hammer.

"Hey, Frank," whispered Billy as they followed him downstairs. "Don't forget. We had seven hundred fifty bucks' worth of clothes on the back seat before the window got broke. When you call Washington, don't forget to tell 'em, so we can get our money back. On the clothes."

Wincelowicz stared at him for a moment, awe-struck, then clattered after Dudley, who was getting ready to attack the factory-mileage Lincoln with his hammer.

"Here, let me do it," Wincelowicz said, because he actually knew how to break a car window with the minimum of fuss and damage.

"No, I got it," said Dudley, aiming to hit the quarterlight with every ounce of his 350 pounds. "Stand back while I give this thing a little tap."

Winding up like a baseball pitcher, he let fly with a round-arm swing of the hammer that would have punched a hole in the Hoover Dam, but the window was made of sterner stuff. The hammer head bounced back off the safety glass with such force that it very nearly toppled him over. Wincelowicz was almost afraid to look for fear that the claws were embedded in Dudley's forehead.

"All right, Elmer," he said, losing patience. "Gimme the hammer."

Snatching it out of his hand, he forced the claws behind the edge of the driver's door and levered it away from the post, grunting and swearing under his breath, until he had enough room to slide in a strip of metal and pop the lock open. By then the party spirit had completely evaporated and they drove to the Green Jacket restaurant for dinner.

"Hey, fellers," said Dudley, burrowing into the trunk of his car as

Billy and Wincelowicz pulled up beside him in the parking lot. "C'mere. Got something to show ya."

As they joined him, screened from general view by the trunk lid, he straightened up with a big .25 caliber pistol in his hand, and for a moment they thought they were gone. A quarter-pound of pressure was all it needed.

"You boys say you want guns?" he asked. "How about this?"

"Yeah," said Billy, releasing his breath. "Yeah, we can use some guns. What have you got? Uzis? Ingrams?"

"Hey, take it easy." Wincelowicz chuckled indulgently. "Don't rush the man. He'll tell ya what he's got."

"Well, I can get you some of these two-five calibers," Dudley said. "Wise guys like 'em when they're gonna make a hit."

"Oh, yeah," said Wincelowicz. "Those are nice. But put it away, Elmer, before somebody sees you. You don't have to show us nothing. Your word's good enough for us."

"No, well, see, you can have this one and I'll get you another. I already sold Jack about eleven of those. I'll get you the silencers, too."

"Hey. Fantastic."

Wincelowicz hesitated. He had no identification on him. He was in the Deep South posing as an Italian from New York. All he needed now was for some redneck sheriff's deputy to come along and catch him with a hit man's gun and he would be dead before he could open his mouth.

"But listen," he said. "I don't wanna take nothing like that on the plane with me—you know what I mean?"

"Sure. No problem."

"No. But how we gonna get 'em up there, then?"

"Well, hell—I'm gonna mail 'em to ya," Dudley said. "Gimme five hundred dollars and I'll mail you the two of 'em."

"You'll *mail* 'em?"

"Do it all the time," he said cheerfully. "Just wrap 'em up in aluminum foil, put 'em in a gift pack, take 'em down to the post office, and drop 'em in the mail. They go book rate."

When Assistant Coordinator Fred Verinder heard it, he called Wincelowicz into his office to explain himself.

"What are you, crazy? I don't believe this. You give the guy five hundred dollars for two guns and he's going to *mail* 'em to you?"

"Yeah, that's right."

"You can't be serious. You're assigned to work con men, and you fall for a scam like that?"

"No, no. No scam. He'll do it."

"Don't hold your breath. Face it, Wincelowicz—you just threw away five hundred dollars of the taxpayers' money. With a pretty bad error of judgment."

"I don't think so. Jack sent me. I'm Jack's boy. If I tell him Elmer screwed me, Elmer's gonna be out a lot more than five hundred. You'll see. He'll send 'em."

"Never going to happen. You'll never see those guns."

The mailman delivered them two mornings later at Investment Capital SA, and Wincelowicz waited all day for an apology. In the end, he called Verinder's office to tell him the guns had arrived.

"Well, he *could* have stiffed you," he was told. "Just don't take chances like that. Could be a sucker play. You got away with it this time. Next time, if it's real money, he'll stiff you for sure."

"Uh-huh."

"Think about it. You got lucky, that's all."

"Uh-huh."

(Dudley was eventually arrested on an assortment of charges, involving guns, narcotics, and bootleg videotapes, and decided to "cooperate" with the government.)

Billy and Wincelowicz also "got lucky" in California.

Jimmy Chypres, another lifelong friend of Jack Mace's, proclaimed himself to be the biggest and the best in the field of false documentation, with a particular interest in providing wanted criminals with new, untraceable identities, and con men with the paperwork necessary for bank fraud, embezzlement, stock swindles, and so on. (In the commission of financial crime, the Chypres team included two hand-reared bank vice presidents and a much-respected Los Angeles CPA.) As sidelines, he also ran a highly profitable business in all-but-authentic "gold" credit cards, and, through an associate in Technicolor's processing laboratories, in prints of new movies prior to their scheduled first-run release dates.

But what burned Billy's tail worse than any of that, Chypres had never spent a day in jail, and the message on his answering machine began, "This is the Voice of America." With Wincelowicz a more or less hapless bystander, and Dale Hackbart next door, taping the encounter, they locked horns in Billy's room at the Bonaventure hotel.

Unlike Elmer Dudley, Chypres combined flamboyance with extreme caution. Although he had no reason to be suspicious, as Mace had vouched fully for both of them, he arrived with a bug detector in his hand, making no attempt to conceal it from Wincelowicz, who let him in. Cylindrical in shape, about four inches long and three inches in diameter, it began to beep as he approached the table where Billy was sitting, and by the time they shook hands, the device was beep-beeping its heart out.

"It's these fluorescent tubes," Chypres said. He held it up toward the light fitting over the table, inducing instant electronic hysteria. "They do it every time."

As the FBI microphone had been installed directly above the light, Billy reached out, removed the detector from Chypres's hand, shook it violently, then started twisting and wrenching at it. Chypres attempted to take it back, but Billy turned away and banged it against the table several times before wrenching at it again.

"Hey," said Chypres. "Don't do that. You'll bust it. That's a delicate piece of equipment."

"I know what it is," Billy replied impatiently. "But mine's a bit different. I just wanna see how this one opens up."

He gave the device another crack against the edge of the table before Chypres snatched it away from him, examined the casing aggrievedly, and put it in his pocket.

From each insisting upon the superior merits of his own electronic equipment, they graduated naturally to comparing their criminal incomes, with Chypres boasting that he was known far and wide as one of the biggest spenders in the state. With that, he lit a Cuban cigar with a twenty-dollar bill.

"Big deal," said Billy, helping himself to a cigar also.

To his horror, Wincelowicz watched him reach for the roll in his pocket and peel off a hundred-dollar bill. "Billy," he said warningly, but was quelled with a glance. "Okay," he sighed. "Suit yourself."

In the first place, Billy did not smoke. In the second place, he evidently imagined he was burning government money. Wrong, glared Wincelowicz, conscious of Hackbart listening to all this and recording it in the next room. Go ahead—knock yourself out, said his indifferent slump. It's *your* hundred. Do whatever you want.

As Chypres had nothing bigger than a hundred, they moved on to the subject of dress and deportment, bragging about the number of suits in their respective closets and capping each other's designer names. Finally, Billy jumped to his feet, wrestling with his belt buckle, and backed away into the center of the room.

"Hah," he snorted, unzipping his fly. "You think *you* got class? I'll show you class, goddammit." With that, he dropped his pants around his ankles and paraded a few hobbled steps up and down. "Okay? Let me see *your* silk drawers."

Wincelowicz shaded his eyes. Here he was, a responsible government agent, one of several brought together in a Los Angeles hotel at no small expense, watching two grown men show each other their underwear.

"Okay," he said wearily. "You done now? Anybody mind if we talk a little business?"

As Chypres had nothing to beat Billy's silk shorts, he talked a little business. He showed them two American Express Gold credit cards, and Wincelowicz ordered one in the name of Frank Kohler. Offered a choice of ID cards for American Airlines and Japan Airlines that Chypres swore would stand up to any check at any security point in any airport used by those airlines, they also bought a Japanese card, in the name of Kohler, and a special hairspray can for smuggling cocaine. (Or, in conjunction with the ID card, plastic explosives?)

In the top compartment of the can there was just enough hairspray under pressure to provide a few trial squirts for Customs or security officials conducting a thorough search, but the rest of it was hollow and constructed to screw into the top counter-clockwise, so that any attempt to unscrew the two sections in the usual way would in fact tighten them.

Again overcome by caution, or perhaps just to irritate, Chypres now went into a colored-balloon routine. Having demonstrated the can in dumb show, he looked at them expectantly, and when Billy asked if they could buy it, Chypres pulled a little green balloon out of the secret compartment blew it up and waved it at them.

"Excuse me," said Wincelowicz, who needed something on tape. "What's with the balloon?"

"It's green," Chypres said. "You know what green means, don't you?"

"It means go, right?" said Billy. "Frank says, 'Can we buy the smuggling can?' You wave a green balloon, and that means yes. Right?"

"Right." Chypres rolled his eyes at the dumbness of some people.

"Okay. You got any more of those?"

Chypres picked out a red balloon, blew it up and tied it off.

"Okay. You're showing me a red balloon so that means no. You just got the one smuggling can?"

Chypres selected another green balloon.

"Well, how much is it?" Wincelowicz asked cunningly.

Chypres held up two fingers.

"Twenty dollars?"

The other lashed out at him with the red balloon.

"Two hundred?" suggested Billy, and was rewarded with a green.

"Okay, Jimmy," Wincelowicz sighed. "We'll buy the cocaine smuggling can for two hundred. But I still don't get the balloons."

"You'll get the balloons," said Chypres. "I'll *give* you the balloons. The balloons are included."

"No, I mean, why the balloon language all of a sudden?"

Chypres found a yellow one and blew it up. "You know what yellow means?"

"Oh, yeah. It means caution, right?"

The other shook his head in mock despair, relieved them of three hundred dollars for the dummy hairspray can and ID card, and departed, promising to keep in touch.

"Phew," said Billy, collapsing in a chair. "You know something, Frank? I got a little bit concerned there."

"Yeah? What about?" Wincelowicz asked. "You mean when he started with the balloon bit?"

"Well, yeah. See, I worked Jimmy Chypres before. About ten years ago."

The other stared. "You *what*?"

"Yeah. And for a minute there, I thought he recognized me."

"Goddammit, Billy," Wincelowicz gargled. He was pretty certain that Chypres had been carrying a piece. "You could at least have *told* me."

Billy shrugged. "What's the use of getting us *both* nervous?"

In Bristol, Tennessee, they opened a file on a local businessman manufacturing counterfeit Calvin Klein jeans on a grand scale. In Oklahoma City, they went after another source of bootleg videotapes, and in Texas, struck oil.

Through his web of connections in that state, Billy arranged for Wincelowicz to meet Robert Hutchings, a con man from St. Louis, Missouri, who was in the process of swindling the First National Bank of Abilene out of $20 million in order to buy the La Jolla Oil Company, of Midland, Texas. As the NYCON team was not in a position to start making out-of-town arrests—they had their undercover identities to protect, their relationship with Mace to exploit, and already some thirty other cases to develop—Wincelowicz managed to engineer just enough official interest in the deal to make Hutchings back off without arousing his suspicions.

But the idea of letting him take a walk rankled to such an extent that Billy decided to take him down another way. He telephoned Hutchings from New York, baiting his call with hints of a $3 million loan from Chemical Bank, and when Hutchings flew in to collect, encouraged him to go for $5 million on the strength of his (wholly fictitious) statement of assets. All he had to do, said Billy, was pay a finder's fee to him and a 1 percent "commission" to "bank vice president" Dale Hackbart.

Scarcely believing his luck, Hutchings met with the president of Chemical Bank and "vice president" Hackbart at 52 Broadway to agree on terms and afterward went off for a celebratory lunch with

Billy and Wincelowicz. When they returned later to pick up his letter of credit, Hackbart produced an arrest warrant instead.

With other prosecutions pending against him in Missouri, Hutchings eventually agreed to plead guilty to a minor charge carrying a nominal two-year sentence, but for reasons no one could comprehend, he later reneged on the deal, went to trial, and was convicted on all counts.

"It was pathetic," Billy said later. "Talked his way out of two on a kiddy farm into seventeen years in the penitentiary. We laughed, but it wasn't funny. He deserved to be off the street. He'd been fleecing people all over. He was worse than Tommy Duke."

Which was saying something. Although Billy had specifically forbidden him to do anything with the deed to his Florida property, Duke had secretly put it up as collateral for a fifteen-thousand-dollar loan from a money-lender named Joseph Bistrix while Billy and Wincelowicz were out on their four-week road trip.

Since joining the NYCON team, Billy's appearances at Cowboy Palace had been necessarily brief and erratic, but the loss of day-to-day touch, while giving Duke more scope for mischief, had also meant less day-to-day friction—so much so that Supervisor Walt Smith and his squad were now clearly convinced that the two of them were working some swindle together.

For his part, Billy did not care *what* they thought. He had taken the case as far as he could. He was still turning over tapes of every phone conversation he had with those involved, and he knew the Bureau still had its wires up in Cowboy Palace and in Resource Capital's offices.

"Did you find Agent Nye to be a liar?" asked Breitbart, still trying to drive a wedge between Billy and the Bureau.

"No, sir."

"Did you find Agent Nye to be an efficient officer of the United States Government?"

"I never had any dealings with him."

"Well, he interviewed you with regard to this case, isn't that true?"

"He was the case agent. I never worked with him."

"Did you tell Agent Nye, sir, that you got involved in the Cowboy Palace to make money?" Breitbart insisted.

"Yes, sir." He really could not remember telling Nye that, but he might have. It was at least partly true.

Breitbart nodded. "Did Agent Nye threaten you?"

"No, sir."

"Did Agent Nye tell you that if you lied to a federal agent, you could go to jail just for that—if it was in a criminal prosecution?"

"No, sir,"

"Did other agents tell you that and threaten you?"

"No, sir."

"How about the agents from the Office of Professional Responsibility? Didn't they threaten you when you accused Stowe of using cocaine?"

Billy and Baird protested together. Billy had never accused Stowe of anything. All he had done was report a malicious statement by Duke that he and Stowe had snorted cocaine together in Cowboy Palace. After the trial record had been corrected, Breitbart worked his way back to firmer ground via lengthy digressions into Duke's extravagant lifestyle.

"As a matter of fact, the agents tried to convince you that Tom Duke was a bum?"

"Yes, sir."

"The FBI agents told you he was an arsonist?"

"Yes."

"They told you he was a flimflam man?"

"Yes, sir."

"They told you he was a thief? What is a flimflam man?"

"I don't think they ever told me that he was a thief."

"They told you that you shouldn't talk to him?"

"Nobody could tell me who to talk to."

"They tried to, didn't they?"

"They didn't succeed."

"No one can tell you anything, isn't that correct?"

"That's correct," said Billy.

He could hardly have put it better himself. After laboring for days to demonstrate that Billy was a common informer who would say or do anything for money, to save his skin or to appease the government, Breitbart had just shot himself in the foot by suggesting that Billy was his own man who took instruction from nobody.

21

Surviving a brief coolness with Mace after his refusal of the Florida invitation, Wincelowicz was now back in tighter than ever, and all Forty-seventh Street knew it. People went out of their way to do him favors, as a mark of respect for his sponsor, and nobody more insistently than Vinnie DiCicci, whose father, Tony, was a power in Teamsters Local 804—Rotondo's union.

Although the Bureau ordered Wincelowicz to decline their offer of a no-show job (counting trucks) in the interests of "program purity," it became an offer he could not refuse when Mace overrode his objections and confirmed his union "appointment" with Paul Castellano, then boss of the Gambino family. With or without official approval, Wincelowicz found himself being propelled into labor racketeering, with an unprecedented opportunity to explore the relationship between labor unions and crime families in New York City.

When he explained this to Verinder, the Bureau again made its attitude clear. NYCON had been set up to go after con men, he was told. Anything else was off-limits.

"But it's all crime," said Wincelowicz. "If I see a bank robbery in progress, what am I supposed to do? Walk away?"

No. He was supposed to take appropriate action, then hand over to the bank robbery squad. In the present case, he should report DiCicci's offer of a no-show job to the labor racketeering squad and leave it to them.

"But I can get in and they can't," he protested. "It's like the Salerno thing. I've got Jack Mace's okay—and it's not transferable. Why don't I see how far I can go with it and *then* bring them in?"

No. If agents were allowed to run down every lead they uncovered, the result would be chaos. He was going great with NYCON. Better he should concentrate on his own cases and let his colleagues do the same.

Al Cohen, purveyor of bootleg videotapes and counterfeit designer clothes, was another old friend of Mace's. As a mark of *his* respect, he invited Frankie and Billy to consider the possibilities of bringing together senior government figures in Hawaii and a wholesale meat-packing firm run by the Carlos Marcello family in New Orleans. Meat exports from the mainland to Hawaii were government controlled, but a modest tribute of so much per pound could open up the islands' beef market for his Louisiana friends, to the benefit of all concerned.

It was a suggestion that the NYCON team was inclined to take seriously. Cohen had already demonstrated his connections with organized crime in Hawaii by arranging for Wincelowicz and Billy to buy as much "pakalolo" from syndicate growers in Maui as they could pay for—no small favor in itself, for no other variety of marijuana was more highly prized by connoisseurs or in shorter supply. But with Assistant Coordinator Fred Verinder's attitude toward out-of-town cases, there seemed little point even in asking him to authorize an investigation until early in March 1983, when Billy was approached by Special Agent Ray Hamilton in Honolulu. Would he be interested in flying out there to help Hamilton with an investigation into organized crime in the islands?

Is a magnet interested in pointing north?

Hamilton met him in Honolulu and gave him a copy of an FBI memorandum setting out the general aims of the operation.

"This plan is being submitted to demonstrate a means by which the organized crime syndicate on the island of Maui specifically, and in the state of Hawaii generally, can be infiltrated, exposed, and prosecuted," it began. "The intent will be to penetrate the upper echelon of the organized crime faction on the island of Maui, and once this is done, 'Project Hale Auau,' through the use of informants and undercover agents (UCAs), will investigate the numerous ramifications of organized crime activities in Hawaii. It is anticipated UCAs will contact U.S. mainland and Japanese organized crime figures as well as become involved with the Hawaii criminal element. The 'spinoff' potential appears promising."

"Did you write this?" asked Billy, pleased to find a less blinkered approach than he was used to in New York.

"I had some input," Hamilton said modestly.

"The initial phase will begin with involvement in production and marketing of 'pakalolo,' the Hawaiian word for marijuana," the document went on. "This will include, upon successful development of the initial phase, the identification of producers, extent of production, organization of production, shipping and marketing of pakalolo and its relationship to organized crime activities, including narcotics, gambling, extortion, bribery, kickbacks, political corruption, labor unions, Yakuza (Japanese organized crime, which has infiltrated Hawaii), police corruption, land fraud matters, and conspiracy.

"This operation will initially be a joint FBI/DEA/U.S. Customs/Honolulu P.D./Maui County P.D. operation with the possibility of including, as developments occur, all other state of Hawaii county police departments, plus the U.S. Postal Service. Other FBI divisions may be called upon to provide supporting service in this operation as the project develops."

Billy snorted. "If you mean New York, you can save your breath. If it was up to them, I wouldn't even *be* here."

"No, but what do you think?" Hamilton asked. "You think you can get in there? With what you got?"

"Oh, yeah," said Billy. "No problem. I done a lot of that already."

"A lot of what?"

"Identifying pakalolo growers and how they tie in with the syndicate and the Yakuza and all that stuff."

As Billy had just stepped off the plane, Hamilton assumed he was joking, but in fact he was exaggerating only slightly. To show that the gods were with him, the Pan Am reservations clerk in Los Angeles had allocated Billy a seat next to Jake Conte* on Flight 811 to Honolulu.

A deal in bullion and uncut diamonds (for income-tax purposes), Conte was a walking advertisement for high-octane after-shave, a tanned, Teflon-smooth parody of a soap-opera star who not only knew everybody worth knowing in Hawaii but could not resist proving it to out-of-shape hicks like Billy—particularly when Billy introduced himself as a senior partner of Investment Capital SA.

In an expansive mood, after a successful business trip to Africa and Zurich, Conte was soon persuaded to reveal himself as a one-man chamber of commerce, representing both independent *and* syndicate pakalolo growers as well as the state's leading cocaine import/export merchants. If Billy was looking to make any kind of high- or

---

*Although the events in this chapter are true, because the investigations did not lead to indictments of those involved, names have been changed to avoid meritless lawsuits.

low-life connection in the state of Hawaii, he suggested, then Conte was his man.

Pakalolo—"crazy smoke"—was Hawaii's number-one cash crop, selling in Honolulu at eighty to one hundred dollars an ounce, but he had enough in his refrigerator at home for Billy's personal use. This private supply came from Millie and Patrick Lamar, on Maui. As independents, they were good only for small quantities, but he could easily arrange through Takeo Yamauchi, boss of the Yakuza syndicate on Maui, for Billy to buy a whole field, if he needed that much. The routine would be to make a down payment on the crop and deposit the rest of the purchase price in a bank, preferably in Switzerland, where they would handle any amount of money for 1.5 percent and no questions asked.

When Billy brought up the subject of "Operation Green Harvest," the much-touted federal campaign against the pakalolo industry, Conte dismissed it as a joke. The helicopters and ground-support crews were being used by the syndicate in preference to their own enforcers, he said. The only growers being hit were independents, deliberately fingered by the syndicate to keep down the competition and keep up the price

"There's something else you oughta look at," Conte went on, as Billy reluctantly released the champagne stewardess after relieving her of several splits. "You know, you can get all the pakalolo you want in exchange for coke."

"You kidding? Shit. Nobody's gonna catch me flying in with *that* stuff."

"Nah, nah. You don't haveta. You'd make the switch in L.A."

"Yeah?" Billy filled the other's glass encouragingly.

"Yeah. Chuck Hauser knows how to do it. He's a good friend of mine. Runs a travel agency. I'll introduce ya."

"I'll drink to that."

They toasted each other solemnly.

"How come you know all these people?" asked Billy, reaching for his notebook. "Lemme write that name down. So I can remind ya."

"I won't forget," said Conte, with a superior chuckle. "And then there's this other guy I want ya to meet—Herb Wilson. Big wheel. He's like state commander for the Veterans of Foreign Wars."

"Yeah?" Billy blinked. "Why do I wanna meet *him*?"

"Why?" Conte leaned forward. "Because he runs all the syndicate casino games and whores on the island," he murmured.

"Ah-*hah*!" said Billy. "Jake, you're a good man to know."

By the time they reached Honolulu, Conte had half-filled Billy's notebook with names, addresses, and telephone numbers.

Suitably amazed, Special Agent Ray Hamilton and his colleagues installed Billy in a condominium on Maui and wired him up with a Nagra body recorder for a visit to the State Liquor Commission. As William Murphy, ex-con, he was to see if he could bribe his way into a liquor license for a Korean bar he wanted to open on Maui. Hamilton prepared the way with a monitored call, and before getting out of the car to keep the appointment, Billy checked the Nagra, as he always did, to make sure it was working properly.

He was inside for three hours, long enough to establish the equivalent of a lifelong relationship with one senior official, who admitted he had been corrupt but was now born again in Christ, and with another, who felt he could probably bring himself to overlook William Murphy's criminal past after he saw the size of the "flash" roll Billy had prepared for the occasion. Ranging far and wide through the Who's Who of politics, business, and organized crime on Maui, the conversation ended in protestations of mutual esteem and a date for drinks on Friday, at which time they would introduce Billy to Charlie, muscle man for syndicate boss Takeo Yamauchi and a big-time narcotics trafficker in his own right.

Conscious that he had established a solid beachhead even by his own exacting standards, Billy went back to the condominium to explain what he had to Hamilton and the other agents waiting to relieve him of the Nagra.

"You don't want to hear it all again, do you, Billy?" asked Hamilton. "Go take in the sights or something while we run through this thing. We can talk about it when you get back."

"Sure," said Billy. They probably knew all the names that had come up in conversation better than he did. "Why not?"

He gave them three full hours, and returned to the condominium to find Hamilton waiting there alone. He looked uneasy, which was wrong.

"You're not going to believe this, Billy," he said, shaking his head. "They forgot to put a tape in the machine."

Billy looked at him for a long time, trying to figure it out. Not only had he *seen* them put a tape in, he had checked it himself. If they were going to lie about it, why did it have to be such a stupid lie? Was Hamilton trying to disassociate himself from a decision to suppress the tape? And why suppress it anyway? Had the wrong names cropped up? If so, what did that tell him about the FBI's Honolulu office? And what did it mean in terms of his personal safety?

"Gee," he said. "That's too bad."

On full red alert, he called Conte. Any encounter with strangers now had to be treated as a possible setup, but the Lamars turned out to be more nervous of him than he was of them. As independent growers, their main fear was not of the police or the federal government but of the syndicate. Before talking business, Billy had to promise not to discuss pakalolo with anyone else, and to deal only through Jake Conte. Working with other growers, they thought they might spare him twenty-five to thirty pounds at $1,500 a pound.

By their third meeting, the Lamars had thawed out a little. Now they thought they could manage perhaps thirty-five to fifty pounds, although that represented seventy to one hundred plants. Normally, they cultivated about eighty plants at a time, yielding around $60,000 a crop. Jake sold the stuff in Honolulu and paid them by check, being careful to keep each installment under $10,000 so that the banks would not be obliged to report it. They even agreed to mail a six-ounce trial pakalolo package to Billy in New York, on the understanding that he would pay for it, if satisfied, with an Investment Capital SA check.

Billy was satisfied. Besides the Lamars, he now had a useful list of names, descriptions, and phone numbers of growers on Maui, and of the syndicate members who represented their main occupational hazard. He also had a reasonable grasp of the syndicate's infrastructure, and its extensive interests in gambling, extortion, and prostitution.

Through Conte, who had remained consistently, almost recklessly, helpful, he had met for drinks with Herb Wilson, who apologized for not joining them for dinner as he had a prior engagement with the local head of U.S. Customs and an FBI agent he did not identify (except that Billy gathered he had a Japanese wife). And again through Conte, he had held serious discussions with Chuck Hauser.

Indeed, in just a week, and to the astonishment of everybody connected with Project Hale Auau, Billy was able to draw Special Agent Hamilton a chart of organized crime on the island with most of the names penciled in.

"And now I'm gonna top it off for yez," he said fondly. Nothing was ever too much trouble for agents who appreciated him. "I'm gonna give ya two big syndicate dealers as a going-away present."

Hamilton smiled. "Do we know 'em, Billy?"

"You will if you do like I tell ya. They wanna talk about swapping pakalolo for coke."

"Okay. So what do you need?"

"Nothing. Just a nice room someplace with a TV camera in it and your wires up. All you gotta do is sit back and watch."

Knowing to within a few minutes when he and the dealers would show up, Billy also asked for a surveillance team to be waiting in the lobby to take photographs, but when he arrived, exactly on time, he saw no one there. Unarmed, and suddenly uneasy, he rode up to his room with the two syndicate operators wondering what could have happened, but soon settled into the swing of a three-hour discussion in which he took them through every incriminating detail of the barter deal they intended to carry out in Los Angeles. He also called room service three or four times so that an assortment of waiters could not only confirm that the meeting had taken place but later identify his visitors.

When the dealers left, radiating goodwill, he gave them a few minutes to get clear, then called the adjoining room to accept the compliments of the agents who had been listening in. But there was nobody there either. And they had "forgotten" to switch on the video camera and tape recorder.

It seemed like a good time to get the hell out of Hawaii.

A few weeks later, when Ray Hamilton called from Honolulu to arrange for Billy's follow-up visit, possibly with Wincelowicz, Assistant Coordinator Fred Verinder put his foot down. Billy was a New York source, he said, and for as long as he stayed on the books, New York was where he would work. As for Wincelowicz, there had never been any question of his going to Hawaii with Billy. New York was short enough already of manpower and resources without having to "loan" agents to other divisions.

Hamilton was horrified. He simply could not accept the idea of Billy's high-speed penetration of Hawaii's organized crime going so completely to waste. Indeed, he was so outspoken on the telephone in condemning Verinder's refusal to let Billy finish what he had started that Billy, dismayed himself by the decision, taped some of Hamilton's angrier criticisms for future reference (without telling him he was doing so). He did tell Wincelowicz and Hackbart, however, thereby presenting them with a tricky little problem in professional ethics even though they agreed with him wholeheartedly. Nobody was supposed to tape telephone conversations with FBI agents, not even when they lied or broke solemn promises or declined to pay his expenses.

As Billy's case agent, Dale Hackbart was beginning to feel personally compromised by the Bureau's failure to keep its word. Indeed, he was by now so outspoken in his criticism of its managerial deficiencies, and of the laid-back, ten-till-five, sportsbag-toting playboys among his colleagues in New York that some suspected he was "ratting them out," and left dimes on his desk in mute accusation. Hackbart's response was to pin a note to the bulletin board drawing their attention to the fact that the price of a local call was now twenty-five cents.

On April 20, 1983, at some risk to his career prospects, he sat down and addressed the following memorandum on the subject of NY 20376 C to the agent in charge of the New York divisional office:

> This source has been opened by the New York office officially for about one month. He has, however, worked with this office on an almost full-time basis since October/November, 1982, while he was a source for Atlanta (AT 4321 OC). His primary duties have been to work, assist and instruct the UCA [undercover agents] of the NYCON undercover operation. This source has so far accomplished so many things for the New York office and the Bureau that it is impossible to relate all of them here. I will relate some of the more recent activities he has been involved in handling.

First, and foremost in Hackbart's estimation, was NYCON's invasion of Forty-seventh Street. "To the best of our knowledge," he wrote, after listing Billy's achievements to date, "there has never before been a successful undercover operation in the Diamond District by any law-enforcement organization, be it state, local, or federal."

The NYCON team was almost equally impressed with Billy's exploits in Hawaii. "He has been able to identify, meet and do business with at least seven major crime figures in the islands," Hackbart reported. "The individuals contacted were higher in the crime chain of command than the Honolulu office ever thought they could reach."

It was the same story in Texas, where Billy "was able to introduce the NYCON UCA to a Robert Hutchings, who was negotiating to purchase the La Jolla Oil Company, Midland, Texas, for $20 million. Through this introduction, the UCA was able to kill the oil deal, thereby saving $20 million for the company. Through this contact, the source and UCA were instrumental in bringing Hutchings to New York, where he was arrested on 4/18/83 for submitting a false loan application to a bank in connection with a $5 million loan. Hutchings will be indicted for the false loan, mail fraud, fraud by wire, and bribery of a bank official. He is also under investigation by the St. Louis, El Paso, Dallas, Cincinnati, Boston, and Chicago Divisions as well as the U.S. Postal Inspectors. He was, however, arrested here in New York first, even though this office has been working him for less than a month. This was largely due to the efforts of the source."

Special Agent Hackbart went on in similar vein for several more paragraphs before getting to the point:

> With all the work and activity of the source, we, the Bureau and the New York office, have not and will not pay this individual for work and expenses owed. He accompanied two agents on a four-week trip

in January. During this trip, a number of contacts were made. He spent about $1,200 of his own money; this has never been reimbursed to him, even though the request for reimbursement of expenses has been submitted at least five times.

During the first week of March 1983, source was in New York to coordinate the apartment activities of Mace, as well as to firm up the meetings and contacts with people in Texas for the UCA to travel to meet Robert Hutchings. His expenses for that period were $671. This, too, has been submitted twice with no payment forthcoming.

During the later part of March 1983, source again came to New York. He recontacted people in Hawaii, arranging to obtain a shipment of narcotics to New York. He also met other contacts of Mace, including Al Cohen, who has access to the governor of Hawaii. On his return home, he met Marilyn Damore, and had discussions with her. He is still awaiting payment for his expenses for that period.

He was not authorized to come into New York during the week of April 11. The airtel requesting his travel to New York was never sent. He discussed the matter with the above agent [Hackbart] who said come anyway. As a result of the trip, Calabrese came into town, and there is a chance to get into the organized crime picture in Cleveland as has never been done before; he met with Marilyn Damore, who is going to sell him narcotics and take him into a bank for a $3 million line of credit, and he participated in the arrest of Robert Hutchings. He, through Marilyn Damore, had a chance to negotiate with the brother of the Bronx district attorney, Mario Merola. He has no chance to get paid for his expenses on this trip because it was not Bureau authorized.

It would seem to me as an agent that the Bureau, and particularly the New York office, would want to do everything in its power to keep an informant of this caliber in New York. There appears to be something wrong with the system when I cannot even get the source a return of his expenses that he has had to take from his own pocket or borrow from friends to work for the Bureau. In addition, he has not been paid an adequate amount for the services he has performed. If I ask for weekly payments, I get a reply that we should pay for results. If he has results, I cannot even get him paid for that because the results are too many and the funds requested are too high. If something is not done in the very near future to improve the method this source is handled by this office and the Bureau as a whole, he will leave the service of the Bureau, which will be a great loss to the Bureau as a whole.

I recommend that this source be placed on a weekly salary by the Bureau, wherein he is paid a fixed salary, possibly $1,000 per week for every week or part of it when he works for the Bureau in any division. This payment would be over and above expenses incurred.

Hackbart's recommendations were ignored.

Billy never recovered the sums that Hackbart mentioned. Nor the $10,000 plus expenses that Supervisor Damon Taylor had promised for his work on Cowboy Palace. He got nothing for Hutchings. By the NYCON team's own accounting, the New York office eventually owed Billy some $41,000, of which he received in total just over $13,000.

And it was not because the Bureau's senior management was unaware of his contribution. Vinnie Wincelowicz received a well-deserved incentive award with a letter of commendation from the director of the FBI, which he hung on the wall of his office. Billy copied it down one day while waiting to see him.

> I have been informed of your outstanding multidirectional efforts incident to the Group 1 undercover operation, code-named NYCON, and I would like to offer you the enclosed incentive award in recognition of your extreme professionalism.
>
> This undercover operation was targeted specifically on "advance fee" swindles and "confidence"-type schemers who prey on the business and private communities. I am particularly impressed by the manner in which you: effected the arrest and conviction of five individuals who tried to use $500 million in fraudulent bonds as loan collateral; prevented the fraudulent takeover of a Texas oil company; and pretended to be a former prison inmate in a highly sensitive matter.
>
> Your undercover role and your handling of the attendant administrative details were conscientiously maintained, and I deeply appreciate the great personal sacrifice you unselfishly bore in the furtherance of this project. The Bureau is indeed fortunate to have a fine investigator like you working on its behalf, and I thank you for a job well done.
>
> Sincerely,
> William H. Webster, Director.

The tribute was entirely deserved, but Billy would have liked one, too. All that stopped him from turning his back on the Bureau in disgust, as Hackbart feared, was a chance to clean up Cleveland.

David Breitbart was also concerned about Billy's financial arrangements with the government. "You applied for a $50,000 reward with regard to Kearns, didn't you?"

"No, sir," said Billy.

"You were turned down, weren't you?"

"I was promised $125,000."

"Did you get it?"

"No, sir."

"How many hundreds of thousands of dollars have you told people the federal government owed you?"

"I have not told a lot of people, but they do owe me money."

"How much does the federal government owe you?"

"A total of $150,000, as far as my figures total up to."

He was glad of the chance to put this on record. By bringing out Billy's grievances against the Bureau, Breitbart was again undermining his own contention that Billy's testimony against Doc Hyman and the others had been bought.

"Was that for out-of-pocket expenses?"

Helpful again. *"There are cases that I worked on that they promised me expenses."*

"These are cases that you were a catalyst for?"

"And convictions were made," agreed Billy.

"That you worked on?"

Billy nodded. *"And recovery was over $300 million in the cases in New York City. Not one case—several cases."*

Earlier on in the cross-examination, he would have suspected some subtle trap behind all this, but he knew better now.

"Is that all it was?" said Breitbart sarcastically.

Billy shrugged. *"I could have put my hand in the cookie jar, as you say, and stole all I wanted to steal."*

"But you didn't?"

In retrospect, that was the moment when Billy knew with absolute certainty that Doc Hyman, for one, was going down.

"That's absolutely correct," he agreed.

22

Billy had felt strangely drawn to Cleveland ever since hearing about the 10 percent reward on offer for the $6 million worth of stolen diamonds that Doc Hyman and his partner, Curly Montana, were ready to sell him. After Supervisor Damon Taylor declined the case, Billy had taken a trip out there to see if he could interest U.S. Customs in a sting operation to recover the stones, and while the local office was more than willing to help, it had no undercover agent available to work with him, and there was no way he could pull it off on his own.

Art Krinsky, performing his last official act as far as Billy was concerned, tagged along for the ride, and to justify his presence, he introduced Billy to some of the FBI's Cleveland division agents, including Don Lungren and his supervisor, Bob Fredericks. Thinking he might set up a plausible reason for coming back with Wincelowicz, Billy asked them about Alfred "Ali" Calabrese, the only significant organized-crime figure from Cleveland whom he could remember meeting in the joint. An early prototype of the new-style punk mobster, Calabrese had to be up to *some*thing worthy of a federal indictment (if he was out), and as a fellow graduate of the same Atlanta cell block, Billy was as confident of a welcome from Calabrese as he had been from Jack Mace.

"Yeah, he's out," they said. "But nothing's happening. He's quiet. Cleveland's not a mob town anymore."

"If he's out," said Billy flatly, "he ain't quiet."

But they were right about Cleveland, where the institutions of organized crime had been destroyed by a gang war between the incumbent family, led by the veteran James "Blackie" Licavoli, and an insurgent group headed by John Nardi and Danny Greene, boss of the city's Irish mob. Although the incumbents eventually won, blowing Nardi and Greene to bits in the process, the FBI had arrested most of the survivors, including Licavoli, Ali Calabrese, and—significantly—Jimmy "The Weasel" Fratianno, who rolled over after being charged with conspiracy to murder and blew the whistle on practically everybody he had ever known in his long, homicidal career. After that, despite occasional attempts by the Pittsburgh and Detroit families to move in, there had been little but disorganized crime in Cleveland. There was no one left, no native son with the heart, the brains, or the balls, to take control.

"Calabrese could do it," said Billy, but nobody in the FBI's Cleveland office knew where he lived, or seemed sufficiently interested to find out.

Predictably, Assistant Coordinator Fred Verinder was even less enthusiastic, refusing several requests for a follow-up visit, but Wincelowicz and Hackbart both felt that Billy's hunch was worth at least the price of a few phone calls. After leaving messages for Calabrese at every likely hangout he could think of, Billy finally ran him to earth at the Dorchester Club. But at that point, with the NYCON road trip about to begin, the Cowboy Palace saga in its terminal stages, and the Jack Mace connection still proliferating wildly, Billy could do little more than exchange telephone numbers. It was April 15, 1983, before he finally picked up the trail again with a recorded phone call from Investment Capital SA.

"Who is this?" asked Calabrese.

"Billy B."

"Hey, Bill. What's up?"

"All right. How you doing?"

"Okay."

"I wanted to let the winter get by—"

"Yeah, I can see that," Calabrese interrupted, laughing.

"I wouldn't go up there in the winter in a million years." Billy winked at Wincelowicz. "Listen, I was down at the Open. I was gonna give you a call because we coulda did something."

"Oh. Oh, yeah. Where you at now?"

"Huh? I'm in New York. I got a little thing going in New York."

"Good."

"You never come into the city, huh?"

"Nah, nah, nah."

"Why don't you come in?"

"Ah, I don't know. What are we gonna do?"

"What do you *wanna* do? Tell me what you want."

"I want some, uh—cash. Waddya mean, what do I want?"

"You want cash. You got anything we can turn into cash?"

"Huh? Yeah, well—*that's* no problem."

Billy smiled. "What you got?"

"Oh, I ain't got nothing *now*."

"Can ya get?"

"Uh-huh."

"Can you get a lot of that?"

"Uh, it all depends, you know? I gotta see a coupla guys, you know?"

"Right. But you oughta come into the city once in a while so we can go out and have a good time and then talk about this shit."

"Yeah, we—I can do that. I can do that in a coupla weeks."

"In a coupla weeks?" Billy looked at Wincelowicz inquiringly.

"Yeah," said Calabrese. "But you gotta give me addresses where to go, you know? I get lost over there."

"Oh, yeah. Well, we'll pick you up at the airport."

"Yeah."

"I got a fat friend that's with me." He easily evaded a mock swipe from Wincelowicz. "He just—he got out of Auburn a little while ago."

"All right, then. Uh, that sounds good."

"You tell me when."

"Yeah, maybe next week."

That was at around 11:30 A.M. At noon, Calabrese called back.

"All right, listen," he said. "Maybe I can take a flight out today."

"Take a flight out today?" Billy repeated, raising his eyebrows at Wincelowicz and Hackbart, who both nodded vigorously.

"Maybe. I'll call and find out."

"Oh, perfect," said Billy.

At 12:15, Calabrese called again to say he had a reservation in the name of Debaltzo on United Airlines flight 1010, arriving at La Guardia at 6:00 P.M.

There was only one problem. After all these years, Billy could not remember what Calabrese looked like. And as they had never had much to do with each other in Atlanta, he was pretty sure that Calabrese would not recognize him either. But he was not about to undermine his master/pupil relationship with Wincelowicz by expressing doubts of any kind.

"Sure, I'll know him," he insisted, as they stood at the gate watching the passengers stream past from flight 1010. "I mean, I *know* the guy, all right? Don't worry about it."

But Wincelowicz could see he was getting uneasy.

"I was just going to bug him again," he recalled later, "when Billy grabs my arm. 'That's him,'" he says, pointing to some guy already half-hidden in the crowd. 'Get him, Frank,' he says. 'Go on, *run*—or we're gonna lose him.'

"So I'm chasing this guy along the exit ramp, charging through the crowd, and when I finally catch up with him, he looks at me as if to say, 'What the hell's wrong with you?' He's like six-four, two hundred pounds, grayish hair. 'Are you Ali?' I says. He says, 'Huh?' So now I go back, and Billy says, 'No, no, Frank'—like it's all *my* fault. 'Here he comes now,' he says. And here's this punk, about five-six, hundred forty pounds, jet-black hair. . . . 'Oh, yeah,' I'm saying to myself. 'I'm in big shit now.' "

But the rest went off without a hitch. Shoehorned into a Camaro, the only undercover car wired for sound that the New York office could find at short notice, Billy and Calabrese chatted so freely as Wincelowicz drove into the city that by the time they reached the Sheraton Center, where NYCON had reserved Calabrese a room for the night, they had also reserved him a cell in a federal penitentiary for at least thirty years.

After a bit of social small talk about the parole time each still had left, Billy got down to business before they had even left the airport parking lot, laying out a requirement for a hundred kilos a week.

"That's how strong we can go," he said.

Calabrese blinked. "That's all coke?"

"Yeah."

"Man, that's a lot."

"Well, I'm just saying . . ."

"Yeah."

Billy could see he was impressed. "We got access to like—if we needed a million dollars, we got," he went on.

"Yeah."

"We need five hundred thousand, we got."

"Yeah. Credit line, right?"

"No. Nothing. We don't want no credit."

"No, I'm saying, you talking about—"

"No, we got cash."

"I mean, the guy's giving it to you up front, that's what I mean."

"No, no, no—we don't want no front. We buy. If you got, we buy. We pay cash."

"Right. Exactly."

"I don't want nothing for nothing.

To give this a chance to sink in, Billy allowed him to describe what had been happening in Cleveland lately.

"See, all them guys that got pinched, I don't fuck with none of them," Calabrese explained. "I was on the outs with them. We had a little war over there for about two years, you know what I mean?"

"Is that right?"

"Yeah, so, uh, then they merged after a while. They made peace and they merged, so I didn't wanta, uh, make no peace with them motherfuckers. They put a bomb in my car. They kill the wrong guy, you know? What the fuck. Yeah, who the fuck am I to, uh—"

"They put a bomb on the wrong guy?"

"No, they knew they put it in my car. It's just that the wrong guy kicked it over—started the car, you know?"

"Uh-huh."

"He got annihilated, but, uh—"

"No kidding."

"See, I thought all that shit was over with the trials and all that bullshit, and now they merged. They made friends, you know what I mean?"

"Right."

"I'm gonna hang around with guys now that try to put me in a casket? You know what I mean? I say, fuck it."

"You think the war's all over with you, huh?"

"Oh, yeah. Yeah, there's no problem. They're all in the fucking can. Most of them guys are dead anyway, you know?"

"Yeah. Did you get even?"

Calabrese laughed modestly. "I always get even. 'Cause I was with the old man over there. Licavoli, you know? The boss. And one fraction was, you know, fucking with the other fraction—you know what I mean? It's an Italian guy and Irish guy hooked up with these mad bombers. They started bombing every motherfucking thing, you know? They wanted to take over, you know?"

"Uh-huh. But you was with the right people, though."

"Oh, yeah. I was with the old man.Yeah. Fuck."

"Is, uh, Cleveland wide open now, huh?"

"Yeah, well, they say a guy's been moving in from Pittsburgh, and this and that, ba-ba-ba. I mean, who gives a fuck, you know? Ain't interested in them fucking battles no more, and that's it. Unless they're personal, you know? Other than that, fuck. I just wanna make some fucking money, you know what I mean?"

Being thus brought back to business, they went into a little more detail this time, step two in the usual narcotics minuet.

"Can you get me footballs?" asked Billy.

Calabrese looked puzzled. "What are them?"

"That's untouched. Not even opened."

"That's what, uh, that's what he can get."

"He can get footballs?"

"Yeah, yeah."

"See, that's what I need. That's all wrapped up in brown paper, the whole package."

"Right, right. Never been touched."

Billy settled back expansively. "If he can get that, why . . ."

"Yeah."

". . . then, uh . . ."

"Oh, then you can make some money."

"Yeah, well . . . What kinda mark-up he's got? What's he asking for, so I consider what I can meet?"

"He told me fifty-five."

Billy nodded judiciously. "Okay. That's all right."

"You know, that's what he told me, so, uh . . . I said, well . . ."

"Fifty-five's a little high, but we'll handle it."

"Well, if it's brand-new, like that there's, I says, if he gives it to me, now I'm gonna fuck with it. Like try to make a—"

Billy threw up his hands in horror. "Don't open—don't, don't mess with it," he said. "I'd rather pay the fifty-five."

"Yeah."

"All right with you, Frank?"

"Yeah, that's good," said Wincelowicz, taken by surprise.

"It ain't good," Billy said reprovingly, "but I mean it's better than having 'em mess with it."

"Well, nobody's . . ."

But Billy had acknowledged his existence, and that was enough. "Listen, I don't want—lemme tell ya—I don't want any that's in Ziploc bags. You understand what I'm saying? I don't want nothing that's so—"

"Oh, yeah," said Calabrese. "Yeah, yeah, yeah. I can understand that, sure."

"Uh, and if you, uh, you can move twenty, if you tell me you got to have a million dollars, we'll put it where you can count, you can do what you want with it."

"Yeah," breathed Calabrese.

Billy nodded. The secret was just to let these people do it to themselves. "Money ain't gonna be anywhere where we can—nobody's gonna rip us off, okay?"

Now Calabrese was horrified. "Ah, no. Fuck, no. I'll meet ya myself, me and you, him or something—know what I mean? Take care of business. We'll meet at a neutral spot, we'll meet there, make a move, and that's it."

"Okay."

"He gets the shit from California, you know what I'm saying?"

"If it came in from California," said Billy, "it's gonna be footballs."

Calabrese was on the hook. Now he had to bring Wincelowicz into play.

"Huh, Frank, waddiya think?"

"Yeah." Wincelowicz was busy with the traffic.

"You say yeah," Billy said crossly. "Waddiya—say something. Am I saying wrong? You know? Because you don't know—this guy's a friend of mine."

"Well, if you say he's, uh, a friend of yours, that's all I need to know, you know?"

"We been outa contact a little bit, but, uh, the guy's a two thousand percent guy, you understand?"

"Well, that's all I need to know," Wincelowicz said, now beset on all sides. "You tell me the guy's a good guy."

"I mean, but you got any questions that—you know, I want you to speak up, too."

"All right. Now you covered everything."

"Well, say—"

"Ya miss something, I'll tell ya you missed something," he said irritably.

Billy smiled. "The reason I say this, Ali, in case I'm not in town . . ."

"Right."

". . . you talk to him like you're talking to me."

"All right. It's no problem. All right."

That settled, they discussed how long it would take Calabrese to drive in from Cleveland with the stuff. He reckoned about seven and a half hours, which brought up the question of his commission on the deal.

"Be honest with me," Billy said. "How much you on already?"

"Pardon me?" said Calabrese, pretending not to understand the suggestion that he had already loaded the price from the seller.

"Three? How much you on there now? Three? Are you on three thousand each one now?"

Calabrese hesitated. "It's about around there," he conceded.

"Okay. So we'll go, uh—what do you want to do, Frank? If they're untouched, unopened . . ."

"Yeah."

"You know what I can get . . ."

"How much more do you want to give him? Now we're fifty-five. We can't go too much longer, see, because we could have bought here. I don't want—a lot of wise guys here I don't want to deal with. Uh, I don't—nobody knows my business. I don't tell nobody nothing."

"That's the way," agreed Calabrese. "Me, either."

"Well, if he could do it right away, we could unload right away. Uh, you wanna tap on three?"

"If he can do it right away, yeah," agreed Wincelowicz. "Because, you know, we got that thing, uh . . . You know, that guy?"

"Yeah," said Billy, but he shook his head. "That's a lot. That's fifty-eight. That'd mean . . ."

"Yeah," Wincelowicz said.

"Let me see, uh . . . okay. All right with you, Frank?"

"Should have waited till he had a couple of drinks," Wincelowicz said slyly to Calabrese, restoring Billy's faith in him.

Calabrese laughed. "Yeah. He might have went to four. But I gotta bring it down here, you know what I mean?"

"Yeah, right. Well, that's good."

"Well, that's all right," said Billy, for Wincelowicz had missed the nuance. "We'll pay the gas."

Calabrese nodded. "You got the expenses? You got expenses covered and everything?"

"Yeah, I'll give expenses," said Wincelowicz. "Don't worry about expenses."

It was not just expenses—from that moment on, Calabrese had nothing left in life to worry about. With step two of the minuet completed, they decided to drop him off at his hotel so that he could get changed for dinner at Romeo Salta's, and the conversation turned again to Calabrese's war memoirs.

"I had a new Lincoln at the time," he said, "and, uh, I used to park it across the street in this guy's driveway, and used to have this kid move the car. I used to tell him, 'Look,' I says, 'look for this.' I used to tell him where to look for the packages, you know what I mean?"

"Yeah," said Wincelowicz, fascinated.

"Sometimes they put them in the dry walls. Sometimes hook 'em up to the fucking wheel with some mercury and, uh, as soon as the wheels move, uh, you're gone, you know?"

"Uh-huh."

"So he used to look every fucking morning. But one day, his old man says, 'I'll move the car.' So he says, 'Nah, I'll move it. You don't know what to look for.' "

"Yeah, yeah."

" 'Let me move the car.' And the poor guy got in the fucking car, and I was taking a shit, and the motherfucker had ten sticks of dynamite in there."

"No kidding," said Billy.

"Va-va-varoom! His fucking head went through the moon roof. All that was in there was his torso, you know?"

"Oh, boy."

"Nice fucking guy, too."

"Well, that's terrible. You still mad? You *should* still be mad."

Calabrese shrugged philosophically. "There's nobody to be mad at, you know? They're all gone."

They were silent for a moment, in memory of the bad old days.

"You got a team?" Billy asked.

"Yeah, I've got a coupla guys that'll move, you know? I ain't gonna go for no, uh . . ."

"No. There's a lot of money in Cleveland, right?"

Calabrese considered this. "Ah, there ain't that fucking much over there as far as like, uh, making a move on a heist or something— know what I mean? Unless you wanna run on drugs, or grab one of them trucks, you know?"

"Yeah," Wincelowicz said, with feeling.

"Mm-huh," said Billy. "Well, Frank, you know, uh . . ."

"Yeah, I know." Wincelowicz grinned at Calabrese. "The last time I did that, I took a truckload of Campbell's soup, and he had my ass for a week."

"Yeah, but I mean, you know?" Billy invited Calabrese's sympathy, as one old pro to another.

"Uh, friends of mine heisted a truck . . ." Calabrese began, cutting across Wincelowicz, who was trying to finish his story.

"We were supposed to take TV sets," he was saying.

"Yeah," Calabrese said encouragingly.

"And it was, uh, Campbell's soup."

"Campbell soup." Calabrese shook his head. "These guys, they had the same thing. It was supposed to be whiskey—"

"Yeah," said Wincelowicz.

"It was Pepto-Bismol."

"Oh, shit."

"Pepto-Bismol. They all did a bit, too. They were set up. The agents were in the truck, waiting for 'em."

They shook their heads over the perfidy of government agents.

Then Billy thought that a federal firearms charge to go with the dope violations would be nice, and asked Calabrese if he could get machine guns in Cleveland.

"Yeah. You want—what do you like, a Uzi or a Ingram or something?"

"Yeah," said Billy. "A Uzi I'd rather have."

"I just had a fucking nice Ingram," Calabrese said fondly. "With a silencer on it, too."

"Yeah? What do they go for up there?"

"I paid a G note for it myself. Yeah, it's beautiful It's brand-new. Never been shot, you know? With a factory-made silencer on it."

"Uh-huh."

"Come with it. Come in a little box. Everything was laid out in a little valise—like a little briefcase, you know? I just flip it open, and just screw it on, and it's, you know, like ready. I got two clips with it."

"Yeah?"

"I keep it, you know—shit, I just like to look at it. It's nice, you know? It's pretty. It's good to have it. If I need it. Ain't nothing better than a shotgun though."

"Yeah, right," said Billy.

"Ain't gonna miss with that."

They continued in this vein, part business, part shop talk, part reminiscence, all through dinner at Romeo Salta's. And as they worked their way through bottle after bottle, so Calabrese warmed to them both as to long-lost cousins. Since beating the homicide rap, he said, he had dreamed of taking over Cleveland, Youngstown, and northern Ohio, but until Billy and Frank came along, he had lacked the manpower to do it.

No problem, said Billy. He belonged to the IRA. A couple of phone calls and he could have twenty or thirty guys up there with machine guns, plastic explosives—anything Calabrese wanted. And Frank hung out with a bunch of Italians he could bring in as well, if they needed more help. The best thing to do would be to visit him there and size up the situation.

Anytime, said Calabrese. Scenting blood, he pawed the ground like a warhorse out to pasture It would not take that much. He had his enemies in Cleveland (including Curly Montana, who was tight with the Teamsters) but the serious opposition, like Danny Greene, was long gone.

Mentioning Greene reminded him of the time when he and his buddy, an ex–Vietnam demolitions expert, had blown up the three-story apartment building where Greene lived, reducing it to a pile of bricks. As the dust settled, they started their car, convinced that the guy was dead and buried at last, only to see Greene totter out of the ruins, brushing himself down. They had succeeded only in killing his cat.

On a previous occasion, Calabrese went on, he had decided to make the hit, Chicago-style, from a stolen car. After staking out Greene's apartment for hours, they followed him as he drove away and at the first suitable stretch of road, speeded up alongside so that Calabrese could let him have it through the open window. But the stolen car had electric windows, and the one Calabrese had to use resolutely refused to open.

In the end, Jimmy "The Weasel" Fratianno had turned them all in—and that was the last time anybody would take him alive, Calabrese told them. Now, when he was working, he always carried a hand grenade on his belt. Anybody tried to arrest him, he would grab the guy in a bear hug and pull the pin. Nudged by Billy, he admitted flying to New York with a Colt .45 automatic pistol in his suitcase, and to be worried about taking it home again as airport security at La Guardia looked a lot tighter than it was in Cleveland.

Billy and Wincelowicz eyed each other. If they could get hold of the evidence, at least two more federal charges could be added to the Calabrese account. But first they had to lock up the cocaine deal—and the supplier, too, if they could coax Calabrese into identifying his source.

"You'd know him if I told you his name." he said. "Best bug man in the country."

"Yeah, okay—so you got the connection," Billy said. "But does he trust you enough? To, like, front you ten keys a week, I mean?"

"Oh, yeah. Comes from Cleveland. I known him for years. He's famous. Most famous burglar in the country. He can do any kinda bug or alarm there is. Went to California and got big out there."

"What's his name? Canada?"

"No. I know him—not Canada. This guy's name is Velotta."

"Who?"

"Velotta. Frank Velotta. And the kid's a genius. Well, he's not a kid—he's gotta be forty—but like I say, he's the best second-story man in the country."

"Then why doesn't he do that? What's he fucking around with narcotics fur?"

"He retired, you know? Now he's doing' what you're doin'."

The next morning, before they picked Calabrese up at his hotel, Wincelowicz established that Frank "Skinny" Velotta was indeed famous. Starting out as Jimmy "The Weasel" Fratianno's driver, he was now underboss of the organized crime family in San Francisco, where Special Agent Max Noel, of the local FBI divisional office, was working on an assortment of cases against him.

"Hey, Ali," said Billy, on the way out to La Guardia airport. "I been thinking. Now we got something goin', you're gonna be in and outa New York all the time and you're gonna need a piece here, right? If you're worried about taking it on the plane wit'ya, give it to Frank here and then every time he picks you up at the airport or wherever, he can bring it with him and give it to ya."

"Hey," said Calabrese, producing the big .45 automatic from under his jacket. "That's a great idea."

Billy and Wincelowicz thought so, too. Besides the parole violations, they now had him for carrying a firearm during the commission of felony offenses, and as a convicted felon, for carrying a firearm across state lines.

That was Saturday. On Tuesday, Calabrese called Billy from Cleveland to say that he had been in touch with Velotta, who was eager to extend his Los Angeles–Las Vegas–Cleveland cocaine network to New York. Barring accidents, they would probably have ten or twelve "footballs" for him by the end of the week. They would bring the stuff to New Jersey, where Velotta also had four thousand pounds of marijuana stashed in a warehouse operated by Tommy Pecora, the organized-crime figure whom Billy already knew as the carpet supplier to Cowboy Palace.

Come ahead, he said. Bring everything you got.

He could hardly say anything else, but in fact the case was moving too fast. Unless he and Wincelowicz left for Cleveland at once, there would be no time for them to get into Calabrese's crew before they had to take him and Velotta down for the cocaine sale.

George Dyer and the NYCON team agreed; the FBI's middle management at 26 Federal Plaza did not.

Calabrese might be a big fish in Cleveland, said Assistant Coordinator Fred Verinder, but he was nobody in New York. Nor was Velotta, who was already being worked by the San Francisco office. If those two wanted the deal to go down in New Jersey, there would be nothing in that for New York either. And even if there were, none of it had anything to do with the NYCON program. It was strictly a case for organized crime and narcotics.

It was a case for the *FBI*, the NYCON team insisted. If they dropped it now, how would New York explain that to the San Francisco and Cleveland offices, both of which had been kept informed of what was going on? Billy had provided the Bureau with a one-shot, untransferable opportunity to wipe out organized crime in Cleveland. Surely it had to be worth a few brownie points if New York could pull it off? Certainly nobody else could.

Okay, said Verinder. Suppose he let them fly out there—Calabrese was never going to introduce them to his people. Whatever else he was, he couldn't be as dumb as *that*.

"You don't understand," Billy told him kindly. "We're going out there to help him take over the city. He asked us to do that. So naturally he's gonna introduce us to his people. He's gotta show us what he's got, right?"

After a lot more argument, Verinder finally agreed to allow them Thursday and Friday to clean up Cleveland.

Which brought Billy to the subject of his fee for the case. Somebody thought a fair reward would be one thousand dollars for every kilo of cocaine seized when the bust went down, and when nobody dissented, Billy assumed this was agreed.

"Okay, Frank," he said after the meeting, only half in jest. "We'll go for fifty keys."

When Supervisor George Dyer heard the joke, Billy was informed that his fee for the Calabrese/Velotta case would be seventy-five hundred dollars, regardless of the amount seized, and it was Billy's turn not to laugh. But with two major crime figures in his sights, he would have walked to Cleveland barefoot to take them down, if that was the only way to do it—and for a while it seemed it might be. He and Wincelowicz were halfway to the airport on Wednesday evening when Verinder recalled them to 26 Federal Plaza.

He had been thinking. He was still certain that Calabrese would never introduce them to his people, in which case the trip would be useless. On the other hand, if Calabrese *did* introduce them, then the trip would be dangerous. Either way, he probably should not allow them to go.

After further argument, Billy and Wincelowicz caught a later flight and checked into rooms reserved for them by the Cleveland office at the Sheraton Beachwood Hotel. By the time they had taken delivery of an FBI undercover car wired with microphones and recording devices it was 10:45 P.M., but with so little time to spare, Billy decided to call Calabrese right away rather than wait until morning.

Surprised, even irritable at first, that they had flown in without warning him in advance, Calabrese told them to wait at the hotel, and came over to pick them up for a late dinner at the nearby Ground Floor Restaurant on Chagrin Boulevard.

The reason for his ill humor, they discovered, was that Velotta had just advised him of a holdup in the cocaine shipment that Calabrese had expected to deliver by the end of the week. As the delay suited them perfectly, Billy and Wincelowicz were prepared to be gracious about it, and by the time they reached the restaurant, Calabrese was not just his usual ebullient self but more expansive than ever in the additional role of host.

"See, it don't mean nothing," he said. "Fucking Colombians hang him up sometimes, but Skinny's got this town by the balls. You want coke—you know, the real good shit—then you gotta go to Skinny. So he says to me, 'Sure. We'll go to New York. Why not? But those guys'—meaning you and Frankie—'they gotta take like fifty keys a week if I'm gonna do it.' "

"No problem," purred Billy.

"I told him that. So then he says, 'We'll use Tommy Pecora's warehouse on the Jersey side.' You know Tommy?"

"Oh, sure," said Billy. "See him around all the time." On the last occasion, he had ripped up Pecora's carpet in Cowboy Palace.

"Well, that's good. Because Tommy's got the law fixed over there, so everything's nice and quiet."

That led them to consider Calabrese's relationship with the law in Cleveland, a matter of some importance if they aimed to take over the city. Well, first of all, he said, he knew all the government agents in Cleveland by sight, so he wasn't much worried about FBI surveillance.

Uh-uh, said Wincelowicz, with an appreciative nod for Billy, who had strenuously declined all offers of local assistance, other than technical.

As for the Cleveland cops, Calabrese went on, he played golf almost every day with his man Butch, a police captain who would take care of any other cops they needed to fix for local protection.

Good, Billy said. It would be important to have the cops looking the other way when they moved in on the city's crap and barbut games and the bookmakers and fences. But he didn't want no violence because of the heat that might bring down. Calabrese agreed, although he was doubtful about the fences. They might have to do a little bit of the violence thing with them. Not much. Just one or two guys was all. And his friend Petey Boy Sanzo could take care of it. He was only a little guy, and since getting shot in the face he no longer played with a full deck, but he was reliable and like real dangerous. They would meet him tomorrow.

Billy and Wincelowicz said they were looking forward to it.

The following morning, Billy and Wincelowicz set out with Calabrese to meet his people, and in particular his "full-blown maniac" of a partner, Petey Boy Sanzo.

"All right, stay in the car," Calabrese said as they drew up outside Sanzo's home on Orchard Street. "Don't get out till I tell ya or he might start shooting. Wait till he sees me and *then* come in."

"Yeah, right," said Billy and Wincelowicz in unison.

A little over five feet, and a lot over two hundred pounds, Sanzo had not been quite himself since sustaining a serious head wound in a gunfight over a parking space outside a convenience store. Although Licavoli had often employed him as a contract burglar and hit man, Sanzo had never been considered stable enough to become a made man, and since his injury, his temperament has proved more volatile than ever. Even Calabrese treated him like an unexploded bomb.

In making the introductions, he explained at some length that Billy was an old friend he had done time with in Atlanta, and that Wincelowicz was Billy's partner from New York. When Sanzo finally grasped the relationship, he sized them up over a can of beer in his kitchen and decided that he liked them, which was a considerable relief to everybody.

Endorsing their plans to reclaim Cleveland for organized crime, he told them he already had the connections necessary to start working in Ashtabula and Geneva, where various high-level county and law enforcement officials were on his payroll, he said. He had a good supply of poker machines, obtained "on the arm," and his workers were getting them into bars and restaurants for a flat fee of fifty dollars each to the local cops. But they were not real workers, like Calabrese, Billy, and Wincelowicz. They were small-time guys who liked to play at being gangsters. They weren't willing to take risks and swallow the nut.

Sanzo personally fetched them another beer as a mark of approval. His main business at the moment, he went on, was the numbers, gambling and sports betting, with a little shylocking on the side, but he was ready to open up if they decided to work together. So far, he had kept the Detroit and Pittsburgh families off his turf—Cleveland was still open—but they would have to dump a lot of independents before they took over.

From Sanzo's, they went to Southgate Park to talk to Sandy and Sonny, two more of Calabrese's ready-and-willing hotshots, and so they continued, meeting most of his business friends and associates through the Thursday and Friday allotted by Verinder and the Saturday and Sunday donated by Wincelowicz and Billy. They charted the crime scene in northern Ohio; identified its principal targets, along with possible ways of taking them down, and firmed up a deal that would put Calabrese and Velotta behind bars for the rest of their criminal careers.

Mission accomplished. Having pulled it off with the same dazzling speed as he had shown in Hawaii, Billy had every reason to feel pleased with himself. Instead, he went home in disgust. Out of the blue, and quite by chance, he had learned that U.S. Attorney Rudolph Giuliani and the FBI had pulled the plug on Cowboy Palace.

To schedule the raid during Billy's two-day absence in Cleveland seemed more than a simple coincidence—and for all the government knew, Billy and Wincelowicz could have been tied up with Curly Montana at the time. Luckily, they had been too busy with Calabrese and his friends to do much about the diamonds, but Billy had fully intended to connect with Montana before leaving Cleveland. If Wincelowicz had not casually inquired about Cowboy Palace while making a routine call to New York, they might well have walked unwittingly into a trap. Beside being Doc Hyman's partner, Montana was listed in the FBI's intelligence files as a contract killer.

In his fury, Billy was tempted to think the Bureau had set him up, but he knew of no one at management level clever enough to make that sort of calculation. It was just more of the same old arrogant indifference he had come to expect of the Bureau—but enough was enough.

As case agent, Dale Hackbart prepared a memorandum for the FBI Director in Washington. After a three-page listing of Billy's achievements in Cleveland with Wincelowicz, he wrote:

"At the present time, the status of the Cleveland case as well as the Honolulu case entitled Hale Auau and New York case entitled NYCON is unknown. Because of problems within the New York Division in obtaining adequate and timely payment of expenses and services for NY 20376 C, the source has left the city. At the present time, he is reluctant to work for either the New York Division or any other division of the FBI. New York will continue efforts to maintain a working relationship with this source. Receiving offices [Washington, Cleveland, Honolulu, San Francisco] will be kept advised."

Hackbart knew that money was really the least of the reasons for Billy's "reluctance," but Washington was unlikely to understand the others. In any case, Hackbart's career prospects had been eroded enough already by his contempt for New York's divisional management without piling on insults gratuitously. What he was counting on to bring Billy back was Billy's inability to trust anybody to work a case properly without him.

On May 6, after two weeks of little or no progress on the coke deal, Billy showed up at Investment Capital SA and called Cleveland to flush Calabrese out.

"Hey, good-lookin'."

"Hey," said Calabrese warmly, recognizing his voice at once. "What's happening?"

"All right. How *you* doing?"

"Okay, buddy."

"Everything in order?"

"Uh, I'm waiting for the guy to, uh, give me a buzz."

"Okay. Well, the only reason I . . ." He broke off, as if annoyed with himself. "Can you go to a pay phone?"

The call was being recorded, of course, but it was little touches like this that made him the best in the business.

"Right now?"

"Yeah."

"Uh, yeah. All right."

"How much time you need?"

"Gimme about five, six minutes."

Billy waited for ten, then called the pay phone number and started over.

"Okay," he said. "The only reason I called, Ali . . ."

"Yeah?"

". . . the only reason I called is that, if it's coming this weekend, I gotta have the ash-kay out for ya."

"Yeah, right."

"You know? But I don't wanna take it out if it ain't coming."

"Well, I gotcha. He said—he told me Saturday for sure, you know? The guy's gonna drive to Jersey."

"Oh, he's gonna drive it up to Jersey?"

"Yeah. My friend will be there, too. I'll meet him there. That's where it's going to be. Newark."

"Okay. Uh, what are you gonna bring me? Ten or twelve, Ali?"

"Uh, right around that figure. I don't know for exactly."

"Okay. That's all right. As long as I know . . . And then you gotta tell me how you wanna do it."

"Yeah. All right. Here's what I'll do. When I get there . . . right?"

"Right."

". . . I'll just call you up."

"All right, kid."

"All right. Tell Frank I said hello."

"All right, baby."

"Hey, when you come, bring that—bring my thing wit'ya."

"Yeah, Positively."

"Okay, babe."

Billy handed the phone to Wincelowicz to hang up for him. "Well, that's it," he said. "We're all set."

"Yeah, well . . ." Wincelowicz and Hackbart exchanged glances. "Not exactly."

Billy studied first one, then the other. "Now what?"

Wincelowicz sighed. "Well, number one, we can't do it in Jersey. Boss says we gotta take 'em down in New York."

"Frank," Billy said patiently. "It don't *matter* what he says. You heard the guy. They wanna do it in New Jersey."

"Yeah, I know, Billy. I know. And there's something else. Another squad has got the case. It's not a NYCON deal anymore."

They looked at one another in silence.

"Frank, nobody's got the case unless I give it to 'em," Billy said, still not losing his temper.

"No. Well, see, they want you and me to handle the deal, but then this other squad'll make the bust."

"What other squad? I don't want nothing to do with Walt Smith or Damon Taylor or any of them guys."

"No, no. This is John Walzer. This is the President's Organized Crime Drug Enforcement Task Force we're talking about."

"You're shitting me."

"No, that's who it is."

Billy shrugged. "Well, I don't give a fuck—as long as they do like I tell 'em. But I don't know I can get Calabrese and his guy to bring it into the city. I'll see."

He certainly tried. He spoke to Calabrese again the next morning, the Saturday on which they were supposed to deliver.

"Oh, shit," said Billy. "I was hoping you weren't at home."

"Monday for sure," Calabrese replied. "At three o'clock. I made the reservations and everything, and I'll call you when I get in."

"Are you coming here or there?"

"I'll meet you over there. I'll tell you where I'm at then."

"Meet us over where?"

"Uh, Jersey."

"Ain't you gonna bring it in here for me?"

"Well, I thought you . . . Maybe you come over there then?"

"Nah. Bring it in to me."

"You sure?" Calabrese's reluctance was unmistakable.

"Sure." Sensing a standoff, Billy slackened the line a little. "Either way, I don't give a fuck. But I'd rather have it come over here for me because . . . that's why I was telling you before. I don't like to move it around too fucking much, you know?"

"Yeah, I know what you're saying. Yeah. Well . . ."

Calabrese was ready to come in. The problem had to be Velotta.

"What's your man say?" Billy asked.

"That's where he wants to meet," said Calabrese. "The spot where he stays. His hotel, you know?"

Calabrese was saying it was Velotta's stuff, and Velotta was calling the shots.

"So don't fuck around with it," Billy told the task force agents when they met at NYCON's undercover office to discuss where and how to take them down. "The guy's got connections over there. He's got protection over there. He's got a hotel he knows—he's comfortable. Why would he wanna come into the city? It don't make sense."

"Yeah, I know, Billy." Wincelowicz intervened before anybody could say something that might put him off entirely. "But I seen you handle bigger problems than this before you put your pants on."

"Yeah, well . . ." He shrugged modestly. "Even if I *did* get 'em over here, we don't have anyplace to do it."

"How about the Sheraton we put him in last time?"

Billy was prepared to consider this, but the suggestion was immediately vetoed by Special Agent Greg Meacham, who preferred someplace quiet. Like the CBS pier on the Hudson. Billy looked at him incredulously.

"On a *pier?*" he said. "This is not a fucking movie, you know. These are real mob guys."

"Right. Armed and dangerous. So I want you and undercover agent Wincelowicz to get 'em down the far end of the pier before you make the exchange."

Billy frowned. Then he laughed. "You mean, you want Frank and me in the middle? Between the good guys and the bad guys? What happens if they start shooting?"

"You'll be okay. If there's a shoot-out, the bullets'll go in the water."

Billy's smile slowly died as he realized that Meacham was serious. "Forget about it, pal." They were going to fuck this one up, too.

They all looked at Wincelowicz.

"Can you handle it without Breen?" Meacham asked. "One of my guys can go in with you."

"Frank," said Billy. You listen to these people and I'm gonna buy ya a nice white T-shirt with a target painted on it."

Wincelowicz was no happier with the pier idea than Billy was, and after a prolonged wrangle, Meacham and the others reluctantly abandoned it in favor of their second choice, the Market Diner on West Street.

"A *diner?*" said Billy. "I don't believe this. I mean, why don'cha do it in fucking McDonald's? Then at least we can get a bag of fries and a milkshake."

"Billy—"

"No, come on, Frank. These guys stay in the best hotels. They eat in the best restaurants. You wanna ask 'em to meet ya in some greasy spoon on the waterfront? Fine. Go ahead."

"Right," said Meacham coldly. "Then I guess we'll have to manage without you."

"Sure. If I'm not there, you don't have to pay me, right?"

"You'll get your money, Breen. Whichever way it does down."

Billy sniffed. After all his years of working with the Bureau, he should not have been surprised, but it still got to him every time.

"They're gonna fuck it up, Frank," he said. "You know that, don'cha?"

Wincelowicz shrugged helplessly.

And they fucked it up.

Standing in for Billy, Wincelowicz finally managed to persuade Calabrese to bring Velotta through the Holland Tunnel to meet him at the Market Diner, but they came reluctantly and brought nothing with them. The guy driving the stuff in from Cleveland was running late, they told Wincelowicz and Special Agent Frank Miele, Jr., whom Wincelowicz introduced as one of "Billy's boys." After Miele showed Velotta the money, $430,000, in the trunk of a rental car guarded by another of "Billy's boys," Special Agent Phillip Armand, they adjourned to the diner and sat around for an hour making conversation.

The only reason he had come over, Velotta said, was because he liked to know whom he was dealing with, and Billy's absence evidently pleased him no more than the surroundings. Three times he got up to call an unspecified hotel in New Jersey, purportedly to see if the footballs had arrived, and three times he returned to the table to say his driver had not yet shown up. On the third and last occasion, he said that he and Calabrese might as well go back to Jersey and wait for him there, and with no possible pretext for detaining them, the agents stood outside and watched them drive away, closely followed by FBI surveillance teams.

Too closely, as it turned out. Around 9:00 A.M., just over an hour after leaving the Market Diner, Calabrese telephoned Billy at the NYCON office, where he and Wincelowicz were commiserating with each other.

"Hey, what's going on, baby?"

"Not much," said Calabrese. "Listen, that friend of mine broke down in Binghamton."

"No shit."

"Yeah. So we're gonna take a ride out there and see what's happening, and, uh . . . By the way, I think we had a little tail, too, you know?"

"You had a little tail?" Billy repeated, looking at Wincelowicz, who covered his eyes and bowed his head.

"Yeah, I think so."

"What makes you say that?"

"Well, uh, looks like, uh, it was a tail, you know? Cars and whatnot."

"Is that right?"

"Yeah. So I'll call you tomorrow. This way, I'm gonna go over there and straighten him out."

"What—here's what, Frank is running around with that money in the back of that car."

"Yeah. All right. Well, there's nothing I can do with it now, you know? I'll call you tomorrow."

They both knew the deal was off.

"We lost 'em, Frank," said Billy, slamming down the phone. "Didn't I tell ya? They botched it."

Even so, he called Calabrese the next day to try to save it for them, but he was wasting his breath. Despite a highly circumstantial tale about finding out that a heroin bust had gone down earlier in the day by the Market Diner, and about Frank also picking up a tail and not getting back with the money until three in the morning, Calabrese remained cool, distant, and monosyllabic. As Billy explained afterward—unnecessarily but at some length—you didn't have to draw guys like that a picture. They were shy little creatures. One little sniff of something wrong, and *poof!* they were gone forever.

"Shit, Frank. We had it all. We had Calabrese and Velotta. We had fifty keys of uncut coke every week for as long as we liked. We had the Pecora crew. We had a warehouse full of grass and stuff. And what happens? They bring in these guys, they take it away from us, and what do they get? Nothing. No arrests. No coke. No Pecoras. Nothing."

"I know, Billy. I know."

With no arrests and no seizures, there was no pay for Billy either. Agents in Ohio and California who had expected the case to help them with their own investigations thought the whole affair was scandalous.

"You did everything you told them you would do," said Special Agent Max Noel, who had been working on Velotta in San Francisco. "You fulfilled your part of the bargain, and their administrative people screwed it up. As a result, they didn't want to pay you the money because that would bring their screw-up to light. Rather than do that—I don't know how they appeased you, but they probably said they couldn't justify giving you anything until he was prosecuted, and he couldn't be prosecuted because of our pending investigation out here, and that's bullshit. You got an Assistant Special Agent in charge and a group supervisor back there that are blowing smoke in."

"They went to Washington, and Washington approved seventy-five hundred dollars for bringing them in," Billy grumbled. "We could have caught as much as fifty keys, easy."

"I know it. I know it. You brought them in and they fucked it up by not getting a good prosecution, by changing the meeting site. The Hudson River to them is a cement wall. They changed it because Newark would get the credit for it. They wanted it all to be credited to NYC. That's self-serving stuff. That's never your fault, for Christ's sake. That's coming from guys in a world apart."

Almost another year went by before Calabrese and Velotta were indicted and taken off the streets—an entirely avoidable year of large-scale cocaine peddling, racketeering, and violence at an entirely unnecessary cost to the public in Cleveland, San Francisco, and elsewhere.

Charged with narcotics conspiracy, attempting to distribute eight kilos of cocaine, and interstate racketeering (plus a couple of gun charges against Calabrese for the .45 automatic Billy had volunteered to hold for him), they were both found guilty on July 13, 1984, after a seven-day trial in the Southern District of New York and sentenced to fifteen years' imprisonment. Billy was not required to testify, which was just as well in view of his opinion of the government's conduct, but Jimmy "The Weasel" Fratianno helped bang a few nails in their caskets as a (bad) character witness.

Faced with the overwhelming evidence of the telephone calls and other conversations Billy and Wincelowicz had recorded, Calabrese and Velotta maintained that they had only pretended to deal in drugs in order to rip off a drug dealer who had turned out to be working for the FBI.

"I'm guilty of conspiracy to heist this guy, that's all," Calabrese told the judge, who failed to regard this as a mitigating circumstance.

Expressing his satisfaction with the outcome of the case, Rudolph Giuliani, then U.S. Attorney for the Southern District of New York, said that the indictment had arisen "out of an undercover investigation conducted by agents of the FBI in New York City and Cleveland as part of the President's Organized Crime Drug Enforcement Task Force."

Which probably explains why Billy never did get his seventy-five hundred dollars.

David Breitbart also had money problems. "Let me ask you something. You said that Duke told you that he borrowed over half a million dollars, is that correct? From the people through Resource Capital?"

"Yes, sir."

"You saw documents which indicated that that loan was at 24 percent per year?"

Billy shook his head vigorously. "I never seen no 24 percent a year document. I saw something that said 2 percent a month, but it had nothing to do with Resource Capital."

Breitbart sighed. "Do you know what twelve times two is?" he asked, with elaborate patience.

"That's correct."

"How much is that?"

"Twenty-four." Billy glanced appealingly at the government table.

"Two percent a month is 24 percent a year?"

"That is correct."

"Do you know how much 24 percent of half a million dollars is?"

"That is not the way the loans came down through Resource Capital," said Billy severely. "The loans—do you want me to explain? I will explain how it came down."

"I want you to answer my question and then you can say whatever you like. Do you know how much 24 percent of half a million dollars is? Can you divide 500,000 by 4 in your head?"

"Objection," cried Baird.

"Isn't it a fact, Mr. Breen," said Breitbart, coming to the point, "that $125,000 a year is the legal rate of interest on half a million dollars?"

"The money was not given at a legal rate of interest," Billy insisted. "It was given at 2 percent a week. Plus there was 23 shares taken from Cowboy Palace in the first closing, where there wasn't even $50,000 passed."

Apparently oblivious to the damage Billy was doing, Breitbart clung to his mental arithmetic. "Mr. Breen, isn't it a fact, sir, that $125,000 is 25 percent of half a million dollars?"

"That is a legitimate margin, if there was one. But there never was one."

Unable to find an opening, Breitbart fumbled the ball. "You understand—you say there was no legitimate loan, right?"

"I was at the closings," said Billy.

"I think we are getting argumentative," Judge Sand observed placidly. "Suppose we move on."

23

If it had bungled the Calabrese/Velotta affair, the government was making an even bigger hash of the Cowboy Palace case, in spite of the importance that the FBI's New York office now attached to it.

"We were impressed by the magnitude of the operation," Thomas L. Sheer, head of its criminal division, told *The New York Times* when the indictment was unsealed. "It shows that organized crime in this region has grown from the traditional concept of giving small loans to poor slobs, who are beaten up by the system and need a few hundred bucks, to a corporate level of substantial loans to businessmen. . . . This was a super-shylock operation."

Lee F. Laster, assistant director of the FBI in charge of the New York office, was equally impressed by the fact that at least four of the region's major crime families had an interest in Resource Capital. "When it comes to making money," he said, "they'll work together."

U.S. Attorney Rudolph Giuliani had also grasped the potential of the case. As a curtain-raiser for a New York mafia-busting campaign, it not only cast him as the Thomas Dewey of the 1980s but, by focusing on the traditional public enemy, served to divert attention from the less tractable problems of runaway white-collar crime and the virtual surrender of three of New York's five boroughs to dope-financed street gangs.

Although gratified that the government had finally seen the light, after twice rejecting his story, Billy was nevertheless mystified by its strategy. Obviously the best witness to any crime is its victim, but instead of cultivating Tom Duke for his well-nigh unanswerable testimony against Hyman, Cooper, and the procession of mobsters who funded Resource Capital, who owned the contractors who worked on Cowboy Palace, who ran the unions their men belonged to, who supplied the goods and services that Duke depended upon, from laundry and liquor to meat and garbage disposal, and who slapped him around when he failed to meet his fourteen-thousand-dollar-a-week interest payments, the FBI did almost everything it could to turn him into a witness for the defense.

With an obsessional dishonesty that led him to commit fraud, forgery, and embezzlement even when he had no need to, the 24-year-old Duke was certainly no model for the nation's youth, but prosecutors cut deals with murderers and rapists every day. Instead of trying to overcome Duke's natural fear of testifying in open court against senior members of five major crime families, the Bureau hounded him to the point where, as a hostile witness, his testimony did the government's case more harm than good.

Even more curiously, the FBI also did its best to alienate its other key witness, William Clifford Breen—the man who had brought them the case in the first place, the man who stood to lose his property as a result of it, and possibly his life if he consented to testify. He was certainly under no compulsion to do so, and the Bureau certainly offered him no incentive to do so. Ignoring Special Agent Walt Stowe's attempts to set them straight from his own firsthand knowledge of the situation, Supervisor Walt Smith and case agent Stanley Nye preferred to treat Billy and Duke from the start as if they were engaged on some joint, fraudulent enterprise in Cowboy Palace that was no less culpable in its way than that of Hyman and Cooper in Resource Capital.

"Who is Walter Smith?" asked Breitbart.

"Supervisor with the FBI."

"Did Walter Smith tell you that he would not permit Tom Duke to do anything in New York City?"

"Yes, sir."

"Was that because the FBI felt that Tom Duke was a crook, an arsonist, and a thief and everything but a human being?"

"Yes, sir."

"Did you get orders to stop talking to Tom Duke?"

"Did I get—?"

"Which you refused?"

"That is correct."

Running low on ammunition now, and still without a significant breakthrough to show for his three-day assault, Breitbart took another prowl around Billy's defenses and returned to the question of motivation.

"When you got involved in the Cowboy Palace, did you get involved to make money?" he asked, for the fourth or fifth time.

"No, sir," said Billy. For the fourth or fifth time.

"Did you tell Stanley—oh, Mr. Nye is here today. Do you recognize him?"

"Yes, I do," said Billy, humoring him.

"Did you ever meet him in his office?"

"I did, sir."

"Remember telling us you didn't on Monday?"

Billy waited in vain for Baird to object. "I never said that," he retorted. "I said I refused to talk to him in his office."

"Did you talk to him in his office?"

"I walked away from him."

"Did you speak to him in his office?"

Talk, no. Speak, yes. "Yes, sir." What difference did it make?

"Did he ask you facts about the Resource Capital thing in Cowboy Palace?"

"The interview was short-lived."

"Did he interview you on the phone with regard to the Cowboy Palace situation?"

"I don't remember what the conversations were." The last of them had been almost a year earlier.

"Haven't you had an opportunity to refresh your recollection by looking at papers?"

"No, sir."

Breitbart was disconcerted. "Prior to testifying here, you haven't looked at any documents?"

"No, sir."

On the brink of yet another morass, Breitbart stepped back. "May I just have a moment, Judge?" he asked, and returned to his table.

"Do you remember telling people that Stanley Nye was a fool?" he asked after a lengthy pause, evidently forgetting he had already done that bit.

"Did I tell people? I might have told some people, yes, sir."

"Do you remember telling them, is the question."

"Yes, sir." Billy directed another mute appeal to the government table.

"Your Honor," said Baird. "Haven't we been through this already?"

Judge Sand nodded. "I believe it is repetitious."

"Did you know in October, November, or December that Stanley Nye had taken over the case?" Breitbart continued grimly.

"Yes, sir. I found that out after they removed Walt Stowe. I knew that somebody else had taken over the case."

"When did you find out it was Stanley Nye?"

"Later on, when he tried to interview me."

"Did you refuse to be interviewed by him?"

"I asked him, 'What about my properties?' He couldn't give me an answer, so I terminated the interview."

Billy got on better with the prosecutors, Bruce Baird and Aaron Marcu, who were appalled to hear about the tapes that had been destroyed or turned away by the FBI. A search they ordered turned up about a dozen in the Bureau's New York office that had been left untranscribed, some of them of Billy in conversation with Tony Napoli, and four or five were subsequently used at the trial. But while he remained the government's star witness, nobody troubled to take him through his testimony or refresh his memory of the documentary evidence. Nor did any one seem much concerned with his safety, in spite of the high mortality rate among those with damaging information against ranking members of the New York mobs. More often than not during the trial, Billy would bump into the accused in the public lobbies of the federal courthouse and have to take care to avoid sharing an elevator with them.

As for Duke, his relations with the FBI had by now collapsed irredeemably. Retreating to Miami, he filed suit in U.S. District Court against the U.S. government, the FBI's Director, William H. Webster, and, among others, Special Agents Stanley Nye, Walter Smith, Damon Taylor, and Walter Stowe for $8.5 million in damages, alleging that they had "negligently and knowingly permitted the plaintiff to become a victim of a criminal extortion ring."

The action was never heard, of course, and could never have succeeded, but it probably helped reassure Hyman, Cooper, and the others. Caught between the Bureau's uncompromising hostility and the lethal sanctions of the mob, Duke had little choice but to cozy up to his former tormentors and show that they had nothing to fear from his (enforced) testimony. One night, before finally abandoning New York for Florida, Duke and Billy got drunk at Gallagher's, although Billy was not as drunk as Duke thought.

"We ate a five-pound lobster between us," Billy recalled later. "Then he pushes my head in my plate and puts the claws in my ear. So I says, 'You fucker. I'll fix you for that. Let's go over to the corner.' I'd told Mike, the bartender, to keep sending over martinis, and I says, 'You know, you're about the lowest motherfucker I ever met.' He says, 'You wait until you hear what the investigator's got on *you*.' 'What are you talking about?' I says. He says, 'The wise guys went and hired this P.I. named McNally.' 'Who?' I says. 'Where's he at?' 'Out on the island,' he says. 'I seen his report. How you beat the living shit out of some broad in Maxwell's Plum. How you got arrested in Atlanta for the drug money, and all that stuff. They know you been in prison, and you robbed a bank. They got everything on you, so you might as well throw the fucking rag in as far as Cowboy Palace is concerned, and going up against those guys.'

"Tommy had it all. He thought I was too drunk to remember and gave me everything in the report. Next day, I told Bruce Baird they had an investigator working on me and maybe I shouldn't testify, but my tapes were pretty much the whole case, so I had to take my lumps. Every fucking thing they hit me with, but at least I was prepared."

In spite of the broken promises, the worthless agreements, the stack of dud checks for a mythical $400,000, the forged deeds, and the glib assurances that the next deal would be the one to set the others straight, Billy was still not prepared for the final treachery. He had managed—just—to save the house in Virginia and his own home in Dallas by reconveying the properties in the nick of time, but the house on Croton Road, North Miami, empty since "the Cuban invasion" by Mike Delgado and his followers, was still in jeopardy. The IRS had a lien on the property for its still-escalating claims against him, and Resource Capital's attorneys were holding the deeds as collateral for shylock money advanced to Duke.

Before Billy left on his FBI mission to Hawaii, Duke claimed to have found a buyer for the house, and signed an agreement with Billy promising to pay him $100,000 on March 21 and the balance of $80,000 (plus the amount of the outstanding mortgage) six months later. He also undertook not to apply any of the money from the sale to the now-lost cause of Cowboy Palace. With this assurance Billy signed a blank quit-claim deed.

No sooner had he departed for Hawaii than Duke called Helen in Dallas to say that Billy had left some papers with him for her to sign. In all innocence, she added her signature to the quit-claim deed and other documents and Duke left immediately for Florida, where he first pledged the property as collateral for a $15,000 loan from a Miami moneylender, Joseph Bistrix, and then instructed a local realtor to sell it for the best price he could get.

Billy found out about this only because a neighbor keeping an eye on the house for him spotted the For Sale sign on the front lawn. As soon as he heard, Billy flew down to take the property off the market, just in time to prevent the realtor from accepting an offer of $130,000 (although later, he wished he had not). Seething all the way back to New York, he rode in from La Guardia determined to straighten Duke out once and for all.

This time, there was no lobster dinner at Gallagher's. Instead, it was knuckle sandwiches for one in Duke's latest apartment, on West Sixty-second Street. But even with a split lip, he still managed to talk Billy into yet another ride on his merry-go-round. Yes, there *was* a buyer waiting in the wings. And of *course* the property could be reregistered in Billy's name. He simply had to be patient a little while longer and he would have the money in his hand and all his debts paid off.

Told what he wanted to hear, Billy waited. And the next thing he heard was that the house on Croton Road had been sold on the courthouse steps for a mere $16,000 to pay off Duke's $15,000 loan from Joseph Bistrix. No one had troubled to notify him, officially or otherwise—not even the IRS, which had a prior, and much larger, lien on the house and which now received nothing. When Billy, distraught, appealed to the Miami FBI office for help, he was, of course, referred to New York. On taking it up with the New York office, he was naturally referred back to Miami.

Although some may feel that Billy deserved to lose his house for letting Duke con him, not just once or twice but on a daily basis for almost eighteen months, the fact remains that he lost it while working alone to develop a case against as dangerous a group of public enemies as the FBI's New York office ever interrupted its volleyball practice to target. As he said later, "This was the first case I ever worked with banks and real estate, and I didn't know nothing about it."

He could have used some help.

Without it, the Cowboy Palace case cost him not only $220,000 (the last appraised value of the Miami house) but at least $10,000 in legal fees trying to get it back. He was never fully reimbursed for his travel and subsistence expenses in the two and a half years from his first meeting with the principals of Resource Capital to their eventual conviction for loan-sharking, nor did he ever receive from the FBI the $10,000 that Supervisor Damon Taylor had promised him in the hearing of other agents. In working Billy over on the witness stand, the one thing that defense counsel could *not* suggest to his detriment was that the government had bought his testimony.

He had also pretty well given up hope of seeing any part of the $125,000 he had been promised originally for his work in unraveling the attempted assassination of Assistant U.S. Attorney James Kerr in San Antonio. The trials of Jimmy Chagra and his hit man, Charles Harrelson, for the murder of Judge John H. Wood, Jr., were now over, and there were only a few months to go to the fifth anniversary of the Kerr assassination attempt, on November 21, when the statute of limitations would remove the last possibility of a prosecution in the case.

Just before Christmas 1982, when Harrelson, his wife, and Jimmy Chagra's wife, Liz, were found guilty of murder and conspiracy to murder, Billy had been busy with Napoli in Brooklyn. When a jury in Jacksonville, Florida, subsequently found Jimmy Chagra *not* guilty of hiring Harrelson to carry out the contract, Billy had been setting up the Calabrese/Velotta case. (On top of the thirty years he was already serving, Chagra drew another fifteen years for obstructing justice and conspiracy to smuggle narcotics.) And when, in mid-March 1983, Harrelson drew two consecutive life sentences for the Wood murder from Judge William S. Sessions (soon to be appointed Director of the FBI), Billy figured that a settlement in the Kerr case was past due in more ways than one.

"How about it, Ron?" he asked Special Agent Iden. "Are we gonna make it? Anything I can help you with, maybe?"

"No, I don't think so, Billy. We're getting there. Like I say, we're going to put Bobby Piccolo in as an unindicted co-conspirator, and he can nail Chagra on his own. Kearns, too—if we ever find the sonuvabitch."

"Yeah. Right." After loading Piccolo up with sixty years of jail time, Billy was not entirely pleased with the way the guy was cutting deals all over the place and generally making himself indispensable.

"But now that you mention it," Iden went on, "there is just *one* thing. Couple of details in your story don't jibe exactly with what Bobby's telling us. Nothing major, but it's the kind of thing that gives the defense something to work with, you know? I'd like to fix that, if we can."

"Fix what?"

"What you're going to tell the grand jury, Billy. I want to go over that again with you. Make sure we get rid of any discrepancies. You know, so your story agrees with Bobby's."

"Hey, Ron." He knew what discrepancies meant. "How about getting Bobby to change *his* story?"

"Billy—"

"No, no. Forget about it. I know what I know. And I don't lie for nobody."

"Billy, I'm not asking you to *lie*. I'm just saying—"

"I hear ya. I know what you're saying. And I don't understand what the fuck's going on. First, you guys make me take a polygraph before you believe me. Now you know I'm telling you the truth, you want me to lie?"

He was so annoyed over Iden's suggestion that he complained to Dave Jellison about it.

"Billy didn't have the whole thing," Jellison said afterward. "He had what he knew about. And they said, 'Well, it doesn't fit with what we've got. Can you say this?' He says, 'No, I can't. I got to testify to what I know, and that's not part of it. I'm gonna have to tell this story ten times. I gotta be telling the truth.' And he backed 'em down. As it turned out, two more years went by and they proved that he was right."

In June 1983, with barely five months to go before the statute of limitations wiped the slate clean, the case suddenly lurched forward with the arrest of Jimmy Kearns in Lake Havasu City, a few hours after his partner, Billy Kelly, had been picked up in Miami. Both had gone to ground nineteen months earlier, after jumping bail in the North Carolina marijuana case with Murdo Margeson, of whom there was still no sign.

The Bureau found Kearns by leaning on his wife, Catherine— "Rene"—who, while living with her five children at the family home in Revere, Massachusetts, had managed to combine her domestic duties with a money-laundering business on the side. About to begin a four-month federal stretch for failing to declare $100,000 on arrival at Miami airport from the Cayman Islands, she was now also under indictment in Arizona for harboring her fugitive husband.

Asking for bail of $250,000 after her arrest in July on this charge, the U.S. attorney in Boston revealed for the first time in public that Jimmy Kearns was "a prime suspect" in the attempted assassination of Assistant U.S. Attorney James Kerr, and that Rene had already testified five times (with immunity) before the federal grand jury inquiring into the case in San Antonio.

"Investigators believe she may have accompanied her husband to San Antonio in connection with the attack on Kerr," wrote Richard J. Connolly in the *Boston Globe*, some three and a half years after Billy had flatly informed Ron Iden that the kids had gone along, too. Having seen her in action, Billy had no doubt that Rene was perfectly capable of having handled the shotgun that was also fired at Kerr when her husband cut loose with a fusillade of nineteen rounds from his .30 caliber carbine.

Another candidate for the role of shotgun rider during the attack was Billy Kelly, but no one was inclined to waste much effort on testing *that* theory, as he was already booked to stand trial for the contract murder of Charles Von Maxcy, of Sebring, Florida, in 1966— not to mention the North Carolina marijuana case and a wide assortment of other offenses.

Just over two weeks later, the last senior member of the Godfrey

Gang not to have been questioned about the attempt on Kerr's life was traced to Santo Domingo. On July 25, Peter White, Billy's former "partner" in the marijuana business, was deported to San Juan, Puerto Rico, where FBI agents were waiting to take him back to Massachusetts as a parole violator with five years still to serve for a 1969 bank robbery in Somerville.

"Investigators were reported last night to be trying to determine if White had any knowledge of an underworld meeting where the so-called 'contract' to murder Kerr was discussed," wrote Connolly in the *Globe*. "There have been reports among law-enforcement officers that a former Massachusetts man was offered a 'contract' to kill Kerr, and that he recommended another criminal from this state for the job."

Billy was pleased that they had picked up White, and looked forward to testifying against him when the time came, but it was irritating to read these tentative suggestions about what might have happened, when he had given the Bureau the plain facts of the matter several years earlier.

"Now all you gotta do is find Murdo," he told Iden, who knew that already. He also knew he was going to have a hard time getting Billy his money, now that the government's case against Chagra and Kearns looked as if it would succeed without his testimony.

"We'll get him," Iden said. "Don't worry about it."

"Who's worried?"

Billy had hardly spared a serious thought for Kearns, Kelly, or Margeson in months. The chances of accidentally bumping into one or another of them while working undercover were remote. Margeson, in particular, had made such a good job of his disappearance that he was still missing on November 20, 1983, when Jamiel Chagra and James Kearns were at long last indicted for the attempted murder of James Kerr—just one day before the statute of limitations would have lowered the boom on the case.

"What about the others?" Billy demanded. "Where's Piccolo? I don't see Bobby in there."

"He's in as an unindicted co-conspirator," said Iden. "So is Margeson. And Joe Chagra—Jimmy's brother."

"I know who he is. How about Peter White? And Billy Painter? They taking a walk, too?"

"Billy, I don't make those decisions. That's up to the U.S. attorney's office. I guess they figure they can't make it stick against those guys."

It was always the same, complained Billy. He would bring in a case. They would behave like they could catch a disease from it. He would persuade them to take it on, and they would get all excited, promising this and that. And as soon as they made a little progress, they would figure they didn't need him anymore. They would leave him out of the picture, and pretty soon the promises were all forgotten and they had botched the case.

"Ron, all you gotta do is tell me what you want," he said, "and I'll get it for yez."

But it was too late for that. And the *Boston Globe* went on rubbing salt in the wound.

"A Texan identified only as Robert Piccolo was named in the indictment as the middleman who gave Kearns money from Chagra," wrote Richard J. Connolly on November 30. "There are reports in law-enforcement circles in San Antonio that Piccolo, who is not a defendant, has turned government witness and is in protective custody."

Like any professional performer, Billy resented the absence of proper credits, even though they might have proved embarrassing. He had to be satisfied with an off-handed reference in the *Globe* to "another alleged conspirator in the marijuana case, William Clifford Breen, formerly of Somerville, [who] reportedly has been questioned about any knowledge he has about the plot to kill Kerr."

Billy knew it was not Connolly's fault. He was simply passing on what he had heard from some government source determined to relegate Billy to the smallest of walk-on parts. And that was all right, too. He was not eager to go public in a Texas courtroom with the story of his life if they could convict Chagra and Kearns without him. Piccolo was primed and waiting, and, according to Iden, Peter White had also agreed to testify. That, everybody agreed, would probably be enough.

And it was. More than enough. On June 16, Jimmy Chagra appeared before District Judge William Sessions to plead guilty to conspiring with Kearns to kill Kerr—and it was all over.

After living with the case for five and a half years, Billy felt suddenly bereft. Kearns was still holding out, but there was no way he could beat the charge now that his paymaster had confessed to it. On June 26, the second day of his trial in Waco District Court, Kearns changed his plea to guilty, on condition that the government dropped charges of perjury and obstruction of justice against his wife. (This was not so much chivalry as determination to wring *some* advantage from an otherwise hopeless situation.)

A month later, Jimmy Chagra drew another life term, to run concurrently with the forty-seven years he was already serving, and Kearns was sentenced to life plus ten and, oddly, fined ten thousand dollars. As Billy Kelly by this time was sitting on death row in Florida awaiting execution for the murder of Charles Von Maxcy, everybody was now accounted for except Murdo Margeson. The FBI had failed to turn up anybody who had seen or heard from him in years.

There was no sign of Billy's agreed fee, either.

Nor very much left in the way of job satisfaction, although working undercover alongside Wincelowicz, with Dale Hackbart as case agent, was still a pleasure. Time and again, the NYCON team made believers out of the Bureau's skeptics, not excluding Assistant Coordinators Fred Verinder and Julian Perez. For a time, a photograph of Billy with other members of the NYCON group actually hung on the wall of Verinder's office, among the framed commendations and signed pictures of past and present FBI directors, but it soon went into the waste basket when Billy finally took his grievances to Washington.

There was nowhere else to go with them.

In the late summer of 1983, Billy and Wincelowicz were so close to Jack Mace that he wanted to put them in charge of his affairs so as to have more free time. It was the best offer ever made to a government agent. From such a position, Billy and Wincelowicz would have enjoyed a general overview of property crime, and with it the ability to target every significant ring of thieves, armed robbers, hijackers, and receivers then operating in the continental United States.

The work would have been dangerous, but police work at that level *is* dangerous. They were aware of the risks and prepared to accept them.

All this was explained in detail to senior management in the FBI's New York divisional office, *but permission to accept Mace's offer was denied.*

One of the reasons why Jack Mace was eager to hand over the reins of his business was that he had decided to marry again. Testament to the matchmaking powers of his mob friends, he had proposed to, and been accepted by, Anne Galante, widow of Carmine Galante, former head of the Bonanno family. It was to be the mob wedding of the year, attended by top crime bosses in the East and powerful delegations from the Midwest, Florida, Las Vegas, and California.

As Mace's old friend and his new heir apparent, Billy and Wincelowicz were among the first to be invited.

Again, they were aware of the risks and prepared to accept them. As honored guests of the groom, they would have rubbed shoulders with the aristocracy of crime, meeting many of the FBI's hitherto untouchable targets face to face in circumstances where mistrust or suspicion were unthinkable. From then on, Billy and Wincelowicz could have enjoyed privileged access to organized crime in any state of the union, and the ability to guide the efforts of federal, state, and local law-enforcement agencies *from within.*

All this was explained in detail to senior management in the FBI's New York divisional office, but *permission to accept the invitation to Mace's wedding was denied.*

There was little anyone could do about it. As government agents, subject to FBI discipline and procedures, the NYCON team was obliged to work through channels. And the harder they pushed against the bureaucratic fat, the more resistance they encountered—until finally New York management solved its problem by pulling the plug. Billy, Wincelowicz, and Hackbart had gone out of program (exceeded their terms of reference).

It was the classic bureaucratic response to imagination and initiative. If an investigation (or an agent) fails to fit in the space provided, put a stop to it (or him).

Wincelowicz was called in and asked if NYCON could continue with white-collar crime. He replied that he would *try* for more con men, but suspected that about 90 percent of the work would continue to be with organized crime, labor racketeering, and property crime. In that case, they said, they would shut NYCON down and put him with an O.C. squad for sixty days to work on Mace's friend Matty "The Horse" Ionello.

Wincelowicz protested that the chance to do that was long gone, but he was assigned to an organized-crime squad anyway.

"Ironically, after that," he recalls, "all the stuff that Jack Mace was sending me was stocks and bonds from First Boston—about five hundred million dollars' worth. And a tractor-trailer load of Kodak film worth a hundred thousand which I could have had for six thousand. But the response from the organized crime people was, 'No, we're not interested in any of that,' so I just said, 'That's it. I'm coming in.' After forty-five days of the sixty. Very disappointing."

After NYCON closed, Wincelowicz and Hackbart placed some of the cases left dangling with other FBI offices, calling them up to explain what they had, then sending on the tapes and files. Wincelowicz rarely had to testify. Once the defendants learned who Frank Kohler was, they would usually try to cop a plea—and there was some satisfaction in that, even though he and Hackbart were reprimanded by the New York bosses for making cases for other divisions. But it was not enough for Billy.

First, he attempted to draft a letter of protest to Assistant Coordinator Fred Verinder, but choked up after accusing him of obstruction of justice. Then he decided to go over Verinder's head and lay out his entire catalog of grievances before the FBI director himself, William H. Webster, together with a concise summary of the cases that had been refused, botched, or abandoned without explanation by the New York office. After working on this for several weeks (it eventually cost Billy three hundred dollars just to get his final draft typed up), he was gratefully diverted from his yellow legal pads by a call from Dave Jellison in Miami.

Would he be interested in talking to Jellison's friend Special Agent Glenn Tuttle in Washington about working a bunch of Italians chased out of the Bahamas for cheating casinos in Freeport and now getting big in the restaurant business?

Sure, said Billy. He liked Italian food. But since when was eating pasta a crime?

Since they started serving it with cocaine, Jellison replied.

24

Things were not much different in the Washington field office.

As soon as Dave Jellison introduced him to Supervisor Kirby Major, he knew he was in trouble. It was Damon Taylor all over again. By the time they sat down with Special Agents Glenn Tuttle, Tom Carter, and a gaggle of other Bureau officials, including an "expert" on organized crime and an undercover agent named Joe, Billy was ready to go home.

"Does the name Giulio Santillo mean anything to you?" asked Major, to get the meeting started.

"That's why I'm here, right?"

Expecting more, Major glanced inquiringly at Jellison.

"Billy worked Santillo in the old days," Jellison explained. "After a whole bunch of 'em got kicked out of Freeport. Right, Billy?"

"Right," he said grudgingly. "I worked him and Valentino Mordini and a coupla other guys—I forget their names. Big gamblers. Liked to bet sports. I got a whole mess of intelligence on 'em for the Miami office and Metro-Dade County."

Major grunted. "Well, we've reason to suspect that Santillo is linked with organized crime," he said. "And he's now a target of the *Washington* field office. I should like to emphasize that."

He went on to explain that Santillo owned Tiberio's, at 1915 K Street, Washington; Tiberio's in Bal Harbor, Florida, and the Ter-

razza in Alexandria, Virginia—three high-class restaurants for customers with coke-user profiles. As Santillo's closest associates were
also big in the restaurant business, it looked like they had a whole
network building up. After busting the Pizza Connection, they were
now beginning to see the outlines of a Trattoria Connection. The first
thing they had to do, therefore, was to lay out a plan.

"Excuse me," said Billy. "The first thing we gotta do is decide
how I'm gonna get paid. I want a thousand a week regardless. I don't
care if it's for seven minutes or seven days, I get a thousand a week
plus expenses."

After some discussion, they agreed on $750 a week plus expenses.

"All right," Major said. "Now can we get on? We need a game
plan here."

"Excuse me," said Billy. "Why do you need me fur? You got your
own undercover agent. You brought in these organized-crime people—I mean, I don't know why I'm here fur. What do you want *me* to
do?"

"You're here to listen," Major replied sharply. "When we've laid
out a game plan, we'll *tell* you what to do."

Billy turned to Jellison, who was closely studying the doodles on
his scratch pad.

"Forget about it," Billy said, almost kindly. "I don't work that
way. If you want this case done, I'll do it. But if you wanna tell me
how to do it, then let me go home. Tell your own undercover guy
what to do. Dave? Take me away from these people."

After some more discussion—in Billy's absence, then in his presence, then in his absence again—Jellison came out of Major's office
with the verdict.

"Go work 'em, Billy," he said. "Don't worry about these guys. Just
tell 'em what you got in mind, then work the case any way you want."

What Billy had in mind was to get over with the Italians by
exploiting their weakness for gambling.

"We're not interested in gambling," Major said coldly.

"Well, *I* am," said Billy. "And if you don't wanna work that side
of the case, I know somebody who will."

"Do what you want with it." Major was finding this increasingly
hard to take. "We're interested in *serious* crimes."

"Okay. In that case, I'm gonna need a good, hardworking undercover agent. And I know just the guy. Special Agent Vincent Wincelowicz."

"You'll work with Joe," said Major.

Billy was inclined to doubt it. Joe had already told him he never
wore a body recorder and not to plan anything after 5:00 P.M., when
his working day ended. As Billy's normally *began* several hours later

than that, his debut at Santillo's Terrazza restaurant in Alexandria was a solo act as usual—the big-time, high-rolling bookie/gambler with cocaine connections. Dressed for the part in flashy resort clothes and festooned with gold jewelry, including a gold Rolex President with a diamond bezel (courtesy of the late George Mitchell), he swaggered in, greeted the maitre d' with a hundred-dollar bill peeled from his roll as though it were toilet paper, and demanded the best table in the joint.

Once seated, he ordered vintage champagne and the most expensive dishes on the menu, sending some of them back to keep the kitchen on its toes, and handsomely tipping everybody who came within range. By the end of the evening, as he prepared to leave in another flurry of high-denomination currency, the staff would probably have carried him to his car, had he wished it.

They had certainly not forgotten him by the following evening, when he showed up to sow the ground he had cultivated the night before, and when Santillo himself remembered him as a bookie he had bet with in Florida, Billy was formally installed as Customer of the Year, with every waiter and busboy in the place eager to stop by his table for a chat.

And very interesting chat it was, too. About betting sports with major mob figures in Florida. About how restaurant owners were even better placed than bookies for evading federal and state taxes. And how the fresh red roses placed on the tables every day were shipped up from Peru in boxes that often contained a little something extra.

With nothing more solid to go on, Kirby Major could see all this lavish expenditure contributing only to the federal deficit, but then Valentino Mordini showed up one day from Florida, and the Breen bandwagon began to roll. A gentle, peace-loving ex-croupier, Mordini was a compulsive gambler and born loser, but he was such a nice man that every wise guy he knew tried to help him out with a piece of his action—and Mordini knew a lot of wise guys. Although he told Billy he was employed mainly as a courier between Santillo and his friends in Washington and their mob bookies in Florida, Anthony Acceturo and Demus "Joey" Covello, he also had a connection for everything—loan-sharking, collection and enforcement, extortion, stolen goods, interstate shipment of liquor to avoid state taxes (a popular "economy" measure among restaurant owners), stolen credit cards, stolen automobiles, guns, including automatic weapons, and virtually unlimited quantities of dope.

Bounced out of the Bahamas ten years earlier with Santillo and half a dozen others, Mordini had survived by waiting tables in Miami and by trying to win money from Billy, who was then running his poker game and sports book under the auspices of Sergeant Dave Green and Special Agent Dave Jellison. When Mordini eventually went to work at Tiberio's in Bal Harbor, the first in Santillo's restaurant chain, Billy made a practice of dining there two or three nights a week, getting to know Mordini really well, but after he moved to Texas they had inevitably lost contact. It was an unfeigned pleasure for both, therefore, when they bumped into each other again at the Terrazza—particularly for Billy. As far as he was concerned, the whole character of the case now changed, with a shift in its center of gravity from Washington to Florida, where Mordini still lived.

Kirby Major did not see it that way. Like his colleagues in New York, he perceived no advantage in making cases for other divisions. But after Mordini had vouched for Billy among the key players around Santillo, and in particular with Angelo Puccinelli, a waiter at the Terrazza who would have informed on his own mother if he had thought it would help him get a restaurant of his own, Billy was satisfied that Santillo was as much a victim of the mob as an accomplice. The only organized-crime connection he could find was between Santillo and his heavyweight bookmakers. Nor, in spite of his trawling, had Billy managed to catch Santillo at cocaine trafficking, unlike Puccinelli, who seemed eager to deal. If the government wanted Santillo, he told Glenn Tuttle and Kirby Major, its best bet would be to look at his tax returns. Unless he was up to something in Miami . . .

After consulting Dave Green, then with the Florida Department of Law Enforcement, Billy flew down to find out. With what they already knew of Santillo, coupled with Mordini's account of what his boss was up to, Green obtained a court order for wiretaps in Tiberio's at Bal Harbor, and on the strength of the conversations he recorded there, he soon had wires up in other favored Italian hangouts around town. That done, Billy then took Joe, Major's undercover agent, to dinner with Mordini at Tiberio's to pull the net tighter.

In such circumstances, if a body recorder is to be used, it is customary for the agent to wear it rather than the source, but Joe had already made all the concessions he was prepared to consider by agreeing to work after 5:00 P.M. It was Billy who had the Nagra taped to his body when they sat down at the table, and Billy who steered the conversation from dope operations in South Florida—Mordini knew of a warehouse full of cocaine in the Kendall area—through the rackets worked by local organized-crime groups, to the availability of stolen cars, credit cards, typewriters, and firearms.

Beaming with satisfaction, Billy sat back and allowed Joe to take his pick from the rich array of cases now open to him. And after due thought, Joe said he would like to buy some typewriters.

"Keep that idiot away from me," Billy bellowed at Kirby Major, as soon as he could get to a telephone. "He coulda had a ton of coke. He coulda bought automatic weapons. He coulda had interstate theft of automobiles. He coulda got into Acceturo and Covello. The asshole coulda done anything he wanted. And what does he want? He wants to buy a couple of IBM golfballs."

Major did not care for his tone and summoned them both back to Washington, where Billy was assigned to work with a woman under-cover agent named Gerry Smith. Again Billy put in a plea for Wince-lowicz (although Smith was tall, dark, and better-looking), and again he was directed to follow instructions. Either he took her with him for his next meeting with Mordini at the Terrazza in Alexandria or he would be dropped from the case, and probably by the Bureau as a whole, for being "out of control."

Billy had never responded well to threats, but he was not about to throw in a good hand because he disliked the dealer. As a cover, he had let it be known that he ran a sports book in the Washington metropolitan area and was looking for connections to lay off some of his heavier bets. To back this story up, the FBI had put in a call-forwarding system, so that when Mordini or any of the others dialed the Washington number Billy had given them, the call was automatically transferred to his home in Dallas or anywhere else he happened to be.

Over dinner, he and Mordini talked sports, with Santillo, Pucci-nelli, and others sitting in from time to time to help Billy with his growing collection of Dom Perignon bottles, and Gerry Smith, a Nagra hidden in her purse, moving it adroitly around the table to record his most productive, and expensive, session yet at the Ter-razza. As the evening wore on and tongues loosened, so the conversa-tion turned to dope and stolen goods and how to beat taxes, until Billy himself put a stop to such careless talk in a public place. He wanted it in a private place, where the Bureau could get everything on videotape, including the stolen furs he had just been offered.

Protesting that he was having too good a time to talk business, he suggested that Mordini and Puccinelli bring the goods to a motel in a couple of days, and when they agreed, ordered a magnum.

After watching the tapes of the motel meeting, even Kirby Major had to admit he was showing results. Although Billy had been obliged to nudge Gerry Smith out of the way of the camera once or twice, the surveillance crew had covered not only their inspection of the furs but a serious discussion of cocaine sources, supplies and prices, and a detailed account of how, by pocketing the cash receipts and dou-bling up on his food and liquor bills, Santillo was able to bet up to

$20,000 a game during the football season, and sometimes as much as $150,000 in a single weekend.

"I'm not interested in gambling," Major said. "I told you that. What about narcotics? Is he into narcotics?"

"You heard the tapes," replied Billy. "Mordini can get a ton of it."

"That's in Florida."

"Right. And you oughta tell Customs about them roses from Peru."

"Billy, this is a *Washington* case. And Santillo is the target. Can we get him for dope?"

"I don't know. Maybe. If he's into it. I can get Puccinelli for sure. And for a big load if you wanna. If it's real big, he might have to go through Valentino for it, and then we can lock *his* people up, too."

"Let's just think Washington, okay? Go for Puccinelli. Maybe *he* can get Santillo for us."

"Maybe." Billy was not disposed to argue. "I'll put the deal together in the Terrazza and see what happens."

By Billy's standards, nothing happened. After firing him up to the point where they were talking fifty-kilo deals, Puccinelli agreed to sell Billy a sample ounce of uncut cocaine for eighteen hundred dollars from his local source, Savino Recine, owner of Washington's Galileo Restaurant at 2014 P Street NW.

No arrests were to be made until the undercover operation had been completed, and it had only just started, but every transaction was to be photographed, taped, and fully documented so that when the time came, obtaining convictions would be the merest formality. Billy, accordingly, gave Puccinelli the money and sent his "girl," Special Agent Gerry Smith, to meet Puccinelli and Recine outside the Terrazza to take delivery of the sample ounce, which turned out to be 98 percent pure.

"No shit," said Billy, when he heard the lab report from Glenn Tuttle. "I better find out where he's getting it and grab off all I can."

"Billy—"

"I'll tell Pucci my people loved it, and we'll take all he can get. Could be twenty keys a week, from what he's telling me. Maybe more."

"Billy, we got all we need, okay? An ounce is as good as twenty keys. They're still looking at fifteen years each."

Billy shook the phone to make sure it was working properly. "You're gonna leave all that shit out there? Is that what you're telling me, Glenn?"

"Kirby doesn't want to spend the money," said Tuttle. He sounded awkward. "Maybe we can set 'em up for a big one when we're ready to take the whole crew down."

Billy retreated in disgust to Florida, where at least they could see the sense of seizing as much dope as they could before it hit the streets. In charge of the local spin-off from the Washington investigation, Special Agent Tony Ameroso put him to work with undercover agent Jerry Sullivan, an amiable, hard-bitten Irishman whom Billy took to on sight. After bringing them up to date with "progress" in Washington, Billy took Sullivan along to meet Mordini and put him in play as his man in South Florida.

Stay in touch, he told them, insisting they exchange telephone numbers. Have dinner. Meet for cocktails. Get to know each other. There was money to be made. Mordini had the connections. Billy and Jerry had the customers.

Sullivan, naturally, needed no urging—nor, indeed, did Mordini, who had also taken an immediate shine to him. Even so, Billy still called Mordini at least three times a week from wherever he happened to be to make another half-hour recording of the latest news from the Italian front, forwarding the tapes to Tuttle and Carter in Washington and Ameroso in Fort Lauderdale. And by one of those seeming coincidences that sometimes encouraged Billy to think he was working for a higher power than the FBI, the Italians now surfaced in Tampa, where, quite independently, he was working for Dave Green in a task-force case code-named Operation Super Bowl.

Green had brought Billy in to play the part of an Irish gang boss in a sting directed against two groups of predominantly Cuban bookmakers grossing around $2.5 million a week. As a front for the investigation, the task force had bought a bar in West Tampa, which it operated for almost a year as O'Ryan's, an archetypal cinderblock Irish-American pub providing Billy with such a comfortable setting in which to work that he would probably have done so for nothing (which, in the end, turned out to be the case anyway). From the day it opened for business, word got around that O'Ryan's was the place for sports betting action, and the bookies flocked there like moths to a flame, bringing their drugs, weapons, and racketeering connections with them.

Wired for sound and vision and flourishing under Billy's "protection," O'Ryan's also turned into a general clearinghouse for criminal intelligence data of all kinds, and some familiar names were soon cropping up. Tina Cesar was down from Washington, looking to open a high-class Italian restaurant named Donatello's. And Angelo Puccinelli was in town. Then Valentino Mordini. Before long, what with Jerry Sullivan's tunneling into the Italian network on the Atlantic coast and Billy's enlisting the Tampa task force to unravel Mordini's connections on the Gulf coast, the Florida tail was vigorously wagging the Washington dog.

Kirby Major was furious. It was Billy's fault. A flurry of teletypes went out reminding all the FBI offices now involved that the investigation had originated in Washington, that Billy was being paid by Washington, and that no matter where or how additional defendants were identified, whether in Miami, Fort Lauderdale, Tampa, New York, or anywhere else, the cases were to be filed and processed in Washington.

When Billy heard how he had been characterized in Major's teletypes, he complained about it bitterly to Special Agent Tom Carter, who did his best to keep the peace.

"Kirby believes you're doing a good job," he assured him. "He just gets hung up in his management philosophy."

This prompted Billy to suggest a few suitable repositories for Kirby's management philosophy, and Carter into promises of support.

"I will not be a party to shafting you in the back," he said flatly. "I'll go to bat for you."

Billy grunted. "I don't like teletypes that say I'm uncontrollable," he said. "I know what I'm doing. I can get the job done. If they can't do it the way it should be done, that knocks me dead. I'm handicapping myself. Every time they come up and take a shot at me, I tell 'em, 'Take a shot at the bad guy. I'm trying to help you.' "

"I know, Billy."

"I'm trying to box 'em in for 'em, but they don't know how to do it."

"I know. They want you to take one step at a time. Unfortunately, you can't go in there and tell Mordini you only want to talk about Santillo today, and you only want to talk about Pucci the next time. He's going to give you all the shit he's got. . . ."

And he had a load of it, as Jerry Sullivan was finding out.

Mordini was now begging Billy and Sullivan to take any quantity of uncut cocaine they wanted—as much as five hundred kilos was mentioned—with no money up front. His principal source was Carlos Lehder Rivas, who had relatives in the Kendall area guarding a warehouse piled high with at least twenty thousand pounds of the stuff. All Billy had to do was go and get it. And if that was not enough, he could also put him in touch with a Colombian senator from Santa Marta who again had almost unlimited supplies, or with a third major trafficker with substantial quantities already landed in the United States. What more could he say? If they asked him for a ton of jelly beans, Mordini would have a problem. But a ton of coke? No problem.

With the Bureau unwilling to finance a major buy, and the undercover operation still turning up new targets, all Billy and

Sullivan could do was stall, although this made an already difficult and dangerous game little short of suicidal. After they had pressed Mordini and his connections for all they could supply, to do no business with them was to court disaster.

Kirby Major was no help. Still asserting his authority over the case, he sent Gerry Smith, Billy's undercover "girl", to Alexandria to meet with Mordini alone at Tiberio's. The first Billy knew of it was when Mordini called to warn him that his "girl" was probably a cop!

And that was just the beginning. Piqued when Billy complained, and without even warning the Fort Lauderdale office to call in Jerry Sullivan, Kirby Major abruptly canceled the call-forwarding system that had enabled Billy to take his Washington calls on any phone in the country. As of that moment, without a Washington number, his cover story was as good as blown.

So was Jerry Sullivan's—and he was lucky to survive. Richard Del Gaudio, top muscle man for Acceturo and Covello, leaned on him heavily for news of Billy's whereabouts.

"Asshole," he said, poking his finger in Sullivan's chest. "You'll take us up to D.C. and we'll fix Breen's head."

Sullivan managed to fob Del Gaudio off, but it was all over. In the middle of a brilliantly daring undercover run, he and Billy had been brought down by a twitch of bureaucratic petulance in Washington— and without an arrest to show for it.

Even so, Billy refused to accept that bungling and petty jealousy had put the Trattoria Connection completely out of reach. What he needed was a way around Kirby Major. He needed to talk to a state or local law-enforcement officer with as low an opinion of the FBI as *he* had, and found just the man in Carl Shoffler, a sixteen-year veteran with the Washington Metro police. A tough, straight, street-wise cop with a lot of experience in federal task forces around the country, Shoffler had locked horns with the Bureau too many times to be even mildly surprised by what had happened.

"I think you should bury that three-letter group," he told Billy on the phone one day, after they had worked together for several months. "I never expected to find myself on this side of the fence, attacking them, but somewhere along the line, someone has got to do something. It's the system. Instead of sharing information and working together, the bosses are always looking to get *all* the credit, so they can put it on their résumés and move up the ladder. As long as the system works that way, they're always gonna pull that kind of shit."

Billy grunted sympathetically.

"I spent sixteen years busting my ass," Shoffler went on warmly. "I'm hated by every top gangster in this area, who at one time or another has planned my demise, and all the while those fools were sitting over there saying these guys weren't nothing, okay? Then, when they found out they were wrong, then they jump on the bandwagon and steamroller over me. Typical FBI arrogance."

"Oh, boy," said Billy. "Tell me about it. I told Verinder up in New York when he was blocking all my cases, I said, 'If I did—or any civilian did—what you people did in NYC and other places, I'd be locked up for obstruction of justice.' "

After Billy explained what had happened to the Trattoria Connection, he was put to work on a parallel investigation by the Washington Metro police into a number of other leading Italian restaurants, among them Filomena's and Peppino's in the Georgetown section of the capital. Billy's role was to establish probable cause for the vice squad to apply for court-ordered wires and phone taps, a job at which he was now so practiced that two or three plates of osso buco or pollo parmigiana were usually enough. On the strength of the tapes recorded by these bugs, Shoffler and his colleagues were eventually able to arrest and convict half a dozen organized-crime figures, most of them linked to Santo Trafficante, the Tampa mob boss, and to Meyer Lansky.

Kirby Major was not particularly pleased when he heard about it, which increased Carl Shoffler's pleasure proportionately.

"Billy is in his own little category," he said afterward. "He's a professional. He goes about doing his job, and if he tells you something, you can take it to the bank. He's got a lot of integrity. But he's not controllable in the strictest sense, so as far as the FBI is concerned, he's also potentially dangerous. If they want him to go one way and he thinks it's the wrong way, he'll be very, very forceful about not doing it. Some of them can't handle that. He also goes too fast for most of 'em. If you can keep up with him, he can make your career. If you can't, he represents a danger to it. There's a good probability that if you don't get your butt out there and work twelve or fourteen hours a day, seven days a week, you're gonna wind up floundering. I don't know if it's stupidity or what, but Billy has a fearlessness about him I don't find in a lot of people."

Shoffler was being whimsical, of course, about Billy's fearlessness. Like most of the other dedicated law-enforcement officers who have worked with him, Shoffler attributes perhaps 90 percent of Billy's motivation to various forms of competitive egotism, ranging from the thrill of the hunt, through hyperactive dislike of being beaten by anyone at anything, to general adrenaline addiction—all of which are undoubtedly present—but the remaining 10 percent eludes him, as it sometimes eludes Billy himself.

What made Billy run beyond the point where any rational person would have weighed cost against effect and backed off was not a desire for money, praise, or public recognition, however welcome those things might be, but moral passion. For Billy, an old-fashioned Catholic conception of absolute good and evil carries with it an absolute requirement to fight the enemy to the last breath.

This was the incalculable element that made him not only dangerous to career-conscious bureaucrats but lethal among the criminal community, which had nothing in its armory that he had not already encountered and survived. Like their opposite numbers in the FBI, his targets in organized crime simply could not conceive of anyone going against his own apparent best interests for the sake of principle.

Before Kirby Major closed all the doors against him in the Trattoria Connection case, Billy went back to Tampa for a final fling at Angelo Puccinelli, who was now living there, and who reluctantly agreed to meet him for dinner at the Villa Nova by Lauro restaurant.

Knowing it was his last chance to show how big a case it *could* be, Billy needed to record their conversation, but he also knew that Puccinelli, after hearing the rumors about him, would have nothing useful to say if he thought Billy was wired. The only answer was to have someone else wear the Nagra, and luckily Billy knew just the man. Working with the Tampa task force on the bookie sting was an undercover agent from the Hillsbrough County Sheriff's office, Al Grosser, who jumped at the chance of champagne and oysters at the Villa Nova after months of beer and burgers at O'Ryan's.

To calm Puccinelli's suspicions, and give Grosser a chance to play himself in as his man in Tampa, Billy kept the conversation going with sports and barroom gossip until they finished eating. Then, relaxed as they were ever likely to be over coffee and Sambuca, he gently steered the talk around to business, eventually inquiring in a casual tone if Puccinelli was interested in taking a thousand pounds of marijuana in exchange for cocaine.

Puccinelli fidgeted.

Pretending not to notice, Billy carried on with his circumstantial tale of how the grass came to be surplus to requirements until Puccinelli at last cut him short.

"Billy," he said, shaking his head. "The word on the street is that you're The Man."

Billy rocked back. Then he leaped up in a rage, knocking his chair over, grabbed Puccinelli by the shirt, and dragged him to his feet. Reaching for his wallet with the other hand, he slapped him about the face with it. He had once seen George Raft do something similar in an old movie.

"Okay," he snarled. "You're under arrest."

Grosser gaped, but before he could say anything to spoil the effect, Billy pushed Puccinelli back in his seat.

"Asshole." He righted his chair, glaring around at their fellow diners. "If I were The Man," he growled, "I'd have busted your ass in Alexandria that time you sold us an ounce."

Puccinelli rearranged his clothing indignantly. "I'm only telling you what I hear. How do I know what happens to you? You could be in trouble. You could be wearing a wire."

"A *wire*?" For a moment, Billy seemed set to repeat his George Raft routine, but subsided in disgust. "No, no—not me. But *he* is," he added mischievously, winking at the unfortunate Grosser. "Al's a cop."

Billy always liked to tell the truth, but even in the subdued lighting of the restaurant, he could see his partner turn pale.

"Tell you what," he went on, as Puccinelli and Grosser looked at each other uncertainly. He was beginning to enjoy himself. "This is what we're gonna do. We'll all go into the men's room and strip off, okay? And if anybody's wearing a wire, the other two will kill him. Waddiya say? That's fair, ain't it?"

As Grosser evidently did not think so, Billy stood up, unbuttoning his shirt, and started to undress at the table. Grosser slid lower in his chair, grinning around weakly.

"All right, all right—sit down," said Puccinelli, equally embarrassed. "Let's cut out the bullshit, okay? Sit down and tell me what you want."

Sensing no further sales resistance, Billy tucked in his shirttails and sat. "I told you what I want. I wanna trade a thousand pounds of grass for coke."

"Well, I don't know about the grass, but I can get you all the coke you want."

It was a good tape—so good that Dave Green still uses it as a teaching aid in law-enforcement seminars. But that was the only benefit derived from Billy's meeting that night with Puccinelli. When Billy tried to report what he had learned to the FBI, he found he had been blacklisted.

Nobody would talk to him or even take his calls.

Tired of the Bureau's broken promises, and without really understanding how much its bureaucrats detested him, Billy had let it be known that in the future he intended to tape his telephone conversations with agents so as to have some record of what had been agreed between them. He knew agents did it to him, so why should he not do the same?

The New York divisional office supplied a reason.

As soon as management heard of his intentions, a teletype was sent to headquarters in Washington and all FBI divisional offices declaring Billy "out of control." Agents were accordingly instructed to accept no more calls or have any further dealings with him.

"But, Dale, that's *crazy*," he told Hackbart, who thought Billy was at least entitled to an explanation. "I got a giant planeload of coke coming in. Carlos Lehder Rivas is bringing it into South Florida someplace. And it's like twenty-five thousand kilos."

Silence. "Twenty-five *thousand*?" Hackbart laughed. "Come on, Billy. That's like fifty *tons*."

"Yeah, right," he said. "But how am I supposed to work it if nobody takes my calls? Dave Green can't handle a deal this big. The Florida Department of Law Enforcement don't *do* drugs. I won't go to the DEA with it, because you know why. I called Customs, and they won't touch it because they think I'm with the Bureau. So what am I supposed to do?"

"Leave it with me, Billy," Hackbart said. "I'll get back to you."

If the case had gone forward, it would have resulted in the biggest cocaine seizure ever, *but Hackbart could find no one to take it on.*

No FBI division would touch it, after Kirby Major and the New York office had closed Billy down, nor would the DEA, which besides doubting his word refused it because no heroin was involved. The Vice President's South Florida Task Force passed for the same reason, and although the New York Task Force expressed an interest, it was a bit outside their jurisdiction.

Sometime later, Billy heard that the twenty-five thousand kilos had been landed, fed into the national distribution network at a wholesale price of around $1.3 billion, and thence, over the next six months or so, up several million noses for at least ten times as much.

He had no better luck with his next hot lead from Puccinelli, although this involved a mere *one* thousand kilos, worth around $55 million wholesale, to be landed on an airstrip in the Everglades near Tampa. Special Agent Dale Hackbart could find no one interested enough to intercept that load either. In the end, Puccinelli was arrested, tried, and convicted for the one-*ounce* sale in Washington.

There was nothing left for Billy to do now except appeal directly to William H. Webster, Director of the FBI.

"Do you think Walt Stowe is the greatest FBI agent that has ever walked the face of the earth?" asked Breitbart.

Billy blinked. "Yes, sir." With the end in sight, why split hairs?

"Do you trust him?"

"With my life."

"You trust his judgment?"

"Yes, sir."

"Do you like him better, and do you trust him more, than you did Special Agent Jack Fishman of the CID-IRS?"

"There's no comparison."

"You trust Walter Stowe with your life?"

"Yes, sir."

"You wouldn't trust Mr. Fishman of the IRS with a nickel?"

"No, sir."

"And how about Revenue Agent Truluck? Do you trust him?"

"No, sir."

"Would it be fair to say, sir, that you put Walter Stowe, this FBI agent, into a completely different class as far as efficiency as an FBI agent?"

"Walt Stowe is good. Yes, sir."

"And Truluck and Fishman are no good, right?"

"I had no dealings with them, except in my interview." Billy was still not sure where Breitbart was taking him.

"But you told us that you thought that they were bums and they lied to you and you misled them?"

"That is correct."

"You wouldn't trust them with your life?"

"No, sir."

"You would trust Walter Stowe with your life?"

"Yes."

"And if Walt Stowe asked you to lie against Linda Holden, would you?"

"No, sir."

"If Walt Stowe asked you to lie against Dr. Jesse David Hyman, would you?"

Billy shook his head. *"I don't have to lie against Jesse Hyman,"* he said. *"I was in the first person with Doc Jesse Hyman."*

"I see. But when Fishman and Truluck asked you to lie about Linda Holden, you were willing to do that?"

"Yes, sir."

"But Walter Stowe, who you would put your life in his hands, you wouldn't do anything he asked you to do?"

Billy frowned. That was a pretty good one, even by Breitbart's standards. *"You want to repeat that?"* he asked.

The other abruptly threw in the towel. *"I have no more questions for this witness."*

25

On April 19, 1985, the government's deficiencies in preparing and prosecuting the Cowboy Palace case became as evident to the jury as they had been all along to Billy.

Dr. Jesse D. Hyman and Melvin Cooper were, of course, convicted—with the Albengas, Anthony C. Capo, Jr., and three other lesser players—but Vincent Rotondo, Carlo Vaccarezza, Antonio Napoli, and the other four "high-ranking members of organized crime families" associated with Resource Capital were acquitted.

U.S. Attorney Rudolph W. Giuliani described the jury's verdict as "a compromise."

"The defendants they convicted were on tape," he told *The New York Times*, "and they were the defendants against whom the most evidence was admitted. They acquitted those where there was somewhat less evidence. We are, of course, quite pleased with the conviction of the eight who were the day-to-day operators of this illegal enterprise."

Billy was far from pleased. There *would* have been more evidence against those acquitted if the FBI had not destroyed it.

He had worked his heart out on this case. He had paid his own expenses and lost his Miami house along the way. He had been mocked, reviled, and tormented—by those to whom he had brought the case as well as on the witness stand. By agreeing to testify, with no offer of protection from the government, he had also blown his cover on network television, leaving himself and his family more dangerously exposed to reprisals than ever before. (At previous trials, his testimony had attracted very little attention outside of the local media.) Worst of all, he had almost certainly sacrificed his mission in life to little purpose.

And Giuliani had the nerve to feel "quite pleased"?

It offended his sense of justice. The FBI had gone public with him. Now it was his turn to go public with them.

Hackbart and Wincelowicz helped Billy compose a letter to FBI Director William H. Webster.

> Dear Mr. Webster,
>
> My name is William Clifford Breen, and I presently live in the Dallas, Texas, area. Although I realize your time is valuable and limited, it is not my intention to impose. However, I feel my situation, as well as my past services to the Federal Bureau of Investigation, warrants bringing certain matters to your attention.
>
> For over 25 years, I have worked diligently with many different law-enforcement agencies, including the FBI, in a sincere and total effort to assist our government's fight against organized crime. I have given instruction to various law-enforcement groups and agencies in Texas, New Mexico, Florida, Massachusetts, and New York City. Through my sources, personal capabilities, and understanding of the law, I have been instrumental in developing many significant cases for the FBI, resulting in many organized-crime figures being brought to justice, tried and convicted.

He went on to mention a few examples: Cowboy Palace; the Wald/Litsky dope case that had led the Bureau into ever-widening circles of narcotics trafficking and resulted in $3.5 billion worth of seizures; the Johnson City casino case; the Haitian guns-for-dope case; the Piccolo/Chagra case, with over 125 defendants, and the attempted assassination of James Kerr.

So that Webster would understand how dangerous a game he had played, Billy also listed some of the contracts out on his life.

> It has been recently stated to me by S.A. Ron Iden that he had learned through his investigations that James Kearns . . . had tried on three different occasions to kill me, with the assistance of Peter White. I also learned from law-enforcement agencies in Boston that my name had been passed on to

several men in the Boston area for a hit on me. I learned from
S.A. Dale Hackbart, of the New York City division, that a high-
ranking LCN figure from Boston, Mike Caruana, a friend of
James Kearns and Jamiel Chagra . . . has a hit out on me, and
is also personally looking to kill me. This came to S.A. Hackbart from Joe Williams, Department of Paroles, Boston, Another man in the Boston area plotting to kill me is Hobart
Willis. This is James Kearns's personal friend. . . . I have also
learned that several Canadians have placed contracts on me.
I recently received a telephone call from the Miami FBI office
informing me that a top LCN figure was looking to harm me.
Another more recent incident involved Joe Covello and Tony
Acceturo. These threatening situations are just a few examples of the many that have occurred over the years.

But the difficulties and dangers of the work arose not solely from
the subjects of his investigations, as Billy proceeded to explain in a
blow-by-blow account of his tribulations in the Cowboy Palace case,
"one of the most troublesome situations I have been in." He also
touched briefly on his problems with Kirby Major in Washington,
whose actions, Billy claimed, "placed my life and the life of S.A.
Jerry Sullivan in grave danger."

Regardless of the threats made against my life, the hard-
ships and inconveniences placed upon my family and personal life, and the constant mental and physical strain of
such a lifestyle, I have always lived up to my end of the
programs I was involved in, and will continue to do so. My
track record speaks for itself—I always go the extra mile. I
have never worked a case, whether it be federal, state, or local
level, that has been a loser. Unfortunately, this has not been
the case on many of the projects I have worked on as regards
the financial and other arrangements made with the FBI.

This brought Billy to the nub of his grievances against the Bureau:
the broken promises.
Re: The reward offered in the case of the attempted assassination
of James Kerr in San Antonio. "I recently was informed by S.A. Iden
that he had requested I be paid $50,000 for my part in the case. This
is far from the $125,000 I was promised and which I rightfully
expected to receive."
Re: Cowboy Palace. "For my participation in the case, I was
promised $10,000 by Supervisor Damon Taylor. I received only
$2,000 of that amount."

Re: NYCON. "I went deeply into debt staying in hotels, eating out, taxis, etc. My personal phone bills have amounted to over $350 a month and sometimes up to $500 a month—this was due to my making tapes, etc. I was reimbursed in part for only some of this. My travels with just one airline was over 148,000 miles, and I've flown several others. I was informed . . . that management in the FBI office, New York City, requested an accounting of, not what I was promised, *but what I was owed.* This came to $41,000. I was then paid $14,000— less $900 for a telephone bill not belonging to me."

(As Billy was already on page 9 of a single-spaced letter with much more to come, he attached a separate, 25-page, "synopsis of the NYCON undercover operation to illustrate my actions, involvement, frustrations, and other thoughts concerning the investigation.")

Re: Calabrese/Velotta. "Management in the New York City office promised that if I was able to bring kilos of cocaine to the area from [these] two LCN figures I would receive $1,000 a kilo. . . . When management became aware that I could accomplish this, they dropped the full amount to a total of $7,500, which I have not received."

Topping off his financial complaints with criticism of the Bureau's handling of the Haitian case and the aborted Hawaiian expedition, Billy began the final page of his letter—number 11—with a plea for advice.

"Recently, I have been informed that FBI agents were not allowed to talk to me. May I ask what I am now to do when I have a problem? I never have called any agent unless it was about a case or concerning a serious personal problem. I intend to have my attorney contact the U.S. Marshal and attempt to have them check out my home periodically."

That paragraph was the subject of long and earnest debate with Dale Hackbart, who felt that to keep the letter within reasonable bounds, Billy should stick to the question of his personal safety and deal with the problems of what to do with his unfinished cases in the separate enclosure on NYCON.

"The way they have it now," Billy said, "they have completely deserted me."

"That's right."

"If anybody comes to kill me, my wife, or my family, I have no one to turn to."

"If that happens, you call me." Hackbart was emphatic. "Call me or Frank. That's bullshit. We'll worry about it after the fact."

"As long as you and Frank can't get scolded—that's my biggest concern."

"So what? What can they do to me that they haven't already done? I'm going to get fired? For what? I hope somebody up in Washington is smart enough to say, 'Hey, something's wrong here.'"

"What did we ever do that was wrong except try to make cases?"

"I don't know, Billy. I really don't."

For the memorandum on NYCON, Hackbart and Wincelowicz both felt Billy's criticisms of the Bureau should be as constructive as possible.

"What you should say is, in your experience of twenty years, the success of the NYCON operation was based on the fact that the agent and source could travel throughout the U.S., thus covering themselves as bad guys," Wincelowicz suggested. "Nobody's done that before. Some of our success was due to the fact that we could immediately obtain funds to buy stolen goods through Dale Hackbart. A flying squad should be set up, and you would be more than willing to blend your experience and expertise with the squad. If they had a squad like that, run out of Washington with an assistant director in charge, can you imagine how effective that would be?"

"You kidding me? We showed 'em it would work, right?"

"Yeah. Then get into the unfinished business."

Dale Hackbart endorsed this approach. "I think that's absolutely right," he said. "You can say I'm ready to accept information from you at any time on any matter and present it to officials either in New York division or any other division, including Bureau headquarters, so that the information can be acted upon in the best interests of seeing that individuals are prosecuted. 'The NYCON operation being closed, there is no way for my contact agent, the former undercover agent, or myself to complete any investigation on many of the individuals listed above.'"

"You think they'll buy that, Dale?"

"I think you've got to put it to them. And I think you've got to say that 'based on my records, it is my understanding that my part of the NYCON operation, and the cases I brought to the attention of New York office, resulted in at least a dozen arrests and convictions and the recovery or saving of hundreds of millions of dollars. And this is only a portion of the cases that should have been worked.'"

After saying all that, and including a three-page addendum on his unresolved problems with the IRS (for which he also held the FBI responsible), Billy wound up his epic letter with an emotional appeal for the Director's understanding:

"As you can see, I have devoted a maximum effort at a very high risk to myself and my family in my assistance to many law-enforcement agencies in support of their efforts against organized crime. None more so than for the FBI. The activities and incidents contained in this letter are just with the FBI. I have worked with local and state agencies, the Department of Labor, the DEA, and the ROCIC. For my part, however—and I feel I have illustrated this sufficiently—I have been maligned, used, deceived, and, in my mind, cheated financially, by most notably the FBI. Just the examples I have written indicate well over $150,000 that I was promised and am still waiting for.

I am appealing to you now for your assistance in helping me get at least a number I can call if my family is threatened—they need this protection from the FBI. I also need your help in gaining payment of the money that I was promised and am owed for the many cases in which I have assisted and worked closely with your agency.

Lastly, I need your help to regain the respect for your fine organization that I seem to have lost along the way.

I remain,
Respectfully yours,
William Clifford Breen

With its enclosures, it was quite a document, running to thirty-nine single-spaced pages. By the time he finished tinkering with it, he had paid his local secretarial agency another three hundred dollars in typing bills.

"You think he'll answer it?" he asked Dale Hackbart.

"They've got to, Billy. They can't ignore you. It's an important letter. Addressed to the Director. You set out the facts. You suggest a solution. You ask for help. Sure, they'll answer you. I don't see how they can sidestep it."

"Neither do I," agreed Wincelowicz. "And anyway, the Bureau's got a policy on that. Every letter has to be answered or acknowledged."

Billy's letter was neither answered nor acknowledged.

Nor was a follow-up letter he sent to Webster a year later.

Nor yet a third letter that he eventually addressed to Webster's successor, William Sessions, whom Billy already knew as the former U.S. district judge who had presided over the Chagra/Kearns trial.

The discourtesy was clearly deliberate. His letters were not only received but acted upon—to the extent that many of the agents he had mentioned were censured.

Understandably discouraged but not yet ready for retirement,

Billy asked Hackbart to present the Bureau with yet another spectacular opportunity to put a crimp in the drug trade.

Still active in Tampa, where the state task force had finally wound
up its O'Ryan's sting with sixty-nine arrests, Billy had been offered a
concession in Belize for refueling smugglers' aircraft before they took
off on the last leg of their journey across the Caribbean. With two or
three men to help him, perhaps from the Bureau or the Delta Force,
his idea was to attach a transponder to each plane as he gassed it up
so that the load could be tracked by radar every foot of the way to its
final destination in the United States.

For six months or a year, or for as long as Billy's ingenuity held
out, the government would have been able to identify everybody
involved in the Belize traffic, from smugglers to street-corner push-
ers, and/or to intercept perhaps as much as a third of all the cocaine
entering the country.

Once again, Hackbart could find no takers.

26

William Clifford Breen is an original.

There has been no one like him in the annals of law enforcement, nor is there likely to be another, for the world that shaped him is history.

Billy's crusade against "the animals" he got to know so dangerously well as a cop, as a confidante of the Winter Hill mob, and, almost terminally, as a convict, probably took a thousand professional criminals off the streets, and for that alone he deserves a decent measure of respect. But as the final tally should have been two or three times higher, perhaps his most durable achievement will be to have laid bare the inadequacies of the FBI.

Of necessity, and by its nature, the Bureau is a secretive organization. The mob cartels and the informal groups of "independents" who coalesce and dissolve around shifting patterns of criminal opportunity already enjoy too big an edge without also being kept advised of the FBI's latest strategy, targets, and available forces. Absolute confidentiality, trust in the Bureau's integrity, and ruthless efficiency in the field are minimum requirements against an enemy that usually holds the initiative and, as often as not, a tactical advantage in money, technology, and manpower.

The problem is that this necessary secrecy can also hide the Bureau's mistakes and weaknesses, and shelter idle, incompetent, timid, cynical, complacent, self-seeking, or self-righteous bureaucrats from public scrutiny.

No serving agent can afford to blow the whistle on his bosses. No retired agent would wish to undermine public confidence in his former colleagues or risk being accused of keeping his mouth shut until safely drawing a pension. It had to wait for someone like Billy to go public—someone with no personal or financial stake in the Bureau to protect, with no traditions of solidarity to respect, with half a lifetime's experience of working with agents and trying to deal with their bosses—before an unvarnished picture could emerge of how the FBI's criminal division actually works in the field.

And the picture is not reassuring.

The Bureau's besetting sin is hubris, bred in the bone by its founding Director, J. Edgar Hoover. No one stands outside its remit, not even the President. As in Hoover's day, the FBI will listen—to the White House, the Congress, the Justice Department, the media, and even to public opinion—but in the end, the Bureau knows best. And, no doubt, it does—at times. But applied as a general principle, the effect is stultifying. To criticize the FBI, to question its policy and actions, or to resist its decisions is to stand revealed, if not as a public enemy then at least as someone to be watched. Its only visible response to criticism is to close ranks.

There is something in the air at Quantico, some implication of being admitted to an elite with access to the awesome powers of the state, that combines with the tangible proofs of authority—the badge, credentials, and gun—to inspire agents who have a true sense of vocation and to corrupt those who do not. In police work, motivation is everything, and those who join the FBI to fight crime are increasingly hampered by those who join for a secure government job with a pension after twenty years. Agents who sign up for that reason are dead wood from the start, for fighting crime is essentially a risk-taking business. By protecting their careers from risk, they frustrate the Bureau's purpose.

Screened from any real accountability, the FBI under Hoover evolved into a kind of secular priesthood that saw itself not as a body of privileged cops but as superior beings endowed with superior wisdom—and enough of that feeling has survived to account for what Carl Shoffler, formerly of the Washington Metro police, describes as the Bureau's "arrogance." In fact, it is both more and less than that. Within the FBI priesthood, an agent's badge is still an icon to which every right-minded citizen, regardless of rank or position, is expected to defer. The duties of the Director and his agents, like those of the Pope and his clergy, are to defend the faith, as embodied in the rituals and traditions of the Bureau; to advance its power and interests, to keep its image bright, to root out heresy, to recruit and train like-minded novitiates as keepers of the flame, and to fight the devil in all his forms—more or less in that order. Any time left over from that can be spent in the gym or brown-nosing superiors.

Divorced from firsthand experience of crime, it is perhaps not surprising, therefore, that the FBI's midlevel Jesuits become obsessed with the abstractions of management at the expense of its mission. An astounding number of supervisory agents actually *hate* informants, even though (or perhaps because) they know that without them the Bureau would be deaf, blind, and helpless as a beached whale.

To be dependent on one's inferiors while building a career is not only humiliating but potentially dangerous. Better by far for ambitious agents to avoid the street altogether, if they can, and get into administration, planning, coordination, finance, number-crunching, or any other controllable management function where life is delivered, prepackaged, to an in-tray.

When asked how they feel about this, street agents tend to shrug philosophically. Already treated with caution—as oddballs contaminated by exposure to people like Billy—most of them have learned to live with it. But not Special Agent Vincent Wincelowicz, even after he came in from the cold and made supervisor.

"This causes me great personal aggravation," he says. "Up to 1987, when I finished my last undercover job, I had never been considered part of the system. I wanted to move up because I wanted to change things, but if I wanted to move up, I had to sit at a desk. An undercover agent can change nothing. You have to play the corporate game to get into a position where you can actually do some good. So I came out and sat at my desk for six months, twiddling my thumbs, jogging in the park, working out in the gym, and shuffling papers until everybody figured I *was* part of the system again. I had to purge myself. I had to show I was no longer a rogue agent involved in all this uncontrollable stuff. And that's got to be wrong.

"You get agents who go straight into management at headquarters to get out of doing field work, before they've gained any experience of life. You get FBI clerks who become FBI agents—who never worked anyplace else. You get people coming straight from college with master's degrees in accounting, or straight from law school. Nothing wrong with that, of course—but you can't expect them to know the streets. You can't expect them to understand what it takes to work a case out there in the field.

"I came across a unit in headquarters, called our Undercover Unit, that monitors all our undercover agents and operations. For most of the time it has been in existence, it's been staffed by agents who have no undercover experience at all and have never worked as a case agent. These guys have no way of knowing what is a good undercover operation and what is a bad one. They applied for the job because it was a management slot, and that's how the system works. But at least I've done that kind of work and know what it entails."

Most agents who joined the Bureau to catch crooks would probably agree with that assessment. Those who stay in the field from choice are not only penalized in their pay and promotion prospects, but have to endure far too often the frustration of seeing their work go to waste as a result of arbitrary, inept, or ignorant decisions at a higher level (although not as often or as painfully as Billy has). With America generating criminals as fast as it generates other kinds of trash, the need to revitalize the one government agency with the mandate and resources to arrest its decline into a lawless society is not simply urgent but critical.

The first requirement is a change of attitude. The FBI was not ordained by God. Its function as a national police agency is the sole reason for its existence, and the one measure of its usefulness is society's compliance with federal law. Despite its lofty pretensions, the FBI is in the garbage-disposal business—and not doing too well at it, to judge from the ethical state of the union.

The most important reason for its mediocre performance is reflected in its treatment of Billy, who knows better than most that you can't ride a garbage truck without getting your suit dirty. As a rule, only field agents understand this—and a lot of *them* tend to forget once they come in from the cold and start playing executive Monopoly.

By and large, a police agency is as good as its sources of information. The quality of its manpower, the size of its budget, and the extent of its technical resources may determine its scope and efficiency (and here the application of modern management theory is entirely appropriate), but the quality of its results is directly proportionate to the quality of its input—and, no less crucially, to the ability of agents and management to *recognize* quality when they see it.

To satisfy this requirement, the FBI needs to get off its high horse and join Billy on the shit pile.

Behind the headlines, almost every successful skirmish with serious crime begins with an informant. Although the credit will attach to the agents who make the case or the prosecutors who try it, the whole system of criminal justice ultimately hangs on a supply of reliable information from unofficial sources who, for one reason or another, are prepared to cooperate with law-enforcement agencies.

The world has moved on, and is unlikely to produce another professional "catalyst" of Billy's caliber or to repeat the opportunities for penetrating organized crime that the FBI squandered in the course of his career, but the Bureau still depends as much as ever on its "assets." It still needs them to bring in cases, to create openings, and to nurse investigators through the early stages of its undercover operations. It still needs them to help with probable cause, to get the wires up, to wear body recorders, and to fill the gaps in its data banks.

And after all these years, it still needs a coherent policy for recruiting, supporting and rewarding confidential informants.

If the Bureau were to devote a fraction of the time, effort and money spent on "managing" itself to fostering new sources of criminal intelligence, it would not only improve its clear-up rate but probably reduce its present unhealthy dependence on cutting deals with convicted felons. Far too often, serious offenders are invited to barter away their sentences in return for testimony against former associates. If the Bureau were to put more of its manpower and resources into the field, the greater certainty of a full-term sentence upon conviction of a major crime might restore some of prison's deterrent value.

More agents would then have to get their hands dirty, but this does not necessarily mean a corresponding increase in the cruder forms of corruption. For years, Hoover steered the FBI clear of narcotics and organized crime in case his boys became tainted by contact with the criminal classes, but after twenty-five years of intimate observation, Billy can point to no solid evidence of favors bought and sold, although he occasionally had his suspicions.

"The average agent is ninety percent better than the average cop," he says. "But the average agent is seventy-five percent stealing his wages. He comes in at nine, ten o'clock in the morning with his sweatsuit and tennis racket and by noon they're gone. You'll find 'em in the gym or the volleyball court or the golf course. Basically, they're stealing their salaries, and if they don't have a guy like me coming in to give 'em the work and making it easy for 'em, they can't do nothing. Their hands are tied by midlevel management. Even those that *want* to can't work. You got paperwork that's gonna block you. Or if your paperwork is in—uh, uh! You can't work that. That's gotta go over to Joe Soap in white-collar crime or the bank-robbery squad or whatever.

"The problem with the Bureau is not corruption but bureaucracy and laziness. Not so much laziness—most agents just don't have the capability of working, and they don't have the motivation because they know up front they ain't gonna get anyplace. Now I met a lot of exceptions to that, but when I look around and see who's out there— oh, my God! No street sense. So how do you train 'em? Not by putting 'em into police departments, because cops hate 'em. You can't give 'em the power to bulldoze police departments—although if the FBI was half as good as it thinks it is they oughta have it. No, they need fifty guys like me who can take agents out on the streets and smarten 'em up. Like I taught Vinnie. On the job.

"Without that, all they do is sit by the phone and listen to the wires. When they think they got enough evidence, they take it to the U.S. attorney and then it takes *him* another year to get *his* shit together. So they'll all tell ya, 'Billy Breen is too fast.' They can't get the paper up that fast. But it's not that. They just don't know what to look for half the time. I embarrass 'em. They couldn't believe what I had to tell 'em, so they had to go out and verify everything before they moved. Is this for real? Can this happen? They had to backtrack over everything I'd done already to make sure it was really so—and they couldn't even do *that* properly. Except for guys like Vinnie, they don't *work*. Five o'clock, it's all over. Good night."

Billy is convinced that NYCON showed the way to go.

"Working in a team, we started a lotta cases," he says. "And they let us run around the country. If there'd been six or eight agents, an assistant U.S. attorney with us, and a typist, we coulda put a lotta stuff together. But nobody knew about us or what we were doing, so they flubbed it. As usual. And they didn't pay me nothing anyway."

Without exception, every field agent Billy ever worked with believes that NYCON's three-man traveling circus pointed the way to the proper use of high-quality informants. All agree that the whole principle of having a *Federal* Bureau of Investigation is negated by chopping it up into segments that operate only within closely defined territorial divisions and are then further subdivided into squads responsible for particular types of crime and particular groups of criminals. This may look good on an organizational wall chart with colored tabs and pins, but it simply does not correspond to the real world.

To pretend that it does—and to have the authority to force real cases into this unreal framework—is to multiply the paperwork unbearably, to involve a score of agents where perhaps only one or two are needed, and to risk jamming everything up in a bureaucratic gridlock.

One solution might be to put some teeth in the government's rhetoric about a "war on crime" by reorganizing the criminal division of the FBI along military lines rather than continuing to run it as a civil-service department. To have investigations in the field managed from behind a desk by lawyers and accountants makes about as much sense as asking the Pentagon's purchasing agents to direct a platoon-level firefight on the other side of the world. With a clear distinction between "field" agents and "staff" agents, and with a separate command structure for each, the FBI would be free to deploy its resources where they were most needed and to pursue every case to a conclusion regardless of local jealousies.

As its "kill rate" would then be a primary—and publishable—measure of efficiency, this might also concentrate the Bureau's mind wonderfully on ways and means of improving the supply of raw criminal intelligence and backing up its field and case agents. Another useful indicator would be the ratio of field agents to desk agents. If published annually, there might be some incentive to control the spread of bureaucratic flab.

With separate pay and command structures, the steady drift of frontline troops into less demanding staff jobs might also be arrested. Agents who join the FBI because they want to catch crooks could then continue to do so without losing out in pay and promotion prospects to their more sedentary colleagues, a sore point with Vincent Wincelowicz.

"When I left the New York office, I was one of the most senior agents there—and that's kind of pathetic," he says. "What happens is that because of all the psychological hassles of trying to ramrod a case and do a good job, with all the frustrations involved, as soon as agents gain a little knowledge or experience they opt out into one of the many ancillary jobs that have opened up. They come in and sit down. They don't have to do any paper. They don't have any responsibilities. They don't have to argue with U.S. attorneys. They don't have to argue with their supervisors.

"But what it means is, the guys that should be there to teach the new people how to do things are just drifting away from their proper work, and that's a shame. Either that or they're leaving the area because there's no more upward mobility. Down in Quantico, we have people with less than five years' experience teaching new agents—and not because they're Rhodes Scholars.

"Street agents, case agents—they need to be treated like the Special Forces in the army. Everybody else is going to do their time and walk away. What the Bureau needs are people who'll go above and beyond the call of duty *every* day—not just on a need-to day. I think everybody in the Bureau would probably do what they have to do when called upon, but we need people who are self-motivated.

"After running around with Billy for a couple of years, coming in was a real psychological letdown. We got over with Jack Mace and those guys so we could learn exactly what was going on, and when you're doing that kind of work, you've got to be accessible all the time. That's holidays. It's nights. It's Saturdays and Sundays—and there are a lot of people who can't or won't give that time to it. I was working sixteen, seventeen hours a day, seven days a week, and getting zero back because I only *had* to work eight hours a day for five days. One of the reasons why Billy enjoyed working with me was because I never said to him, 'No, Billy, I can't. I got to get the groceries.' I was never too busy to do what had to be done, but a lot of times, personally, it was tough.

"Too many people join the Bureau for the wrong reasons. You get a badge. You get power and position with a pension at the end of it. If you don't get out of line, nothing bad can happen to you. It's as secure a job as you can find anywhere, with all kinds of fringe benefits. But if you also happen to be a highly motivated police officer, then your attitude is entirely different. You expect from the Bureau the kind of backup you don't always get.

"Out in the field, if you want something to succeed, sometimes you have to become a squeaky wheel, and that's not the way it should be. A lot of people in the Bureau want to change what's going on. Some are willing to go to almost any lengths to get it done. There's even one who will let himself be quoted on it."

Special Agent Vincent Wincelowicz has never been afraid to stick his neck out. After the Bureau cut Billy off, Wincelowicz took his calls at home. He was simply too big an asset to let go to waste, even with his cover blown to shreds. There was no one else around with his depth of experience, his ability to "get over," or his general all-around expertise in undercover work. If he could no longer employ those skills himself, there was no reason why he should not try to pass them on to the Bureau's agents in seminars and training sessions. Always provided that Wincelowicz could finesse his way around the bureaucratic obstacles.

It took him a couple of years, but he worked on it so assiduously that at last, in one of those delightful ironies of which only an overweight bureaucracy is capable, he and Billy were invited to the FBI Academy at Quantico, Virginia, to lecture a class of five-year agents on how to get the best out of informants!

Since then, they have been asked back several times to repeat their double act, and have also taken it to St. Louis and New York, where Billy took particular pleasure in pointing out the divisional office's shortcomings to the seventy-odd agents who attended.

"I got no ax to grind," he told them. "Me and my family, we live here in this country same as you do. Crime gets to me the way it gets to you. No— *worse*. I don't wanna see the kind of animal I saw in prison running around loose on the streets. Think what you like—I'm a law-and-order guy. I wanna help *you* lock 'em up, so I make things happen. I'm a catalyst. I do the work *for* ya. Most of the cases I've worked with agents I've put together long before they even knew what it was about. I get the paperwork done and *then* I go to the Bureau."

"That's how he got into trouble," Wincelowicz interposed, trying to get in as their time was running out.

"Not me," said Billy irritably. "*I* didn't get into trouble." He had been too nice to these people. Half of them were not even listening. "It was the Bureau that got into trouble. You all got trouble with the Bureau. With the paperwork. That's all your bosses care about. Never mind about the pinch—where's the paper on it? 'Oh, look. There's a guy robbing a bank.' 'Yeah? Sorry. I'm in white-collar crime. Tell him to wait while I get permission to work the case.'"

Several agents acknowledged this with a nod and chuckle, and Billy shifted up a gear.

"You think that's *funny?*" he bellowed. "Well, lemme tell ya something. It's pathetic. You people ain't shit. Don't raise your hands or nothing, but how many of yez have had a decent pinch in the last three or four years? You don't have to answer that. None of yez. Your record stinks. You *got* no record. Why? Because you got no fucking informants. If you did, you wouldn't be in here listening to me. You'd be out on the street doing your job.

"And *why* ain't you got no informants? I'll tell ya why. Because when you *do* get somebody to take you out like a seeing-eye dog, what do you do? Do you treat him nice? Do you treat him like he's somebody? With respect? Do you go to bat for him if he's in trouble? The hell you do. You treat him like shit. You lie to him. You screw over him and you burn him. People know that. So nobody wants to work with yez. They're afraid of yez.

"Because you all got that attitude. You pull your badge on John Q. Public and you melt him. Don't *melt* people. Be kind to people. Treat 'em like you want to be treated yourself and you'll get informants. Not like me, because there ain't nobody like me. But I could put an ad in the paper for citizens to work with FBI agents and weed out a bunch for you every day. You might have to work through fifty before you found what you was looking for, but then you got one that wants to clean up the world.

"And don't tell him you're working organized crime," he plowed on, ignoring Wincelowicz. "Or white-collar crime. Or public corruption. He don't wanna know that. You're federal agents. *Your* job is to uphold the law, and *his* job is to tell you who's breaking it. So don't say to him, 'I gotta get permission to do this because I'm working drugs this week.' The guy could be putting his life on the line. He don't wanna hear any of that shit. When you're not burning informants, you're turning 'em off.

"You think I'm all right because I do what I do? People look at me like I'm shit. I'm the biggest fucking asshole out there because I help you idiots. And do you help *me?* Like fuck you do. All you ever do is lie to me.

"Don't lie. Three things they teach you at Quantico. Wear a three-piece suit. Keep your weight down. Learn how to lie. It's true. I seen people I worked with get up in court and lie. I tell 'em, 'You lied in that case.' And they say, 'Well, we know he's guilty.' Don't matter. Don't lie. Don't make promises you can't keep. You tell an informant you're going to do something for him, do it. You tell him you're going to pay him X amount of dollars, pay him."

Sensing he had left most of his audience behind, Billy trampled over Wincelowicz's attempts to head him off and started in on the catalog of broken promises that littered his thirty-year association with the Bureau, finishing up with the Calabrese/Velotta debacle.

"I know I'm not easy," he said, yielding to Wincelowicz at last. "But this is important. It's only hard to get informants because you make it hard. You let their names leak out. You make 'em testify. You fuck over 'em. You don't pay 'em. You gotta understand—you can't put people into the kinda trap you put me into and expect 'em to work. I've been told by agents to sue the Bureau for the money it owes me, but you got the Attorney General going for you. So how can I fight yez? I wrote to your bosses, and didn't even get a fucking answer."

He looked at Wincelowicz, and in a moment they both laughed.

"Well," said Billy, dismissing it all with a sweep of his hand. "I woulda done it anyway. God has been good to me. When I need something, He drops it on me."

POSTSCRIPT ONE

God is still dropping it on him.

Not a week goes by without somebody in law enforcement calling Billy from somewhere in the country to ask his advice, chew the fat, or, best of all, to sound him out on another assignment. No more retiring at sixty-five than he was at thirty, he has only to hear of a bookmaking ring that needs taking down in Kansas City or an interstate hijacking crew defying the Bureau in Baltimore or a high-level crack-house operation to be penetrated in Chicago and out comes the $14,000 Rolex and the designer casuals and off goes Billy Murphy or Billy Clyde Walker and his (rented) Lincoln to snow mere criminals blind with savoir faire.

Anybody else would be cowering in the Federal Witness Protection Program. After his multimedia exposure during the Cowboy Palace trial and the subsequent televised interviews and illustrated magazine articles, Billy Breen's mug shots—in bespectacled full-face and double-chinned leprechaun profile—should have been pinned behind the door of every self-respecting criminal household in the United States.

But for Billy, the additional risk that he might be recognized by the next target he confronts is like lemon on his caviar, an extra tingle of anxiety to go with the vanishing margins for error, the utter reliance on his wits, the impossibility of backing out once committed.

342 *DONALD GODDARD*

All the factors that would normally deter a reasonable person from doing what Billy does are precisely the factors that keep him doing it. But after fingering more major mobsters than anyone else alive, he is now seriously pressing his luck.

On January 4, 1988, Vincent Rotondo, the lead defendant in the Cowboy Palace trial, was repeatedly shot in the face at close range outside his home in Brooklyn. The most senior mobster to be assassinated since the hit on Paul Castellano, Rotondo was dispatched, it was thought, for putting Doc Hyman and Mel Cooper in a position to inflict serious damage on the mobs by cooperating with the government after their conviction. And Billy Breen had secured their conviction.

As Vincent Wincelowicz remarked, on hearing the news, "I wouldn't want to have to start Billy's car every morning."

So why is he still out there?

None of the obvious explanations, including his own, is entirely convincing. For Billy is both one of them *and* one of us. Devious *and* loyal. An amoralist devoted to decent values. A case-hardened cynic with sentimental illusions. A wary, reckless, calculating hothead with a big heart and bigger mouth who took on the most dangerous job on earth and left himself nowhere to hide.

In the end, Billy remains an enigma—even to himself—but one that throws some light on a similar engima at the heart of American life.

POSTSCRIPT TWO

So that the Federal Bureau of Investigation might have an opportunity to comment on the criticisms leveled against it in the book, a copy of the manuscript, addressed to Director William S. Sessions, was delivered by courier on June 22, 1991, with the following letter:

June 21, 1991

The Hon. William S. Sessions,
Director,
Federal Bureau of Investigation,
Washington, D.C.

Dear Mr. Sessions,

   I enclose for your attention the manuscript of "The Insider," a book to be published early next year by Pocket Books, about the life and times of Billy Breen, an FBI "asset" who has been involved with the Bureau in one way or another for some 35 years.
   I have taken the liberty of addressing it to you personally, not only because your name appears in the book several times, but also because the work is often highly critical of FBI policy and management with respect to criminal law-enforce-

ment. I would not wish this—I hope, constructive—criticism to be discounted at precisely those mid-management levels that gave rise to it in the first place.

Indeed, my purpose in sending you the manuscript in advance of publication is to allow you an opportunity to consider the charges and allegations that appear in the book, and to respond, if you so wish, in time for the Bureau's comments to be incorporated in the work, possibly as a preface or appendix to it.

While, clearly, a line-by-line rebuttal would not be feasible, I would be happy to include a general statement of your position and policy on the issues raised—without, of course, embellishment, editing or further comment on my part. The exigencies of the publishers' production schedule, however, do require that any such statement be with them by not later than July 31, 1991.

Sincerely,

Donald Goddard

Receipt of the manuscript was eventually acknowledged on July 15, 1991:

Dear Mr. Goddard,

Your June 21, 1991, letter with enclosure to FBI Director William S. Sessions has been referred to my office for response.

Your request for FBI comments in connection with your book entitled "The Insider" is under consideration. I will notify you as soon as a decision has been reached.

Sincerely yours,
Thomas F. Jones,
Inspector in Charge
Office of Public Affairs

There was no further response.

Rather than comment publicly, it may be that the Bureau chose to express its displeasure in a more roundabout way.

Two weeks after the manuscript was delivered to the FBI in Washington, the Internal Revenue Service moved to seize Billy Breen's home in Dallas, having previously allowed its disputed claim against him to lie dormant for over four years.

D. G.